## Alexander Pope

# Alexander Pope

## ☙ THE GENIUS OF SENSE

David B. Morris

Harvard University Press
Cambridge, Massachusetts, and London, England   1984

Publication of this book has been aided by a grant from the Andrew W. Mellon Foundation

This book is printed on acid-free paper, and its binding materials have been chosen for strength and durability.

Library of Congress Cataloging in Publication Data

Morris, David B.
    Alexander Pope, the genius of sense.

    Bibliography: p.
    Includes index.
    1.   Pope, Alexander, 1688–1744—Criticism and
interpretation.    I.   Title.
PR3634.M67   1984        821'.5        83-18577
ISBN 0-674-01522-3 (alk. paper)

*To Ruth Cohen Morris*
*and to the memory of*
*Samuel Holt Monk*

# Acknowledgments

BYRON wrote an extraordinary acknowledgment of his regard for Pope: "Neither time, nor distance, nor grief, nor age can ever diminish my veneration for him who is the great moral poet of all times, of all climes, of all feelings, and of all stages of existence. The delight of my boyhood, the study of my manhood, perhaps (if allowed to me to attain it) he may be the consolation of my age. His poetry is the Book of Life."

For Pope, as Byron understood, books and lives have a way of crossing, interpenetrating. Good books, Pope believed, have the power to sustain and to improve us, while bad writing (by which he understood far more than clumsy style) might damage the quality of human life. Lives and books proceed together for better or for worse.

I began writing this book some twelve years ago. My explanation for such slow work is that I wanted a subject which demanded to be lived with, over a period of years. Pope's body of writing—which includes his five-volume correspondence—is too substantial, too complex, too various to reward the kind of study appropriate in analyzing a brief poem or novel or play. Further, as a writer deeply engaged with his own times, Pope requires that we understand something of the eighteenth century—of the lives it produced as well as the books—without which we will see only the mirror of our own critical preoccupations.

Friends, too, have a habit of slowing down composition—by the possibilities they open for improvement. Small wonder that Pope be-

## Acknowledgments

lieved we are diminished (not simply grieved) by the death of a friend. For me, the death of Samuel Holt Monk will always remain such a loss. For whatever improvements they could force upon the book, three persons deserve special thanks: Marvin Bell, Gerald Bruns, and Ralph Cohen. Ralph Cohen, to whom my debt is greatest, gave the final draft a close reading from first page to last, and suddenly it was no longer final. Gerald Bruns lent his inventiveness to every topic I could tempt him to discuss, and he invariably enriched it. Marvin Bell, without breaking stride, kept my attention on poetry, hills, and what is beautiful inexactly. Shelley Bennett and Judith Hurtig provided generous help at an opportune time. Rose Udics, Michel Nutkiewicz, Misako Hamada, my brother Christopher, my daughter, Ellen, and my mother, Emily, all gave special assistance for which I am deeply grateful.

For a teacher constitutionally unable to do two things at once, several fellowships provided the summers and semesters in which writing was possible. It is a pleasure to thank the American Council of Learned Societies, the American Philosophical Society, the John Simon Guggenheim Foundation, and the National Endowment for the Humanities. For permission to include materials that appeared elsewhere in earlier versions, I am grateful to *Modern Language Quarterly*, *Philological Quarterly*, *Texas Studies in Literature and Language*, and Vision Press Limited. Every scholar of Pope owes an unending debt to the editors of the Twickenham edition of *The Poems of Alexander Pope* (1939–1969), from which I quote liberally.

For some people—I am one—the most profound convergence of books and lives takes place within a marriage. My wife, Ruth, shared the days which went into the making of this book. A collaboration so intimate is not easily unraveled. It is certain that her thoughts helped me at every step and that she understood, with uncanny exactness, when I needed rescuing. Such indispensable assistance would seem enough, but there is more. As Pope knew, it is far easier to improve a book than to improve a life. I am luckily able to say, with confidence and with love, that she has done both.

# ~æ Contents

# ᐕ Illustrations

# Illustrations

Of his intellectual character the constituent and fundamental principle was Good Sense, a prompt and intuitive perception of consonance and propriety. He saw immediately, of his own conceptions, what was to be chosen, and what to be rejected; and, in the works of others, what was to be shunned, and what was to be copied.

But good sense alone is a sedate and quiescent quality, which manages its possessions well, but does not increase them; it collects few materials for its own operations, and preserves safety, but never gains supremacy. Pope had likewise genius; a mind active, ambitious, and adventurous, always investigating, always aspiring; in its widest searches still longing to go forward, in its highest flights still wishing to be higher; always imagining something greater than it knows, always endeavouring more than it can do.

—Samuel Johnson, *Lives of the English Poets*

# Introduction: Imitation and Commerce

The best history of a writer is contained in his writings—these are his chief actions.

—George Eliot

ONLY A HANDFUL of writers are sufficiently central that we name whole ages after them. Thus we speak of an Age of Wordsworth but not an Age of Keats, a Pound Era but not a Williams Era or an Age of Frost. Alexander Pope is the major poet of his century, and the period of his lifetime (1688–1744) might be justly called, give or take a few years, the Age of Pope. Pope's importance, however, extends far beyond his own times. Few major poets remain so unfailingly controversial, for Pope has deeply divided readers in almost every subsequent generation. (His gift for attracting enemies seems inseparable from his poetic virtues and large talent for friendship.) Questions of morality no doubt generate much of the divisiveness; even after two hundred years his motives and conduct still inspire lively dispute. Yet, questions about Pope's morality do not fully explain his knack of transforming readers into passionate advocates or adversaries. He continues to engage us, I believe, especially because his work requires us to clarify and to articulate our differences about literature itself. It demands that we reconsider such primary issues as the uses of tradition, the value of rhyme, and the place of doctrine in poetry. We must redefine what we mean by imitation and originality, by open and closed form. We must test our beliefs about the moral stance of the poet, about the nature of style, about didactic verse, about wit and reason and imagination as poetic resources—about the relation between life and art. Pope is more than a gifted writer from a distant age whose writing still commands attention. He has become fundamental to our ways of thinking about literature.

# Alexander Pope

The purpose of this book is to offer a perspective on Pope which will allow a better understanding of his achievement and importance. Perspective is a crucial matter, because Pope remains identified by many of his readers (and many who have not read his work) with the smallest fragment of his genius: the heroic couplet. Most academic studies have unintentionally helped to distance or to diminish Pope by offering us only two main ways of encountering his work, as in a film that consists entirely of close-ups or panoramas. We view him either through the detailed analysis of individual poems and of special topics or through bird's-eye surveys which glance swiftly and super-ficially over his entire career. In the years since Reuben A. Brower's *Alexander Pope: The Poetry of Allusion* (1959) only a few critical books—introductions aside—have attempted to discuss at length the whole range of Pope's work, and even Brower circumscribed his study by emphasizing Pope's debt to the classical tradition, especially to "Homer and the Roman poets."[1] As in Brower's distinguished study, for example, the emphasis upon a special topic or controlling theme necessarily introduces additional problems of perspective by excluding or by blurring whatever falls outside a unifying focus. (Thus Pope's classicism needs to be understood in relation to his concern—not always disapproving—for contemporary culture and for popular writing: he enjoyed such unclassical works as *Gulliver's Travels*, *The Beggar's Opera*, and *Robinson Crusoe*.) A writer as diverse as Pope demands in his readers a perspective both compre-hensive and flexible, one which offers more than a choice between rapid sketches in bold outline and the scrutiny of magnified pieces. We need a perspective which encourages us to see Pope as a life-size, three-dimensional, changing figure. We need studies which are de-tailed but not fragmentary, extensive but not merely general, which permit us a spectator's freedom to shift our points of view. If no sin-gle study can accomplish such an impossible combination of virtues, it is essential to respect the diversity of such an elusive and many-sided writer.

The problems of perspective are further complicated by Pope's troublesome multiplicity, for his character and art confront us with strangely incongruent figures. There is the bawdy Pope, the polite Pope, Pope the scholar, Pope the gardener. There is the London wit, the country gentleman, the plain-dealer, the genteel equivocator. There is the gallant, the outsider, the man of moderation, the heroic extremist, the faithful son, the devoted enemy, the trickster, the philosopher, and the rake. Like Proteus, his nature seems centered, if a stable center exists, in the power to assume different shapes. It is easier to make sense of Pope if we narrow our gaze to a single fragment of his character, such as the familiar poet of retirement and limitation who gives voice to all the verities of neoclassicism. A more comprehensive study, however, must offer us a less manageable portrait— diverse, copious, changing, contradictory—like mankind as depicted in Pope's two puzzling epistles on human character.

An exhaustive study of Pope might begin with the moment when Pope began his own literary studies, but in a poet so precocious and so devious (who, quoting Ovid, reports that he lisped in verse) such unrecoverable origins recede indefinitely. Even as a child, Pope seems never wholly outside the world of literature. Perhaps the best substitute for a moment of poetic origin—the occasion when the poet first dedicates himself to poetry—is Pope's encounter as a child with the seventy-year-old poet and playwright John Dryden. "I saw Mr. Dryden when I was about twelve years old," Pope recalled to Joseph Spence. "I remember his face, for I looked upon him with the greatest veneration even then, and observed him very particularly."[2] This encounter at Will's Coffee House had not been left to chance. Pope had persuaded a friend to bring him to Will's—where Dryden regularly held court—hoping to see the greatest writer of the age. To the young Pope, Dryden was not simply a celebrated literary man but the epitome of a poet. Pope at twelve was carefully observing not just an individual but a role, a vocation, an archetype.

The "veneration" (implying almost religious awe) with which Pope gazed at Dryden tells us a great deal about Pope. As he once implied in referring to the encounter at Will's, he saw in Dryden something like the legendary dimensions of Virgil. Nor did this patriarchal stature diminish as Pope gained experience in recognizing Dryden's faults. At sixteen he had undertaken with the aging William Wycherley a strained and posturing literary correspondence, and the unpublished young poet needed no prompting to share his thoughts about Dryden. "I think with you," he replied agreeably to Wycherley, "that whatever lesser Wits have risen since his Death, are but like Stars appearing when the Sun is set."[3] So imposing was Dryden to Pope that even his absence seemed, like night, a form of lingering presence. Although Pope spent ten years translating Homer

and editing Shakespeare, although he was one of the earliest admirers
of Milton, and although he borrowed ideas or appropriated phrases
from writers in at least four languages in a literary heritage extending
from the Bible to Matthew Prior, yet, as he worked to secure his character and reputation as a poet, his closest kinship was with the man
(like Pope, a Roman Catholic) who was the most important writer of
the previous age. Dryden's words and rhythms and thoughts make a
continual reappearance throughout the works of his extraordinarily
allusive successor. It is hardly surprising that Pope kept a picture of
Dryden in his chamber, along with portraits of Shakespeare and of
Milton.

The influence of a great writer often causes later writers to experience a form of anxiety. Pope's relation to Dryden, however, does not
reveal the strains of psychic and literary conflict that Harold Bloom
discovers in Romantic and in post-Romantic writers. Pope's emotions
are instead disarmingly direct: "Many people would like my ode on
music better," he states matter-of-factly, "if Dryden had never written on that subject."[4] The judgment is probably correct. It certainly
exposes no dark and intricate turns of anxiety, no oedipal designs on
Dryden's muse, no latent fears of castration, no patricidal desire—
only respect mingled with diffident self-regard. When Pope came to
translate the *Iliad* and the *Odyssey*, he again encountered the looming
presence of Dryden, who had published translations of scattered passages from Homer. "Had he translated the whole Work," Pope confessed sensibly, "I would no more have attempted *Homer* after him
than *Virgil*, his Version of whom (notwithstanding some human
Errors) is the most noble and spirited Translation I know in any
Language."[5] Pope's parenthesis is not an instance of mean-spirited
detraction—damaged praise—but the expression of discriminating
independence—the judicious criticism of one who knows, as opposed
to servile or dutiful flattery. (Dryden himself publicly deplored his
own haste in composition.) It might be possible to uncover traces of
anxiety or envy in Pope's silences, to discover occasions when he
*ought* to have praised Dryden but did not—as in the roll call of exemplary critics which concludes *An Essay on Criticism*. Yet, silent
omissions, where they can be reasonably discovered, prove little.
Pope borrowed more without acknowledgment than any major poet
except Shakespeare. Psychoanalytical speculation about his latent
anxieties, even if fascinating, overlooks the central feature of Pope's

literary relation with Dryden. His relation to the past was not governed by oedipal themes or buried laws of the psyche, but by two
formerly powerful and closely related forces: the classical theory of
mimesis and the mercantile doctrines of trade.

For Pope, the classical theory of imitation specified the poet's main
task not as the pursuit of radical uniqueness—what a later generation
meant by "originality"—but as the imitation of nature. The imitation
of nature, of course, included the imitation of literary works that embodied laws, forms, and sentiments stipulated as "natural." This, for
Pope, was the great lesson of Virgil, whose youthful, spirited contempt for literary models did not survive his later scrutiny of Homer.
As Pope wrote of Virgil's crucial discovery: "*Nature* and *Homer*
were, he found, the *same*."[6] The imitation of specific writers and of
established genres did not imply slavish copying, which Dryden dismissed with scorn: "This is like Merry Andrew on the low rope,
copying lubberly the same tricks which his master is so dexterously
performing on the high."[7] Neoclassical imitation, as Pope and Dryden understood it, implied a process of transformation in which continuities with the past are a means of making change visible. "I might
imitate Virgil, if I were capable of writing an heroic poem," Dryden
modestly remarked, "and yet the invention be my own."[8] For Pope,
as for Dryden, invention—the creative faculty which discovers and
disposes new materials for art—was the indispensable collaborator in
all worthy acts of imitation. ("Without invention," Dryden insisted,
"a painter is but a copier, and a poet but a plagiary of others."[9]) Thus
the past, like nature, is an inexhaustible treasury of matter which the
inventive poet will put to use, mixing genres, adapting characters, reviving imagery, echoing thoughts to create a work simultaneously familiar and new, imitative and original. Although an adversarial
relation with the past often bedeviled (or inspired) writers in the
generations after Pope, Pope was not, as they were, charged with the
burden of an innovation so radical that it reduced the past to a catalogue of exhausted possibilities. Pope, while drawing nourishment
from the past, found his main adversaries in the present—in the corrupt politicians and hack writers whose open rejection of established
values he transformed into a sign of their duncelike irrationality.

It was in genealogy that the theory of imitation found its most
fruitful metaphor for expressing the relation between past and present. Genealogy, of course, was not the only metaphor available, for

neoclassical writers imagined the past in various ways, complementary and sometimes contradictory. The past might seem, for example, like a pastoral scene, a region wholly set apart from the present, inaccessible, fixed in a serene and perfect stillness, as in a classical landscape by Poussin. This is the view Pope reflects in *An Essay on Criticism* when he imagines the great writers of the past as a separate community—"born in *happier* Days" (l. 189)—isolated from the corrupt present by an almost visible gulf. Genealogy as a metaphor for imitation held the power to span the vast distance between past and present without denying the remoteness of antiquity. In fact, the bond linking fathers with sons—sometimes over many generations—becomes the most common way for eighteenth-century writers to express their connection to the past, and Pope invokes this metaphoric bond in *An Essay on Criticism* when he directly allies himself with the great ancient writers as "the last, the meanest of your Sons" (l. 196). For Pope the relation between fathers and sons did not conjure up themes or metaphors of Freudian family romance, but rather it referred mainly to social, legal, and religious duties. Pope imagines the son primarily in the role of heir: the ultimate successor to his father's estate. Imitation becomes the act by which a modern poet appropriates tradition, establishing himself as rightful successor, son and heir, to the great ancient writers. Yet, the social and legal suggestions of inheritance do not exhaust the metaphor of genealogy. Equally important, the father is both guardian and teacher; he protects the son, instructs him, and guides him toward eventual independence and maturity. This filial embrace with the past—far from creating rebellious tensions—serves as a source of support, for the father in his role as tutor and protector performs the office usually attributed, in the traditional development of the artist, to the "master." Imitation is a mode of learning—a source of knowledge—and the tradition of artistic discipleship expects worthy sons eventually to become the fathers and teachers of a new generation. The crucial question for Pope is whether they will have appropriated—made their own—what the past has to teach them. We look in vain for hints of anxiety in Pope's forthright statement that he "learned" the art of versification "wholly from Dryden's works."[10] Dryden, quite simply, was the master.

While the theory of mimesis provided in genealogy one way for modern writers to imagine their relation to the past, a complementary version of the same relationship (with its own cluster of metaphoric terms) was available in contemporary mercantile doctrine. Commerce, as an economic force and a literary subject, holds an importance in the eighteenth century now difficult to reconstruct.[11] Free from its later associations with bourgeois philistinism and distinct from mere shopkeeping or plying a trade, commerce then seemed an unprecedented national adventure—opening new overseas markets, supplying raw materials, generating endless publications, and promising not only personal wealth but also imperial power. Far from denigrating commerce as an activity reserved for the enemies of culture, Augustan writers viewed it as a potentially glorious and civilizing enterprise. Thus Pope's *Windsor-Forest* (1713)—like Dryden's *Annus Mirabilis* (1666), from which it frequently borrows thoughts and images—concludes its vision of British renewal by celebrating commerce as an emblem of harmonious order. Pope would later question the commercial spirit *Windsor-Forest* so readily endorses, but his early celebration of trade was far from unusual. Polite letters had discovered in commerce something like a new species of romance. The merchant as financial daredevil and exotic traveler grew indistinguishable, in some eighteenth-century accounts, from the enterprising heroes who dominated the recently translated *Arabian Nights* (one of Pope's favorite books). Commerce promised the abrupt magical change of fortune that also fed the national passion for lottery tickets and South Sea stock (in which Pope, too, invested). This general celebration of commerce had at least one further effect on the world of writing. It supplied a set of economic metaphors for literary production at a time when literature was just beginning to redefine itself as a commodity. It is not coincidental that Pope was the first English poet to earn a living from the sale of his works or that borrowing (perhaps his most characteristic literary trait) refers, like commerce, to an economic process.

It was probably from Dryden that Pope borrowed the commercial metaphors which help him express his relation to the past. Dryden at times viewed the poet's task as inseparable from the new enterprises of commerce. As he announced openly: "I trade both with the living and the dead, for the enrichment of our native language." These words, meant to explain his linguistic practice in translating the *Aeneid*, offer more than a description of poetic technique. The metaphor of commerce central to Dryden's meaning might be said to encompass a whole theory of literature. His subsequent discussion of poetic language seems to have been developed primarily to explore the richness of this controlling metaphor. "If [re]sounding words are not of our growth and manufacture," he continues, "who shall hinder me to import them from a foreign country? I carry not out the treasure of the nation, which is never to return; but what I bring from Italy, I spend in England: here it remains, and here it circulates; for, if the coin be good, it will pass from one hand to another." Then he concludes his strange discourse on poetic diction with a restatement of mercantile theory that sounds as if it were written by an economist rather than by a poet or literary critic: "We have enough in England to supply our necessity; but, if we will have things of magnificence and splendour, we must get them by commerce."[12] Such literary uses of commerce did not depend upon a realistic understanding of how an economy functions. We are witnessing rather the spell of a metaphor as it shapes and expresses Dryden's attitude toward the relations between present and past. Writing—whether it involves translation or imitation or allusion—seems now absorbed into the general activity of commerce, and the restoration of English literary greatness is seen to depend upon expanded trade with the past. The past, like Virginia or the East Indies, becomes a resource for what Dryden calls national "enrichment." Poets in this alliance find themselves the merchants of a mutual exchange between distant worlds of time.

The idea of the poet as merchant, though hardly a sublime concept and insufficient to represent Pope's larger view of poetry, expresses an outlook wholly appropriate to the materialistic and patriotic spirit of Augustan writing, concerned with rebuilding England's literary reputation after the ruinous violence of seventeenth-century conflict. Such rebuilding is Dryden's theme in his noted essay *Of Dramatick Poesie* (1668). "Be it spoken to the honour of the English," boasts Dryden's usual spokesman, Neander, "our nation can never want in any age such who are able to dispute the empire of wit with any people in the universe." The metaphor representing literature as an empire-in-dispute may seem casual or commonplace until we reflect upon the strange setting in which Dryden places his four speakers. They are drifting down the Thames on a barge, attracted by a distant thunder of cannon. A great naval battle is in progress, we learn, between Dutch and English warships—which "disputed the command of the greater half of the globe, the commerce of nations, and the riches of the universe." By setting his gentlemanly argument against the background of a violent episode in the recurring Anglo-Dutch commercial wars, Dryden emphasizes that *two* empires are in dispute—that English dominance in commerce establishes a paradigm for literary dominion. At times Dryden's metaphors reveal an exploitative attitude toward the past that verges on crude imperialism. For example, Neander says in praise of Ben Jonson's imitation of the ancients: "He has done his robberies so openly, that one may see he fears not to be taxed by any law. He invades authors like a monarch; and what would be theft in other poets, is only victory in him."[13] Here is the opposite of anxiety: a sovereign confidence that the past exists to advance the power and grandeur of the present. This belief, purged of its bellicose tone, is among Dryden's most important legacies to Pope and is the basis of all Pope wrote. "A mutual commerce makes Poetry flourish," the young Pope explained to his mentor, William Walsh. "But then," he added, in enlightened mercantile phrases, "Poets like Merchants, shou'd repay with something of their own what they take from others; not like Pyrates, make prize of all they meet."[14]

What can it mean to "repay" the past? Pope's statement to Walsh helps to answer this paradoxical question when we recognize that Pope's image of mercantile repayment corrects or revises Neander's rough metaphor describing imitation as a form of imperious theft or seizure. For Pope, the present "repays" the past by judiciously correcting or improving its legacy. This process, so crucial for understanding Augustan poetics, is what Pope describes in the ambiguous term *refinement*. Refinement does not imply an indiscriminate or artificial smoothness—as Romantic critics of Pope suggest in their attacks—mere high polish, fancy manners, or elitist taste. In refinement, the purpose of labor is to enhance value already existing in an original material. (It is necessary in refining gold to begin with gold-bearing ore.) The most obvious eighteenth-century models for refinement were the massive building projects which occupied the great landowners of Pope's day, who not only constructed vast country houses in imitation of classical prototypes but also redesigned the landscape, adding artificial lakes or woods or vistas wherever nature proved deficient. This was far from mere polish, even when stretched to absurdity. (The well-placed ruin soon joined Roman temples on the list of desirable aristocratic improvements.) Refinement was a special kind of creation which artfully linked past and present in an improving harmony. Like Pope's famous improvements to the small estate he rented at Twickenham, the changes in landscape and in architecture signified internal refinements of spirit, taste, and knowledge. Ethics and aesthetics thus shared the same general goal, as reflected in *The Spectator*, where the refinements of polite behavior were recommended in a prose so pure that Addison sometimes stopped the presses (legend has it) to correct a comma. An ideal so widely shared has, of course, numerous precedents—in theology, in philosophy, in political theory—but for Pope no precedent was more more conspicuous than the literary career of Dryden. It was Dryden who most influentially defined the modern writer's relation to the past as one of revision, correction, and improvement. Pope would have perfectly understood the reference to Augustus' transformation of Rome when Samuel Johnson wrote of Dryden that he found the language brick and left it marble.[15]

Refinement, as a concept describing the Augustan poet's relation to the past, provides both the subject and structure for Dryden's brief but important poem "To my Dear Friend Mr. Congreve" (1694). The poem is in effect a sustained meditation on the relations between past and present, proposing a clear three-stage vision of English literary history since the time of Elizabeth. First come the great Elizabethan "Syres" (l. 3): unnamed writers of strength and genius, who were also rough, rude, and uncultivated. The second stage commences with the Restoration, which Dryden characterizes as a period of art, skill, and cultivation accompanied by the unwelcome loss of genius and strength. (Dryden modestly includes himself among the writers of this second stage.) Congreve, for Dryden, signals the inception of a third and culminating era, when strength and art, genius and regularity are at last triumphantly united. This is the prophetic moment of transition with which Dryden's poem begins:

> Well then; the promis'd hour is come at last;
> The present Age of Wit obscures the past.[16]

This is a counter *Dunciad*: its plot reveals the long-deferred arrival of light. The light which obscures the past, however, does not bury it in darkness. In Dryden's vision of refining change, the present rejects only the weakness and errors of the past, while maintaining and augmenting its strengths. This mythic history of refinement—with Congreve cast metaphorically as Dryden's "Son" (l. 43) and "lineal" (l. 44) heir—suggests how Pope might have understood his visit to Will's Coffee House. As he gazed at Dryden "with the greatest veneration," he was gazing at the poetic father whose estate he—not Congreve—would soon inherit and improve.

There is no more profound kinship between Pope and Dryden than the belief that poetry advances by refining the achievement of the past. Refinement is so far from mere technique that it enters into the most basic composition of Pope's thought, which his technical improvements might be said to reflect. For Pope the ultimate purpose of poetry is, quite simply, to make men better. The refinements of poetry are a means toward achieving ethical improvements that Pope would consider more valuable than any poem. Toward this goal, he needed to turn his attention to improving the legacy of English verse as inherited from Dryden. Pope, of course, never gave better proof of his debt to Dryden than when improving, and reproving, him. Thus, although he praised the unprecedented variety, energy, and majesty of Dryden's couplets, he also usually rejected the alexandrines and triplet rhymes so characteristic of Dryden. Such silent reproofs, to be sure, do not add up to damaging criticism. They also seem focused upon small points of style. Pope, however, found in Dryden much more serious errors—errors which he could not correct in silence.

Dryden's serious failures shared, in Pope's view, the defects characteristic of most Restoration writing. The charge that Dryden often lapsed into tasteless indecency ("To please a lewd, or un-believing Court") seems slightly hypocritical when issued by the author of *Sober Advice from Horace* (1734)—Pope's seamy analysis of lust. Less pietistic is the explicit claim that Dryden's indecency can be understood as an attempt to win favor at court. In refining the example of Dryden, Pope was less concerned with indecent language than with establishing his independence from all sources of patronage, both in and out of court. This determination not to repeat Dryden's errors is clear, too, in Pope's complaint that Dryden published in haste, failing to revise or correct his own performances. As Pope wrote in mixed praise and blame: "Ev'n copious Dryden, wanted, or forgot, / The last and greatest Art, the Art to blot."[17] Pope, in correcting Dryden, performed what Dryden did not do for himself. Yet, although Pope's pursuit of correctness is notorious, there is one final improvement which clearly distinguishes his work from Dryden's. Dryden, in Johnson's words, "delighted to tread upon the brink of meaning, where light and darkness begin to mingle; to approach the precipice of absurdity, and hover over the abyss of unideal vacancy. This inclination sometimes produced nonsense."[18] Such a description could not apply to Pope. For Pope and his age, the improvement which most clearly measured their distance from the recent past was conveyed in a single, momentous change: the correction of nonsense by sense. Sense, as embodied in the poetry of Pope, became the watchword of a new age.

As I have said, this study of Pope aims to encompass his entire career, treating specific poems at considerable length. In most cases I have chosen to discuss well-known poems rather than works which are seldom read or taught, although this procedure slights some poems which seem to me unjustly neglected. There is no single, central argument or thesis which underlies my discussion of specific poems, such as the claim (by Thomas R. Edwards, Jr.) that Pope's career can be divided into an "Augustan" and a "grotesque" mode. Such overly schematic generalizations tend to dissolve when pressed upon individual works. What gives this book coherence is a series of recurring topics, issues, and themes. The sequence of chapters, while following the basic chronology of Pope's works, is intended to allow the eddying and recursive movement of Pope's thought full play, as later poems extend or modify or affirm earlier positions. A chronological study in thematics seems especially appropriate to Pope's work. Pope, in his concern with ethics, was particularly attracted to the interpenetration of imagery and idea that imparts a concreteness and vitality to abstract propositions. In addition, as a writer whose major work spans three decades, he was constantly revisiting and revising his own compositions. Revision, in its richest sense, is the characteristic activity of Pope's writing. Homer, Virgil, Lucretius, Horace, Donne, Shakespeare, Milton, Dryden—all are in various ways "revised" by Pope as he appropriates their virtues for his work or infuses their writing with his own vision. Even his own previous works become a resource which he draws upon later. For Pope, new poems do not simply follow, but modify and sometimes replace—even retract—what went before. A study in thematics, with its recursive ebb and flow, offers a way of understanding how thoroughly Pope devoted his career to the refinement which comes through repeated acts of perception, with their reopening and shifting of perspectives. Revision for Pope is a great deal more than a technique of composition. It is a mode of thought, a natural rhythm, a way of life.

As a poet dedicated to the principle of refinement, Pope at times necessarily contradicted his earlier positions and statements, since revision can introduce change which is abrupt and radical as well as gradual and continuous. Sometimes, because he is a writer so committed to paradox, his thought is irreconcilably divided, as with his attitude toward women, whose "oppression"—the term is his—he observes, condemns, and, in a milder form, perpetuates. Yet, it is not sufficient to observe contradictions within Pope's thought, whether they emerge over time (as his themes develop and ideas alter) or remain fixed and unalterable. We must also try to understand how and why these conflicts appear at different times in different poems. An understanding of such differences exerts two kinds of pressure: outward, toward history, so that we may see how Pope revises both his own thought and the thinking of his age; and inward, toward detailed literary analysis, so that we may see how Pope develops the resources of his style and vision. Refinement implies both change and consistency, and what remains consistent is no less important than what changes. The unchanged verse or phrase or thought, as it passes through successive stages of approval, contributes an invaluable stability to the text, without which change would be invisible. The scope of such changes may be large or small; size is not crucial. Refinement refers to a process, not to magnitude, and it is in the unremitting refinement of his own thought and language that Pope locates the poet's essential work. My purpose in examining Pope's work is not to argue with him, to condemn or to exaggerate his failures of logic, his ideological blindnesses, his lapses of taste. Rather, I wish to recover the vision and revisions which make his work—including its blindnesses, lapses, failures, and contradictions—ultimately compelling and coherent. Pope's outlook clearly differs from our own. The literary conventions he accepted we no longer accept, much as swords and wigs and sedan chairs, like rhymed couplets, now seem antique. I do not intend to claim for Pope an unusual timeliness or special relevance to the present, if only (as Pope insisted) because the present continually changes. I try instead to present Pope *through* the past, believing that his power to speak to us depends primarily on our power to recover his language and the vision which gives it shape. Neoclassical theorists often emphasized the importance of timeless values and general truths, as in Imlac's famous advice against numbering the streaks of the tulip. Pope, in many ways the most neoclassical of writers, shared the view that art must not lose itself in what is purely idiosyncratic, contemporary, individual, irregular, or untrue. It was also Pope, however, who believed that poets unable to speak to their own times speak, finally, to no one. Historical facts, local details, slang expressions, personal whimsies, unruly (even obscene) verses all find a place in Pope's work—to the distress of readers who seek only what is timeless and uplifting. We cannot understand Pope fully or adequately without immersing ourselves in the historical life which his works helped to create and which they so fully engaged. The challenge in reading Pope arises precisely from the complicated sense in which he agrees with Wallace Stevens that poetry—while not reduced or restricted to its origins—is always, inevitably, "the cry of its occasion."

# I

## The Occasional Self:
## Pope's Minor Verse

If I speak variously of my self, it is, because I consider my self variously. All contrarieties are there to be found, in one corner or another, or after one manner or another. Bashful, Insolent, Chast, Lustful, Prating, Silent, Laborious, Delicate, Ingenious, Heavy, Melancholick, Pleasant, Lying, True, Knowing, Ignorant, Liberal, Covetous, and Prodigal . . . In a word, I have nothing to say of my self entirely, simply, and solidly without mixture, and confusion.

—Montaigne

OCCASION has been consistently underestimated or ignored as a regulating principle in eighteenth-century literature. Scholars still do not sufficiently emphasize how popular journalism, competing theaters, and the pamphleteering of political and religious opponents—as well as the continuous warfare among literary factions— combined to create during Pope's lifetime the great age of occasional writing. Probably the most repeated title of the period is the catchall *Poems On Several Occasions*, an apt name for collections in which sublime translations from the Old Testament mingled with ditties to a sweetheart or a squirrel. The idea of occasion thus provided the sole organizing principle which rescues such volumes from absurdity. It is one measure of their popular appeal that Pope published a miscellany with the requisite title—*Poems On Several Occasions*—in 1717.

Pope's interest in occasion extended beyond the jumbled volumes of forgotten verse which his contemporaries admired. Many of his major poems begin in response to a highly specific occasion, such as a feud inspired by a stolen lock of hair. The major poems always manage to transcend, without renouncing, their origins in specific occasions. What proves remarkable, however, is that even when absorbed in weighty affairs, Pope continually returned to the limited, idle, indecent, humorous, short, solemn, tasteless, inconsequential, friendly or simply miscellaneous occasional verse now collected in the volume entitled *Minor Poems*, in the Twickenham edition of his poems. Occasional poetry, though usually minor, should not be confused with nineteenth-century "light verse," which it sometimes resembles. The concept of light verse depends upon an Arnoldian distinction between poems which are serious and poems which are not. What distinguishes occasional verse is not an index of relative seriousness but the concept of occasion. A number of Pope's minor poems explicitly identify their occasions in long and elaborate titles, such as the unedifying verses "On a Lady who P-st at the Tragedy of *Cato*; Occasion'd by an Epigram on a Lady who wept at it." Although free to poke fun at solemnity, occasional verse is not irreversibly opposed to seriousness, especially if the occasion is religious. The timeless is its only true antagonist. If the mixed nature of occasional verse is among its attractions to Augustan writers, who specialized in such impure forms as the ballad opera, the mock-heroic, and the satiric epistle, Pope's long commitment to occasional poetry encourages us to ask what additional attractions it held for a poet whose ambition directed him toward the more authoritative and prestigious literary genres.

## Occasion and Character

Oddly enough, one of the attractions which occasional verse held for Pope was the range it offered for the exploration of human character, especially of his own character as poet. Pope, of course, is not generally considered a writer who invites us to contemplate the riddles of human character. Many readers still associate him mainly with the distant realms of society, morality, and argumentation, where self-disclosure has no place. It is not unusual to hear that Pope is a public poet, speaking in the official idiom of reason, clear, abstract, and impersonal. Compared with his turbulent and mercurial friend Swift, Pope seems reassuringly stable, a writer whose character is fixed and unproblematic. The sense of Pope's stability, however, is a modern illusion. Although he wished at times to portray in himself a character of lucid simplicity, as if truth compelled him to expose the virtual transparence of his inner life, history reveals a multitude of contrary and competing portraits.

Lytton Strachey, for example, created the most entertaining variant of a stereotype dating from Pope's lifetime when he described the poet as a diabolic monkey, gleefully pouring hot oil onto the harmless victims below his window. In welcome correction, recent scholars and critics portray a more upright figure: Pope the liberal Christian in the style of Erasmus, a generous friend and righteous enemy whose high-minded satire defends a landed, patriarchal, classic civilization against the vulgarity and corruption of modern, amoral, bourgeois opportunists such as Walpole and Cibber. Yet this noble likeness demands that we ignore or explain away the flashes of willful deviousness, crude humor, bravado, irreverence, and vindictive delight in punishment that Pope's works also convey. Further, to these competing images we must add other influential views of Pope, such as William Hazlitt's laureate of artifice, triviality, and the indoors; Joseph Warton's description of a poet wedded to reason, morality, and didacticism, incapable of Miltonic sublimity; the angry sketch by John Dennis of an incompetent upstart whose twisted body mirrored his deformities of art and character; or Byron's defense of the most faultless of poets—and almost of men. Like the diverse portraits of Pope created by eighteenth-century painters, this collection of literary sketches (which could be greatly extended) seems to find in Pope completely different men. The problem is not—as with most major poets—that changes in literary taste and in critical method tend to emphasize differing aspects of Pope and his work. Pope inspires such regular and intense controversy about his character that we cannot help thinking him—not his readers—the main source of confusion. Confusion is indeed the result, as Pope himself implied in a teasing letter to Martha (Patty) Blount: "Every one values Mr Pope, but every one for a different reason. One for his firm adherence to the Catholic Faith, another for his Neglect of Popish Superstition, one for his grave behavior, another for his Whymsicalness. Mr Tydcomb for his pretty Atheistical Jests, Mr Caryl for his moral and christian Sentences, Mrs Teresa [Blount] for his Reflections on Mrs Patty, and Mrs Patty for his Reflections on Mrs Teresa."[1] These few illustrations are sufficient to indicate the dilemma facing readers of Pope. In its apparent self-contradictions, his character—as Pope recognized—provides an instance of the potential for incoherence that always threatens man as an ethical being.

The problematics of character interested Pope not only because character is deeply relevant to ethics, but also because in the Augustan Age writers found that they were a source of unusual curiosity for their readers—a curiosity which has persisted to our own day. "I have observed," writes Addison as Mr. Spectator in the first sentence of his epoch-making series, "that a Reader seldom peruses a Book with Pleasure 'till he knows whether the Writer of it be a black or a fair Man, of a mild or cholerick Disposition, Married or a Batchelor, with other Particulars of the like nature, that conduce very much to the right Understanding of an Author."[2] This statement is a true beginning—it marks a new era. Although Addison's irony is clear, since correct understanding involves more than a knowledge of biographical details, his account also defines an important change in the expectations of contemporary readers. The newly popular autobiographies, journals, letters, and novels of Pope's age owe much of their prominence to the growing demand for information about individual lives—a demand which Edmund Curll exploited in his hack biographies and which Johnson rewarded in his superb *Lives of the English Poets*. Sociologists of literature offer various reasons for this new interest in contemporary lives. (The most popular and facile explanation involves a middle class which was "rising.") Whatever its origins, which are surely mixed, the taste for "Particulars" of a writer's life had added a new dimension to authorship and helped to create, notably in the first-person novel, a literary revolution. Thus, despite his ironies, Addison also supplied a long passage in which Mr. Spectator explains in detail his "History and Character." Authors, even if they invented pseudonyms, masks, or semifictional persons, employed such literary devices to ground their writing in the experience and voice of a distinctive "character."

*Character* is a term we must try to recover, for it avoids certain unsettled and misleading ideas implied in the modern concepts of self, in nineteenth-century notions of personality, and in the Lockean concept of identity. Pope undoubtedly knew about Locke's struggles to redefine human identity as consciousness rather than as substance, for he more than once exploited the comic potential of Locke's definition.[3] Pope also shares the general tendency of Locke and later philosophers to emphasize the inwardness of human experience, with its attention to hidden sources of conduct and to a mental life which finds no outlet in action. "My life in thought and imagination," Pope observed in a telling analogy, "is as much superior to my life in action and reality as the best soul can be to the vilest body."[4] Yet, character—not identity, self, or personality—is the term Pope chooses for his most extensive analysis of human nature, and there are considerable advantages in reconstructing Pope's idea of character free from the contexts of philosophy, psychology, and sociology. He was above all a man of letters, merciless in parodying the jargon of specialties, and character offered him a traditional, ready-made concept which (in his preferred mode of innovation) he could shape and refine to suit his own literary needs.

One literary source available for refinement was the critical tradition of character. Character inside this tradition carries a limited, technical meaning. "Know well each Ancient's proper *Character*," Pope advises in *An Essay on Criticism* (l. 119), and what he means by character is something like distinctive excellence. The term has little psychological or ethical resonance, and thus Pope offers only the most general literary description when he defines the "chief Character" of Homer as "Spirit and Fire."[5] Such formulaic descriptions, which conventionally identified Homer with invention and Virgil with judgment, nonetheless held a possibility for richer development. For example, the influential French theorist Roger de Piles defined character in the painter as follows: " 'Tis the Seal that distinguishes his Works from those of other Men, and which imprints on them the lively Image of his Mind." Here is an emphasis upon character as a lifelike ("lively") quality of mind which might point beyond formulaic descriptions. "This Character," de Piles summarized, "consists then in the manner in which the Painter *thinks* Things."[6]

A manner of thinking, the image of a mind: these are ways of considering character which coincide with Pope's emphasis upon the writer's life in thought and in imagination. Such interest in the mental dimensions of character underlies his response to Swift's proposal shortly following the death of John Gay for a posthumous edition of their friend's work. Wrote Pope: "There is nothing of late which I think of more than mortality, and what you mention of collecting the best monuments we can of our friends, *their own images in their writings:* (for those are the best [monuments], when their *minds* are such as Mr. Gay's was, and as yours is)." Then, referring to the volume of his own miscellaneous prose and verse nearing publication, Pope adds revealingly: "I am preparing also for my own."[7] It is useful to disentangle the ideas Pope compresses here, since they suggest a way of understanding literature directly relevant to his own works.

Pope implies that their writings necessarily convey the "images" of all worthy writers; that these images represent "minds"; and that he, as a worthy writer, is consciously "preparing" the image of his own mind that his works will convey. Mind and character here are closely related and inseparable. What Pope's words fail to suggest is how complex the idea of character grows in his work and how complicated are its modes of expression.

The complications and complexities surrounding Pope's representation of his own character had several sources, and we should consider these sources briefly before exploring the relation of character to occasion. The first source of complication is both literary and historical, for the new interest of writers and readers in authorial character had not solved certain long-standing problems of self-disclosure. "It is a hard and nice Subject," explained Abraham Cowley some twenty years before Pope's birth, "for a Man to write of himself."[8] A generation later—despite the influential self-disclosure of Montaigne's essays—the literary problem remained much as Cowley had formulated it. "Anything, though never so little, which a man speaks of himself," wrote Dryden in 1693, "in my opinion, is still too much."[9] Shaftesbury, some fifteen years later, was equally adamant. Despite his forward-looking thoughts as a philosopher and aesthetician, on this subject he simply repeated the views of Dryden: "I hold it very indecent for any one to publish his meditations, occasional reflections, solitary thoughts, or other such exercises as come under the notion of this self-discoursing practice."[10] We may assume that Shaftesbury did not search out points of agreement with the poet who had satirized his grandfather (the first Earl of Shaftesbury) as the satanic and treasonous statesman Achitophel.

The pressures against autobiographical disclosure required that writers conceal their self-discoursing practices by indirection. For Pope the difficulty was how to speak of himself, as he once put it, "with decency." This was no easy problem to solve in the decades before Rousseau in his *Confessions* utterly transformed the canons of self-disclosure. What were the proper forms, about 1700, for speaking of oneself? In a manuscript version of the preface to his *Works* Pope tried out the following formula: "When a man must speak of himself, the best way is to speak truth of himself, for all manner of Tricks will be discoverd. I'll therfore make this Preface a general Confession of all my Thoughts of my own poetry, resolving with the same freedome to expose myself, as it is in the power of any other to expose that."[11] Something beyond the awkwardness of his prose convinced Pope to delete the entire passage. "General Confession" clearly came to seem an artless and foolhardy means of exposing his thoughts and character. Besides, frankness, he knew, had a long history of misuse as the most subtle form of deception.[12] "In the Cunning," he wrote on good authority, "Truth itself's a lye" (*To Cobham*, l. 127). The real question was not whether to renounce "Tricks" of indirection but how to make self-disclosure both decent and artful. At times, surely, his love of tricks won out, as when a mysterious "P.T." delivered to the piratical bookseller Edmund Curll an apparently stolen selection of Pope's correspondence. Pope—who arranged the "theft," certain that Curll would publish at once and thus (unknowingly) oblige Pope to issue an authorized edition in response—no doubt enjoyed any occasion for outwitting the unprincipled Curll. Yet, this was far more than a prank. The canons of literary decorum made it unthinkable for Pope to initiate publication of his own letters. Disguise, as he noted in praise of Ulysses, is sometimes the mask of prudence (note to *Odyssey* XIII.338).

The ingenuity of Pope's dealing with Curll suggests that concealment was not simply a stratagem but a potent source of pleasure. Hiding, as all children know, offers an almost endless satisfaction to playful spirits. Yet, the "habits of secrecy and cunning" Johnson rightly attributed to Pope were also rooted in a self-protectiveness which seems antithetical to play. Perhaps his early experience as a Roman Catholic, forced to worship in concealment and to disguise his views, contributed to Pope's general guardedness. It is certain that, like Ulysses, he did not hesitate to practice what he praised as "prudent dissimulation" whenever he sensed danger. An absolute or impenetrable concealment, however, was not the stance Pope preferred, even when in danger. His ideal state—mixing self-disclosure with secrecy—resembled the paradox of his amorous nymphs in "Spring," who hid themselves in order to be found. Concealment, in such cases, is not a goal but the means of eventual (if partial or incomplete) revelation. This paradoxical mixture of disclosure and concealment is clearly at work in a note Pope sent to Edward Harley, second Earl of Oxford. "*Here we are to be seen*, is the Motto over my house," he explains, adding in crucial and characteristic modification, "but it is so written that none but such as are worthy & Enlightend can understand it."[13] The motto states that at home, in Twickenham, is where he can be found unconcealed—presumably, free from the social constraints and polite artifice which worldly dealings impose. In this vein Pope often writes of Twickenham as a kind of mythic retreat, endowed with healing and restorative virtues, protective, inaccessible to the world outside, where he may reconstitute and recollect his scattered powers. "Shut, shut the door, good *John!*" begins *An Epistle to Dr. Arbuthnot*, not issuing an ordinary domestic command but protesting the invasion of a sanctuary—the violation of his spiritual peace.

Home, for Pope, is a psychological or spiritual alternative to the world; it collects all the resources seventeenth-century writers had invested in the idea of "retirement." As he wrote soon after the note to Oxford, "One's chief business is to be really at home."[14] Twickenham—where Pope is really "at home"— comes to signify a condition of undisguised self-possession. Like the motto, it holds a promise of ultimate disclosure. Yet the motto is also a device of concealment. The disclosure it promises is paradoxically hidden, transformed (by the manner of its inscription) into a secret, an enigma, which only the virtuous and knowing will understand. Pope more than once in his works employs apparent explicitness as a means of concealing what he wishes to leave unsaid. We must not expect that we will enter into a knowledge of Pope's character without close attention to the concealments which are a precondition and medium of its disclosure.

Occasional verse, with its informality and playfulness, offered (like friendship) a perfect arena for combining self-disclosure and self-protection. It was also especially instrumental in Pope's explorations of authorial character because he viewed character, like poetry, as deeply responsive to the informal but binding laws of occasion. Occasion in eighteenth-century life was an active and directive principle—a power, as we sometimes still speak of the law, that can confer pardon and make demands. It was the acknowledged arbiter of social convention. "Just as I am drunk or Scandalous in Town, according to my Company," wrote the youthful Pope from a temporary retreat in the countryside, "I am for the same reason Grave & Godly here."[15] This is hardly direct confession—for Pope expected the understanding reader to know that he was neither as scandalous nor as godly as he pretended—and quite possibly he was making an ironic protest against the genteel tyranny of occasion, which provided a "reason" for completely antithetical modes of being. Yet, although the ironies of a polite correspondence are difficult to measure, Pope's contrast between London scandal and rural sobriety expresses a conviction that unvarying sameness is unnatural. He regarded literature no less than human conduct as necessarily regulated by the flexible laws of occasion. Thus, in *An Essay on Criticism* he described literary conventions in metaphors borrowed directly from social behavior: "For diff 'rent *Styles* with diff 'rent *Subjects* sort, / As several Garbs with Country, Town, and Court" (ll. 322–323). Like poetic language, character was not fixed in a single mode of action but open to sometimes wildly varying possibilities, according to the occasion. Occasion therefore became for Pope a significant guide to the interpretation of human character, indispensable in unfolding the subtleties and changes that would otherwise remain concealed. His interest in occasion was of course shared by other writers of the age, who helped to fill the shelves with occasional verse, yet, they did not share his understanding of the relations between character and occasion. Perhaps the best evidence of his uniqueness is the distinction Pope drew between two different types of occasional verse—one of which he firmly and thoroughly rejected.

In the absence of an established vocabulary, we might call the two main types of eighteenth-century occasional verse historical and ahistorical. Both presuppose a vision in which time—composed, let us imagine, of an endless flow of events—thrusts forth certain acts or moments of heightened significance: a decisive military victory, the birth of a prince, a great storm or fire or plague, a coronation, a peace treaty, a saint's day, a scientific discovery, an act of heroism, the death of a famous man. Public significance detaches such happenings from the ordinary flow of time and transforms them into historical occasions. Historical occasion implies an event so remarkable—so visibly distinct from everyday affairs—that it virtually *demands* a poetic voice. Many Augustan poets saw it as their function to confer upon each historical occasion the distinctive and ceremonious language which alone could properly express its importance. The poem becomes a kind of command performance, composed at the bidding of history, much as the king's birthday extracted from the poet laureate his yearly ode of tribute. Lesser poets thus stood forever vigilant, scanning the field of events in search of momentous occasions— poised to seize the precise instant when history demanded a poet. "What a pity it is that you printed that poem in your Miscellany!" lamented minor poet Elijah Fenton to minor poet William Broome, concerning verses Broome had published ten years earlier. "*Mutatis mutandis,* if it had been published on the seige of Gibraltar, it would have gained you a great deal of reputation."[16]

Occasion, almost independent of human agency, held the power to make unknown poets famous, at least for a moment, and Pope implicitly acknowledged this power in revising his manuscript version of *Windsor-Forest* to conclude with a tribute to the recent Treaty of Utrecht. The poem's epigraph from Virgil accurately summarizes the aesthetic which governs historical occasion: *non iniussa cano* (not unbidden I sing). History bids the poet sing, in this case through the public person of the Secretary for War—George Granville, Lord Lansdowne. The implicit subordination of poet to history—"*Granville* commands: Your Aid O Muses bring!" (l. 5)—helps explain why, after the single exception of *Windsor-Forest*, Pope consistently rejects the commands of great public events. His silence amounts almost to an act of defiance. The poet's chief office, he decides, is not to celebrate history but to evade or to engage it.

Pope's refusal to celebrate historical occasions coincides with his affection for a kind of writing which thrives on the inversions of grandeur: the trifling, the humdrum, the domestic, the inglorious, the insignificant. Private or ahistorical occasions attract him precisely because they express his aversion to public formalities and the inflated significance of government and civic greatness. Pope's occasional verse usually positions itself in the interstices of history. Historical significance is deliberately excluded, but the exclusion is meant to be obliquely visible; as in the pastoral subplot to heroic drama, we are always conscious of diminishment. Pope's ahistorical occasions do not contrive to annihilate or to deny history but to remind us that history goes on, elsewhere, in a less human dimension. For example, Pope writes no poem to celebrate the coronation of George I. Yet, as if calling attention to this rich refusal, he addresses one of his finest occasional poems to an obscure spectator of the great event—his "Epistle to Miss Blount, on her leaving the Town, after the Coronation" (1717). The phrase "after the Coronation" identifies the point of view which dominates most of Pope's occasional verse. The poems not only focus on what is personal and diminished and ordinary. They deliberately stand apart from history, offering an unspoken critique of greatness, reminding us how much of our lives passes invisible to public gaze. In the case of Miss Blount:

24

She went, to plain-work, and to purling brooks,
Old-fashion'd halls, dull aunts, and croaking rooks,
She went from Op'ra, park, assembly, play,
To morning walks, and pray'rs three hours a day.   (ll. 11–14)

Here is the realm where nothing ever happens. It is a world set apart
from history, where the most momentous action is escapist dreaming.
Thus in the country Miss Blount dreams of London, while in London
the poet (also cut off from happiness) dreams of Miss Blount. The
fantasies of poet and lady intersect but fail to coincide, ending the
poem in a comic dissatisfaction which emphasizes Pope's critique
of greatness, whether literary or civic. Like the "Epistle to Miss
Blount," Pope's occasional poems, in their disregard for history, offer
an indirect plea for the domestic trifles and private affections which,
if we will let them, can truly sustain us.

It would be over-solemn and incorrect to suggest that the evasion
of history and the explorations of character were the sole attractions
occasional verse held for Pope. Like many other pieces collected in
the four-volume *Miscellanies in Prose and Verse* (1732–1734) which
Pope published together with Swift, the occasional poems represent
what the authors call "not our Studies, but our Follies; not our
Works, but our Idlenesses" (I, xiii). Yet, idleness and folly—for writers such as Pope and Swift— do not imply the absence of art. In fact,
for a virtuoso stylist one main attraction of occasional verse was undoubtedly its requirement of flawless technique. "Faults may occasionally be excused in a work of length," explains the well-bred hero
of an eighteenth-century novel, "but a short poem must be correct
and perfect."[17] Pope observed much the same to Joseph Spence—"a
poem on a slight subject requires the greater care to make it considerable enough to be read"[18]—and, although as a critic he explicitly rejected the claim that poems must be faultless, as a poet he willingly
accepted the challenge of occasional verse to attain the flawlessness of
a perfectly played game.

Play, indeed, is the implicit activity of many occasional poems,
which are often forms of personal amusement or social pleasure, entertaining rather than profound, the antitype of epic. A gamelike
spirit frequently prevails, as it does in Pope's "Epigram. Engraved on
the Collar of a *Dog* which I gave to his Royal Highness"—a work
whose title contains as many words as the poem. Occasional verse

challenges Pope to discover what will redeem such unpromising materials. It represents Pope's game against himself. He undertakes a composition in which absolute control and skill are essential, yet this effort succeeds only if the poem gives the impression of being casual, effortless, offhand, even improvised. Sometimes surely they were improvised, spontaneous and unrevised accidents of skill, but they could not simply *be* accidental: they had to *appear* accidental as well. The precision of occasional verse is damaged fatally not only by slight faults of scansion, rhyme, awkwardness, or obscurity but also, ironically, by the evidence of precision itself.[19] We should not underestimate, in considering Pope's interest in occasional verse, the attractions of an art which simultaneously appealed to his genuine love of trifles and exercised what Yeats called the fascination of what is difficult.

Neither the skill occasional poems demanded nor the pleasures they imparted, however, can account for the particular use Pope makes of them. In addition to their other functions, the occasional poems provide a stage where Pope discloses aspects of his character which find little or no place in his major works. Pope acknowledges this indirect function in the preface to the four-volume *Miscellanies*, where, in describing the contents, he explains with Swift that the volumes express "the Gaiety of our Minds at certain Junctures" (I, x). But, a collection that contains *A Modest Proposal* cannot be uniformly gay. The "Minds" of the writers, as expressed at the revealing junctures of occasion, are what provide the true principle of coherence. Thus the authors defend even ribald and offensive pieces as written "according to the Dispositions we were in" (I, x). As a defense of ribaldry, this is not persuasive, yet their illogic calls attention to the importance the authors attribute to disposition.

Disposition, in fact, is a concept crucial not only to Pope's occasional verse but also to his exploration of human character. Character, for Pope, *includes* disposition, by which he means the changing mental and emotional states to which all people are subject. As Johnson wrote: "When Pope murmurs at the world, when he professes contempt of fame, when he speaks of riches and poverty, of success and disappointment, with negligent indifference, he certainly does not express his habitual and settled sentiments, but either wilfully disguises his own character, or, what is more likely, invests himself with temporary qualities, and sallies out in the colours of the present moment.[20] Johnson is correct to discount the likelihood that Pope's "temporary qualities" are willful disguises. They are rather the expression of Pope's belief that character, like poetry, belongs not only to the great events of history, but also to the unstable and unheroic flow of time. The occasional poems allow Pope to give free play to the disparate and unstable dispositions excluded from the major poems and thus to extend and refine his self-disclosure. They make of the poet a central instance of the elusiveness, variance, and vast multiplicity of human character—and of its potential for ultimate coherence.

## The Death of Pope: Self-Modifying Structures

The temporary qualities and varying dispositions of Pope's occasional verse reflect his understanding of how the mind works. Human psychology, he believed, is not like a calm stream, steady and composed. It is a rush of "quick whirls" and "shifting eddies."[21] This extreme fluidity is mirrored in the subjects and sentiments of his occasional verse, as in the bawdy mock-epitaph Pope composed for the rural lovers John Hewet and Sarah Drew, who died by lightning:

> Here lye two poor Lovers, who had the mishap
> Tho very chaste people, to die of a Clap.

In these lines we encounter Pope as worldly realist, superior to sentiment, who undermines pathos with his cold and mischievous pun. Yet, in a noncomic disposition, Pope also composed *two* serious and poignant epitaphs for the same unlucky lovers. Misfortune does not evoke a uniform, unvarying, single response but instead provides an occasion for representing the multiplicity of poet and of poetry.

Pope could use a single occasion to illustrate or call forth widely different dispositions and responses, but he could also experiment (as his fame grew) with poems which employ widely differing occasions to dramatize what seem almost separable fragments of his character. The same poet could write, little more than a year apart, both a slyly indecent parody entitled "A Roman Catholick Version of the *First Psalm*, For the Use of a Young Lady":

> *She* shall bring forth most Pleasant Fruit,
> *He* Flourish still and Stand,

Alexander Pope

> Ev'n so all Things shall prosper well,
> That this Maid takes in Hand                    (ll. 9–12)

—and, for another occasion, perhaps his most beautiful and reverent religious poem *The Universal Prayer:*

> Mean tho' I am, not wholly so
>   Since quicken'd by thy Breath,
> O lead me wheresoe'er I go,
>   Thro' this day's Life, or Death.              (ll. 41–44)

An identical meter, stanza, and level of diction convey almost totally opposite spirits. Sometimes the divisions of character are less extreme but inextricably tangled or combined within a single work. Thus, *An Epistle to Dr. Arbuthnot* incorporates at least three related figures: the historical Alexander Pope, whose life the poem (with some exaggeration) describes; the dramatic speaker of the poem (Alexander Pope) who is bounded by the language of the text and whose dispositions vary from indignant rage to pious resignation; and the author of the poem, Alexander Pope, who creates both speaker and text, and whose character cannot be bounded by a single poem or duplicated in a biographical portrait. All are rightly—and perplexingly—called Pope. Some critics would encourage us in the desperate exercise of dividing Pope into more manageable pieces (the man, the persona, the speaker, the character, the poet, and so on) but the difficulty with such neat separations is that they keep breaking down. Pope, in fact, deliberately strains their boundaries, even as he follows Horace and Montaigne in deliberately expanding the perimeters of normal literary experience until his house, dogs, friends, garden, diet, appearance, and innumerable personal details all make their way into his verse. To this slow, complex unfolding of a verse self-portrait the occasional poems contribute their own small but essential refinements.

The little-known "Epitaph. On Himself" (1741) offers us an occasion to explore at some length the problems created by Pope's interpenetrating literary and historical character. The speaker of the "Epitaph" must be Pope, speaking about himself. But which Pope is speaking about which?

> Under this Marble, or under this Sill,
> Or under this Turf, or e'en what they will;

28

Whatever an Heir, or a Friend in his stead,
Or any good Creature shall lay o'er my Head;
Lies He who ne'er car'd, and still cares not a Pin,
What they said, or may say of the Mortal within.

The problems of character explored in the "Epitaph" might have been thrust upon Pope rather than selected coolly for their intrinsic philosophical interest. "No authours," noted Johnson, "ever had so much fame in their own life-time as Pope and Voltaire."[22] The phenomenon of unprecedented notoriety held for Pope a unique peril. No longer did fame pose simply the familiar moral question of whether the artist (tempted by pride) would remain uncorrupted. For Pope fame added a psychological dilemma far more perplexing: could the artist remain unsplintered or whole? Fame, in the new era of print and publicity, splits off from the artist a sizable fragment of character that sometimes seemed to attain nearly an independent existence. It might be adorned, nourished, defended, manipulated, attacked, and even destroyed—as if it were a separate person. Pope belongs in the forefront of a distinct group of writers, including Sterne, Byron, and Wilde, whose contemporary fame created in effect public alter egos.[23] The relation between the artist and his public alter ego can lead to many disorders—from narcissism to suicide—but fame in its modern versions has done more than add such psychic perils. It has changed the aesthetics of self-portraiture. The "Epitaph. On Himself" is among Pope's attempts to repossess the fragment of character he had lost to fame.

The multiplicity of character is what makes careful reading of the "Epitaph" unavoidably vertiginous, because Pope makes us aware of two figures simultaneously: the living poet who composes the words, and the dead poet who utters them. The shifting temporal perspective keeps the reader uncertain not only about the occasion but also about the speaker, who seems so difficult to pin down. In effect, uncertainty accelerates line by line. The funereal explicitness of the opening three words ("Under this Marble") seems to point to a specific slab of white stone. But certainty yields at once to doubt as the marble gravestone suddenly loses its concreteness. Perhaps the body lies under a sill (probably a rough-hewn, common stone like the stone sill at the foot of a barn door)—or in an unmarked plot of turf—or, in the progression from engraved marble to indeterminacy, anywhere. The voice of the dead fails to possess the knowledge we normally attribute to posthumous speakers. But doubt concerning the place of burial is simply prelude to further uncertainty concerning the agents. Who arranges the interment? An heir? or friend? or kindly stranger? The syntactic emblem of this general slippage of certainty is the equivocal conjunction *or*—which Pope repeats five times in the first four lines. Here its semantic function is not to delineate known alternatives (this *or* that) but to evoke the openness of an indefinite series (this *or* that *or* that *or* ... ). The sequence of verbs is equally fluid, shifting from future to present to past to present to past to future, and diction too works to undermine consistency. The abrupt shift from ceremonious dignity to colloquialism ("cares not a Pin") creates a verbal analogue for the multiple modifying structures which control the poem.

Why should Pope pretend total ignorance about his place of burial? (Two years later he specified that he be buried in Twickenham Church, beside his parents, with no epitaph.[24]) Several possible explanations help to illuminate the poem. First, Pope is writing in a tiny subgenre of occasional verse that toyed with the normally solemn conventions of the epitaph. Swift and Gay both preceded Pope in this seriocomic form, which might be called "the author's verses on his death." Second, and more important, Pope's exaggerated pretense of not-knowing supports the tone of not-caring that the poem deliberately cultivates. The speaker's nonchalance concerning his own death parallels the disregard he claims to feel about his worldly reputation. The very creation of a memorial—the poet's epitaph—is contradicted by the poem's express disdain for monuments and reputation. Pope composes an epitaph which, in its shifting perspectives, refuses to adhere to the propriety of a solemn occasion. The refusal acknowledges a paradox that governs the entire poem: Pope wishes to be remembered as not caring how he is remembered.

The "Epitaph" embraces at least one other self-modifying paradox. No honest biographer could claim that a disregard for reputation was ever characteristic of Pope. "It is evident," writes Johnson, "that his own importance swells often in his mind."[25] The "Epitaph" depends upon such public knowledge of Pope's reputed vanity. (The attacks on Pope were legion, and an implicit defense of his modesty by a poet whom everyone believes to be modest is, after all, hardly an occasion for song.) With its paradoxical modifications, the "Epitaph" is not simply an idealized picture designed to correct the slanderous images of Pope circulated by fame. It also reflects an ambivalence central to his character. "The Love of Praise," as *The Spectator* (no. 467) reminded its readers, "is a Passion deeply fix'd in the Mind of every extraordinary Person, and those who are most affected with it, seem most to partake of that Particle of Divinity which distinguishes Mankind from the inferior Creation." Pope not only expressed repeatedly a philosophical detachment from fame, but also, clearly, courted and cherished the fame he disowned. The "Epitaph" simply does not support the sympathetic discrimination between a true or just fame that Pope seeks and a vulgar reputation that he rejects. It is unnecessary to explain away the paradox of simultaneous desire and revulsion. Such contradictory impulses, in Pope's view, go to make up the "riddle" of human nature, reflecting not only our inability to persevere in a single, unchanging conduct but also our secret love of contradiction.

Assumptions about their triviality encourage us to overlook the complex modifications of tone and of content that often accompany the development of Pope's occasional poems. For example, one of the few modern critics to discuss the "Epitaph. On Himself," John Paul Russo, provides this unmixed summary: "Pope trifles with death, like Voiture, and he writes up his own epitaph in a gay moment."[26] The claim for trifling is somewhat weakened, however, when Russo quotes only the six lines we have already examined. The poem, of course, is eight lines long. An accurate summary of the speaker's disposition requires our looking at the complete poem:

> Under this Marble, or under this Sill,
> Or under this Turf, or e'en what they will;
> Whatever an Heir, or a Friend in his stead,
> Or any good Creature shall lay o'er my Head;
> Lies He who ne'er car'd, and still cares not a Pin,
> What they said, or may say of the Mortal within.
> But who living and dying, serene still and free,
> Trusts in God, that as well as he was, he shall be.

The first six lines certainly contain moments of playfulness, but Pope's final couplet changes the poem from play to earnest. It modifies everything that has gone before.

The final couplet concludes in unmistakable reverence, as the earlier confusions of temporal sequence are clarified and resolved. The poem ends in the present-tense action of trusting in God, and the poet's previously-unsettling detachment now reveals to us its source in a vision which understands living *and* dying as aspects of a single, continuous process, subordinated to God's will. (This vision helps to explain the unsettling erasure of distinctions which underlie *The Universal Prayer*, written two decades earlier: "O lead me where-soe'er I go, / Thro' this day's Life, *or* Death.") The religious serenity of Pope's conclusion, nevertheless, does not create a uniformly serene or religious poem, just as his earlier moments of playfulness do not make the "Epitaph" merely trifling. Instead, the "Epitaph" traces a movement from doubt to certainty, from play to earnestness, arriving finally at a statement of plain and unshakable faith, where the process of modification stops.

The modifying structures which govern the development of Pope's "Epitaph" find impressive and subtle support in even such easily ig-nored details as meter. Readers certainly differ in where they would locate stressed and semistressed syllables, but everyone should agree that the opening couplet contains lines of ten syllables each, while (strangely) the concluding lines each contain twelve. In addition, the first line has three perfect dactyls and a final stressed syllable, while the last line changes to an unusual meter for Pope: perfectly com-posed anapests. The change closely imitates the movement of thought in the poem from the false certainty of Pope's opening dactyls, through the unstable metrical variations of the middle couplets, to the final equipoise of his concluding regular anapestic tetrameters. In ef-fect, we see the opening meter gradually modified into its mirror op-posite. I will not attempt to trace the intervening stages of modification, because the latitude for disagreement is too great, but the harmony between Pope's unexpected last statement of faith and the unusual, flawless, closing anapests prompts one final comment. Refinement for Pope is not a process of merely random change or purposeless variety. It points always toward correctness, comprehen-siveness, and conclusiveness. It seeks the repose offered by a stance where further refinement is either pointless or, as in a final "perfect" edition of a work or in the poet's actual death, impossible.

## Character Refined: "A Standish and Two Pens"

We know from many sources, including his self-portrait in *An Epistle to Dr. Arbuthnot*, that Pope was not always serene and free in the face of hostile criticism. A deep conflict of will and emotion underlies his composure in the anecdote recounted by Johnson: "I have heard Mr. Richardson relate that he attended his father the painter on a visit, when one of Cibber's pamphlets came into the hands of Pope, who said, 'These things are my diversion.' They sat by him while he perused it, and saw his features writhen with anguish."[27] The "Epitaph. On Himself" does not cancel such public knowledge of Pope's agitated temper—as if the poem were contradicting a falsehood—but instead exposes any such single characterization as inadequate, incomplete, in need of refinement. The "Epitaph"—like Johnson's anecdote—reminds us that on the subject of fame Pope was not of one mind. The occasional poems, in fact, sometimes establish an open and deliberate counterpoint to the more single-minded self-characterizations developed in the major works, as if together they belonged to an undeclared, inescapable dialectic.

Modification of Pope's self-portraiture in his major works is one purpose of his occasional poem "On receiving from the Right Hon. the Lady Frances Shirley a Standish and Two Pens," which was written about 1739 and has seldom been reprinted. Long neglect leaves no alternative to quoting it fully here. The poem acknowledges the gift of an inkstand and two pens, one tipped with steel and one with gold—the "radiant weapons" of stanza 2. Bertrand's was a toy shop which sold such domestic curios.

> Yes, I beheld th' Athenian Queen
>     Descend in all her sober charms;
> —"And take (she said, and smil'd serene)
>     Take at this hand celestial arms:
>
> Secure the radiant weapons wield;
>     This golden lance shall guard Desert,
> And if a Vice dares keep the field,
>     This steel shall stab it to the heart."
>
> Aw'd, on my bended knees I fell,
>     Receiv'd the weapons of the sky;
> And dipt them in the sable Well,
>     The fount of Fame or Infamy.
>
> —"What *well?* what *weapon?* (Flavia cries)
>     A standish, steel and golden pen;
> It came from Bertrand's, not the skies;
>     I gave it you to write again.

33

But, Friend, take heed whom you attack;
    You'll bring a House (I mean of Peers)
Red, Blue, and Green, nay white and black,
    L. . . . . . and all about your ears.

You'd write as smooth again on glass,
    And run, on ivory, so glib,
As not to stick at fool or ass,
    Nor stop at Flattery or Fib.

*Athenian Queen!* and *sober charms!*
    I tell ye, fool, there's nothing in't:
'Tis Venus, Venus gives these arms;
    In Dryden's Virgil see the print.

Come, if you'll be a quiet soul,
    That dares tell neither Truth nor Lies,
I'll list you in the harmless roll
    Of those that sing of these poor eyes."[28]

Like many of his occasional poems, Pope's lines carry immediate practical and personal significance, returning gift for gift. Mythological allusion supplies a mock-heroic dazzle to what is plainly a private and ahistoric event. But, unlike the situation in *The Rape of the Lock*, this occasion has the poet (not the lady) appearing faintly ridiculous in epic dress. Dryden, in Swift's *Battle of the Books* (1704), had appeared to similar disadvantage, decked out in the armor of the ancients, wearing a helmet unfortunately nine times too large for his head.

The mock-heroic moments belong to Pope's strategy of indirect compliment. (Direct compliment might have looked like flattery and implied an unwillingness or inability to rise above witless gratitude.) The self-deprecating extravagance creates an impression of playful intimacy, as England's most famous poet clowns for the amusement of an aristocratic Twickenham neighbor. But the poem contains more than good-natured fun. Quite possibly at Pope's direction, William Warburton, Pope's chosen editor, placed it as an appendix or coda to the fierce *Epilogue to the Satires*, for which Pope had been threatened with prosecution in the House of Lords. (The symbolic colors of stanza 5 represent the united lords and bishops reduced to their lowest level of reality.) In a postscript first published after his death, Pope explained something of the pressure that had induced him to abandon Horatian satire, saying: "This was the last poem of the kind printed by our author, with a resolution to publish no more; but to enter thus, in the most plain and solemn manner he could, a sort of PROTEST against that insuperable corruption and depravity of manners, which he had been so unhappy as to live to see." Silence—which Pope utilized earlier in his refusal to celebrate the great public events of history—here becomes the poet's ultimate (but most desperate) form of expression. It is also the direct occasion for Lady Shirley's practical gift: "I gave it you to write again." Pope, we should notice, does not resolve to be *totally* silent, at least not until the epic apocalypse of *The Dunciad*, where wit is finally silenced by the reign of "Universal Darkness" (IV.656). Rather, he chooses a form of modified speech, enlisting the playful spirit of occasional verse in his serious campaign against corrupt politics, depraved morals, and fraudulent art.

The mixture of play and seriousness in "A Standish and Two Pens" extends throughout the poem, altering our sense of characters and tone until nothing remains unqualified or pure. For example, the poem's controlling allusion directs us to a scene of solemn and dynastic gift-giving: the descent of Venus, who brings to Aeneas the divine weapons with which he will establish the future greatness of Rome. This is the famous scene—illustrated in Dryden's translation of Virgil—to which Flavia specifically refers in stanza 7. Her literary reference, however, is not the sign of a poetic temperament but expresses her good sense and respect for plain facts, as she openly rejects the speaker's preposterous delusion that the pens are weapons supplied by an "Athenian Queen." It is Flavia's task to counter his delusions with practicality: "what *well*? what *weapons*?" This underlying contrast between the deluded poet and the lady of sense allows Pope to manipulate self-parody for the purposes of social praise. First, he pays Lady Shirley the indirect compliment of comparing her to Athena. Then he allows her the modesty and intelligence to reject such poetical flattering: "*Athenian Queen! and sober charms!* / I tell ye, fool, there's nothing in't." She even enjoys an opportunity to correct the translator of Homer in a detail of classical learning—with the reminder that it is Venus, not Athena, who descends to arm the hero. There is no taint of illusion about Flavia. The conflict of contrary

35

styles and visions creates an impression of divided worlds. By characterizing himself as delusive, vain, and ridiculous, Pope grants Lady Shirley the high privilege of appearing, by contrast, both practical and wise.

But the separation between the poet and the lady—when we look beyond the purposes of social compliment—does not remain a fixed line dividing wisdom from folly. Close attention to Flavia's language reveals the limits, as well as the attractions, of practicality and good sense. Her affectionate manner and friendly concern should not disable us from recognizing what ignoble projects (for his safety) she commends to the daring poet of the *Epilogue to the Satires*: "glib" and "smooth" social pleasantries, innocuous love poetry, and versified equivocation ("neither Truth nor Lies"). Her gift, however well intended, is deadly. It lures the poet toward a comfortable form of emasculation and self-betrayal. As we begin to examine Flavia's recommendation, the speaker's delusion reveals at least glimpses of a wisdom beyond the reach of worldliness. His refusal to acknowledge the triviality of Flavia's little gift is more than Pope's well-engineered compliment to Lady Shirley. It also conveys an indirect reminder of art's high calling. "To write well, lastingly well, Immortally well," Pope emphasized, "must not one leave Father and Mother and cleave unto the Muse? Must not one be prepared to endure the reproaches of Men, want and much Fasting, nay Martyrdom in its Cause."[29] A pen-and-ink set is merely a trivial domestic object—or, if embellished, a luxurious gadget—but it is also the instrument by which writers exercise their capacity for courage and virtue. Only when used for trivial purposes is the poet's gift ever trivial. Why should it seem extravagant to serve the goddess of wisdom? to reject self-serving worldliness? On reflection, the roles of poet and lady look now almost reversed. Extravagance and delusion suggest integrity, while practicality and good sense have an air of knavish calculation.

A reversal of the values normally assigned to delusion and to good sense, however, is not entirely accurate as a description of the movement we have traced. The poet is not fully transformed from fool to hero, nor the lady reduced from affectionate friend to knave. "A Standish and Two Pens" develops instead through a modification in which neither figure, alone, monopolizes virtue or folly. Their merits and deficiencies prove so thoroughly mixed that no pure or unaltered final summary of character is possible. We are left with a speaker compounded of wisdom and folly—both perhaps equally inadvertent—and a lady whose kindness is short-sighted. Standing behind both of these incomplete figures, of course, is their creator, who employs self-parody here as a means of modifying an earlier exaggerated and incomplete portrait of the artist in his *Epilogue to the Satires*. The solitary, embattled, heroic champion of virtue portrayed in the *Epilogue* finds in "A Standish and Two Pens" his parodic alter ego. The reader—confronted with both portraits—encounters a dilemma which is not concerned so much with meaning as with the understanding of human character.

The relation between the *Epilogue* and "A Standish and Two Pens" provides an unusually clear example of how Pope used occasional verse to revise and to enrich our understanding of his character. The vantage they create together allows us to see the poet as completely dedicated to his office as the feared satirist—the sole figure in a landscape of general complacency who "dares" to attack the political machine of Robert Walpole. Yet it also shows us the good-natured, mild-tempered, social gentleman whose wit can be turned equally upon himself, whose self-possession is such that he can afford to poke fun at his high seriousness, at least when the occasion permits. We see a character rich enough not to be utterly consumed or possessed by a public mission. Pope invites us to understand that the feared scourge of Walpole is precisely the self-deprecating and humorous good neighbor of "A Standish and Two Pens"—*driven* to satire by outrageous corruption. Neither figure—the good neighbor or the satiric scourge—should be regarded as the "real" Pope while the other is designated a mere role or pose or mask. Both figures belong to a flexible, composite, and potentially coherent character, who contains and transcends them. "There is one great and consistent genius evident through the whole of your works," wrote the minor poet Henry Brooke to Pope, "but that genius seems smaller by being divided, by being looked upon only in parts." Then he added what modern criticism still needs to understand: "You are truly but one man through many volumes."[30]

## Character as Style: The Language of Refinement

Character in its multiplicity finds expression not only in feeling, thought, and action. Dryden insisted that character is also expressed in a distinctive use of language. The poet's particular manner of thought reveals itself in his diction, versification, and style. Thus for Dryden the main duty of a translator is to understand the "particular turn of thoughts and expression" in each author—which "distinguish, and as it were individuate him from all other writers."[31] Style, for Dryden, possesses almost a personal signature, and no writer can reproduce another poet's individuating stylistic character except by deliberate and skilled imitation. Although Dryden here invokes the same technical tradition of character which Pope honored in *An Essay on Criticism*, Pope at first might seem to disagree with his great predecessor: "There is nothing more foolish," he told Joseph Spence, "than to pretend to be sure of knowing a great writer by his style."[32]

Pope's claim did not convince Spence ("Mr Pope had certainly a style of his own which was very distinguishable"), and it did not convince Swift. Although initially unable to identify the author of the anonymous *Essay on Man*, Swift declared confidently that he could recognize Pope within six lines whenever Pope chose not to write below or above himself. Pope, in turn, was equally confident of his ability to recognize Swift, despite Swift's notorious satirical impersonations. (Wrote Pope: "Your method of concealing your self puts me in mind of the bird I have read of in India, who hides his head in a hole, while all his feathers and tail stick out."[33]) Pope's irritation at critics who claimed to know him by his style involves their failure to understand that he was writing in many *different* styles, from Ovidian dramatic monologue to Horatian familiar conversation to grave philosophical dispute. As Spence and Swift knew, however, certain long-recognized consistencies in Pope's language and technique also gave credence to the idea that he had a distinguishing style or styles. Unfortunately, Pope's style is still discussed mainly as an inventory of rhetorical devices from anaphora to zeugma, so that the possible ways in which his language may represent his character are rarely explored. Yet, the representational possibilities of style are beginning to gain a renewed credit among modern theorists, and this representational power was exactly what Pope described as the principle of selection in determining which pieces to include in the *Miscellanies* he would publish with Swift. As he wrote to Swift: "I would chuse to print none but such as have some peculiarity, and may be distinguish'd for ours, from other writers . . . For unless there be a character in every piece, like the mark of the Elect, I should not care to be one of the Twelve thousand signed."[34] The articulation of his character was one of Pope's major literary projects. It would be surprising—Dryden would hold it impossible—if his mastery as a stylist proved completely unrelated to what distinguishes and "individuates" him.

A brief and unfamiliar occasional poem permits us to see certain techniques of style that were fundamental to Pope's writing throughout his career—Pope's "Epitaph. On Mrs. *Corbet,* Who dyed of a Cancer in her Breast" (1730):

> Here rests a Woman, good without pretence,
> Blest with plain Reason and with sober Sense;
> No Conquests she, but o'er herself desir'd,
> No Arts essay'd, but not to be admir'd.
> Passion and Pride were to her soul unknown,
> Convinc'd, that Virtue only is our own.
> So unaffected, so compos'd a mind,
> So firm yet soft, so strong yet so refin'd,
> Heav'n, as its purest Gold, by Tortures try'd;
> The Saint sustain'd it, but the Woman dy'd.

Johnson considered this poem "the most valuable" of Pope's many epitaphs. "Domestick virtue, as it is exerted without great occasions or conspicuous consequences in an even unnoted tenor," he wrote of the "Epitaph. On Mrs. *Corbet,*" "required the genius of Pope to display it in such a manner as might attract regard, and enforce reverence."[35] As his praise indicates, the chief merit of the poem for Johnson is its manner or style, for the subject otherwise commands little regard. Yet many readers would surely disagree with Johnson's praise. The portrait is sufficiently general to suit almost any virtuous, long-suffering, and obscure woman. (Until recently, scholars believed Pope first wrote the poem for a shadowy and unfortunate woman named Mrs. Cope.) The tone of restraint can suggest a cold detachment, as if the unemotional language had been designed to obliterate all trace of the author's personal feelings. I contend, however, that even where Pope seeks to expunge the traces of a distinctive speaker, even where he strives to celebrate Mrs. Corbet in a personless and passionless (and hence impartial) voice, he cannot succeed. His language reveals him.

Despite its deliberate impersonality, the style of the "Epitaph. On

Mrs. *Corbet*" is dominated by the principles of modification and of refinement so basic to Pope's character and thought. The first couplet provides a model for the subsequent operation of his refining style. In their formulaic bluntness, the first four words ("Here rests a Woman") confront us with the unadorned and unqualified fact of death. The refinement begins immediately with the simple phrase "good without pretence." Crucial discriminations—some obvious, some subtle—are set in motion at once. The adjective "good" certainly divides womankind into two broad, if unequal classes, and thus we learn at the outset to what large subclass Mrs. Corbet belongs. But the initial modifying phrase "good without pretence" distinguishes not only between two classes of women (good and not-good) but also between two kinds of goodness. In her unpretentiousness, she is both modest (distinguishing her from good women who make a show of their virtue) and genuine (distinguishing her from women who merely pretend to goodness). It is slow work, of course, to spell out distinctions which, if not grasped almost intuitively, make explicit commentary ponderous. Yet, modern reading provides little experience in how to understand Pope's refining style with anything like intuition. It may be useful, then, to extend the analysis briefly.

Consider the second line of the opening couplet: "Blest with plain Reason and with sober Sense." Here Pope continues to build up particularity through the accumulation of modifying formulas. The nouns "Reason" and "Sense" may at first seem synonymous—but they are not, even though their alliance is so close that they seem indivisible. In *An Essay on Man*, Pope marvels at the "thin partitions" which divide "Sense from Thought" (i.226). Reason is, of course, a vastly complex concept, for which Johnson's dictionary offers some widely differing definitions, and there are ways in which sense is equally complex. But the combination of sense, reason, and goodness is not all that distinguishes Mrs. Corbet. Each modifying noun is itself modified. Her reason is "plain," distinguishing it from the over-sophisticated intelligence which (*An Essay on Man* insists) creates half the misery of mankind. Like reason, her sense is also modified, as "sober," which adds a range of possible shadings to her character. (For *sober* Johnson offers the relevant meanings: "Temperate"; "Not mad; right in the understanding"; "Regular; calm; free from inordinate passion"; and "Serious; solemn; grave.") The poem's best emblem of Pope's modifying style is undoubtedly the repeated syntactic pattern "so $x$ / yet $y$"—where traditional opposites (firmness and softness, strength and refinement) modify each other. The relation between firmness and softness, between strength and refinement, manages to reconcile extremes customarily attributed to masculine and feminine temperaments, so that Mrs. Corbet's achievement is no ordinary synthesis. Pope's shades of meaning begin to create a study in moral character, which, despite his use of general nouns and adjectives, is more specific and individual than it first appears.

I have no wish to make these small distinctions seem momentous. My point is just the contrary. Because they are not momentous or spectacular, we tend to overlook them altogether. The habit of ignoring Pope's careful refinements of meaning was perhaps inevitable when new poetic values—and thus new demands upon the reader—developed after his death. Wordsworth, for example, in a long commentary on the "Epitaph" complains of Pope's "laborious attempts at discrimination."[36] Yet, this discriminating process at work in Pope's most basic units of syntax is among the most characteristic features of his style and thought. The twentieth-century revival of Pope has encouraged readers to admire his use of techniques now favored by modern poets and critics—metaphor, imagery, allusion, puns, irony, paradox—and these techniques are essential to Pope's art. The "Epitaph. On Mrs. *Corbet*," however, owes little to the honorific devices of modernism. It builds up meaning in a different manner, a manner analogous to the painstaking discriminations of Lockean judgment, with its careful distinction between apparently similar ideas.[37] Our knowledge of Pope does not advance by pretending that the "Epitaph. On Mrs. *Corbet*" is enriched by subtle metaphors, rich imagery, and erudite allusions—or by implying that their absence constitutes failure. The poem's strength depends instead upon minute, prosaic, cautious, discriminating refinements that grant to Mrs. Corbet a praise whose ultimate authority is its own unimpassioned judiciousness.

As he extends his study of moral character, Pope in his measured praise of Mrs. Corbet also establishes a deliberate contrast within the poem between two ideals of conduct:

> No Conquests she, but o'er herself desir'd,
> No Arts essay'd, but not to be admir'd.

41

The modifying syntax (no $x$ / but $x'$) unobtrusively calls into question the entire heroic tradition. Quiet self-mastery is described by comparison with martial conquest, just as private virtue is compared with the arts of worldly reputation. Mrs. Corbet's freedom from "Passion and Pride" suggests, in fact, that the new heroism of retiring self-mastery is an improvement over the traditional pursuit of glory. "Men should know that the noble power of suffering bravely," Pope wrote several decades earlier, "is as far above that of enterprising greatly, as an unblemished conscience and inflexible resolution are above an accidental flow of spirits or a sudden tide of blood."[38] Yet, it is not only traditions of masculine heroism which Pope's poem calls into question. He also describes Mrs. Corbet as standing apart from traditions of feminine conduct which emphasize the "Arts" of pleasing and self-adornment. The admiration which Belinda seeks in *The Rape of the Lock* is always, at last, erotic, arousing envy in women and desire in men. In rejecting the erotic arts of display, Mrs. Corbet assumes a position as far from conventional female behavior as from masculine ideals. Pope sets her on an uneasy, unworldly, indefinite ground where character finds itself in opposition to traditional roles.

While the "Epitaph. On Mrs. *Corbet*" contributes to a general revision of values in its celebration of individual goodness, brave patience, and retired self-possession, its revisionary stance also contributes to a major redefinition of the English elegy, marking a decisive change from the baroque exuberance and learned intricacy represented by Milton's "Lycidas." "The new idea of elegy," explains Rachel Trickett, "was that it should be more concerned with the honest achievements of the dead than with the mystery of death itself. To the Augustans death was a fact to be accepted, not the subject for poetic meditation, and the death of a good man seemed rather to level him with others than to distinguish him with unique glory."[39] These important redefinitions demanded that Pope abandon the exaggerated praise and elevated language traditional in epitaphs, where (as Johnson observed) no man writes under oath. Thus, while the concluding couplet might seem to abuse honesty by comparing Mrs. Corbet's fortitude to the martyrdom of official saints, in a final modification the strained analogy also calls attention to its own limits. Mrs. Corbet's life, despite her great suffering, was not the stuff of hagiography. If her spiritual strength deserves comparison with saintly virtue, some readers will find her virtue sadly cloistered, her life regrettably colorless and forlorn. Pope's restrained diction no doubt encourages reflections about the cost of self-mastery and the isolation of suffering. (Illness filled Pope's life with pain, whose isolating effects he compared with stoic self-denial.) Mrs. Corbet's elevation to the status of saints and martyrs simply will not hold. The concluding down-to-earth words return us to the plain human fact with which the poem began: "the Woman dy'd."

A poem describing the character of Mrs. Corbet might seem remote from the subject of Pope's character, and it would be easy to argue that all poets employ modifying structures, which are not only normal to English syntax but also especially common in eighteenth-century verse.[40] Two points deserve brief consideration. First, Pope's style logically should exhibit features characteristic of eighteenth-century verse because, more than any other writer, he is responsible for refining and for defining the poetic idiom of his age. Any general description of eighteenth-century verse which does not apply to Pope must be flawed. Second, in distinguishing Pope from other poets who worked in a similar style, questions of degree are crucial. No poet but Pope has so thoroughly personalized the modifications native to English syntax and inherent in the traditions of the heroic couplet. Nor is refinement, as we have seen, merely a technique. The syntax and style which so carefully shape the language of the "Epitaph. On Mrs. *Corbet*" correspond to repeated patterns in his work, where opposing concepts and traditions are forced (by the compression of Pope's writing) into close encounters. Sometimes the result is paradox and conflict, sometimes reconciliation and refinement. In the case of Mrs. Corbet, her achievements of character resemble the reconciled and modified virtues which Pope praises in his epitaph "On *John* Lord *Caryll*":

> A manly Form; a bold, yet modest mind;
> Sincere, tho' prudent, constant, yet resign'd     (ll. 1–2)

or in his "Epistle to Mr. Jervas," which celebrates similar achievements in art:

> Soft without weakness, without glaring gay;
> Led by some rule that guides, but not constrains;
> And finish'd more thro' happiness than pains!     (ll. 66–68)

or, leaving the arena of minor verse, in the brilliant portrait of Martha Blount in his epistle *To a Lady*:

> Reserve with Frankness, Art with Truth ally'd,
> Courage with Softness, Modesty with Pride,
> Fix'd Principles, with Fancy ever new.          (ll. 277–279)

Like Mrs. Corbet, Martha Blount avoids the defects of traditional masculine and feminine conduct while she simultaneously unites the traditionally divided virtues of womanly softness and manly strength. Such passages, in their similarities, reveal more than individual portraits of virtue. They also convey, through and beyond style, patterns of thought which are basic to Pope's outlook. The process of refinement which employs traditional opposites as a medium for creating new virtues belongs to his most fundamental modes of vision, feeling, understanding, and expression. These activities deserve a prominent place in any critical discussion which seeks to discover—as he sought—not just the meaning of a poem but the character of the poet.

## "A Perfect Edition": Refinement Concluded

The analysis of several neglected occasional poems can be no more than introductory and suggestive, but the importance of refinement to Pope and his art makes clear that the occasional poems are not simply trifling or marginal pieces of no interest. Despite Pope's sometimes dismissive tone in mentioning them, the occasional poems gave him a freedom unavailable in other literary forms. In certain dispositions Pope could equally dismiss all poetry as a mere jingle of horse-bells, a frivolous distraction from the serious business of living.[41] Trifling is itself a significant act for a poet who normally regarded verse as a lofty and serious vocation, and, as the "Epitaph. On Mrs. *Corbet*" shows, the occasional poems are not uniformly trifling but rather contribute their mixed spirit to the larger drama of character which unfolds throughout Pope's work. "Every hour of my life," he explained to John Caryll, "my mind is strangely divided. This minute, perhaps, I am above the stars, with a thousand systems round about me, looking forward into the vast abyss of eternity, and losing my whole comprehension in the boundless spaces of the extended

Creation, in dialogues with Whiston and the astronomers; the next moment I am below all trifles, even grovelling with Tidcombe in the very center of nonsense."[42] Pope's contemporaries William Whiston (who delivered popular lectures on Newtonian science) and John Tidcombe (whose military background included a preference for rough, broad humor) stand as metaphors for the mind's capacity to stretch, within moments, from the sublime to the ridiculous. The occasional poems reflect this genuine division in Pope's mental economy. Further, they attest to an ideal of character in which coherence must allow for unexpected shifts, for opposite extremes, for eccentric or erratic tangents, for what is loosely connected and oddly juxtaposed, as distinguished from the homogeneous unities in which all is tightly drawn to a center. The danger of such vast internal divisions is that the centrifugal energies of character will disperse in chaotic discord—soaring, plunging, tumbling incoherence. Equally dangerous, however, are the centripetal tendencies which (especially in Pope's late satires) always threaten to reduce human character to a fixed, mechanical, obsessive sameness. Pope's work depicts man, imperiled by the opposite dangers of chaotic dispersal and inhuman contraction, in search of a self-possession rich enough to embrace both extreme multiplicity and ultimate coherence. To this continuing plot or action the occasional poems attach themselves as significant episodes.

"My works will in one respect be like the works of Nature," Pope wrote to Swift, "much more to be liked and understood when consider'd in the relation they bear with each other, than when ignorantly look'd upon one by one."[43] Our understanding of a specific poem changes, he implies, when we recognize its continuities with other works, and Pope sometimes explicitly quotes from or refers to his earlier verse for this reason. This self-revising process certainly applies to our understanding of the occasional poems. They demand to be understood within the larger body of works to which they contribute. An incompleteness, an insufficiency are inherent in their nature, much as snapshots (by their nature) contain an implicit statement of incompleteness. They give us fragments, moments, passing dispositions, experiments, pretense, play. Their importance depends upon the recognition that there is no occasion large or rich enough to call together—to summon, integrate, and embrace—all the diverse possibilities of character. Thus for Pope every act of self-portraiture must contain a measure of incompleteness, and character can best be expressed seriatim, where one disposition, one moment, one occasion yields to the next. "Whatever I write," Pope assured a valued correspondent, "will be the real Thought of that hour, and I know you'll no more expect it of me to persevere till Death in every Sentiment or notion I now sett down, than you would imagine a man's Face should never change after his picture was once drawn."[44] The occasional poems belong, like his letters, to the temporary truths of change. Completeness, if conceivable, is always a project of futurity.

There is, in fact, one occasion which offers Pope the melancholy prospect of completeness. "I *must* make a perfect edition of my works," he exclaimed to Joseph Spence in the year of his death, "and then I shall have nothing to do but to die."[45] The statement implies more than the wish to behold an authorized text containing final emendations, variant readings, and explanatory notes. The fulfillment of a "perfect" edition—not flawless but completed, finished, final (Latin *perficere*, to complete)—would bring to conclusion the portrait of his own mind toward which Pope had told Swift he was steadily "preparing." Although Pope sometimes insisted on the separation of his life and art, here his statement to Spence suggests that writing is so nearly equivalent with living that they reach their conclusion simultaneously: the completion of the work signals the completion of the life. Incompleteness, in this last act of revision, is finally overcome. Unlike certain modern writers who suppose that endings are impossible, that there is no point when composition can be concluded, Pope sees writing, like human character, as moving toward a point at which the process of refining necessarily ends. In a final, perfect edition, refinement can proceed no further; character has received its finishing strokes; the sequence of individual poems in their self-modifying relations, along with their previously deleted lines or passages, represent all that can be expressed of the poet's mind. Perfection in this technical sense does not require the exclusion of what is juvenile or playful or trivial or incomplete. The occasional poems, rather, lend their incompleteness toward a full and final summation. They are not major poems which have mysteriously failed. They are not premature or scaled-down versions of more substantial works. Their diversity is more than neglected evidence of Pope's wide range as a poet. They also, in their explorations of authorial character, help to explain the strange multiplication of history's Alexander Popes.

# II

## Civilized Reading:
## The Act of Judgment
## In *An Essay on Criticism*

Men must be *taught* as if you taught them *not;*
And Things *unknown* propos'd as Things *forgot.*

—Pope

P OPE'S earliest didactic poem, *An Essay on Criticism*, published in 1711, extends his debt to Dryden by consolidat-
ing ideas from Dryden's scattered prefaces and essays within a
unified critical theory. It is also, however, a poem which has proved
so successful in disguising the unfamiliar as the forgotten that its
claims to originality and importance are today automatically dismissed. De Quincey encouraged this fashion in subsequent commentators with his picturesque description of the poem in the seventh
edition of the *Encyclopedia Britannica* (1842): "It is a collection of
independent maxims, tied together into a fasciculus by the printer,
but having no natural order or logical dependency: generally so vague
as to mean nothing."[1] For more than one hundred years docile scholars have repeated this opinion. One standard modern history of criticism summarizes Pope's poem with routine nonchalance: "There are
repetitions and inconsistencies, some conventional pronouncements
along with injunctions of lasting value; but nowhere (and this should
be emphasized) are the principles organized into a coherent whole,
and no cut-and-dried theory therefore emerges."[2] Even readers alert
to Pope's technique of inventive borrowing—the repayment of the
past through the refining of what it provides—find it easy to regard
the *Essay* as merely an urbane collection of platitudes: "What oft was
*Thought*" (l. 298). The poem's ostensible subject evokes so little serious attention that it is regarded as a screen for loftier ambitions.

## Alexander Pope

"Pope's object in the *Essay on Criticism*," we are told, "is not to say something original about criticism, but to announce himself as a poet."[3] Almost no one believes that the twenty-three-year-old prodigy capable of composing such a learned and skillful poem could have thought seriously or cared deeply about the nature of literary criticism. Particularly because modern studies have focused on its treatment of wit, the *Essay* is commonly discussed as a poem about poetry with an unfortunately misleading title.[4] I wish to propose a very different view: that *An Essay on Criticism* is an original and significant contribution to the history of critical theory.

## Authority and Taste

Some of Pope's distinguished contemporaries would seem to support the claim of originality and significance. Addison in *The Spectator* (no. 253) lauded the poem as a "Master-piece." Joseph Warton, adept in the labyrinth of ancient and modern critical tradition, ranked the youthful poet among "the first of critics."[5] Samuel Johnson grew even warmer in his praise, calling the poem one of Pope's "greatest" works. If Pope had written nothing else, he claimed, *An Essay on Criticism* "would have placed him among the first criticks and the first poets."[6] When we recall Johnson's stature as a critic and his contempt for versified platitudes, we might begin to suspect that Pope offered his contemporaries more than a slick cento of traditional lore. Both Johnson and Warton elevated Pope, as a critic, to the level of Horace, Longinus, and Aristotle. Their harsh treatment of other poems by Pope suggests that they had no reason to exaggerate the merits of an early work which one representative modern scholar dismisses as simply "a mosaic of scraps."[7] Clearly they found something in the poem of great value. What they found, I believe, is a stimulating and original (if submerged) theory of literary criticism.

The theory takes some finding—for it is one of the ironies of Pope's discourse on method that it appears casually unmethodical, as if directed mainly by a loose association of ideas. "The Observations follow one another," writes Addison, "like those in *Horace's Art of Poetry*, without that Methodical Regularity which would have been requisite in a Prose Author" (*The Spectator* no. 253). The appearance of irregularity, however, is not equivalent to actual disorder— and we should recall Pope's assertion that he had "digested all the

matter in prose" before composing his poem.[8] Prosaic method and
rigorous argument may simply be disguised for the purpose of instructing readers "as if you taught them *not*." Yet, its substructure of
well-grounded method is not all that the *Essay* conceals. Pope also
disguises his originality, preferring the deceptive method of "anamnesis" which had been a strategy of the new science from Galileo to
Newton.[9] As an interested student of Newtonian physics, which he
encountered in the popular lectures of William Whiston, Pope understood how the method of "anamnesis" avoided controversy by
disguising innovative concepts in the language of traditional thought.
Then, too, concealment was always Pope's favored mode of disclosure. We should not expect him to make a show of his originality.
The unmethodical order of *An Essay on Criticism* imitates (as Addison noted) Horace's prestigious *Ars Poetica*, and this continuing
allusion to Horace is a strategic way of transferring to criticism
(which Swift depicted as a dwarfish parody of its ancient stature) the
dignity and authority of a classical model. It suggested that criticism,
like tragedy or epic, possessed its own poetics, and it reflected Pope's
attempt to establish English criticism, as Horace had established
Roman poetry and drama, on the foundations of a coherent art. The
Herculean difficulty of this labor may help explain why Pope considered his *Essay* a work which "not one gentleman in three score even
of a liberal education can understand."[10] They would not understand
the poem because it proposed a theory of criticism unprecedented in
their experience.

The originality of Pope's *Essay*, in its mixture of tradition and innovation, becomes more apparent when we compare his theory with
the established critical positions. *An Essay on Criticism* offers a clear
alternative to the two main theories prominent in his early years—
theories defining the extremes which Pope felt compelled to reject.
Simplified, these extremes can be described by the terms *authority*
and *taste*. Authority in criticism, for Pope, implied that critics main-
tain a reverent adherence to a set of doctrines derived from Renaissance interpretations of Aristotle and of Horace. These so-called
"rules" were further incrusted with accumulations of critical dogma-
tism, issuing in such petrified constructions as Corneille's treatment
of the three dramatic Unities. With deliberate imprecision, Pope pa-
triotically associated the principle of authority in criticism with the
political tyranny of absolutist France (ll. 711–714). While France

erred at the extreme of slavish authority, England, in Pope's view, failed by indulging the opposite extreme of anarchic taste. Taste as a critical position licensed more than the passing fashions in wit, such as the modish indecency and skepticism that Pope criticized in the reigns of Charles II and William III (ll. 534–553). It also encouraged an idle critical dalliance with secluded "beauties" of poetry, invoked in a vague jargon of *je-ne-sais-quoi* or ecstatic cries, permitting the mystery of individual responsiveness to free a critic from accountability to any principle beyond the self-illuminated ego.[11] This boneless criticism was a form of cant which Pope branded "the perpetual Rapture of such Commentators, who are always giving us Exclamations instead of Criticisms" (note to *Iliad* XV.890). Taste licenses a total freedom from reasons; authority shackles criticism to a set of iron rules. Pope, of course, does not take the foolish position that all insights of taste are vacuous or all rules false. (In refining the past, he did not mean to reject its strengths but only its errors.) He objects instead to accepting either authority or taste as controlling principles of criticism. It is only when wrongly hardened into principles that taste degenerates into exclamatory rapture and authority repeats the mechanical rules that Pope parodies in "A Receit to make an Epick Poem" (*The Guardian* no. 78). Although readers sometimes claim that his compromise with taste and with authority is equivocal or confused, Pope consistently adheres to the clear distinction he makes between practice and principle. In practice, critics can learn much from the personal insights of taste and from the public edicts of authority. Pope does not recommend a merely hybrid criticism, combining in the name of moderation two contradictory principles. Rather, once deprived of their status as absolute laws, authority and taste serve a changed function within Pope's theory. In effect, *An Essay on Criticism* re-employs in a changed role the concepts which it rejects as principles, subordinating them to a new theory that provides an alternative to the past. This alternative might be called the criticism of judgment.

The criticism of judgment, as an alternative to past approaches, provides both the theoretical foundations and the practical principles for a new kind of literary discourse. One might argue, of course, that references to the term "judgment" are commonplace in earlier critical writing, especially because the word "criticism" derives from the Greek *krinein*, "to judge." Certainly Dryden (the most distinguished

English critic before Pope) liberally sprinkles his prefaces and essays
with references to judgment, which for him embraces at least three
distinct but overlapping senses. In Dryden's usage, the main technical senses of *judgment* appropriate to neoclassical criticism are: (1)
the mental faculty which discerns differences, controls the operations of wit, and comprehends the elements of poetic design; (2)
discretion, reasonableness, good sense; and (3) the faculty which
distinguishes excellence in literary works and, hence, an opinion
of the quality of any work.[12] It is clear that Pope understands and
exploits the earlier associations which link criticism with judgment,
for his language, in its repetitions, gradually surrounds criticism
with an idiom of judging that is not present in his other poems.
*An Essay on Criticism*, for example, uses the word *judgment* thir-
teen times, and *reason* only four. By contrast, *An Essay on Man*
uses *reason* forty-four times, and *judgment* none.[13] Yet the traditional associations between criticism and judgment do not require
Pope to use the idiom of judging traditionally. (Pope's art of refinement frequently invests familiar words such as *dullness* and *wit*
with new meaning.) In reading *An Essay on Criticism*, we should
understand that Pope's references to *judgment* (and to other words
which share the same etymology) invoke a familiar, quasi-technical
term. We should also understand, however, that *judgment* had
never referred to a coherent theory. It belonged more to the casual
vocabulary than to the conceptual framework of criticism. This
central, conceptual, defining position is the innovative place that
*judgment* occupies in Pope's *Essay*. In effect, he captures a term
having traditional but casual associations with criticism and transforms it into the primary force behind an original and coherent
critical theory, an alternative to the personal mysticism of taste and
to the fiats of authority.

## Theoretical Foundations: The Search for Universals

Before Pope could develop the practical principles of a criticism of
judgment, he faced the task of explaining how valid judgments are
*possible*. A practical criticism of judgment demands a theory capable
of making clear its sources of validity. Otherwise, differing judgments
about a single work (like differing tastes or conflicting rules) would
be indisputable and indefensible. Thus within his first ten lines Pope

confronts the fundamental dilemma that could overturn his whole
enterprise:

> 'Tis with our *Judgments* as our *Watches*, none
> Go just *alike*, yet each believes his own.        (ll. 9–10)

This basic human fact, the inconsistency and fallibility of our understandings, might suggest that judgment is wholly relative and impossible to verify. A second observation, applying specifically to critics,
compounds the problem of validity:

> *Authors* are partial to their *Wit*, 'tis true,
> But are not *Criticks* to their *Judgment* too?        (ll. 17–18)

The self-love which inclines all people to trust their own judgments
is especially well developed among critics, for whom the exercise of
judgment is a characteristic function. These inherent flaws or weaknesses in judgment would seem enough to stop Pope cold. The case
*against* judgment could hardly be stronger. The cogency of Pope's
fundamental questions about the validity of judgment is what creates
his agenda for the entire first section of the poem. (The three sections—indicated by blank spaces in the text—I will call "parts.")
With allowance for its tangential pursuits, part 1 of *An Essay on Criticism* may be read as an extended, theoretical defense of the very possibility of valid judgment.

For Pope, valid judgment depends not on repairing the inherent
weaknesses of human understanding but on defining fixed, theoretical
standards outside the individual that allow us to reason accurately
about literature. The weakness and variance of human understanding
are facts which, as Locke argued persuasively, do not necessarily preclude the possibility of knowledge. Although individual judgments
are likely to differ, the existence of fixed, theoretical standards establishes a norm against which personal variance can be measured and
corrected. For example, the minor differences from clock to clock do
not preclude the possibility of accurate timekeeping. In Pope's day,
the newfangled pocketwatches which adorned the gentry could be
corrected against the tolling church bells, just as a century later official clocks could be regulated by the standard of Greenwich time.[14]
The possibility of correct time is thus established by the existence of
a fixed standard outside the individual, so that we accept minor

variations as inevitable and inconsequential. If your watch says ten and mine twelve, we can resolve our dispute by appealing to the outside standard which creates the possibility that one of us is correct. Pope's attitude toward judgment is implicit in the simile of clockwork which he introduces. Minor variances prove acceptable and major differences can be adjudicated once criticism has established the possibility of valid judgment by articulating the fixed theoretical standards that govern literary analysis.

Pope's description of the unshakable standards governing literary criticism occupy two parallel passages which mark the rhetorical peaks of part 1. Symmetrically placed and stylistically linked, the passages are far more than fragments of practical advice, which is how they are usually construed. Their task, rather, is to define the norms or standards which make valid judgment possible. Pope's initial standard of validity in criticism is an unsurprising choice:

> First follow NATURE, and your Judgment frame
> By her just Standard, which is still the same:
> *Unerring Nature*, still divinely bright,
> One *clear, unchang'd*, and *Universal* Light,
> Life, Force, and Beauty, must to all impart,
> At once the *Source*, and *End*, and *Test* of *Art*.      (ll. 68–73)

Almost a set piece, the passage is so familiar that readers easily ignore its specific purpose in the *Essay*. Thus, we must remind ourselves that Pope's subject is not the praise of nature but how to "frame" one's judgment. (*To frame:* "To regulate; to adjust," Johnson's *Dictionary.*) Nature is praised specifically because it provides a "just" and changeless "Standard" for ensuring that an individual's judgment can be accurate. The somewhat general or abstract language of Pope's description, for which he is sometimes censured, is perfectly suited to this articulation of a theoretical norm. The fixity and universality of nature provide an indispensable criterion of measurement: all practical exercises of individual judgment derive their validity from its presence and power. Nor does nature's power as a "just" standard derive merely from human choice or arbitrary convention, like Greenwich time or the metric system. As Pope's dominant metaphor implies, the theoretical standard which nature provides for criticism is "just" because its potency, like the sun's, belongs to the inherent order of the world. It is "divinely" ordained.

53

The second theoretical standard validating the possibility of individual judgment shifts the locus of permanence from nature to art. Here Pope justifies, on theoretical grounds, the commerce with the past that is a continuing resource for his work. Art offers its more limited permanence in the figure of the ancients, an informal designation which for Pope evokes the entire classical tradition from Homer to the Latin poets of the Silver Age. Like his earlier praise of nature, Pope's celebration of the ancients is so familiar—the subject so traditional—that readers often fail to notice its specific function within the *Essay*. The purpose is not merely to praise the virtue of past writers but, as befits a poem about criticism, to advise critics how to "steer," or direct, or regulate their literary judgment:

> *You* then whose Judgment the right Course wou'd steer,
> Know well each ANCIENT's proper *Character*,
> His *Fable, Subject, Scope* in ev'ry Page,
> *Religion, Country, Genius* of his *Age*:
> Without all these at once before your Eyes,
> *Cavil* you may, but never *Criticize*.          (ll. 118–123)

If criticism is to become an art—not unresolvable wrangling based upon authority or taste—it requires a firm theoretical foundation, and Pope's purpose in praising the ancients is directly related to the needs of a coherent critical theory. True, other writers had advised reading the ancients, just as they had advised following nature. What matters most is not the source of Pope's ideas, since familiar ideas are always subject to refinement. What matters is the *use* Pope makes of traditional materials, which he often employs in nontraditional ways. Although clearly he did not invent the concepts of nature or the ancients, he employs them to original purpose in defining fixed, universal standards which create the possibility of valid judgment in criticism. "Before the use of the loadstone, or knowledge of the compass," wrote Dryden, reflecting upon his early efforts in criticism, "I was sailing in a vast ocean, without other help than the pole-star of the Ancients, and the rules of the French stage amongst the Moderns."[15] Criticism, despite Dryden's strenuous practice, had not advanced in England to the status of a reliable, self-conscious art, established on firm and clear principles. It was an activity which relied more on precedent than on theory. The province mainly of idle aristocrats or professional hacks, English criticism had as yet failed to reflect upon its character as an art of knowing. In isolating nature and the classics as universal standards for validating the possibility of individual judgment, Pope offered readers something beyond Dryden's tentative explorations as a practicing critic. He offered English criticism the theoretical foundations of an authentic art. His next step, logically, was to sketch the practical principles and methods that would guide the critic's day-to-day encounter with literary texts.

## Judgment as Critical Method: The Logic of Probability

What distinguishes Pope's *Essay* from earlier English discourses on criticism is not only its attention to theory but also its concern with a specific method of reasoning. The rejection of authority and taste involves for Pope the rejection of an entire way of thinking about literature. Authority and taste deal equally in certainties: they do not invite doubt and conflict because they impose an absolute power, personal or impersonal. Pope, as we have seen, is not afraid of proclaiming certainties when he announces nature and the ancients as providing fixed theoretical standards for validating the possibility of judgment. Part 1 consistently treats the act of judgment within a context of universal, certain, permanent, theoretical values. In parts 2 and 3, however, Pope moves from establishing theoretical absolutes to exploring particular, variable, practical aspects of critical activity. This movement from theoretical to practical, from universal to particular, from permanent to variable is reflected in his new concern with a world of mutability and limitation. Although the theoretical standards for criticism are presented as universal and unchanging and certain, the actual texts to be judged and the daily practice of judgment belong to the fluctuating realm of time and change, where abilities differ, customs vary, creeds lapse, and languages decay. The tone of parts 2 and 3 is set decisively by the extended comparison (ll. 219–232)—rare in Pope's work—which contrasts the unknown vastness of human knowledge with the frailty of our individual understandings. Expanded horizons do not so much dispel uncertainty as reveal new vistas of ignorance:

Th' *increasing* Prospect *tires* our wandring Eyes,
Hills peep o'er Hills, and *Alps* on *Alps* arise!     (ll. 231–232)

55

Pope's disheartening image, which so deeply impressed Johnson, is especially appropriate at the beginning of part 2, where certainties are left behind. It creates an implicit contrast with the hymnlike celebration of the *"Immortal"* ancients (l. 190) that had closed part 1, leading the reader artfully from the realm of timelessness to time, from past clarity to present complexities and doubt. Pope's couplets still carry a crisply authoritative tone when defining terms or giving direct advice, but their assurance flows from observation, experience, logic, and tradition—not from indisputable authority. Even his most confident assertions are subtly modified by their placement within a context where certainty has vanished.

The disappearance of certainty—the dominant fact underlying the final two sections of the *Essay*—creates the context for Pope's association between criticism and a method of reasoning appropriate to a science of uncertainties. This is the method of probable reasoning, the method which becomes a distinguishing mark of the period. The pre-eminence which earlier ages awarded to syllogism, to paradox, and to the varieties of rhetorical persuasion yields in Pope's lifetime to a reasoning based, formally or informally, on the concept of probability. Locke in *An Essay Concerning Human Understanding* (1690) had provided a highly influential account of such probabilistic knowledge, but it was not simply the contemporary importance of probable reasoning which attracted Pope. Pope understood that the method of probable reasoning was also indistinguishable from the act of judgment which defines literary criticism. In fact, he viewed probable reasoning as fundamental not only to criticism but also to all forms of literary composition, where it finds its most prominent place in the practice of revision. Thus Pope would describe his later addition of the sylphs to *The Rape of the Lock* as "one of the greatest proofs of judgement of anything I ever did."[16] Judgment, as an activity poets shared with critics, held great significance for Pope precisely because, unlike invention or imagination, it was not a private and unsummoned power but a human capacity which might be cultivated, improved, and refined.

The importance of probable reasoning extended far beyond the boundaries of polite letters. As a means of analysis, probabilistic thought was understood during the eighteenth century as "the most legitimate and valid method—for Locke, in fact, the only possible method—in most of the arts and sciences and in the everyday think-

56

ing of rational people."[17] Yet, its influence upon literary criticism proved especially decisive. In 1764 the young Edward Gibbon could write: "Geometry is employed only in demonstrations peculiar to itself: criticism deliberates between the different degrees of probability."[18] Criticism is thus characterized for Gibbon (as for more experienced critics) by its use of a particular method of reasoning, and his distinction between geometric demonstrations and degrees of probability echoes Locke's discussion. In *An Essay Concerning Human Understanding* Locke distinguishes between two fundamentally different kinds of knowledge: the "clear and certain" knowledge which he imagistically associates with the broad daylight of truth; and a lesser, uncertain, tentative kind of knowing, which he describes as "the twilight . . . of *Probability*."[19] The twilight of probability serves as Locke's metaphor for the normal state of human intelligence, since he believed (as Pope stated in "The Design" prefixed to *An Essay on Man*) that there "are not *many certain truths* in this world." Probable reasoning, in Locke's view, is divine recompense for the absence of certainty. Limited and fallible, it nonetheless guides us through the doubtful twilight realms where demonstrations, proofs, and certainties are chimerical.

Nowhere in *An Essay on Criticism* does Pope argue explicitly that English criticism must henceforth be characterized by the method of probable reasoning. His language conveys such an argument indirectly and implicitly. The final two sections, for example, suffuse an awareness of the human limitation and temporal change that defy certainties and encourage a probabilistic spirit of inquiry. Further, Pope's practical principles of criticism require for their application a spirit and method of probable reasoning. The practicing critic, however informally, constantly assesses degrees of probability and constructs hypotheses about intention or design. But Pope's association of criticism with probabilistic reasoning needed no explicit statement because it was also implicit in his choice of terms. Locke's famous distinction between certain and probable knowledge occurs in the chapter entitled "Of Judgment." There Locke clearly states that the mental power of judgment holds full sway over the operations of probable reasoning. As he declares unequivocally, "the Faculty, which God has given Man to supply the want of clear and certain Knowledge in Cases where that cannot be had, is *Judgment*."[20] In using *judgment* as the key term for his new theory of criticism, Pope gained more than the sum of its traditional meanings. The prestige of Locke's *Essay* had endowed *judgment* with the connotations of an entire method of thought—probabilistic reasoning—which conformed exactly with the spirit and demands of Pope's critical enterprise. Probable reasoning, whether Pope derived its tenets from Locke or from his own thought and reading, underlies his entire approach to the practice of criticism.

The strategic association between criticism and probable reasoning helps considerably to explain the extravagant praise of Pope's *Essay* by eighteenth-century critics such as Johnson, for whom (like Gibbon) the methods of probabilistic thought were inseparable from the methods of criticism. The substitution of probability for the dogmatic certainties of authority and of taste had a profoundly liberating effect. "To judge therefore of Shakespeare by Aristotle's rules," Pope wrote in the spirit of independent, probabilistic inquiry, "is like trying a man by the laws of one country who acted under those of another."[21] The submerged legal metaphor of judging is almost always present, if faintly, in Pope's vocabulary of judgment. Its presence, whether concealed or open, suggests an additional benefit from the emphasis on probabilistic thought, for the English judicial system provides reassurance that uncertainty need not induce a skeptical indifference or relativism, as if all judgments were equally doubtful. Far from clouding critical inquiry in irresolution, probable reasoning grants to critics the same discriminating powers which characterize English law. Most important, the metaphoric equivalence of critic and judge helps to illuminate the final goal of all critical activity. For Pope, the ultimate function of criticism is evaluation. Indeed, no aspect of Pope's critical theory so clearly separates him from modern academic critics as his emphasis upon evaluation as the chief end of criticism.

For most modern critics, interpretation—not evaluation—is what commands their greatest interest. Evaluation is purposely ignored or practiced unknowingly. Often it is openly condemned, especially by science-minded writers who argue that value judgments are an impediment, an impurity, something to be removed from critical writing at all costs. Pope, like most of his contemporaries, considered interpretation the tedious business of commentary, relegated (as in his translations of Homer) to the status of notes. Criticism, as distinguished from mere commentary, rose above detailed inquiry into meaning—a drab pedantic chore—which (he wrote) only "puzzles the text." Pope has short patience for meanings which seem so deeply hidden as to require intricate labors of excavation. "We care not to Study, or Anatomize a Poem," he wrote, "but only to read it for our entertainment."[22] Yet, Pope's breezy contempt for editorial scholarship and textual commentary—even though he edited the plays of Shakespeare and wrote long commentaries in his notes on Homer— not only reveals a widely-shared prejudice but also emphasizes how essential he felt evaluation was. The worthy critic, in Pope's view, must accept the responsibility of making evaluative judgments, even as judges do. It is no accident that the portraits of exemplary ancient critics in *An Essay on Criticism* conclude with Longinus gowned in legality as an "ardent *Judge*" (l. 677). As a judge, the critic necessarily evaluates what is good and bad. Certainly English criticism had often performed this function, although not with notable understanding or distinction. (Thomas Rymer's condemnation of *Othello* as "the tragedy of a handkerchief" is a classic instance.) Where Pope departs from his predecessors and contemporaries is in emphasizing the responsibility of critics to seek a method of evaluation which would make criticism less biased, less arbitrary, less whimsical, and less wrong-headed.

Evaluation for Pope must issue from a responsible method. Thus a crucial function of probabilistic reasoning is to impart the fairness and consistency required when the critic-judge, as a final act, delivers the "Sentence" (l. 678) which evaluation demands. Evaluation as the final purpose of criticism gives the critic not only a personal goal but also a larger social role. The critic's rigorous separation of good writing from bad serves the world of letters in the same way that a wise judge serves a social community, with the added boon that wise critics reward as well as punish. The judge is not Pope's only image of the critic, but the implications of this role are far-reaching, especially because judges and poets were not (as they seem now) almost incompatible figures, who belong to separate realms. They were instead allies in judgment:

> But how severely with themselves proceed
> The Men, who write such Verse as we can read?
> Their own *strict Judges*, not a word they spare.[23]

The good poet internalizes the figure of the judge whom the critic outwardly personifies. Precisely because criticism ends in decisions on value, for poets as well as for critics, Pope must stress the methods by which just evaluations proceed. As a native of twilight uncertainties, his ideal critic endows the act of judgment with a spirit of deliberative reasoning, judiciously weighing the various degrees of probability, and it is this probabilistic thinking—with its frank evaluations of good and bad—which characterizes the best English criticism for the rest of the century.

## Practical Principles of Judgment: Propriety

The association between criticism and reasoning based on probability exerts a powerful influence not only over the general spirit of Pope's enterprise but also over the practical principles of judgment, which he sparingly defines. Despite the swirl of specific maxims, sententious learning, examples, portraits, and anecdotes that pack the last two sections of the *Essay*, Pope subsumes the entire practice of criticism under two all-embracing principles, propriety and generosity, to which almost every precept or fragmentary insight after part I pertains. Like most of the resonant concepts in *An Essay on Criticism*—nature, judgment, wit, the ancients—propriety and generosity assemble, under deceptively plain terms, a complex series of related ideas. Propriety, for example, evokes in modern usage a simple and limited notion of correctness, the counterpart of etiquette in manners. But for Pope the term had very different connotations. "There is hardly any laying down particular rules for writing in our language," he told Spence. "Even Dean Swift's, which seemed to be the best I ever heard, were three or four of them not thoroughly well considered."[24] Propriety, for Pope, is not a set of specific rules but an abstraction filled with a constantly shifting content. Appropriateness consists solely in a flexible harmony among parts, and on differing literary occasions the content of propriety necessarily differs. The changing shapes of propriety, however, despite their variations, all share one thing. They contribute toward a goal which Pope defines as the ideal condition of every literary work. This is the state of poetic "wholeness."

Pope's idea of poetic wholeness does not imply either symmetrical form or hidden unities. Especially when compared with earlier neo-Aristotelian treatments of "the Unities" in drama and epic, his approach has a flexibility that frees criticism from narrow, rigid obsession with the details of "correct" composition, where everything is done by the rules. Poetic wholeness, for Pope, involves a harmonious relationship between the two major elements of composition, which he calls (although not with absolute consistency) conception and execution. Conception, which is close in meaning to the classical term *invention*, denotes the preliminary and essential creative work of the poet which governs the subject, form, and purposes of a text. It includes authorial intention, choice of genre, establishment of an underlying moral, disposition of the structural design, and discovery of plot, characters, argument, and incidents. Execution, on the other hand, involves the actual process of writing. It compasses the lesser details of what Pope calls "the Thoughts, the Expression, and the Numbers."[25] The poet's movement from conception to execution is a descent from the pure ideas of poetry into the materials of language, versification, and statement. Both, of course, are crucial to a finished work. The actual history of composition may not follow a clear sequence from conception to execution, as if the poet worked from blueprints. But, as opposed to most Romantic and modern theories of composition, which imply a necessary fusion between language and thought, for Pope it is the *separability* of conception and execution that creates the precondition for unity.

For Pope, a poet's knowledge of propriety is crucial because the materials of poetry may take so many different shapes. Propriety— not an organic or linguistic determinism—is what selects the final shape that the poem will assume. Thus even a work as fragmented in its form as *The Dunciad* may, where execution and conception coincide, attain a propriety which embraces or supersedes its apparent, satirical improprieties. Despite a discontinuous or extended history of composition, despite changing plans or unplanned changes, the finished poem for Pope always reaches a state in which the harmonious relation between conception and execution creates an appropriate wholeness. Such wholeness does not rule out future revisions; it is not synonymous with completion, finality, or permanence; it is, simply, the point at which a literary work attains the crucial state where we may distinguish poetry from mere verse.

In the formula which determines propriety, the essential and primary term is conception. For Pope no matter how intricate the meter or how polished the style, no matter how vivid the imagery or how witty the language, a work lacking the support of an underlying conception fails to attain wholeness. This idea of poetic wholeness was meant specifically to repudiate the literary amateurs, hacks, and dilettantes who confused genuine poetry with isolated, fragmentary felicities of execution: "pretty conceptions [that is, witty thoughts], fine metaphors, glitt'ring expressions, and something of a neat cast of Verse."[26] In offering a more comprehensive vision of poetry, Pope in the *Essay* equally repudiates the pedants and scribblers in criticism who ignore a poet's governing conception and simply cavil at minor faults of execution—hence Pope's harsh censure of critics who distort their judgment through a *"Love to Parts"* (l. 288). True criticism, for Pope, requires a knowledge of poetic wholeness. Only by understanding the intimate marriage of execution and conception can critics render the valid judgments of propriety that Pope's *Essay* expects.

As a principle of criticism, propriety applies not only to the relation between conception and execution; it extends also to judgments concerning the specific parts of execution: the thoughts, words, and metrical patterns that must be judged in relation to lesser, local harmonies. For example, Pope argues that true wit exists in the harmonious relationship among idea, image, and expression. This argument, in making wit accountable to a standard of propriety, helps to deflect the charge that wit was by nature lawless, excessive, and indecent. It also recognizes the function which context serves in distinguishing true wit from false. Thus, for Pope, the critic judges true wit not by predetermined codes of decency (with their various taboos) but by the demands of a specific context or occasion: even obscene or offensive passages, he would argue, may be perfectly appropriate to their surroundings. A similar, uncramped respect for context also underlies Pope's attitude toward diction, where propriety again supplies a practical standard of judgment. Words must suit both subject and genre. As for versification, which Pope illustrates with famous examples such as his snakelike alexandrine dragging its slow extra syllables, propriety reveals itself in the echoing relationship between sound and sense. In effect, Pope applies to the judgment of particular parts the same subsuming principle of propriety he applies to the judgment of poetic wholeness. The value of propriety, for Pope, lies in its freedom from the absolute and fixed laws of criticism which constrain both poets and critics alike. Propriety gives access to the *varieties* of justness not encompassed by "Aristotle's rules."

Variety, of course, is an aesthetic principle honored in the English and Italian Renaissance, as well as in ancient Greece and Rome, and its meaning has not always remained constant. When Pope told Joseph Spence that "all the beauties of gardening might be comprehended in one word, variety," he imagined variety in gardening very differently than did his Renaissance predecessors.[27] The English landscape garden, which Pope at Twickenham helped to create and to popularize, calls for a fluid mixing of elements—trees, lawn, flowers, water, light, shade—in uneven patterns which break the formal geometry of French gardens, where each distinct part is balanced by a counterpart, where "Grove nods at grove, each Alley has a brother, / And half the platform just reflects the other" (*To Burlington*, ll. 117–118). Variety in gardening demands for Pope the pleasing intricacies and artful wildness which defeat rigid boundaries. So, too, as critic Pope recommends a variety that differs from the bounded and balanced harmonies preferred by earlier writers who emphasized generic purity, symmetrical form, and unities of time, place, and action. In this older tradition, still influential in Pope's day, mixing comedy with tragedy was strictly forbidden; epics contained either twelve or twenty-four books; Rome and Athens were unimaginable on the same stage. Pope's distance from that tradition is noticeable even in the apparently casual metaphors of dress (l. 318) and fashion (l. 333) which he associates with poetic diction. Like his extended lament for the mutability of language (ll. 476–493), such metaphors acknowledge that literature cannot exclude the change and variety intrinsic to social life. Criticism for Pope quickly turns moribund if it fails to incorporate in its most basic principles of judgment the provision for change.

It is not merely the changeable nature of language and of occasion which makes variety an important concept for Pope. All poems, in his view, observe proprieties which are to some degree historical and personal, thus subject to change. For example, he argues that in certain poems we can trace the distinctive proprieties fostered by a particular age, country, and poetic character: "*Homer* hurries and transports us with a commanding impetuosity, *Virgil* leads us with an attractive Majesty: *Homer* scatters with a generous Profusion, *Virgil* bestows with a careful Magnificence: *Homer* like the *Nile*, pours out his Riches with a sudden Overflow; *Virgil* like a River in its Banks, with a gentle and constant Stream."[28] Each writer, in other words, creates a different form of propriety. This view of variety—

implicit in the concept of appropriateness—means that, unlike some of his contemporaries and predecessors, Pope does not feel forced to choose *between* different forms of literary merit: Homer *or* Virgil, Pindar *or* Horace, Shakespeare *or* Jonson. Propriety recognizes and encourages diverse individual possibilities of justness. Only such an elastic and inclusive principle could be appropriate, in Pope's view, to a criticism locked within the world of change, uncertainty, and human limitation. With its generous endorsement of variety, it offers critics an unprecedented freedom to admire the unique proprieties of even the most irregular works in which conception and execution attain a plausible and pleasing harmony. "I had some thoughts of writing a Persian Fable," Pope confessed to Spence, "in which I should have given a full loose to description and imagination. It would have been a very wild thing if I had executed it"—wild, doubtless, and appropriately so.[29]

## Practical Principles of Judgment: Generosity

The undogmatic flexibility implicit in Pope's criticism finds its clearest expression in his treatment of generosity. Generosity is not a concept we would expect to encounter in modern discussions of critical theory. For Pope, however, a person—not a theory or method—is the ultimate source of literary judgment, and no program for criticism would be complete if it failed to discuss the personal, ethical aspects of critical activity. As the opening couplet of part 3 proclaims, the critic's knowledge of propriety must be complemented by equal achievements of character:

> LEARN then what MORALS Criticks ought to show,
> For 'tis but *half* a *Judge's Task*, to *Know*.     (ll. 560–561)

Even in an age of moralists, Pope's emphasis upon the ethics of criticism is extraordinary. He is not demanding, like John Dennis and earlier English critics, that criticism stress the moral qualities of art, as expressed in such critical doctrines as poetic justice (the good triumph, the bad repent or die). He is demanding that critics themselves exemplify and embody individual virtue. Moral character, in fact, comprises fully *"half"* of the critic's equipment and identity. This requirement alone argues for the prominence of Pope's *Essay* in the history of critical theory. It also suggests a strong personal bias, exemplified in Pope's later turn to explicitly ethical verse and his life-long combat with dunce-critics whose characters, as well as criticism, he attacked. Valid criticism, for Pope, is always an expression of vir-tuous character. Why is generosity, however, more prominent than other virtues which critics might possess? If we wish to understand Pope's emphasis on generosity, we need to see how generosity was a virtue particularly relevant and timely in addressing the problems he confronted in *An Essay on Criticism*.

One reason for Pope's stress on generosity is historical. At the turn of the century, two stereotypes dominated the portraits of contempo-rary critics: the coffee-house fop and the ill-tempered crank. The crit-ical fops and butterflies so often satirized in Augustan literature personified for Pope the shallowness and ignorance of modern criti-cism. The parade of Ned Softleys and Dick Minims who mumbled platitudes and flaunted banalities suggests how far English criticism had degenerated from the noble line of Aristotle, Horace, and Lon-ginus. But even more degrading than the coffee-house fop was a contrary image of the critic as a carping, ill-natured, irascible, can-tankerous crank—an outlaw from polite society. Thus Swift was merely alluding to a stock figure when he described criticism in *A Tale of a Tub* (1704) as the allegorical offspring of Pride and Ridi-cule. For Pope, a surly character seemed (along with unsound judg-ment) the inevitable source of all bad criticism. "Sure upon the whole," he wrote in 1717, "a bad Author deserves better usage than a bad Critic; a man may be the former merely thro' the misfortune of an ill judgment, but he cannot be the latter without both that [that is, ill judgment] and an ill temper."[30] While a knowledge of propriety rescued criticism from foppish ignorance, the principle of generosity promised to correct the ill nature that equally disfigured modern crit-icism. The generous critic, for Pope, has resources of character which ensure that sound judgment will operate with temperance and hu-manity. Generosity transforms the Dennis-like crank into a fossil from the less-refined past.

A second reason for Pope's emphasis on generosity of character is, strangely, epistemological. Generosity is indispensable to criticism because valid judgment requires that critics face their own uncertain-ties and imperfect knowledge. "To err is human" remains among the best-known quotations from world literature, but how many readers know that its source is *An Essay on Criticism*? The compression of

Pope's thought suggests not simply that human creatures are prone to error but that error is a distinguishing mark of our humanity. Despite its aphoristic sweep, this idea has specific relevance to Pope's ideas about criticism. Generosity, with its forgiving spirit, implicitly recognizes the human limitations and natural tendency to error which all critics and poets share. As a poet as well as critic, Pope understood that no poem completely satisfies its author: "We grasp some more beautifull Idea in our Brain, than our Endeavors to express it can set to the view of others; & still do but labour to fall short of our first Imagination. The gay Colouring which Fancy gave to our Design at the first transient glance we had of it, goes off in the Execution; like those various Figures in the gilded Clouds, which while we gaze long upon, to seperate [sic] the Parts of each imaginary Image, the whole faints before the Eye, & decays into Confusion."[31] Pope's complaint here echoes his extended lament in the *Essay* at how time damages the poem, blurring its diction and effacing its design (ll. 476–493). Betrayal is the extreme image which he chooses to suggest how far a poem may falsify or contradict the poet's purity of vision and thought. Execution always falls short of conception. Some residue of flaw necessarily accompanies even the most polished work. Time, human weakness, and the nature of poetry—not hostile critics alone—help to account for Pope's plea that readers hasten to "befriend" true merit (l. 74). The metaphor is not entirely conventional. Just as propriety finds figurative expression in the image of the judge, generosity for Pope also calls forth its representative figure: the critic as friend.

Friendship—he called it "the sacred Idea" of friendship—is a concept of unusual significance throughout Pope's work. "There is nothing meritorious," he said on his deathbed, "but Virtue, & Friendship."[32] As his linking of these two terms suggests, Pope understands friendship to pass beyond simple emotion. He shares Aristotle's view that, although affection resembles an emotion, friendship resembles a moral state, implying purpose, choice, and knowledge (*Nicomachean Ethics*, VIII.vii). Further, while providing a source of social pleasure and literary alliance, friendship also offered Pope an ideal of complete protection or guardedness combined with free disclosure, promising a state in which human character is simultaneously accessible and shielded. The nature of friendship, we should recognize, was considerably redefined during Pope's lifetime.[33] No longer the Aristotelian alter ego or mirror of the self, the friend for Pope assumes the new, unclassical, domestic offices of consolation and understanding, and the role which Pope assigns to critics is curiously similar. The critic, like the friend, is understanding, consoling, sympathetic. Further, critics and friends share the responsibility (in Pope's view) to tell us our faults, which foes are likely to exaggerate or conceal. While generosity in critics acknowledges the inescapable presence of error, friendship thus permits and encourages correction. The friendship which Pope imagines linking poets with critics is not a device for withholding or for disarming judgment but for making it more effective. Together friendship and generosity create the means for reviving an ancient ideal in which criticism served as a civilizing power, encouraging poets and enlightening readers in a community of knowledge:

> The gen'rous Critick *fann'd* the *Poet's Fire*,
> And taught the World, *with Reason* to *Admire*.   (ll. 100–101)

Here, two apparent opposites—emotional admiration and analytical reason—are reconciled, even as traditional antagonists—poet and critic—become collaborators. This belief in the reconciliation of traditional opposites reappears in one of the most personal moments of the *Essay*, when Pope directly praises his own mentor, the critic, poet, and statesman William Walsh, as "the Muse's Judge and Friend" (l. 729). Judge and friend together reconcile the potentially conflicting roles that the ideal critic must embody.

Friendship, with its consoling, corrective, and reconciling powers, does not exhaust the benefits from the critic's generosity. In criticism, generosity achieves finally the exalted status of an ethical opposite to pride. Pride—as represented in *An Essay on Man* and *The Dunciad*—is not only the intellectual sin accounting for mankind's basic failures in living. It is also especially relevant to criticism, as the source of a great many errors in critical judgment (ll. 201–204). The effect of pride, within the context of Pope's *Essay*, is always a pressure toward partiality and fragmentation, blocking comprehensiveness of vision. In its pressure against wholeness, pride radically constricts understanding by attaching us to cherished opinions and to favored fragments. The principle of propriety, in demanding a knowledge of poetic wholeness, had offered one means of counteracting the misjudgments of pride expressed in bad critics as a *"Love to Parts."* But partiality takes another threatening form in *An Essay on Criticism*. This mode of fragmentation, rooted in pride, is prejudice.

Prejudice in criticism makes its appearance in two main areas: in the political disputes that divided Augustan writers into Whigs and Tories, and in the equally divisive and prolific literary quarrels. Like the Little-Endians and Big-Endians of *Gulliver's Travels*, Pope's contemporaries seemed capable of transforming almost any human activity into an argument, from saying prayers to cracking egg-shells. Writing usually meant taking sides. Such widespread factionalism is what Pope lamented in the 1717 preface to his *Works* when he described the poet's life as a "warfare upon earth." Thus, while *An Essay on Criticism* censures obsessive fondness for specific "parts" of execution (ll. 289–383), it also attacks at almost equal length partiality, expressed as prejudice, toward writers from one historical period, one political party, one country, or one school of wit (ll. 384–473). What Mr. Spectator condemned as the "Malice of Party" was a pressing threat to sound judgment, in literature as in politics. "If this Party Spirit has so ill an Effect on our Morals," wrote Addison, "it has likewise a very great one on our Judgments. We often hear a poor insipid Paper or Pamphlet cryed up, and sometimes a noble Piece depretiated by those who are of a different Principle from the Author. One who is actuated by this Spirit is almost under an Incapacity of discerning either real Blemishes or Beauties" (*The Spectator* no. 125). Prejudice is regarded by Addison and by Pope as a defect of character which inevitably erodes literary judgment, and for Pope the ethical corrective to prejudice is generosity. Generosity permits the critic to approach an equitable judgment by consciously rejecting whatever is incomplete and partisan. It seeks to move criticism from a warfare of factions to civilized discourse among persons too large-spirited for parties or partiality or prejudice of any kind.

It should be clear that generosity is not for Pope a simple or commonplace virtue like thrift. (Its history as an ethical concept runs back at least to Cicero's *De Officiis*.) Pope's critical theory holds, as we have seen, that judgment consider the *"Whole"* (l. 235). This idea of wholeness also requires us to understand the unstated intentions of the author that contribute to the work's conception. Thus Pope insists that criticism must always regard the writer's purposes (l. 255), judging the performance in the light of intentions. But there is an old problem lurking in this good advice. Readers discover every day that not all authorial intentions and purposes can be clearly reconstructed from an impartial study of the text. How, then, can the critic gain access to the author's mental processes and undeclared purposes which are required for understanding the *"Whole"* work? Pope's answer to this difficult question is the power of sympathy. Sympathy, like friendship and virtue, is a necessary characteristic of the generous critic. As an aspect of generosity, it permits the critic to achieve a close emotional and intellectual kinship with the author under study: "No Longer his *Interpreter,* but *He.*"[34] The generous critic reads with a sympathetic understanding, which, when perfectly attuned, allows a presumptive reconstruction of authorial plans and purposes and processes which complement a judicious study of the text:

> A perfect Judge will *read* each Work of Wit
> With the same Spirit that its Author *writ,*
> Survey the *Whole,* nor seek slight Faults to find,
> Where *Nature moves,* and *Rapture warms* the Mind.
>
> (ll. 233–236)

The "perfect Judge" whom Pope depicts is no ordinary critic. His generous character allows him insights which judgment alone cannot attain. Rather than spend itself in the pointless exclamations of taste, emotion in the ideal critic proves a source of otherwise inaccessible knowledge.

It is not my purpose to debate the soundness of Pope's position, for although generosity solves some critical problems, it also introduces new ones. (How can critics judge or understand a writer with whom they are unsympathetic?) More important, Pope's emphasis upon generosity allows us to reconsider the surprising and neglected prominence which he assigns to emotion in criticism. Judgment alone is not enough. Just as poetry contains "nameless Graces" which gain the heart "without passing thro' the *Judgment*" (l. 156), so, too, criticism cannot rely solely on method but must enlist the powers of feeling without which it proves sterile and mechanical. Such emotional powers are most evident in Pope's portrait of Longinus:

> An ardent *Judge,* who Zealous in his Trust,
> With *Warmth* gives Sentence, yet is always *Just;*

# Alexander Pope

> Whose *own* *Example* strengthens all his Laws,
> And *Is himself* that great *Sublime* he draws.　　(ll. 677–680)

Sublimity, Longinus had said, was the echo of a great soul, and the emotional ardor of Longinus stands in stark contrast to the stifled feeling which Pope depicts in his portrait of Atticus: "Alike reserv'd to blame, or to commend."[35] Atticus, in his unwavering reserve, is an antitype of the generous critic. Generosity, for Pope, always retains its etymological link with noble and spirited character, with a magnanimous soul capable of the ardor, warmth, and zeal Atticus denies. Among its other functions, generosity assures that the final judgments of criticism, whether resting in praise or blame, will not be inhuman and unfeeling.


## Pope as Metacritic

"Criticism," wrote Samuel Johnson in 1751, "reduces those regions of literature under the dominion of science, which have hitherto known only the anarchy of ignorance, the caprices of fancy, and the tyranny of prescription."[36] Johnson's statement is a short history as well as a definition of criticism. It charts the progress in criticism away from the "prescriptions" of authority and the "caprices" of taste—a progress which Pope's *Essay* helped to initiate and secure. Johnson's inclusion of criticism within the "dominion of science" does not imply that criticism now belonged to the disciplines of the new natural philosophy, like chemistry or physics, but that it had established the principles and procedures required of useful knowledge. It was Dryden, in Johnson's view, who deserved credit as "the father of English criticism": "the writer who first taught us to determine *upon principles* the merit of composition."[37] Dryden's primacy is indisputable, for he did more than any writer of his age to free English criticism from the confusions and ignorance in which he found it. But Dryden was most successful as a practicing critic, not as a theorist of criticism. Modern scholars still have trouble making his principles consistent and clear, for his work as a critic ranges from occasional pronouncements to speculative dialogues. With the death of Dryden in 1700, a new generation of writers needed to consolidate his advances and to reflect upon the nature of criticism, to think of it as a coherent discipline conscious of its own aims and methods. John

Dennis, with his meaty tracts *The Advancement and Reformation of Modern Poetry* (1701) and *The Grounds of Criticism in Poetry* (1704), had already begun the task of establishing theoretical foundations for English criticism—in what Pope could only regard as a dogmatic and misguided effort to flood England with swollen imitations of *Paradise Lost. An Essay on Criticism* in effect reclaims and refines the example of Dryden for English critics, endorsing his main principles, backing his often speculative and exploratory spirit, and providing a secure, compact, flexible theory of criticism to stabilize the practice of his English successors.

Historians of criticism and of critical theory should take a fresh look at *An Essay on Criticism*, for it possesses a coherence (despite its unmethodical form) and originality (despite its use of traditional materials) which deserve reappraisal. Some of the apparent familiarity of Pope's ideas derives, like the "clichés" of *An Essay on Man*, from their subsequent absorption into the language of English thought, where they proved powerfully influential. The strength of his poem, contrary to general opinion, is not in its free-floating couplets of specific advice but its consolidation of traditional wisdom and of native sense within a full (if brief) theory of criticism. Specific couplets, however self-contained they *sound*, reverberate in the larger, surrounding system that endows them with additional meaning, as in this example:

> In ev'ry Work regard the *Writer's End,*
> Since none can compass more than they *Intend;*
> And if the *Means* be just, the *Conduct* true,
> Applause, in spite of trivial Faults, is due.       (ll. 255–258)

In this instance, the highly compressed language does more than defend an idea of poetic wholeness achieved by understanding the interdependence of execution (*"Means," "Conduct"*) and conception (*"End"*). It entails an entire sequence of theoretical and practical steps. It is embedded in a theory which defines criticism as an act of judgment; which places this definition within its historical context as an alternative to criticism governed wholly by authority or by taste; which identifies and links, in nature and in the ancients, fixed standards that create the possibility of valid judgment; which associates criticism with the method and spirit of probabilistic reasoning appropriate to a realm of limitation and uncertainty; which articulates, in propriety and in generosity, comprehensive practical principles of criticism embracing both knowledge and ethics; which directs practical criticism toward the goal of fair evaluation; and which justifies such verdicts as helping to revive a true community of discourse, with critics both judges and friends, mediating between writers and readers in a model of ancient civility. Pope's theory may not be "cut-and-dried" (if that is a virtue), but it certainly possesses the rigor and coherence that a useful theory of criticism requires. Where in the previous history of English criticism does one find a more fully integrated model of theory and practice?

It is true that readers must perceive the organization of Pope's critical system without the aid of such prose crutches as statements of purpose, chapter headings, mathematical subdivisions, detailed logical argument, and plain, utilitarian language. These devices, so dear to an age of treatises, encyclopedias, and dictionaries, were too straightforward for Pope. Pope, as Johnson accurately observed, "had great delight in artifice, and endeavoured to attain all his purposes by indirect and unsuspected methods."[38] A writer who advised instructing people "as if you taught them *not*" understood that indirection is a means for overcoming the normal human resistances to instruction. Further, he knew that we are likelier to value knowledge which by our own labors we have helped to discover:

> To Observations which ourselves we make,
> We grow more partial for th' observer's sake;
> To written Wisdom, as another's, less.[39]

If partiality could not be banished from human behavior, at least it could be put to educational uses. Perhaps this explanation accounts for Pope's preference to discuss propriety, for example, mainly through the oblique method of examining various improprieties and errors. Despite its indirections, his treatment gains strength from respecting a basic, even rudimentary, logic of exposition. Part 1 treats the universal standards validating the possibility of judgment. Part 2 treats the principle of propriety. Part 3 treats the principle of generosity. Within this less-than-cunning framework, however, Pope allowed himself the many excursions or informal digressions sanctioned by the term *essay*, and no doubt he hoped that a loose informality might help deflect charges of youthful presumptuousness. (Accusations, hurled like weapons by the wounded Dennis, came anyway.) But finally we should not miss the obvious point. Like his predecessors Horace and Boileau, Pope chose to write a poem, not a prose treatise. *An Essay on Criticism* is a supple, allusive, complex, sometimes dazzling work in which the reader's participation is crucial. In form and in method, it constitutes a test of the specific critical power it celebrates. We must read by constantly exercising our judgment—or find, like De Quincey, merely a heap of fragments.

Pope, I believe, cared deeply and thought seriously about the nature of literary criticism. He was a skillful practicing critic, as his essays, notes, and prefaces amply demonstrate. He was a connoisseur of critical responses to his own poems—and even reviewed his own Pastorals (favorably) when he thought critics had failed to understand their merit. Before the age of twenty, with virtually no formal schooling, he mastered the tradition of classical, Renaissance, and contemporary criticism in at least three languages. There are no grounds for considering him a shallow opportunist looking for an untried, easy field in which to demonstrate his knack of rhyme. *An Essay on Criticism* is a major attempt to place English literary analysis on the foundation of a coherent theory. Like all his works, it is a labor of refinement—both a commerce with the past and an original engagement with the present, viewed in the light of traditional knowledge. In his own time Pope viewed English criticism as a history of darkness and error, punctuated by the ineffectual efforts of a *"Few"* (l. 719) sound minds. The names William Walsh, Wentworth Dillon (Earl of Roscommon), and John Sheffield (Earl of Mulgrave and Duke of Buckingham and Normanby)—Pope's *"sounder Few"*—hardly define a flourishing native criticism. Although his failure to mention Dryden is surely significant, for the immediate past was less dark than Pope in his rhetorical conclusion needed to claim, yet, naming Dryden would not have invalidated Pope's point. While France derived some benefit from the imported rules its writers (in Pope's view) slavishly obeyed, England, by asserting its independence from French and Roman influence, unfortunately decreed its isolation from the improvements of polite learning:

> But *we*, brave *Britons, Foreign Laws* despis'd,
> And kept *unconquer'd*, and *unciviliz'd*.      (ll. 715–716)

The phrase "brave *Britons*" contains both a touch of irony and a trace of pride. Pope's task in *An Essay on Criticism* was to civilize an uncivil discipline. Preserving still the spirit of independence basic to

British liberty, he wished, by identifying the values which British writers shared with their great predecessors in various nations and times, to define the literary principles which would advance criticism from ignorance and incivility to knowledge. The ideal is to be both unconquered *and* civilized. The criticism of judgment represented Pope's first explicit effort, which continued indirectly throughout his lifetime, to civilize the act of reading. Not coincidentally, it provided England with a workable theory of criticism befitting an era that had begun to imagine emulating the achievements of ancient Greece and Rome.

# ·¿· III
## The Aesthetics of Revision
## in *The Rape of the Lock*

To make verses was his first labour, and to mend them was his last.

—Samuel Johnson

BYRON STATES with disarming clarity one of the central tenets of Romantic composition: the myth of spontaneity. "I am like the tyger (in poesy)," he wrote of his method of composition. "If I miss my first Spring—I go growling back to my Jungle.—There is no second.—I can't correct.—I can't—& I won't."[1] All poets revise, of course, even Byron. True improvisation, such as we find in William Carlos Williams' *Kora in Hell*, is a rarely practiced and mostly experimental art. The significant question is not whether poets revise. It is how they revise, what values they attribute to the act of revising, and what they expect revision to achieve. Although a notorious maverick, Byron is representative of Romantic theory in his public attitude toward the act of revising. Because the Romantics transform revision into a symbol of falsification, it finds few apologists or champions among poets who stress original genius, organic form, and the natural language of feeling. As in Byron's image of the springing tiger, poetic composition for the Romantics takes its characteristic metaphors from activities in which revision approaches the unthinkable. A nightingale singing in darkness to cheer its own solitude need not trouble about corrections. Music produced in a wind-harp requires no adjustment of its impulsive harmonies. Reflection in tranquillity may assist the poet, but laborious deliberation is antipoetic. Poetry should come as naturally as leaves to the trees, says Keats, or not at all.

We must recognize that most of the major Romantic poets have left us monuments of actual revision, from Blake's differing illuminated texts to Wordsworth's two versions of *The Prelude*, yet they remained committed to metaphors and to theories of art that associated great writing with the spontaneity of Milton's "unpremeditated" verse. Truly original utterance, even if imperfect, was regarded as almost by definition unimprovable. In its kinship with visionary experience, Romantic poetry is often fragmented, but the fragments, like a perfect ruin, do not invite repair. Byron's refusal to "correct" his verse is not the idiosyncrasy of an ardent temperament. It belongs to a prevailing Romantic equation of spontaneity with poetic genius. In fact, the trust in spontaneity—which fosters a simultaneous dread of the lapse or blockage of unsummoned imaginative power—is founded, authorized, or underwritten by a theory of genius which assumes that truly original poets, as opposed to mere journeymen, cannot abide and do not require the second thoughts intrinsic to refinement. Alexander Pope, by contrast, located revising at the heart of the poetic process.

## Seeing Anew: The Nature of Popean Revision

Writing for Pope was, in its largest sense, always a form of rewriting. Mending verses was not only his last labor (as Johnson states) but accompanied every stage of the lengthy process of composition, which Pope often protracted for years. "The method of Pope," Johnson explains, " . . . was to write his first thoughts in his first words, and gradually to amplify, decorate, rectify, and refine them."[2] Because Pope did not consider revising an implicit confession of failure, his "first words" should not be construed (in a Byronic sense) as more or less successful attempts at finality. Their purpose was often to create the occasions for their own eventual displacement. Indeed, the margins and interlinear spaces of Pope's manuscripts grew so dense with successively displaced improvements that the initial language is sometimes impossible to recover.

The extensiveness of his changes, however, cannot alone indicate the importance of revision for Pope. Even minor adjustments, given his economy of style, may compel major changes of interpretation. "A mighty maze! but not without a plan" is how *An Essay on Man* describes the scene of humankind, as few need to be reminded. Pope's earliest readers encountered a rather different description: "A mighty

Maze! of walks without a plan." The later change is far more than a mere verbal tinkering. It eliminates from Pope's first published version the (doubtless unintended) possibility of viewing the universe as simply a planless or accidental order, like the dance of Lucretian atoms. The example is a bit melodramatic, since most revisions do not create such complete reversals, but it demonstrates that revision for Pope was not limited to matters of style and sound. The correctness attained by mending verses involved also the construction of new meaning.

Meaning is the ultimate object of Popean revision. This claim borders on heresy because—at least since the time of Byron—Popean refinement has been understood mainly as involving the perfection of language. Verbal correctness, not the struggle with meaning, is what most Romantic critics associated with Pope, as when Coleridge argued that in Pope's work "it is the mechanical meter which determines the sense." Leigh Hunt expressed a similar view in asserting that Pope had mistaken "mere smoothness for harmony."[3] Perpetually smooth-sounding verse, however, was not what Pope meant by refinement—"But when loud Surges lash the sounding Shore, / The *hoarse, rough Verse* shou'd like the *Torrent* roar" (*An Essay on Criticism*, ll. 368–369)—and, in asserting that the sound of a verse must seem "an *Eccho*" (l. 365) of its sense, Pope assigned an unmistakable priority to sense. It is meaning which governs the music of his verse, not music which governs meaning.

The long-established view which identifies Popean revision with mere verbal correctness simply misconstrues what Pope meant by refinement. Although refinement includes attention to precise diction, he did not mean that language should monopolize a poet's interest. Writers who preoccupied themselves with verbal ornament ("pretty conceptions, fine metaphors, glitt'ring expressions") Pope denied the title of poets and demoted to the rank of "Versifiers."[4] Further, refinement did not mean that poets must sacrifice their creative energy and boldness. The laboring bard who "strains from hard-bound brains eight lines a-year" (*Arbuthnot*, l. 182) receives no praise from one of England's more prolific writers. As we have seen, Pope did not mean by refinement that English poets must obey the ancient or modern arbiters of criticism with their rules and unities. Nor did he mean that unrevised thought or language is presumably flawed. "Sometimes our first Thoughts are the best, as the first squeezing of the Grapes makes the finest and richest Wine," he replied to William Walsh, who supplied the memorable advice that Pope study correctness.[5] For Pope refinement is a positive state: not the absence of error but a harmony between the poet's execution and guiding conception; not mere verbal smoothness but an appropriate interplay of sound and sense; not an elimination of asymmetries but the achievement of an inclusive variety, amplitude, and wholeness. Refinement rightly construed is what issues at last from a comprehensive process of revision aimed at discovering and disclosing ultimately what the poem means.

Popean revision implies, in its root sense, a seeing again or, more precisely, a seeing anew. Like refinement, revising is a transformation of what is already received and known. Like judgment, it is by nature deliberative and comparative. Because human knowledge for Pope is always fragmentary and limited, the only possible approach to a more complete understanding is through repeated acts of perception, and revising implies the fuller experience and more mature judgment necessary for increased knowledge. It brings to bear upon the past the perspective of the present—and vice versa—in a commerce of mutual exchange. Not every act of revision, of course, has a rational explanation, for poetry to Pope contains *"nameless Graces"* that bypass the judgment and strike the heart directly. The creativity of revision must leave considerable space for strokes of inexplicable rightness.

Nevertheless, revision for Pope is unmistakably under the power of judgment. Critics have long regarded the machinery of sylphs and gnomes which Pope added to *The Rape of the Lock* as (rare) evidence of his powers of fancy or imaginative vision, but Pope did not agree. He emphasized instead the judiciousness of his revision, calling it "one of the greatest proofs of judgement of anything I ever did." Revision, among its other functions, allows the poet to "judge" dispassionately—to add what will improve a work, to reject what is irremediable, and to preserve what is worthy. Although he occasionally violated his own rule, Pope claimed he always waited at least two years before publishing.[6] For less-skilled poets, his advice in *An Epistle to Dr. Arbuthnot* was a blunt "Keep your Piece nine years" (l. 40). Time, in the figure of posterity, would affix proper and ultimate values to literary works, he believed. By allowing opportunity for the personal revisions of judgment, time was also the best insurance for poets that their compositions would be refined and correct.

Although the discovery and disclosure of meaning is the most important purpose of revision, it is not, of course, the only purpose. We must not ignore Pope's attention to details of syntax, sound, and versification simply because critics have usually overemphasized them. Meaning cannot be completely separated from such resources of language. Furthermore, we cannot fully understand the nature of Popean revision until we have some awareness of the relation between what is revised and what is unrevised.[7] Even unrevised passages may undergo subtle or profound changes depending upon the changes introduced *around* them. Revision is a complex process in which the relations between style and sense, between syntax and semantics, between the revised and the unrevised are not easy to disentangle. It is certainly more complicated than Pope implied in offering a piece of good advice to his literary companion Joseph Spence. "After writing a poem," he told Spence with donnish clarity, "one should correct it all over with one single view at a time."[8] He apparently meant that a poet should correct once for versification, once for diction, once for character, and so on. While emphasizing the value of revision, the statement does not correspond to what we know of Pope's practice, which was hardly so regimented. For example, the editor of one manuscript version of *Windsor-Forest* deduces about Pope's revising that "grammar, organization, imagery, fact, diction, prosody, puns, punctuation, and politics were forever jostling one another for attention."[9] In the case of *Windsor-Forest*, they jostled for some nine years, according to Pope, before the impending Treaty of Utrecht created both the occasion and the logic for his resolving image of *concordia discors*. The advice to Spence has the final defect of completely obscuring a question of serious consequence for the study of Popean revision: When is a poem finished?

There were really two separate stages of revision for Pope, even though the same procedures might have appeared in each stage. The first stage involved the usual drafts and improvements that his manuscripts preserved and that preceded publication. Here Pope was unusual only in the thoroughness of his revisions. Pope's practice, however, included also a second stage of changes—sometimes quite extensive and significant—introduced *after* a work is published. For most poets publication is a sign of closure, and each work reaches a state of public fixity before the next work appears. Yet, for Pope, publication was not an inevitable sign of finality. Poems were rarely finished but were perpetually finishing. He may have abandoned works that no longer interested him, as with certain minor poems he preferred to forget. But a major poem seemed always open to change, never achieving more than a temporary or tentative or approximate completion.

This openness to change sometimes created almost entirely new poems, leaving posterity the troublesome pleasure of two quite different works sharing the same title. *The Dunciad* of 1728, for example, contains many lines that survive in successive revisions, but it differs massively in aims and achievement from *The Dunciad* of 1743. Other poems, such as *An Essay on Criticism*, were developed through a series of relatively minor alterations added in successive editions. Sometimes fragments published separately (like portions of *An Epistle to Dr. Arbuthnot*) gained new significance when implanted in a superseding work. Even unchanged poems could undergo a form of revision simply by being placed in new relation to each other, as Pope's "Messiah" (1713) became through its placement in the *Works* of 1717 the culmination of his earlier sequence of Pastorals.[10] We must not assume that this openness to change meant that revision was an endless process and that poems were never, in principle, capable of completion: Popean refinement always sought a point of repose at which further refinement was pointless or impossible. Some poems quite early achieved a published state from which Pope did not vary. In practice, however, finishing a poem became for Pope the labor of a lifetime. For him, truly final revisions were possible only as a form of last rite.

Pope's answer to the question of when a poem is finished would demand the recognition of a paradox. A poem is finished when it can no longer be revised, and all poems are open to continuing revision. Clearly the stage of revision preceding publication may prove so thorough that little need exists for improvement; the second stage of revision can then occupy itself with minor details of technique or nuances of meaning. My intention is not to claim a special importance for revision after publication but—on the contrary—to suggest that it is part of a single comprehensive process whose primary object is the discovery and disclosure of meaning. Revising for Pope is far more than an unavoidable procedure that he shares with almost all writers. Joseph Warton did not intend unqualified praise when he wrote that Pope was "a most excellent IMPROVER, if no great original INVEN-TOR."[11] It would be more accurate to say that Popean invention takes the form of improvements so thorough that revision is inseparable from imaginative power. The improvements of revision, whether small or large, constitute for Pope not simply a program for correcting errors but a way of uniting imagination with judgment in the creation of meaning.

## Modes of Revision in *The Rape of the Lock*

No better poem for the study of Popean revision exists than *The Rape of the Lock*. The original version was, by his own account, "written fast."[12] Its two cantos in 344 lines grew to the familiar five-canto poem, well over twice as long. The poem developed over an extended period. The two-canto version appeared in 1712; Pope expanded it to five cantos in 1714. In 1715 he made a few minor corrections; in 1717 he continued minor corrections and added Clarissa's lengthy speech. In 1736 he altered three lines and several words. The Twickenham edition includes, as "probably" authorized by Pope, several slight variants from the version in Warburton's 1751 *Works of Alexander Pope*, so that Pope in effect revised the poem even beyond the grave. For our purposes, the specific timing of these revisions matters far less than the general process of correction itself, and we can study this process most effectively by comparing two texts: the original poem of 1712 and the authoritative five-canto version, incorporating all of Pope's changes, in the Twickenham edition. In analyzing these changes, we have an opportunity to examine how revision contributes to a cumulative, decisive change of meaning.

Pope's most extensive and intricate revisions in *The Rape of the Lock* have little to do with the verbal "smoothness" that Leigh Hunt associated with refinement. Detailed repair to the wording of the original poem proves quite unusual. Many of the wittiest and most quoted lines come directly from the initial version, which Pope claimed to have finished in two weeks. A comparison between what was revised and what was unrevised shows that about half of the original verse paragraphs received no change whatever (except for the addition of new couplets). Very few whole lines disappeared. One was rejected to avoid a Drydenesque triplet rhyme (ii.177), and another dropped out of an overcrowded catalogue (i.56). But in general the same law of conservation that governed Pope's personal thrift also governed his revisions. Little was wasted.

Perhaps most surprising, rhyme, Pope's modern trademark, received slight attention. Indeed, his concern with rhyme can be easily overestimated. Complex or extravagant or ingenious rhymes, like the famous pair "chaste/embrac'd," are always noteworthy in *The Rape of the Lock* because they are comparatively infrequent. They owe their prominence to Pope's usual practice of rhyming common monosyllables that not only call little attention to themselves but seem almost self-effacing—ray/day, lay/say, air/care, sky/die—some repeated with scandalous regularity. The degree of self-effacement is not greatly altered when, as often happens, one or both of the pair is a dissyllable. Such ordinary rhymes are important mainly in providing the norm against which his more significant pairings can be measured.[13] Pope's unsurpassed skill, as demonstrated, for example, in *An Essay on Man*, lies less in the sustained ingenuity of his rhyming than in his use of rhyme to compress great richness of sense within the patterns of normal English syntax. It was rhyme alone, Pope argued, that allowed him to be so concise.

To multiply examples of Pope's obvious technical repairs would be pointless because they tell us so little about Pope. Such corrections, adjusted only slightly, are what we would expect to find in the practice of many writers. The following practical advice, for instance, summarizes Pope's technical guides to revision and could be duplicated in almost any modern handbook of style: (1) delete all expletives and unnecessary predication, such as *do* before a main verb; (2) remove redundancies of expression and fact; (3) emphasize forms of contrast through parallel syntax and rhetorical antithesis; (4) make verbs active and vivid; (5) avoid awkward constructions; (6) clarify unintentional ambiguities; (7) keep main units of sense relatively brief; and (8) alter punctuation to express continuity and discontinuity. If we feel disappointed with such a conventional list, we might also appreciate a modernity in Pope's style which we too seldom recognize: an identical list of guidelines could not be composed for Chaucer, Spenser, Shakespeare, Donne, Herbert, or Milton. We might also observe—in defense of Matthew Arnold's judgment concerning Pope and Dryden as "classics of our prose"—that Pope's techniques for revising poetry emphasize values normally admired in modern expository writing. Perhaps most disconcerting, because it reflects Pope's practice of revision, is what the list does not contain. In *The Rape of the Lock* Pope does not introduce changes merely to create alliteration, euphony, or metrical variety, all of which (like rhyme) comprise distinctive features of his style. After his extensive labor to refine the versification of his Pastorals—preceding their publication—he may have found it almost second nature to observe what he called the "great rule" of verse: "to be musical."[14] Sense, not sound, is what concerns him most in revising *The Rape of the Lock*.

Even minor technical repairs usually influence meaning. Only one word in the passage below has been changed:

*Original*

    But when to Mischief Mortals bend their Mind,
    How soon fit Instruments of Ill they find?      (i.105–106)

*Revision*

    But when to Mischief Mortals bend their Will,
    How soon they find fit Instruments of Ill!      (iii.125–126)

Probably the most passionate interpreter would fail to convince us that the change from "Mind" to "Will" veils a profound intent, since both words convey the idea of conscious choice. (The slight metaphorical strain suggested by the idea of bending a mind is not notably improved by the concept of a bent will.) Pope's revision has an evident and unforced explanation. In transposing the phrase "fit Instruments of Ill" to the final position, Pope avoids syntactic inversion and achieves a normal word order of subject–verb–object. The normal word order also allows the final word of the couplet to shift emphasis from the process of finding to the thing which is found. In its concluding position, Pope's ironic phrase "fit Instruments of Ill," which unites the disparate concepts of fitness and evil, now locks itself into place, doubly secured by syntax and by rhyme, transforming the earlier weak half-question into an affirmative exclamation. So far, the gains seem mainly stylistic or technical.

When we look closer at Pope's change of rhyme, however, the relation between meaning and style reveals its intrinsic complexity. As Nelson Goodman rightly observes, "What is said, how it is said, what is expressed, and how it is expressed, are all intimately interrelated and involved in style."[15] Style and meaning are, at last, inseparable. In this instance, the rhyming of "Will" with "Ill"—though not so

83

witty as "chaste" and "embrac'd"—is significant, for it invites us to realize that Pope's characters, no matter how comic and two-dimensional, are moral agents, responsible for (willing) their (good or ill) actions. The original couplet contained this implication, but in shifting the word "Will" to a final position Pope's change adds extra emphasis, because *will* specifically denotes the faculty of moral choice. Further, in its newly prominent position, "Ill" creates an internal allusion which associates the rape with another revised passage: the added episode of impending disaster in which, facing defeat at the card game ombre, Belinda "sees, and trembles at th' approaching Ill" (iii.91). The linked passages contrast a simple misfortune at cards, which Belinda sees and fears and escapes, with a calculated (if trivial) evil which she cannot foresee and cannot avoid. Pope's one-word revision thus creates verbal and thematic filaments which help integrate the added episode of Belinda's card game into the original poem. Such continuities affect the meaning of the poem by supplying new and richer contexts for interpretation.

The interrelation of technical and semantic change is easier to follow if we distinguish the four maneuvers possible in revising: addition, deletion, substitution, and transposition. We have just seen, in Pope's shifting of the phrase "fit Instruments of Ill," how the transposition of exisiting words or phrases can alter emphasis and create new possibilities of internal allusion. Later I will examine the transposition of an entire couplet from a speech by Thalestris to one by Belinda, where the rearrangement decisively alters our understanding of Belinda's character. Transposition, however, usually does not occur in isolation but in combination with other techniques of revision. Of these, deletion—"The last and greatest Art"—is the technique Pope uses least in revising the published editions of *The Rape of the Lock* (though in revision which *precedes* publication it is considerably more frequent).[16] Once a poem had been published, Pope revised not by pruning but mainly by substitution and addition.

Among the more interesting examples of Pope's economical substitutions is a passage describing his heroine, Belinda:

*Original*
> If to her share some Female Errors fall,
> Look on her Face, and you'll forgive 'em all.     (i.33–34)

*Revision*
>      If to her share some Female Errors fall,
>      Look on her Face, and you'll forget 'em all.          (ii.17–18)

Here too only one word is changed, but the slight change in wording has unmistakably altered the meaning. The difference between forgiving and forgetting is the difference between voluntary and involuntary action. Forgiveness is an act of the will, usually reflecting credit on the person who forgives; forgetting is something which, unwillingly, happens *to* us, suggesting weakness and discredit. Both of Pope's couplets imply that "Female Errors" are inconsequential. In both cases it is Belinda's remarkable beauty that outshines her trivial faults. In the version of 1712, however, the verb *forgive* suggests that we knowingly and willingly absolve her. The verb *forget* implies, instead, that we have no choice: beauty will always dazzle judgment. Our will is simply overmastered by a superior force.

These few differences do not complete Pope's readjustment of meaning, for it is not entirely correct to claim that forgetting is an involuntary act in which judgment plays no part. Here again one revision alludes to another. Consider Ariel's recitation of the possible disasters threatening Belinda: losing her chastity or breaking a china jar, falling in love or misplacing her necklace, staining her honor or her new brocade. Among this celebrated jumble of serious and trivial dangers, which exposes the folly of a world that assigns them equal weight, is the possibility that Belinda may "Forget her Pray'rs, or miss a Masquerade" (ii.108). In this instance the act of forgetting implies a careless indifference and irresponsibility. "It is, indeed, the faculty of remembrance," writes Samuel Johnson, "which may be said to place us in the class of moral agents" (*The Rambler* no. 41). We remember what we *choose* to remember. Against the entropy of involuntary forgetfulness mankind can, if it chooses, oppose its judicious, willing, moral capacity for remembrance. This is a fertile theme, which Pope explores most thoroughly in *The Dunciad*. Here the substitution of *forget* for *forgive* not only alters the meaning of a single couplet but helps to create a new allusive context within which the original actions become more meaningful.

Addition, as Byron was among the first to observe, accounts for the great majority of Pope's changes in *The Rape of the Lock*. Seeing anew for Pope was primarily an art of expansion. Addition, however, should not be mistaken in Pope's practice for simple embellishment. When embellishment is artful, it enhances our appreciation but does not alter our understanding. For Pope, by contrast, addition discovers, modifies, and discloses meaning. It alters the ways in which actions and ideas are understood. The most obvious example of such an addition is Clarissa's speech on good humor and good sense. In a note, Pope explains that the speech was added *"to open more clearly"* the moral of the poem. Indeed, meaning might be considered less a product of addition than a generating force. In seeing the poem anew, Pope in effect read between the lines, discovering what larger meaning his story possessed, and this discovery of meaning generated the additions that expressed it. Yet, before I examine how several of Pope's largest additions directly influence the meaning of the poem, we should consider the *indirect* influence of additive revisions as they introduce changes in narrative form and technique.

An odd detail is worth considering. In the poem of 1712 the adverb *now* appeared three times; the final version contains seventeen uses of *now*. This isolated fact, when supported by alterations in verb tense and by the addition of new speeches, reflects a noticeable change in Pope's poetic technique. The revised poem considerably increases the sense of narrative immediacy. Immediacy—a concept related to the Greek critical term *enargeia*—was a value Pope understood from his reading of Longinus. The practical changes in his art of narration, however, should probably be attributed to his study of Homer, a study which coincided with the period of his most substantial revisions to *The Rape of the Lock*. By adding the orations of Ariel, Umbriel, and Clarissa, Pope substantially increased the presence of direct speech in the poem, thus placing the reader in immediate relation to the speaker. Pope noted this technique in Homer: "What *Virgil* does by two words of a Narration," he wrote, "*Homer* brings about by a Speech; he hardly raises one of his Heroes out of Bed without some Talk concerning it" (note to *Iliad* XIII.353). Pope's dry humor, while here perhaps favoring Virgilian economy over Homeric "Talk," reminds us that the speech making begins in the revised *Rape of the Lock* even *before* his heroine rises from her bed. The continual mock-heroic allusions to the *Iliad* and the *Odyssey* reflect only one aspect of Pope's commerce with Homer. His most pervasive and most subtle debt involves insights into the art of narrative, for Homer offered Pope not only a rich store of epic conventions but also a model of vivid narration. "What he writes," Pope observes of Homer as storyteller, "is of the most animated Nature imaginable; every thing moves, every thing lives, and is put in Action. If a Council be call'd, or a Battle fought, you are not coldly inform'd of what was said or done as from a third Person; the Reader is hurry'd out of himself by the Force of the Poet's Imagination, and turns in one place to a Hearer, in another to a Spectator."[17] We can best judge Pope's appreciation of Homeric immediacy if we turn to another revision, small, but far from insignificant.

Pope's new emphasis upon narrative immediacy governs his revised description of the Baron at the exact instant of the rape:

*Original*

> He first expands the glitt'ring *Forfex* wide
> T'inclose the Lock; then joins it, to divide.          (i.115–116)

*Revision*

> The Peer now spreads the glitt'ring *Forfex* wide,
> T'inclose the Lock; now joins it, to divide.          (iii.147–148)

Both passages rely on the wit of a spatial paradox: spreading encloses and joining divides. Both also achieve forms of internal harmony (*ex*pands / For*fex* : *P*eer / *sp*reads). The most significant feature of Pope's revision, however, beyond its possible gains in sexual innuendo, is the new reference to time. The substitution of "now/now" for "first/then" reflects a general change in Pope's narrative strategy. The original formula "first/then" implies a retrospective stance, an orderly temporal sequence, a narrator who relates what has *already* happened. The shift to "now/now" creates the illusion of a narrator who tells the story *as* it is happening, with no gap between the experience and the tale, no stance for reflective ordering. Immediate observation supplants reflective memory as the poet's source of speech, and we are brought directly into the present as spectators. In a narrative which proceeds on the model of "first/then," we are (in Pope's phrase) coldly informed; "now/now" invites a breathless hurrying out of ourselves, an impassioned involvement with the fiction that creates both suspense and sympathy. Pope does not everywhere sustain the illusion of present action. Memory and foresight are also

87

available to the narrator as he chooses to temper Homeric immediacy with Virgilian reflectiveness, and Pope emphasizes his moments of immediacy by contrasting them with other modes of narration. These refinements of narrative technique create a work which mediates selectively among past, present, and future, allowing us at crucial junctures to share the involvement as impassioned eyewitnesses.

Pace or tempo is another aspect of narrative technique affected by Pope's additions. The original description of the rape occupied only two couplets—the first of which we have just examined—appearing at the end of a rather shapeless fourteen-line paragraph. Pope's revision intensifies the drama of Belinda's loss by describing the rape in a separate paragraph that amplifies the two original couplets through the addition of four intervening lines (iii.147–154):

> The Peer now spreads the glitt'ring *Forfex* wide, }  *original*
> T'inclose the Lock; now joins it, to divide.
> Ev'n then, before the fatal Engine clos'd,
> A wretched *Sylph* too fondly interpos'd; }  *revision*
> Fate urg'd the Sheers, and cut the *Sylph* in twain,
> (But Airy Substance soon unites again)
> The meeting Points the sacred Hair dissever }  *original*
> From the fair Head, for ever and for ever!

By interposing the history of the bisected sylph, Pope's symmetrical paragraph both shapes and prolongs the moment of crisis, delaying our otherwise direct progress from action (as the scissors join) to consequence (when the lock falls). The past tenses of Pope's addition do not propel the narrative back into the past. Rather, as nearly as linear print and English syntax can express, Pope's history of the sylph opens up the present, expands it, revealing in its dilation (as if the film of a foot race suddenly changed to slow motion) action ordinarily invisible even to an eyewitness. The addition effectively changes the pace of narration, prolonging the present, building suspense, in a process duplicated in Pope's more substantial additions. In the original version Belinda rises from bed and finds herself launched upon the Thames within the space of two lines (i.19–20). Among their other functions, the added Rites of Pride (which divide her rising and boating) serve, like Pope's other added episodes, to slow down the action, to open possibilities for speech and description, to create an impression of dilatory indolence soon to be shattered by the methodical world of fate.

Pope's largest additions, while altering the pace or tempo, also greatly change the poem's narrative form. The form of the original version is a simple, two-part, before-and-after structure, with the rape marking the obvious point of division between the first canto and the second. In the final five-canto version Pope transforms the rape from a dividing point to the center of an elaborate, symmetrical architectonics of contrasting values and events. The final poem, in fact, closely follows the structure of a neoclassical play, which Pope would have known from many sources, among them Dryden's compendious *Of Dramatick Poesie*. Dryden can supply all the necessary technical terms for describing how Pope has divided his action:

canto 1—*protasis*: { Ariel on self-love
The Rites of Pride
canto 2—*epitasis*: Sylphs (upperworld)
canto 3—*peripetia*: { Ombre (play/victory)
Rape (seriousness/loss)
canto 4—*catastasis*: Gnomes (underworld)
canto 5—*catastrophe*: { Battle of the Sexes
Clarissa on good sense

Schematic diagrams of literary works are always suspect, but the important point is that Pope's original version does not lend itself to similar analysis.

Form in the revised poem reflects the new infusion of drama into epic. The central canto, with its vivid reversal, creates the pattern for Pope's elaboration of dramatic contrasts that extend even to such paired details as Belinda's "Shouts" (iii.99) of victory at ombre and her "Screams" (iii.156) of dismay following the rape.[18] Canto 2 is suffused with an atmosphere of delicate beauty, epitomized by Ariel and the radiant sylphs; its reverse is canto 4 where the sooty gnome Umbriel and the deformities of Spleen plunge us into subterranean gloom. Cantos 1 and 5 present a similar contrast. Ariel's indulgent celebration of self-love, in contrast to Clarissa's homily on good sense, provides a kind of antimoral, while the private order of Belinda's ceremonious dressing culminates finally in the public disorder of a general melee. This new intricacy of form derives entirely from Pope's additions to the original poem. Nor is formal intricacy a purely aesthetic achievement. Aesthetic order for Pope has cognitive functions. His symmetries link otherwise disparate and isolated episodes to form allusive commentaries, thus embedding the original action in a context that makes it not only suspenseful and interesting but, more important, intelligible.

Three large additions which help generate much of the revised meaning and refined comedy of Pope's completed poem are the Rites of Pride, the Game of Ombre, and the Cave of Spleen. These episodes do not significantly advance the plot but instead guide our understanding of its meaning, especially by developing the thematically resonant concepts of play, ritual, and sexuality. There is no reason why analyzing Pope's treatment of sexuality, ritual, and play should prevent our appreciating the poem's comic spirit, for of course Pope did not think of sense and meaning as literary killjoys. In fact, Rabelais annoyed Pope precisely because "there were so many things in his works in which I could not see any manner of meaning driven at."[19] The *Rape* of 1712, with its accelerated pace and senseless action, seems closer to farce than to the rich comedy of Pope's revised poem. In revising the original version, Pope sought to explore and to expand its significance, to unite comedy with meaning, so that the reader could experience both pleasure *and* knowledge—an experience that would stand as a judgment upon the mindless diversion of the beau monde.

## The Mirror and the Cave

With her treasured lock suddenly cut, Belinda concludes her lament upon the vanity of courts with a complaint addressed directly to the Baron that gains added prominence in its new place as the final couplet of canto 4:

> Oh hadst thou, Cruel! been content to seize
> Hairs less in sight, or any Hairs but these!     (ll. 175–176)

In the version of 1712 these indelicate lines had belonged to the forgettable minor character Thalestris. Pope's decision to transpose the couplet to Belinda's speech, placing it where few readers could miss its indecent suggestion, was a risky piece of revision. Because intentional indecency is quite out of character for Belinda, Pope's purpose must depend on our interpreting her cry as an unknowing slip. The slip certainly exposes a truth about Belinda's tacit system of values. In the beau monde rape or sexual misconduct, if discreet, is less dishonorable than public unsightliness. Yet Belinda's superficial values hardly required exposure in such an unsettling manner. What her slip unquestionably allows us to observe—an observation possible in the revised poem only—is a sexual content to her speech of which Belinda is apparently unaware. Her language reveals what she herself is unwilling or unable to say.

Belinda's delicate but bawdy words not only provide a glimpse into her character but also repeat a pattern central to the revised *Rape of the Lock*. This pattern can be described as a pairing of rudeness and refinement. In Belinda's lament to the Baron a coarse sexual content irrupts in the refined social speech; her composed and formal rhetoric is disfigured by an unseen force. Ironically, the refined abstractness of "any Hairs"—inviting the widest possible interpretation—carries only one relevant meaning, rude and blatantly unabstract. In the rape, the central action of the poem, the stylized composure of Belinda's world also shatters from the force of rude violence. Rudeness and refinement in the revised poem are inescapably locked together in ways which not only generate comedy but also invite subsequent reflection. Why should this most refined of virgins, in her delicate words, express such a rude and bawdy meaning?

Refinement is the regulating virtue of the beau monde; however, for Pope, virtues are often more complex than they sound, and the virtue of refinement is no exception. His habitual modes of thought identify true refinement as the golden mean between two forms of excess, rudeness and overrefinement. On reflection, it seems clear that the artificial manners valued by the beau monde are precisely what Pope would define as false refinement or overrefinement—an excess that, in its flight from rudeness and vulgarity, passes through the bounds of true refinement and, paradoxically, becomes entangled with the rude and vulgar—its own opposite. Just as the Catholic Peter and the Calvinist Jack in Swift's *Tale of a Tub* are continually mistaken for each other, so too in *The Rape of the Lock* opposites prove strangely linked. Rudeness and overrefinement cannot get free from each other's company. What we do not yet understand is how Pope's revisions help to identify the overrefinement of the beau monde with the rudeness of sexual desire which finds its main symbol and victim in Belinda.

Pope, we might say, depicts sexuality in the beau monde as rig-

orously abstracted—"drawn away" from its natural, physical base—
through such overrefinements of fashion as card parties, masquer-
ades, and billets-doux. The fashionable abstraction of desire in turn
brings its own inevitable irruption of rude passions. In the beau
monde, we should notice, sexual passion has been attenuated rather
than expunged or extinguished. Belinda's bawdy slip and (another
revision) the "Earthly Lover" who lurks in her heart (iii.144) both
assure us that natural desire is not entirely absent from the powdery
world of beaux and coquettes. "One of the vicissitudes an instinctual
impulse may undergo," wrote Freud, "is to meet with resistances
which seek to make it inoperative."[20] The abstraction of sexuality in
the beau monde is a form of resistance aimed not at denying desire
but at rendering it "inoperative" in a curious way—by somehow purifying it, elevating it, maintaining it in a state of disembodied arrest,
so that it is never contaminated by the carnal cycle of gratification
and satiety. Belinda is the nearly perfect image of this cultural ideal.

It is the sylphs, however, added to the original poem in 1714, who
perfectly represent the abstracted sexuality of the beau monde. These
airy creatures have achieved a state of virtual disembodiment. Although less "refin'd" (ii.81) than pure angelic spirits, they have shed
the flesh and blood of their previous existence as coquettes (i.65) and
function now as the reigning deities of fashion. They characterize a
world of folly which Pope depicts as a refraction of its prototype in
Restoration comedy. Sexuality in Restoration comic drama adheres
to a strict code of hypocrisy. For example, the public decorum of
Horner and of Lady Wishfort in Wycherley's *The Country Wife*
masks an enormous private lust. In the sylph-governed realm of the
beau monde, by contrast, sexual desire is not satisfied in concealment
but endlessly and openly deferred through perpetual displacements
onto objects, images, and words. Thus the marbled cane and name-
sake feather of Sir Plume—the phallic emblems of his overrefinement—display something like a self-induced impotence, comically
duplicated in his blustering speech. In the revised *Rape*, the abstraction of natural desire grows so intricate and copious as to produce almost an anatomy of sexual dysfunction. No male character proves
virile enough to threaten the chastity of the most willing female. The
Baron, as befits a figure of heroic refinement, has transmuted the
rudeness of natural desire into an elegant and effete fetishism.[21] It is
only our assumptions about why men *normally* pursue women which
allows us to misconstrue the rape (which is only, abstractly, a seiz-

ing) as a symbolic sexual assault. The armor of slain enemies was a sign of conquest for Homeric warriors, but the Baron's prize ringlet does not signify carnal knowledge of Belinda's person. A harmless trophy-hunter, he gets exactly what he prays for—not sexual pleasure but (to embellish his collection of gloves and garters) a lock of hair.

The Rites of Pride and the Cave of Spleen are, through Pope's revisions, extended metaphors for the inseparable union of refinement and rudeness that characterize sexuality in the beau monde. At her mirror, Belinda produces a disembodied and refined image of herself which ultimately will call forth its own deformed reflections in the realm of Spleen. Normally the Rites of Pride have been assigned a simple, moral significance as depicting Belinda's narcissism, which they do. We might also recall, however, that Freud discusses narcissism as a form of sexual (not moral) disorder, and his account of female narcissism helps to illuminate Belinda's function and power within the beau monde.[22] Her special role as an object of worship requires not only her own proud contrivances but also the confusion and complicity of those who worship her:

> Fair Nymphs, and well-drest Youths around her shone,
> But ev'ry Eye was fix'd on her alone. (ii.5–6)

Pope's dazzling (added) catalogues of gewgaws confirm that Belinda inhabits a culture literally in love with objects—objects refined beyond all use—even as the erotic attachment to other persons (what Freud meant by object-love) is beyond its power. It is the coquette, of course, who best fulfills Freud's description of female narcissism: the woman simultaneously attractive and invulnerable, whose eminence depends upon a refusal to gratify the desire she arouses, thereby maintaining sexual passion in a state of uninterrupted and unsatisfied longing. (By keeping men off, as Mrs. Peachum sings in *The Beggar's Opera*, you keep them on.) Belinda seems to know that one slip of answering desire will cause her power to vanish:

> Favours to none, to all she Smiles extends,
> Oft she rejects, but never once offends. (ii.11–12)

Her cool economy of favor is certainly one source of power. Yet, we should not let her calculated smiles betray us into the error of imagining Belinda the simple object of Pope's satire.

Pope's revisions prevent us from reducing Belinda to a satirical stereotype, for, despite her airs, Belinda is not identical with the empty-hearted creatures Addison ridicules for coquetry in *The Spectator*. The true coquette, as Addison informs us, has no feelings to hide. Her heart is impervious to desire.[23] Belinda, however, lacking the true coquette's protection of insensibility, is vulnerable to her own erotic nature. She is *not*, as another revision tells us, "predestin'd" (i.80) to the sterile life of coquetry—hence Ariel's panic when he views the "Earthly Lover" concealed in her heart. In the revised poem, Belinda holds the awkward position of a woman who plays a role for which she is ill-equipped, so that she must inevitably fail. Her theatrical swoons and cries certainly expose a comic superficiality (the antithesis of the tragic self-consciousness which Pope portrays in Eloisa). Indeed, Pope depicts Belinda as someone who has no genuine consciousness of self on which to rely, a woman conscious only of her beauty, who cannot understand her own feelings or the conduct which might guide them. Yet, Pope's revisions emphasize that Belinda's folly is not merely a personal failing. No one in the beau monde applauds Clarissa's moral speech. An often ignored addition (i.83–90) employs the language of pedagogy ("Instruct," "Teach," "bidden," "know") to suggest that young women like Belinda are deliberately *schooled* in absurdity. (In other poems Pope takes pains to sympathize with women as "confin'd" by forms, "Bred to disguise," and cursed "by Man's oppression."[24]) Although she justly suffers for her undeniable mistakes, Belinda's folly coincides with a general pattern of cultural error—one that incriminates even "Peers and Dukes, and all their sweeping Train" (i.84). It is this wider, centrifugal pattern of folly which permits us to understand the Rites of Pride as linked, like reverse images, with the rudely grotesque Cave of Spleen.

Pope's revisions deal in causes, sources, origins. The Cave of Spleen thus provides, in its gothic parody of classical underworld scenes, more than merely another epic allusion. While Belinda's fashionable mirror refines, idealizes, and abstracts, the Cave of Spleen collects the coarse and disfigured victims of fashion, who are reduced to disease, matter, and deformity. The "Unnumber'd Throngs" (iv.47) confined there suffer from a variety of disorders, not all explicitly sexual. But sexual disfigurement supplies some of Pope's cruelest and most grimly comic shapes:

Men prove with Child, as pow'rful Fancy works,
And Maids turn'd Bottels, call aloud for Corks.    (iv.53–54)

The abstraction of erotic desire in the beau monde finds its ironic embodiment in young women transformed into mere receptacles, holes, denied even mechanical satisfaction. Just as Umbriel is the dark counterpart or rude double of Ariel, the misshapen figures of Spleen reveal how far the "graceful Ease" (ii.15) of the beau monde is linked with forms of psychic and sexual disorder. The 1712 poem catches some, but not much, of the deferred, deflected, and deformed sexuality that is a major presence in the revised version. In Pope's revision, however, Umbriel's downward flight to the Cave of Spleen reveals a disorder far more significant than the fuss about Belinda's lock. It releases into the poem disturbing new images, which implicitly condemn the fashionable culture that is their source.

All readers can agree that the beau monde is a trivial society characterized by absurd rites and ceremonies. But what makes the beau monde trivial? In what does its absurdity consist? We should notice that a curious transformation has occurred in the beau monde. Speech and behavior have grown invariably ritualized, formulaic, so that ritual has become indistinguishable from nonritual. Every phrase and gesture in the world of fashion repeats the meaningless ceremonies which constitute its only action. Everything that can happen has already happened, has been absorbed into the indiscriminate formality of a world which runs like clockwork. There is truth as well as comedy in Pope's exposure of courtly life. As Lord Hervey wrote to his mother from the court at Windsor, "What can I tell your Ladyship from hence? The Circle of our employments moves in such unchangeable Revolutions that you have but to look at your watch any Hour in the four & twenty & tell your-self what we are doing as well as if you were here, *for as it was in the beginning is now & ever shall be, Court without end, Amen.*"[25] The formulaic phrases of prayer exactly suit an ironic description of life at court, where everything is repetition. Unlike his arch-foe Hervey, Pope could understand what was wrong—not simply tedious—about the mindless repetitions of a courtly elite.

The forms of repeated activity and language with which Pope's revisions fill *The Rape of the Lock*—even in such minor details as the "thrice" rung bell (i.17), the "thrice" twitched ear (iii.137), the heroine who "thrice" looks back and the hero who "thrice" draws near (iii.138)—accomplish far more than the imitation of epic, where nothing worth doing is done only once. Imitation itself is a mode of repetition, just as writing always for Pope incorporates rewriting. The challenge Pope sees—in literature as in life—is how to distinguish sterile or servile repetition from a repetition which is fruitful and renewing, which permits both continuity and change. Here Pope's practice of revision suggests a model by which to judge the activity of the beau monde, for Pope's revisions, as we have seen, do not merely repeat or embellish but serve to generate new meaning. They extend and refine what was previously undeveloped. By contrast, ritual and ceremony in the beau monde are empty forms, foolish and reductive, without the power to connect man with the wider realms of nature and community. Meals in Homer serve a vital function: they impart strength, they unite guest-suppliant with host, they do honor to the gods. In *The Rape of the Lock* all significance dwindles away in the fashionable chitchat of the coffee table. Like Belinda's ceremonious dressing or the Baron's sacrificing alone before dawn, the imitation of epic ceremonies now emphasizes private ends. Pope's new emphasis in his revisions upon the hermetic self-enclosure of the beau monde is so successful that there seems nothing outside its perimeters: "Belinda smil'd, and all the World was gay" (ii. 52). It is not the heroine alone but an entire society that sees only what it wishes to see. Belinda's smile might be considered the act of repetition—practiced, deliberate, exclusive—on which her world is founded. The strategy of exclusion has reduced human life to the dimensions of a private social set.

The exclusiveness of the beau monde is by no means a Popean invention. As the historian J. H. Plumb writes: "The whole of London's social life revolved around the Court; its gaiety, wit and malice were inbred; it was a closed yet glittering world which dazzled all who did not belong to it by birth."[26] In developing his comic exposure of a society whose sole activity is endless repetition, Pope preserves from his original version stark evidence of the wider community that the beau monde conveniently forgets or deliberately excludes from thought:

> Mean while declining from the Noon of Day,
> The Sun obliquely shoots his burning Ray;

The hungry Judges soon the Sentence sign,
And Wretches hang that Jury-men may Dine.        (iii.19–22)

The intrusive presence of the hanged wretches, like Pope's emblematic "Merchant" (iii.23) and like the creatures deformed by Spleen, acknowledges (however fleetingly) a world of enterprise and suffering wider than the toy microcosm warmed by Belinda's smile. A coarseness and confusion in the dim world beyond the beau monde, where the ceremonies of dining preempt justice, help to explain why Belinda and her admirers choose to exclude it, shrinking reality to the small circle of courtly pleasures. The fragile order of the beau monde demands such exclusions—especially, of course, the exclusion of time, with its unrelenting process of aging and death. Repetition and refinement in the beau monde might be best described as an attempt to stop time, to replace the natural cycle of procreation, growth, and death—which incorporates change and renewal—with a circle of unending sameness. Within its artificial environment the beau monde has achieved through the power of repetition an almost perfect ceremonial self-sufficiency. Almost, because where all is repetition the only truly momentous event possible is the intrusion of change—an irruption of the unexpected. It is the achievement of complete predictability and undisturbed sameness that accounts for much of the comic frenzy following the Baron's assault. His violation is precisely the violence of change—unexpected, intolerable, unthinkable—as it breaks in upon and disfigures the sphere of unchanging repetition.

## Ombre: Life as Game—Game as Form

If Pope in his revisions had wished to create a single image emblematic of the meaningless repetitions and deliberate exclusions central to Belinda's artificial cosmos, he could not have chosen better than the Game of Ombre. More than one writer has noted the gamelike qualities of life in the beau monde.[27] In excluding whatever threatens its repetitious forms and in isolating itself from surrounding realities, the beau monde occupies the charmed circle or playground that Johan Huizinga describes as a main feature of games. Belinda's world, like any game, is a rule-bound and ceremonious realm of arbitrary order, with penalties (shame and ostracism) reserved for players who break the rules. The recognized roles of cheat and spoilsport, as Huizinga

97

analyzes various types of players, match rather eerily the behavior of the Baron and Clarissa. The Baron as cheat is finally tolerated because, however rudely he violates the rules of propriety, his cheating does not call into question the worth or primacy of the game. Thus his formal speech following the rape perfectly upholds the values of the private world he has temporarily outraged ("As long as *Atalantis* shall be read, / Or the small Pillow grace a Lady's Bed"). A spoil-sport like Clarissa is ultimately a much greater peril, because she attacks the game itself, reminding the players of realities that their playing excludes, insisting that the game is *merely* a game. The spoil-sport, in effect, threatens the illusion inherent in play by invoking the world outside the game, just as Clarissa invokes the facts of aging and death that the beau monde rigorously excludes. Her role, like her speech, emphasizes how far play and game have become in Belinda's world a comprehensive metaphor for living.

An aura of unaccountable significance has long attracted scholars to the Game of Ombre, as if the sequence of play must conceal a key to interpretation, and Pope doubtless enjoyed setting this trap for over-solemn and deep-reading critics. In his mock-treatise *A Key to the Lock* (1715) he further helped to inflame critical passions by pretending to uncover hidden political meaning in each card. Yet Belinda's playing holds an obvious moral which requires no intricate decoding. She does not err in her skill at cards: "I question whether Hoyle could have played it better," marveled Joseph Warton.[28] Pope contrives the Game of Ombre not to test her intelligence or technique but to examine her character and conduct. It is, after all, blind luck which ultimately decides Belinda's fate. Her only choice, as the Baron runs his winning diamonds, involves what to discard. Given the incomplete deck and absence of preliminary bidding that characterize ombre, Belinda has little reliable data on which to base her decisions about discards. Denied even the Lockean twilight of probable reasoning, she must make crucial decisions without sufficient information to enable judgment to do its work. What inspires her to retain her final victorious king of hearts cannot be skill or reason. (Sentiment is the likely explanation, since Belinda's king still mourns his fallen queen.) Indeed, its unpredictability makes ombre for Pope a ready-made image of Fortune, and Belinda's playing provides us with the scarcely arcane wisdom that we must encounter chance and change with equanimity. "Human Life (as Plutarch just now told me) is like a Game at Tables," Pope wrote in an early letter, "where every one may wish for the best Cast; but after all he is to make his best of that which happens, and go on contentedly."[29] For someone with Pope's physical deformities and debility, contentment in the face of misfortune was a less complacent virtue than his sententious comparison implies. Belinda's sudden shifts from burning anticipation to fearful palor to wild exultation indicate how far she has strayed from such philosophical conduct. If a "Game at Tables" can serve as an image of "Human Life," Belinda's playing points to failures that her lucky victory at ombre momentarily obscures.

We diminish the importance of the Game of Ombre, however, if, like critical Clarissas, we attend to its moral meaning only. The game serves a dramatic function far more effective than providing the revelation that Belinda has failed to study Plutarch's *Moralia*. If we pursue Plutarch's observation that life is like a game, Pope places an actual game—which (luckily) Belinda wins—within the context of a metaphorical game which (unluckily) she must lose. In the metaphorical game of human life, Belinda has only two choices. As Clarissa rightly tells her, she can either marry or "die a maid" (v.28). The options both involve loss. Choosing a husband means resigning much of her independence and power, legally, socially, sexually. Dying a maid, in the nonfeminist culture of eighteenth-century England, evokes fears of living in isolation and sterility. Belinda has no choice but to play out a (serious) game which, like Hector, she is fated to lose. Her only leeway is in which loss to accept (for they are not equal) and in what spirit to accept it. Here is a dilemma which her folly, pride, and miseducation have not caused. In fact, she faces a feminine version of the general dilemma which poet and reader must also confront. As Pope tells a correspondent, "They say, 'tis in the conduct of life as in that of picquette, one shows most skill in the discarding part of the game."[30] Life (if we are lucky) may include moments of triumph, but (unluckily) it *must* include discarding and loss. It is as a fellow creature facing inevitable loss—loss of beauty, freedom, power, youth, and of life itself—that Belinda merits sympathy, even where she fails to command admiration. Pope's revisions thus create a perspective on the action that is noticeably absent from the original poem. Whereas the 1712 version forced us to recognize Belinda's folly, the revised poem makes it possible also to understand her plight.

# Alexander Pope

Pope's treatment of Belinda in the revised poem encompasses Johnson's observation on women that "the custom of the world seems to have been formed in a kind of conspiracy against them" (*The Rambler* no. 39). The poem, however, while it recognizes the conspiracy of custom, also depicts Belinda's willing and thoughtless acquiescence—so unlike the resistance to custom which Pope praises later in Martha Blount. As a result, Pope cannot offer Belinda more than a mixed or incomplete consolation. He invites her to understand that the theft of a lock is truly inconsequential and that her more serious forms of loss unite her with all mankind. This perspective, like Pope's pose in the awkwardly "gallant" letter to (the real-life Belinda) Arabella Fermor that introduces the revised poem, may be criticized as conveniently male-centered, even though the men in *The Rape of the Lock* prove as foolish as the women. Yet, the reconciling vision of Pope's ending is meant to pass beyond distinctions of gender to a universal inclusiveness. Thus the poem concludes in an elegiac, Virgilian sadness at the conspiracy of loss in which all people—the wise and foolish, the plain and beautiful—are inescapably entangled:

> For, after all the Murders of your Eye,
> When, after Millions slain, your self shall die;
> When those fair Suns shall sett, as sett they must,
> And all those Tresses shall be laid in Dust;
> *This Lock*, the Muse shall consecrate to Fame,
> And mid'st the Stars inscribe *Belinda*'s Name!

It is not surprising that Pope did not revise a single word in these eloquent concluding lines, with their tribute to art as a valid means for opposing the ruins of time. Poets display their judgment, Pope believed, not only in what they revise but in what they choose to leave unrevised.

Its descriptive beauty is what makes the Game of Ombre, in Pope's masterly addition, so expressive of the mixed attitudes which characterize the revised poem. Games, however inadequate they prove as substitutes for living, however foolish to nonplayers the players sometimes seem, nonetheless offer a formal grace and fictive pleasure that Pope as an artist did not fail to appreciate. "Into an imperfect world and into the confusion of life," Huizinga writes of play, "it brings a temporary, a limited perfection." "Play," he adds, "has a tendency to be beautiful."[31] Inside the larger world, which contains wretches, grimness, injustice, suffering, and death, the miniature perfection of play creates a momentary stay against confusion—a resistance to time and change—which art also pursues. His poem (*"This Lock"*), Pope tells Belinda, will provide her a consoling measure of permanence in a world of flux. It is, of course, the folly of the beau monde to seek its permanence in idle games or attractive women or modish fashions, where beauty is always fleeting. False refinement or overrefinement are also delusive in that they cannot achieve genuine beauty but merely its pale simulations. Yet the beau monde, where aesthetic form so frequently opposes rather than follows nature, also possesses a charm that survives disapproval. Belinda is foolish, but nature has also made her beautiful. The beau monde is ridiculous, but Pope's art has made folly pleasing. A poem which can embrace such linked facts—without condemning beauty or approving folly—must achieve a perspective wider than that of the mistaken critics who find merely the satire of a coquette or nostalgic longings for a world of pure artifice.[32] Pope's moral stance, like Spenser's, does not require us to disparage beauty in order to love truth, although both writers challenge us with the careful discriminations necessary to distinguish genuine beauty from its deceptive counterfeits. Pope does not endorse the easy judgment that Belinda's beauty, enhanced by *"Cosmetic* Pow'rs" (i.124) as his revision explains, is necessarily false or tawdry. Nowhere does he imply that all women must face society with a milkmaid's fresh-scrubbed look. Instead, while valuing what is lovely and fragile in Belinda's world, while lavishing his own art in describing trifles, Pope also invites us to understand that beauty alone is inadequate, that formal order may prove hollow or constricting, that visual symmetries can veil disorder and disfigurement.

The creation of a perspective wide enough to embrace appreciation, exposure, understanding, laughter, and regret is the final achievement of all Pope's revisions in *The Rape of the Lock*. In seeing the poem anew, he did not reject the playful whimsy of the original—intended, as he said, to "make a jest" of an actual event that the Fermor and Petre families had taken "too seriously."[33] Play and pleasure, as in the occasional poems, are poetic resources Pope greatly respected. He was even ready to assign them an exaggerated importance, once claiming (in half truth) that he wrote to amuse himself and revised because he found revision as "pleasant" as writing.[34] Beginning as an occasional poem, savoring the domestic farce of actions too insignificant for history, *The Rape of the Lock* defeats seriousness in its constant play of wit, which is why Addison had cautioned Pope against revising it. Yet, in revising a work of "pure wit," as Addison had called it, Pope not only preserved the playfulness of the original but also, as I have argued, tempered his jesting with additions calculated to make us think, to revise human behavior. "This whimsical piece of work, as I have now brought it up to my first design," Pope in 1714 wrote of the revised poem, "is at once the most a satire, and the most inoffensive, of anything of mine. People who would rather it were let alone laugh at it, and seem heartily merry, at the same time that they are uneasy."[35] The power to make us uneasy is something that the mirth of the original poem cannot achieve because the events are depicted as meaningless. Subsequently, in seeing the poem anew, Pope discovered the richness of meaning that even trivial events disclose. The discovery creates a poem that provokes uneasy reflections as well as comic and satiric laughter, and it helps to explain Pope's commitment to the nonspontaneous process of refinement and correction that marks a lifetime of mending verses.

# ⚝ IV

## Virgilian Attitudes
## in *Windsor-Forest*

Let others better mold the running Mass
Of Mettals, and inform the breathing Brass;
And soften into Flesh a Marble Face:
Plead better at the Bar; describe the Skies,
And when the Stars descend, and when they rise.
But, *Rome*, 'tis thine alone, with awful sway,
To rule Mankind; and make the World obey;
Disposing Peace, and War, thy own Majestick Way.
To tame the Proud, the fetter'd Slave to free;
These are Imperial Arts, and worthy thee.

—Virgil

T HE MIXED attitudes so characteristic of *The Rape of the Lock* also find expression in *Windsor-Forest* (1713), where history and politics become for the first time important issues in Pope's verse. Like *The Rape of the Lock*, *Windsor-Forest* went through a lengthy process of revision and did not receive final form until George Granville—the current Secretary for War, who was raised to the peerage as Lord Lansdowne in 1713—asked Pope to compose a poem in celebration of the Treaty of Utrecht. If *The Rape of the Lock* begins in a trivial, private, ahistorical occasion (the feud over a lock of hair), *Windsor-Forest* may be said to conclude in an occasion which is solemn and public and historical. Pope's concluding reference to the peace at Utrecht and to the treaty that ended the long War of the Spanish Succession (1701–1714) is more than opportunism or a concession to the power of Granville. As Earl R. Wasserman has shown, *Windsor-Forest* is a thoroughly political poem in which landscape becomes the vehicle for reflections on English history both recent and distant.[1]

The poem's historical and political materials sometimes lead readers to believe that Pope's intentions were narrowly partisan. Yet, his veiled, caustic attack upon Queen Anne's predecessor, William III, did not necessarily identify *Windsor-Forest* as Tory propaganda. The unpopularity of William crossed party lines. Although Pope clearly aligned himself with the Stuart monarchy restored with Anne, he tried to avoid taking positions which would identify him as spokesman for a specific political interest or point of view. In a period when party loyalties divided writers into opposing camps, he deliberately remained nonpartisan in his friendships. As he wrote to John Caryll several months after the publication of *Windsor-Forest*: "To tell you the bottom of my heart, I am no ways displeased that I have offended the *violent* of all parties already."[2] He was indirectly quoting Dryden (" 'Tis not the violent I design to please"), but the sentiment was also deeply rooted in Pope's own character and experience. Violence is a central theme in *Windsor-Forest*, and the threat of violence was especially pressing in the political context of 1713, with the childless queen in poor health (she died in August), with the succession in doubt, and with the Pretender (son of the deposed Roman Catholic king, James II) sheltering at the French court and actively plotting his return. Two years later ten thousand Jacobite forces in England and Scotland were poised to support the Pretender's planned invasion. The occasion of peace at Utrecht, as the young poet recognized, called for something more reflective than an occasional poem.

## Fathers and Sons: Imitating Virgil

"Mr Pope has publishd a fine Poem calld Windsor Forrest," wrote Swift to Esther Johnson, adding in his magisterial style: "read it."[3] The poem has remained, despite Swift's commanding praise, probably the least familiar of Pope's major works. Yet it is a complex and rewarding poem that reveals much about his development as a poet—particularly about his relationship to Virgil. Although Homer and Horace soon absorbed Pope's attention—claiming the years of Homeric translations from 1715 to 1726 and the extended period of Horatian imitations in the 1730s—Virgil was unmistakably the poet of his youth. Dryden's famous translation of Virgil had appeared in 1697, shortly before Pope at twelve made his pilgrimage to Will's

Coffee House, and all of Pope's major works written before 1715—
the Pastorals, "Messiah," *Windsor-Forest*, and *The Rape of the
Lock*—reflect a style and vision dominated by his familiarity with
Virgil. Even *An Essay on Criticism*, which is strongly indebted to
Horace and Boileau, and which advises writers to make Homer's
works their study and delight, nevertheless carries an entirely Virgilian message to poets: "Learn hence for Ancient *Rules* a just Esteem; / To copy *Nature* is to copy *Them*" (ll. 139–140). Pope derives
this precept from Virgil's practice, and, as the ancient poet renowned
for his "judgment," Virgil is in some sense the aesthetic patron of *An
Essay on Criticism*. Pope in the *Essay* does not merely repeat
Horace's advice that writers should study Greek models (*exem-
plaria Graeca*). He adds a crucial recommendation—not present in
Horace—concerning the proper *means* for studying Homer:

> Still with *It self compar'd*, his *Text* peruse;
> And let your *Comment* be the *Mantuan Muse*.   (ll. 128–129)

Virgil—"the *Mantuan Muse*"—becomes for Pope the modern poet's
best commentary on Homer, revealing how Homeric fecundity can
be reconciled with the judicious strategies of self-conscious art.

Even as he recommended reading Homer through the lenses of
Virgil, Pope labored to infuse into his own translations of Homer a
recognizably Virgilian spirit. "The narrative style, the heroes, and
the gods," one scholar tells us, "all became more Virgilian than Homeric."[4] In the notes to his translations of Homer, Pope everywhere
proved himself a perfect Virgilian commentator by searching out examples of Homer's "art" and "judgment," emphasizing instances of
humanizing pathos, deploring the violence of Homeric manners. Significantly, the passion for Homer which Pope felt from his earliest
days never expressed itself, as it sometimes did among his contemporaries, in a depreciation of Virgil's gifts. Virgil, in Pope's view, was
"undoubtedly the greatest Poet" after Homer—giving him a position
above Shakespeare, Milton, and Dryden, all of whom Pope revered
(note to *Iliad* XX.270). The highest praise he could bestow upon his
own youthful Pastorals was the sly opinion, delivered anonymously,
that "Mr. *Pope* hath fallen into the same Error with *Virgil*."[5] To err
with Virgil was to approach perfection.

Despite Pope's fame as the translator of Homer, the qualities of
Virgil's work were in many ways uniquely suited to Pope's character

and literary ambitions. Virgil's commitment to revision (legend reported he would work all day over a single line) made him an obvious model for Pope, and the Virgilian technique of literary allusion, which wove into his own language images and phrases from earlier writers, was a method that Pope thoroughly appropriated. As he explained in what could be a summary of his own practice: "Virgil's great judgement appears in putting things together, and in picking gold out of the dunghills of the old Roman writers."[6] In following Walsh's advice to become England's first "correct" poet, Pope naturally looked to Virgil as the classical paragon of correctness both in art and in morality. A humane and forgiving pathos consistent with the ideals of Christianity saved Virgil's works, in Pope's view, from the unfortunate "Spirit of Cruelty" in Homer, which he explained as the residue of a barbarous era (note to *Iliad* XIII.471). But, there was one over-riding difference that separated Pope from Homer and drew Pope toward a Virgilian poetics.

Virgil was preeminently the model for the learned (*doctus*) poet, whose vocation as a writer honored the classical ideal of the poet as a teacher and sage. In fact, Virgil's correctness was thought to extend beyond literary decorum to an almost devout piety, which helps to explain why throughout his life Pope continued to use a copy of the handsome Elzevir edition of Virgil, just as many families used the Bible, to record the names of his departed relations and friends. Certainly this ritual suggests that his lines addressed to Charles Jervas, who instructed him in painting, expressed a kinship of spirit with Virgil that transformed his borrowings into far more than exercises in learned allusion:

> Thou oer thy Raphaels monument should mourn
> I wait inspiring dreams at Maros urn.[7]

In this pictorial image Pope implicitly defines his poetic genealogy, choosing the spiritual father from a distant age who will revisit him, bestowing the visions which are a form of "repayment" for his filial devotion. The image of Pope at the urn of Virgil is a variation on the metaphors of poetic commerce and literary exchange. Pope is not simply mourning but drawing sustenance, emphasizing his devotion to the past, his commitment to a vanished master. Vividly, the image reminds us how Pope in his early career followed the pattern of Virgil's poetic development, from pastoral to georgic to epic. Pope's lines to Jervas can be dated about 1713, the year in which *Windsor-Forest* appeared—when the conclusion to a tedious European war (longer than the Greek siege of Troy) finally turned men's thoughts to peace. It was in such a climate, with some contemporaries openly comparing him with Virgil, that Pope published his georgic vision of "*Albion's* Golden Days" (l. 424).

The fidelity of Pope's youthful imitation of Virgil—including a verbatim quotation from his own Pastorals in the final line, a technique that imitated Virgil's self-referential conclusion to the *Georgics*—no doubt helped to foster the critics' neglect of *Windsor-Forest*. The poem seems vulnerable to the charge Johnson leveled at Pope's Pastorals: "The imitations are so ambitiously frequent that the writer evidently means rather to shew his literature than his wit."[8] The view that *Windsor-Forest* was a piece of imitative and decorative juvenilia prevailed until Wasserman in *The Subtler Language* brilliantly demonstrated the intricacy and significance of Pope's design. Arguing that *Windsor-Forest*, like Denham's *Cooper's Hill* (1665), uses descriptions of nature as a metaphorical language of politics, Wasserman traced Pope's manipulation of the philosophical doctrine of *concordia discors*—which held that harmony in the state, as in the cosmos, requires the creative tension of opposing forces. In its emphasis on political and philosophical matters, however, Wasserman's analysis of *Windsor-Forest* neglects somewhat the equally important moral and literary dimensions of the poem, particularly as they are related to Pope's imitation of Virgil.

Most existing treatments of Pope's debt to Virgil are brief and general. The Twickenham editors, for example, relied mainly upon E. K. Rand's *The Magical Art of Virgil* (1931) to sketch a parallel between *Windsor-Forest* and the *Georgics*: "The movement of Pope's poem from the shades and glades of Windsor Forest to the villas and public buildings of London and to the 'Golden Days' inaugurated by Queen Anne is nothing less than a direct imitation of the way Virgil in the *Georgics* moves 'from crops to towns and from the works of men to the men themselves, the older heroes and the hero [Augustus] of the age, in which the golden days of Saturn have come again.' Pope's subject, too, is the same as Virgil's: his country's 'need of peace, well typified by the simplicity of rural life.' "[9] This broad pattern of similarity tells us nothing about the fluctuations of thought

and feeling that give both poems an eddying as well as a straightforward movement. Further, it provides no hint that the "direct imitation" was at all creative or original, even though Pope's imitations
usually refine and revise—not simply reproduce—his original source,
for words, images, and general patterns borrowed from earlier poets,
like fragments of ancient stained glass set in a modern window, take
on different values when skillfully integrated with the contemporary.
Although some of the defects of the account in the Twickenham edition are corrected by Reuben Brower, who adds to the criticism of
the poem a sensitive appreciation of its Virgilian qualities that are
more elusive than theme and large design, he too tends to emphasize
Pope's use of specific images, devices, and motifs—such as the "Virgilian tradition of the Golden Age."[10]

*Windsor-Forest* is Virgilian, however, not primarily because Pope
borrows certain structural, thematic, and ornamental features from
the *Georgics*, but because he expresses a general outlook upon life—
certain "attitudes"—characteristic of the Roman poet. Although
Pope may have begun his apprenticeship to poetry, as he told Joseph
Spence, by "copying good strokes from others," he soon advanced to
the subtler and more fruitful idea of imitation that Longinus among
the ancients and Roscommon among Pope's immediate predecessors
had both recommended. A member of the select company of critic-
heroes praised at the end of *An Essay on Criticism*, Roscommon advised authors, whether translators or poets, to choose exemplars who
shared an identical *"Ruling Passion"*:

> Then seek a *Poet* who *your* way do's bend,
> And chuse an *Author* as you chuse a *Friend*:
> United by this *Sympathetick Bond*,
> You grow *Familiar, Intimate*, and *Fond*;
> Your *thoughts*, your *Words*, your *Stiles*, your *Souls* agree,
> No Longer his *Interpreter*, but *He*.[11]

Like Longinus, Roscommon recommends imitating the spirit of ancient poets, rather than specific details of composition, and the *"Sym-
pathetick Bond"* he imagines linking the souls of two writers could
well describe the relationship between Pope and Virgil in *Windsor-
Forest*. To say that Pope alludes to the *Georgics* as a means of giving
his poem generic coherence or literary resonance is an insufficient explanation of his debt. His borrowings, in fact, extend over the whole

body of Virgil's work: they are neither necessary for generic identification of the poem (which has a notoriously mixed form) nor effective in creating a unified tone (which, like the form, is complex and shifting). Instead, as Pope's classically schooled readers would have recognized, Pope embodies through his poem the *spirit* of Virgil—not as an act of proud impersonation, not as a literary convenience, but as an expression of the deep affinity between their ways of viewing experience. *Windsor-Forest*, unlike a modern "copy" of the *Eclogues* or *Georgics*, is an original and contemporary work which remains nonetheless profoundly Virgilian.

In understanding Pope's characteristic use of allusion we need to recognize a peculiar form of intertextual relation. In normal literary reference, a specific English passage recalls a specific earlier counterpart. *The Dunciad*, for example, contains what Pope in his annotations calls "particular allusions infinite." When the traveling chaperon says that his young charge "greatly-daring din'd" (IV.318), we are meant to recall Ovid's praise of Phaethon, who "greatly-daring *died*" (*magnis excidit ausis*).[12] It is possible to debate at great length the *significance* of this bilingual allusion—to trace its possible meanings through postclassical commentators on Ovid or to reject entirely all meaning that is not explicit—but such discussion nonetheless agrees in defining allusion as the relation between two or more *specific* passages.

At least as important for Pope, however, is a very different type of allusiveness, such as we find in *Windsor-Forest*, where the interplay of texts cannot be limited to specific passages. In describing what he calls the "modern humanist text" descended from Petrarch, Thomas M. Greene calls attention to relations among ancient authors and Renaissance imitators that extend beyond specific borrowings to "subtle interpenetrations, an interflowing and tingeing, an exchange of minute gradations, that cannot be measured wholly or formulated."[13] Pope's imitation of Virgil in *Windsor-Forest* challenges the reader not only to understand specific literary references but also to recognize a form of allusiveness that Petrarch described as "the resemblance of a son to his father": "Therein is often a great divergence in particular features, but . . . as soon as we see the son, he recalls the father to us, although if we should measure every feature we should find them all different."[14] Pope's idea of imitation and refinement as a filial relation to the past—like his own relation to Virgil—would find in Petrarch's analogy an appealing image. Indeed, in describing the pleasure that flows from recognizing in modern works the imitation of ancient authors, Pope found a way to refine or improve upon Petrarch's analogy. "Such Copyings as these," he wrote, "give that kind of double Delight which we perceive when we look upon the Children of a beautiful Couple; where the Eye is not more charm'd with the Symmetry of the Parts, than the Mind by observing the Resemblance transmitted from Parents to their Offspring, and the mingled Features of the Father and the Mother."[15] Popean allusiveness often reveals such a "mingled" parentage, much as his imitation of Virgil in *Windsor-Forest* also reflects the features of Virgil's great English imitator and translator, John Dryden. The line of descent from Virgil to Dryden to Pope finds its expression in *Windsor-Forest* in the mysteriously inexact resemblances of a family likeness.

## Discord and Furor

If the specific occasion of *Windsor-Forest* is the transition from violence to concord with the signing of the Treaty of Utrecht, Pope elevates mere occasion to a general theme when he portrays Queen Anne as a figure of almost biblical power:

> At length great ANNA said—Let Discord cease!
> She said, the World obey'd, and all was *Peace!*   (ll. 327–328)

The development of the poem, mirrored in these pivotal lines, comprises a series of sharp contrasts between conditions of discord and of harmony, leading ultimately to the vision of a new golden age. Anna's creative fiat, then, foreshadows the conclusion of the poem, in which Discord (grown from an intellectual abstraction into a personified monster) is actually banished by the hands of Peace. It is Peace—also personified—whom Pope addresses in describing this final victory over Discord:

> Exil'd by Thee from Earth to deepest Hell,
> In Brazen Bonds shall barb'rous *Discord* dwell:
> Gigantick *Pride*, pale *Terror*, gloomy *Care*,
> And mad *Ambition*, shall attend her there.
> There purple *Vengeance* bath'd in Gore retires,
> Her Weapons blunted, and extinct her Fires:

There hateful *Envy* her own Snakes shall feel,
And *Persecution* mourn her broken Wheel:
There *Faction* roar, *Rebellion* bite her Chain,
And gasping Furies thirst for Blood in vain.     (ll. 413–422)

The actual accomplishment of Anna's earlier command now assumes
the concreteness of ritual. Around the central figure of Discord, as in
a monument or statuary, Pope groups all the related evils that have
suffered similar exclusion. The idea of exile is significant. Nowhere in
*Windsor-Forest* does Pope imply that the uncivilizing ("barb'rous")
power of Discord can be tamed into a creative harmony. He nowhere
states, as he does later in a passage from *An Essay on Man*, that Discord is a component of universal rightness, "Harmony, not understood" (i.291). Rather, in *Windsor-Forest* harmony is possible only
when Discord and its attendants have been utterly overcome. Here
Pope and Virgil are completely agreed.

Pope's agreement with Virgil extends to the allusive resemblance
that, in his description of the exile of Discord, summons up two passages from the *Aeneid*. The cast of personified terrors banished by
Peace recalls the specters, from book VI, which Aeneas meets just
within the jaws of the underworld. Even more explicit, however, is
Pope's evocation of another Virgilian scene. In book I, Jupiter pre-
dicts the triumph of Aeneas' Roman descendants, who will transform
an era of "impious War" into a time of peace. Dryden translates the
passage as follows:

*Janus* himself before his Fane shall wait,
And keep the dreadful issues of his Gate,
With Bolts and Iron Bars: within remains
Imprison'd Fury, bound in brazen Chains.     (ll. 402–405)

The image of Fury (*Furor* in Virgil) chained within the Temple of
Janus, whose closed gates signified peace to the Romans, clearly underlies Pope's bondage of Discord. In fact, the poet who claimed to
have learned versification "wholly from Dryden's works" seems purposely to echo the language of Dryden's famous translation: except
for an alliterative change, the "Brazen Bonds" of Discord are surely
the same "brazen Chains" that manacle Fury. The similarity serves a
purpose more serious than allusive ornament or elevation. In this
case, as so often in Virgil's works, allusion superimposes one literary

context upon another, creating a transparency or a lucid fusion of the
two. The effect here is the creation of a composite figure: Pope's Discord assumes the identity and function of Virgil's Furor.

Why would Pope wish to associate the two figures? A probable explanation is that Pope considered Discord—as Virgil considered
Furor—the ultimate personification of human irrationality—hence
its central position in the cluster of exiles. The attendant and associate powers also merit exile, however, because they represent the main
causes or embodiments of discord. In this sense, Patricia Meyer
Spacks seems correct in writing that the image of the Furies, which
concludes the list of personifications, "finally sums up all of them."[16]
From classical drama to Restoration panegyric, the Furies have regularly presided over scenes of chaos and destruction, often accompanying manifestations of violence as if they were the personal agents
or splintered images of Discord. By Pope's time, however, much of
the meaning behind this association had disappeared, and too often
the Furies were employed merely as a grotesque embellishment, the
classical equivalent of buzzards.[17] Pope in *Windsor-Forest* renews
the significance of the Furies by using them to suggest that Discord is
not an independent, external force like the allegorical figure Plague,
who "stalks" through innumerable eighteenth-century poems of disaster, but the embodiment of passions located fundamentally within
the human heart. Associates of Discord such as faction and rebellion—no less than pride, vengeance, and envy—are to Pope and his
age the expression of forces deeply rooted in man's dark interior regions. The traditional association between Discord and the Furies,
then, becomes in *Windsor-Forest* a means of suggesting the relationship between outer and inner, between disorder in the state and its
sources within the individual. The evidence for this view consists
partly in an unobtrusive pattern of reference linking Pope's image of
the Furies to the Virgilian concept of *furor*.

Throughout his works Virgil depicts the irrational power of *furor*
as constantly threatening to destroy the precarious balance of civilized values. Because of its direct influence upon action, the role of
*furor* is particularly clear in the *Aeneid*, where it represents the negation of the complex religious and social virtues which Virgil sym-
bolizes in the concept of *pietas*.[18] When in a moment of mindless rage
Aeneas seizes arms amid the fires of Troy, it is *furor* which blinds
him to the firm directive of the gods. When Turnus later breaks faith

with the Trojans, it is *furor* (personified as Alecto, one of the Furies) which thrusts the burning torch into his breast. It is *furor* which dooms the heroic mission of Nisus and Euryalus. These instances, reflecting a motif well known to scholars of Virgil, give special significance to the image with which Jupiter describes the peace of Augustus: *Furor impius* (I.294) at last chained within the sturdy temple of classical order. The epithet *impius* epitomizes the basic antagonism in the *Aeneid* between Aeneas, always associated with *pietas*, and the power of *Furor*, whose bloody mouth (*ore cruento*) denotes the same savage impulses embodied in *Windsor-Forest* in the figure of the blood-thirsty Furies.

The diction of *Windsor-Forest*, like the contrasting episodes of harmony and strife, helps to reveal Pope's concern with the antagonism between civilized peace and the irrationality of *furor*. The adjective *furious*—which of course derives from *furor*—always occurs in contexts that imply frenzy bordering upon madness. (If we disregard his Homeric translations, *furious* appears nine times in Pope's verse, three of them in *Windsor-Forest*.) When Pope describes the tyranny of William the Conqueror, for example, his language suggests not only the oppressed condition of the people but also the human source of their oppression:

> To Savage Beasts and Savage Laws a Prey,
> And Kings more furious and severe than they.     (ll. 45–46)

It is the dehumanizing *furor* of its rulers which reduces law to bestiality, initiating the transformation of England into a "dreary Desart and a gloomy Waste" (l. 44). But the cottages and temples which crumble into "Heaps of Ruin" (l. 70), like the falling towers of Eliot's *The Waste Land*, are more than images of destruction. Just as Eliot's allusive mode emphasizes the disintegration of the present by recalling simultaneously the high civilization of the past, Pope's image of devastation recalls the "heaps of Ruins" described in Dryden's *Aeneid* (VIII.467), where Virgil's context celebrates the continuity, rather than the radical disruption, of civilizing values.

The irrationalism of *furor* is again Pope's theme in the mythological episode describing the nymph Lodona. Straying beyond her proper "Limits" (l. 182), Lodona discovers that excess does not lead to the palace of wisdom but to the amoral world of absolute power.

Transformed from huntress to prey, she desperately flees from the rapacious Pan, who is in hot pursuit:

> Not half so swift the trembling Doves can fly,
> When the fierce Eagle cleaves the liquid Sky;
> Not half so swiftly the fierce Eagle moves,
> When thro' the Clouds he drives the trembling Doves;
> As from the God she flew with furious Pace,
> Or as the God, more furious, urg'd the Chace.    (ll. 185–190)

The stylized description plays out a fatal, unchanging scene of power and violence in the world of nature, where doves are always prey to eagles. It also implies the certainty of a parallel situation in the human world when individuals like Lodona fail to observe the limits of sense and judgment. *Furor*, if it gains mastery over intelligence, inevitably erases the boundaries separating man from beast. Pope's concluding lines—by applying the same adjective both to Pan and to Lodona—deftly suggest the blurring of distinctions, the convergence of opposites, which inevitably follows the victory of *furor*. The repetition of "furious" is, in fact, a significant addition to the 1712 manuscript, in which the simile concluded:

> As from the God with headlong Speed she flew,
> As did the God with equal Speed pursue.[19]

Pope's revision substitutes normal word order for inverted syntax and discards an unwanted *did*, but (as in *The Rape of the Lock*) meaning as well as expression is at stake. The revised couplet, in substituting *furious* for *headlong*, manages not only to express speed but also to suggest causation. Disregarding her proper limits, Lodona in her excess calls forth the violence that is always possible in nature. Yet Pope also insists that nature is not irreconcilably hostile to man but, on the contrary, can serve and nurture him—a fact established early in *Windsor-Forest* when Pan appears in his peaceful role as shepherd (l. 37). Pan's two roles emphasize the divided possibilities nature offers. Like the episode describing the hunting of William, Lodona's frenzied chase and abrupt metamorphosis affirm that discord in nature can often be traced directly to human failures.

The close relationship Pope establishes between discord and *furor* is unmistakable when we examine the version of Anna's fiat in the manuscript of 1712:

Till ANNA rose, and bade the Furies cease;
*Let there be Peace*—She said; and all was *Peace*.[20]

The revision most evident in the published version of this passage is
the shift from a direct to an indirect means of creating harmony. *"Let
there be Peace"* becomes, in the poem of 1713, the more oblique
command "Let Discord cease!" Because the effect of both commands
is almost identical, however, this change has little influence on meaning. A much more fundamental, if less obvious, change occurs with
Pope's substitution of Discord for the Furies. The change from "bade
the Furies cease" to "Let Discord cease" is consistent with the attitude toward violence that Pope expresses throughout the poem. Discord, as an outward manifestation of violence, can indeed be stilled
by fiat (or, what is the same thing, by treaty). But the human sources
of discord, represented by the Furies, cannot be corrected or contained merely by the promulgation of law. Monarchs may sign peace
treaties—thus stilling Discord—but they cannot legislate changes in
the mind or heart. Like the extralegal offenses traditionally punished
by the satirist, the interior "sins" of pride, envy, ambition, and vengeance require a different language of correction. In *Windsor-Forest*,
written before Pope turned to the punitive and deterrent power of
satire, he addressed the causes of discord through literary strategies
particularly appropriate to his Virgilian idea of the poet's role. He
uses poetic language, beyond simple purposes of praise or blame, to
mirror the complexity—sometimes even the ambiguity—of human
experience. He attempts to challenge and to improve readers by en-
larging their vision, by refining their sensibilities. Here too Pope
looked to Virgil as his mentor and model.

## The Art of Correction

The poet as sage and teacher had no finer representative among the
ancients than Virgil. As a moral and didactic poet, Virgil was praised
in particular for his art of indirection: eighteenth-century critics admired not only his wisdom but also his ability to half-conceal it in the
obliqueness of a descriptive style. Addison, in a well-known essay,
praised Virgil as a poet "who loves to suggest a truth indirectly, and
without giving us a full and open view of it, to let us see just so much
as will naturally lead the imagination into all the parts that lie con-

cealed."[21] Poetic concealment, however, was not all that Pope could learn from Virgil. For Virgil, as for Pope, it was the voice of the poet—expressed in all the nuances of style—which carried, indirectly, a form of moral understanding. "A man who devises new rhythms," wrote T. S. Eliot, "is a man who extends and refines our sensibility; and that is not merely a matter of 'technique.' "[22] The refinements of language and meter for which Virgil and Pope are famous have much to do with their opposition to modes of thought which to them seemed coarse or rude or undiscriminating. Improvements in literary technique, for Pope and Virgil, are associated with means of correcting human action, feeling, and perception.

Their complex vision helps to generate, in Pope's work and in Virgil's, a poetic language in which ambiguous or multiple meanings are a crucial feature. Wherever a single event requires a plural interpretation, the poet's language transforms allusion, ambiguity, and polysemy into techniques for describing the complicated, layered, composite nature of human experience. Man's condition, as Pope describes it in *An Essay on Man*, is one of constant doubt; he "hangs between" the divided possibilities of his own nature; his understanding is always a compromise between knowledge and ignorance (ii. 1–18). Such a creature, living amid mysteries beyond his grasp, has an obvious need for the didactic clarifications poetry can provide, dispelling uncertainty through the authoritative maxims of a well-turned couplet. In a world of doubt, however, literature can perform an equally valuable function in unsimplifying the sense we normally make of experience. Pope did not admire in critics the ingenuity that merely multiplies possibilities. In fact, he explicitly denounced commentators who, through pride or ignorance, were "apt to fancy Two Meanings for want of knowing One" (headnote to book I of the *Iliad*). In his own work he constantly implied that literature may be complex without being unclear. For Pope, understanding man's social and political condition is possible, as *Windsor-Forest* proposes to show, but only if one engages the subtle Virgilian indirections and allusive polysemy that complicate the search for meaning.

The attitudes that Pope shares with Virgil are not limited to a general outlook on experience or to an understanding of style. He also follows Virgil in his specific political attitudes. There have always been readers who claim that *Windsor-Forest*, like the poetry of Virgil, shamelessly flatters a contemporary regime and whitewashes the sins of nascent imperialism. Yet, although moved to celebrate contemporary rulers, Pope and Virgil both profess their independence; they carefully moderate well-deserved praise with disquieting intimations. (Only the extreme value he placed upon his own independence could inspire Pope, late in his career, to misrepresent Virgil as a "party-writer."[23]) Further, political optimism in the works of Virgil and of Pope is usually conveyed in a vision of the future. Praise of Augustus or of Anne never obscures a sobering awareness of the imperfections of past and present. The vision of a possible golden future coexists with the melancholy consciousness of the tears of things (*lacrimae rerum*) that, in a world still far from civilized, accompany even the most heroic victories. Virgil's praise of Augustan Rome is rarely unambiguous and cannot alter the dominant impression of loss and perplexity conveyed by the *Aeneid*. If fate impersonally requires the deaths of Dido and of Turnus, we are not allowed to dismiss their human significance: Virgil compels us to understand that empires exact a cruel toll in human sorrow. Even in the *Georgics*, Virgil reminds us that natural events have human, personal significance; the advent of the mating season evokes sentiments transcending any national pride in the multiplication of livestock:

> In Youth alone, unhappy Mortals live;
> But, ah! the mighty Bliss is fugitive;
> Discolour'd Sickness, anxious Labours come,
> And Age, and Death's inexorable Doom.          (III.108–111)

Careful attention to *Windsor-Forest* shows that Pope's attitude toward national grandeur is very close to Virgil's. Both poets, of course, associate general harmony with enlightened government. Although both discover in contemporary rulers grounds for hope in future peace and order, they do not encourage partisan or utopian claims, nor do they forget that their subject is the imperfect state of human nature. The reader moves toward clarity and affirmation, but only through an ambiguous and disturbing process in which the voice of the poet is a guide to disillusionment.

"We oftner think of the Author himself when we read *Virgil*," Pope wrote, "than when we are engag'd in *Homer*."[24] In place of Homeric objectivity, the works of Virgil embody a distinctive yet restrained subjectiveness. The narrative voice expresses a civilized sensibility which in effect enriches the action of the poem by surrounding it with what one critic has called an "empathetic style." "The most obvious key to Virgil's 'psychological identification' of himself with the characters," Brooks Otis asserts, "is the tell-tale phrase or word which either describes the character's feelings or Virgil's own feeling for him or—what is nearest to the fact—a subtle blend of both."[25] It seems likely that Pope understood this aspect of Virgil's art, for he practiced it himself in *Windsor-Forest*. The language of the poem, far from glorifying conquest, conveys the poet's individual sense that the achievements of civilization often require disheartening sacrifices of natural beauty. Through the process of reading, we share, if only momentarily, the poet's heightened powers of sympathy and understanding.

The best place to examine Pope's empathetic language is in the seasons-of-sport passage (ll. 93–164), which uses hunting, in Wasserman's words, as "a metaphor for the recommended norm of human activity, in contrast to the excessive and uncontrolled activity of William."[26] Hunting also is regarded traditionally as an art and can thus represent the civilizing process which redeems man from artless barbarity. Art, discipline, and skill, however, are aspects of hunting that Pope does not emphasize in *Windsor-Forest*, choosing instead to remain close to the practice of Virgil, who employs scenes or imagery of hunting in the *Aeneid* to mark the regression into irrational states of being.[27] Pope's language, while praising the hunt, manages at the same time to suggest the ambiguity of most human norms. The "eager" youths (l. 148) who rush headlong to the "Sylvan War" ominously resemble the "eager" huntress Lodona (l. 181), especially when Pope describes the "eager Speed" (l. 157) of their horses in a famous line that he borrowed from Statius' epic about civil war. The energy compressed in the word *eager* is reflected in Johnson's definition: "Struck with desire; ardently wishing; keenly desirous; vehement in desire; hotly longing." Although some readers have argued that the excessive energies of youth *require* hunting as a form of release or exercise, Pope's language suggests the peril of such violent therapy. The scent of the partridge carries on "tainted" breezes which "betray" (l. 101); the fields are "unfaithful" (l. 103); the beagles "learn of Man" the pastime of sportive killing (l. 124). Rebecca Price Parkin rightly asserts that the ambiguity of Pope's diction conveys one of the principal insights of *Windsor-Forest*: "that there is a case to be made for both the hunter and the hunted. The reader is made to enter imaginatively into the sentiments of both."[28] Through this empathetic widening of perspective, we not only extend our powers of feeling but enlarge our understanding as well. The poem deprives us of a single-minded vision.

Pope's Virgilian attitudes and empathetic style in *Windsor-Forest* belong to his deliberate effort to portray the mixed state of human experience in which there is no gain without accompanying loss, no energy without the danger of excess, no peace without the wars that limit it. This representation of mixed states is easiest to follow in two related vignettes within the seasons-of-sport passage. The first is Pope's description of the dying pheasant, a scene simultaneously elegiac and objective. Its objectivity derives mainly from the brilliant pictorial detail—a vivid attention to surfaces—similar to the often passionless virtuosity of a French or Flemish *nature morte*:

> See! from the Brake the whirring Pheasant springs,
> And mounts exulting on triumphant Wings;
> Short is his Joy! he feels the fiery Wound,
> Flutters in Blood, and panting beats the Ground.
> Ah! what avail his glossie, varying Dyes,
> His Purple Crest, and Scarlet-circled Eyes,
> The vivid Green his shining Plumes unfold;
> His painted Wings, and Breast that flames with Gold?
>
> (ll. 111–118)

Pope, like the hunters, might seem to be treating the pheasant simply as an object on which to exercise his art. But the language offers more than objective description. Its concurrent elegiac tone exerts a humanizing counterbalance which takes us beyond surfaces, which prevents us from viewing the pheasant solely as an object for the sublimation of warlike energies. As a closer analysis of the passage reveals, Pope's language successfully recreates the intricate blend of acceptance and regret characteristic of Virgilian pathos.

In tempering his objective description with an empathy and subjectivity, Pope uses a variety of techniques, including a jolting inverted metrics (as in "Shórt is his Jóy"), an emphasis upon pain, a pathos (expressed in such words as "flutters" and "panting") that contrasts with the vigor of the earlier verb forms, and the openly elegiac "Ah!" But Pope's most subtle techniques are implicit in the same painterly skills which lend the passage its objectivity. The opening command "See!" could well have reminded an eighteenth-century critic of the traditional argument of rhetoricians, which was then being revived with the translation of Longinus, that feeling is best evoked through visual imagery. By careful attention to pictorial detail, the poet transforms the reader into a spectator who can then respond with the emotional immediacy of an eyewitness. We have already noticed this emphasis on immediacy in Pope's revisions of *The Rape of the Lock*, where its source or chief analogue was Homer. Here it is not narrative but descriptive technique which concerns Pope, and his language seems clearly Virgilian. For at least one of Pope's admirers, the poem's descriptions were a direct source of emotion:

> Ah! how I melt with pity, when I spy
> On the cold earth the flutt'ring Pheasant lie;
> His gawdy robes in dazling lines appear,
> And ev'ry feather shines and varies there.[29]

Pathos is induced not by maudlin diction but by its opposite: precise, visual description which transforms a passive reader into an active spectator, for whom seeing clearly is the occasion for strong feeling.

Pope's use of color, so conspicuous in his portrayal, conveys throughout his works a special value or range of meaning that helps to complicate the description of the dying pheasant. Just as Pope consistently associates an absolute or immutable truth with the unrefracted purity of light, so color for him frequently signifies the sad but inevitable link between beauty and death.[30] The pattern linking color and beauty and death is not rigid—elsewhere in *Windsor-Forest* the colors of the landscape express plenitude, order, and stability. Like other features of his style, color bears or suggests more than a single meaning. In his description of the dying pheasant, however, Pope's language emphasizes the transience implicit in all natural beauty. The pheasant's "gawdy robes" are an image of the impermanence its death signifies. Mortality is present even where life seems most vibrant. In Pope's "whirring" pheasant, the brilliant, lifelike hues create a striking contrast with the abrupt blackness of death. Like the "transient Colours" (ii.67) which tint the wings of Belinda's delicate guardians in *The Rape of the Lock*, the purples, greens, and golds of the bloody pheasant reflect the fragility of all natural beauty.

We misread Pope if we linger too long, as his poetical admirer did, in the pathos of the dying pheasant. Pope did not wish to exaggerate the elegiac nature of the passage but to balance feeling with objectivity. His language, encompassing the dual perspectives of hunter and hunted, invites us to experience the death of the pheasant as a phenomenon requiring the abandonment of a single, unmodified viewpoint. We are made to sense an intricate, perplexing nexus of loss and gain as the passage confronts us with a situation demanding a complex response. It is not surprising that two learned eighteenth-century commentators, William Warburton and Joseph Warton, both glossed Pope's description of the pheasant with different passages from Virgil. In what Petrarch might have called such "filial" imitations, a single source is probably impossible to specify. The attitude expressed in the passage is, however, unmistakably Virgilian.

A second vignette of equally disturbing complexity immediately follows and complements Pope's description of the pheasant: the capture by English troops of an "amaz'd, defenceless" (l. 109) little town. Just as the sudden, colorful flight of the pheasant parallels the abrupt hoisting of the Union Jack, the situation of the town, ringed by attackers, resembles that of the pheasant, trapped by dogs and hunters. The conjunction of powerlessness with raw power should trouble at least slightly even the most patriotic reader, for England's "eager Sons" (l. 106) are hardly ennobled by such an effortless conquest. Eagerness may link them allusively with the eager Lodona, whose fate suggests the wisdom of forethought and restraint. Further, in a poem ostensibly celebrating peace, the almost gleeful description of the capture seems to jar with other passages that suggest the futility and madness of war. The jarring, however, is functional. Pope uses such discordances for the serious, civilizing, Virgilian purpose of unsimplifying our assumptions about how clear-cut the relationship is between victor and vanquished.

Gilbert Wakefield, who edited Pope's works in the 1790s, provided an explanation for the disquieting quality of the "capture" passage in his comment on the poem's later celebration of peace: "This fine panegyric on *peace*, in opposition to the horrors and devastations of war, was in part occasioned, I presume, by our author's politics; by his hostility to the name of *Marlborough*, and an uneasiness at the glory of his victories."[31] *Windsor-Forest* says little about the victories of war, and Pope's scant praise of conquest seems calculated to provoke "uneasiness" in the reader. His method is like Virgil's when describing Aeneas, just on the point of sparing his fallen enemy Turnus, as suddenly "inflamed with fury and dreadful in his wrath" (*furiis accensus et ira / terribilis*). Victory through force, even when force is justified, is undercut by the poet's allusive language. There seems no ultimate victory over the uncivilizing power of fury. Indeed, Virgil's doubts about Rome's history of blood and *furor* are dramatized in the indecision—the deep suspense between compassion and vengeance—that seizes Aeneas as he hesitates over his defeated foe. "Turnus stands for the world of Italy," writes Michael C. J. Putnam, "that strange combination of wildness and pastoral order. In spite of Juno's plea to Jupiter, it is this world which Aeneas destroys, and with a lack of mercy singularly pronounced because it gives the lie both to Anchises' utterances about the future nobility of Roman conduct and to Jupiter's scarcely finished declaration about the happy union to be attained. The tragedy of the destruction of Turnus and his world does much to negate any romantic notion of the *Aeneid* as an ideal vision of the greatness of Augustan Rome, and it negates, too, the image of Virgil as its poet-laureate."[32]

Pope's extended analogies between warfare and hunting express a similar view that the course of English civilization embraces, even with its triumphs, a history of waste and violence. Not only Marlborough's victories but conquest itself made Pope uneasy. "True Courage," he wrote in a Virgilian commentary on a passage in Homer, "is inseparable from Humanity, and all generous Warriors regret the very Victories they gain, when they reflect what a Price of Blood they cost" (note to *Iliad* XIII.471). Through its Virgilian language, *Windsor-Forest* encourages readers to reflect upon the "Price of Blood" which civilization exacts. The spirit of generosity which Pope praised in *An Essay on Criticism* extends, in his view, beyond reading to activities where understanding and misunderstanding are equally significant. Like hunting, war is one of the "various Arts" (I.217) which Virgil in the *Georgics* sees as the consequence of man's fall from golden-age harmonies. But, as the language of *Windsor-Forest* attests, both warfare and hunting are, for Pope, arts that are unworthy of England's potential for civilized improvement.

Resemblance between the death of the pheasant and the capture of the little town must not finally blind us to their real differences. It is the Lockean task of judgment, after all, to make necessary discriminations among apparently similar ideas. Thus, although the capture of the defenseless town (like the death of the pheasant) contains disquieting elements, the main thrust of the passage is affirmative, and close attention to Pope's language reveals why. The town is described as "thoughtless" (l. 107). Although this condition is natural in the pheasant, an irrational creature, it is unnatural and irresponsible and dangerous in man, for whom civilization is the outward expression of social reason. Further, although the town seems blessed with "Ease and Plenty" (l. 107), the phrase begs comparison with Pope's earlier description of the landscape of modern England:

> Rich Industry sits smiling on the Plains,
> And Peace and Plenty tell, a STUART reigns.     (ll. 41–42)

The phrase "Peace and Plenty" was a cliché of contemporary political rhetoric, but Pope would also have encountered it in Dryden's description, from the *Aeneid*, of the golden age of Saturn (VIII. 431). Its similarity to the phrase "Ease and Plenty" calls attention to important differences and reminds us that times have changed: for modern man, peace, though it inevitably creates a state of plenty, is by no means synonymous with ease. As Virgil expressed this fundamental creed in the *Georgics*, the fate of iron-age man is labor and art:

> The Sire of Gods and Men, with hard Decrees,
> Forbids our Plenty to be bought with Ease.     (I.183–184)

For Pope, true peace, like plenty, requires work, both the labor of intelligence necessary to good government and the labor of refinement necessary to civilized conduct. The specious ease and plenty of the little town, by contrast, is simply the transient product of chance, as unthinking and vulnerable as the pheasant. Its image of false peace complements the disquieting descriptions of the hunt. Together they form a background for Pope's vision of a truly civilized era.

## Transformations: Human, Social, Literary

"No writing is good that does not tend to better mankind some way or other," Pope told Joseph Spence, probably recalling a similar assertion in Knightly Chetwood's "Life of *Virgil*," which was prefixed to Dryden's translation.[33] Amelioration, of course, has many sources—including increased knowledge—and men are less likely to glorify war if they understand something of its human costs. But Pope also viewed experience as a theater of moral action, where the perception of complexity can be debilitating if it paralyzes the will. Thus Pope is rarely content to leave his readers in ambiguity, and *Windsor-Forest*, like much of his work, moves toward a point of reconciliation.[34] This corrective movement is embodied in the poem's vision of historical change: from an idealized distant past, irrecoverably lost, through a mixed era which vacillates between peace and discord, to the prospect of an idealized but attainable future, in which ambiguity is transformed into affirmation.

The transformation of Lodona, as Wasserman has shown, stands as the central, transitional episode of *Windsor-Forest*, moving the poem from the discord and ambiguity of hunting to the peaceful activities of meditation, poetry, and commerce. As huntress, Lodona embodies the energy necessary to the active life; as river, she mirrors and composes the beauty of her surroundings, suggesting virtues necessary to the contemplative life. Neither state alone, however, is entirely satisfactory. For example, her slow waters assume something of her former energy only when they "rush into the *Thames*" (l. 218). Similarly, the forest achieves its greatest glory only when half its trees, as Father Thames remarks, "rush into my Floods" (l. 386) to form England's new commercial navy. The emphasis on rushing suggests that the fatal eagerness of Lodona must be transformed into a positive, directed motion. Wasserman, in fact, finds in Lodona's progress an image of the poem's thematic movement from unsatisfactory conditions of discord represented by hunting to the fulfillment of a true *concordia discors* through "the strifeful peace of foreign commerce, instead of foreign war."[35] But, although Pope's celebration of commerce resolves his main political and philosophical themes, his consistent "imitation" of Virgil also creates an appropriate moral and literary resolution.

Although Virgil in the *Georgics* celebrates agriculture rather than commerce, both he and Pope are equally interested in the symbolic uses of work, and their use of commerce and agriculture as symbols is profoundly similar. For Virgil, the concluding episode of the *Georgics*, a "resurrection" of bees from a decaying carcass, provides an image of natural renewal that fittingly concludes the poem. The full meaning of this episode, however, is incomplete when the imagery of natural renewal is separated from the accompanying episode of Orpheus and Eurydice. The bitter fate of Eurydice depends upon Orpheus' failure to control his passions, to part from Eurydice without looking back. "What fury seiz'd on thee, / Unhappy Man!" Eurydice cries out, "to lose thy self and Me?" (IV.714–715). All the power of Orpheus' art proves unavailing without a simultaneous discipline over his own nature, just as nature's powers of fecundity and renewal (symbolized by the bees) are wasted until they are cultivated and improved by art. For Virgil, both the improvements of art and the discipline over human passions must be integrated with the regenerating cycles of natural change if man is to achieve a truly civilized ("cultivated") state. Like agriculture for Virgil, commerce for Pope provides an image in which man can harmonize art and discipline with the dynamics of nature. Like Virgil, he associates this ideal condition with the myth of the golden age. Father Thames's prophecy of an era of peace and commerce, in fact, is modeled mainly on Anchises' prediction in the *Aeneid* foretelling the peaceful reign of Augustus:

> Sent to the Realm that *Saturn* rul'd of old;
> Born to restore a better Age of Gold.          (VI.1080–81)

The concept of a "better" golden age underlies Pope's choice of commerce as a reconciling image of harmony and reflects an attitude wholly, if not exclusively, Virgilian. It affirms the argument of the *Georgics* that the new Age of Gold will not be achieved through nostalgia and pastoral ease but through the refining, improving disciplines of art and labor.

Pope's choice of commerce as a reconciling image of *concordia discors* recalls the importance he attributed to mercantile exchange as a metaphor for poetry. His own "exchanges" with Virgil in *Windsor-Forest* provide a perfect example of such poetical commerce. As an economic activity, commerce also provided (at least in theory) a mechanism for transforming violence into peaceful competition and mutual benefit. Yet, the function of commerce in *Windsor-Forest* cannot be fully understood until we trace two related literary motifs that the poem unobtrusively develops. These two motifs are Pope's imagery of blood or bleeding and his myth of social change. The imagery of bloodshed occcurs so frequently in *Windsor-Forest* that it gains an almost primal, cumulative force. Until the appearance of Queen Anne introduces the prophetic vision of Father Thames, the poem conveys the painful impression of a land virtually bleeding to death:

> Oh Fact accurst! What Tears has *Albion* shed,
> Heav'ns! what new Wounds, and how her old have bled?
>
> (ll. 321–322)

From early references to the "bloody Chace" (l. 61) begun by Nimrod, biblical archetype of the hunter and the tyrant, Pope continually associates the actual and potential violence of *furor* with bloodshed. Not even the composing power of Granville's art can alter the burden of the past:

> Still in thy Song shou'd vanquish'd *France* appear,
> And bleed for ever under *Britain*'s Spear.     (ll. 309–310)

Ironically, the poem suggests that Britain rather than France seems most likely to bleed forever. The dying pheasant which "Flutters in Blood" probably summarizes better than any other single image the poem's spectacle of waste. To understand how Pope integrates this literary motif with his use of commerce, we must first examine his related development of a myth of social change.

*An Essay on Man*, although published in 1733–34, offers a clear view of Pope's earlier ideas on the origin and progress of society—ideas which underlie his resolution of *Windsor-Forest*. The movement of both poems is curiously similar. "Beginning with a reminder of a paradise man has lost," Maynard Mack has written of *An Essay on Man*, "the poem ends with a paradise he can regain."[36] *Windsor-Forest* likewise begins with a reference to Eden—"vanish'd now so long" (l. 7)—and concludes with the vision of a future golden age. Both poems also establish a context within which human discord is understood as a stage of arrested moral growth. Far from offering a philosophical vindication of the status quo, which denies the possibility or desirability of change, *An Essay on Man* charts a potentially progressive development from innocence, through corruption, to possible regeneration. This progress, applied to the development of man in society, also provides the basis for Pope's vision of future amelioration in *Windsor-Forest*.

Pope's myth of social change begins with the premise that the original state of nature, which Hobbes had described as warring, was in fact the "reign of God" (iii.148), a peaceful golden age in which self-love and social interest were in perfect harmony: "Union the bond of all things, and of Man" (iii.150). This unity extended even to man's relationship with the animals—a fact which bears upon Pope's description of hunting in *Windsor-Forest*:

> Pride then was not; nor Arts, that Pride to aid;
> Man walk'd with beast, joint tenant of the shade;
> The same his table, and the same his bed;
> No murder cloath'd him, and no murder fed.
> In the same temple, the resounding wood,
> All vocal beings hymn'd their equal God:
> The shrine with gore unstain'd, with gold undrest,
> Unbrib'd, unbloody, stood the blameless priest:
> Heav'n's attribute was Universal Care,
> And Man's prerogative to rule, but spare.　　(iii.151–160)

The passage, through its use of negative constructions, both documents man's fall from harmony and suggests a possible return to concord. In this movement, the linked images "gold" and "gore" (l. 157) provide an emblematic picture of human corruption. Elsewhere in *An Essay on Man* Pope returns to these linked images in describing man's apparently inextinguishable capacity for greed and violence:

> Now Europe's laurels on their brows behold,
> But stain'd with blood, or ill exchang'd for gold.　(iv.295–296)

Like the blood-stained pheasant of *Windsor-Forest* whose breast "flames with Gold," the laurels of heroic conquest in *An Essay on Man* are an unworthy prize. Generosity and power—ruling and sparing—have become dissociated. Such opposition proceeds so far in *An Essay on Man* that humankind is cast in the role of universal adversary: a "foe to Nature" (iii.163).

The "murder" (iii.154) of animals in *An Essay on Man* is not only a sign of man's fall from harmony but also a prelude to grosser corruptions. Blood-sacrifice in Pope's account actually breeds war:

> The Fury-passions from that blood began,
> And turn'd on Man a fiercer savage, Man.　　(iii.167–168)

## Alexander Pope

We should distinguish these "Fury-passions" from the natural appe-
tites that Pope calls, simply, passions. Passions, of course, are a positive force in *An Essay on Man*, the innate principle inspiring all
human action. Such passion is necessary and essential, although it is
equally necessary for passion to be guided (not suppressed or controlled) by reason, for without the guidance of reason man would be
"active to no end" (ii.62). The destructive "Fury-passions," then,
represent passion unguided or misguided. They are another name for
the irrational power of *furor*, which plunges man from innocence and
charity into an uncivilized ("savage") history of bloodshed.

*An Essay on Man* holds out two paradigms of transformation: one
historical and social, the other timeless and personal. The personal
transformation comes through charity—not narrowly understood as
alms but broadly interpreted to signify a sympathetic union between
man and nature. Self-love, redirected outward, works in the rational
mind like a pebble dropped into a peaceful lake, radiating successive
circles of inclusion:

> Wide and more wide, th'o'erflowings of the mind
> Take ev'ry creature in, of ev'ry kind;
> Earth smiles around, with boundless bounty blest,
> And Heav'n beholds its image in his breast.      (iv.369–372)

This imagery of inclusiveness contrasts vividly with the exclusive,
elite, hermetic contractions of society that Pope depicts in *The Rape
of the Lock*. The charitable man creates a paradise within himself
that mirrors the harmony of an original state when man and beast
walked together as "joint tenants" of the wood. Since this kindred
feeling embraces all creatures, clearly the charitable man cannot easily reconcile himself to the sport of hunting. But personal charity is
not the only alternative that Pope offers to the dehumanizing "Fury-
passions." The age of patriarchs is a model for the social transformations possible when mankind heeds, rather than opposes or ignores,
the voice of nature:

> Great Nature spoke; observant Men obey'd;
> Cities were built, Societies were made:
> Here rose one little state; another near
> Grew by like means, and join'd, thro' love or fear.
> Did here the trees with ruddier burdens bend,

And there the streams in purer rills descend?
What War could ravish, Commerce could bestow,
And he return'd a friend, who came a foe.          (iii.199–206)

The transformation of foes into friends, of war into peace, of plunder into commerce returns us to the contemporary world of *Windsor-Forest*, where commerce again becomes both means and symbol of harmony restored.

The reconciling power of commerce, which creates the same union among nations that charity creates among individuals, is pictured in *Windsor-Forest* as initiating a new era, an image of man's original unity. The new golden age can justifiably be called "better" than the first, however, because it boasts all the fruits of art and industry previously unknown. Best of all, it implies, too, progressive social development and the wisdom earned by experience that make the possibility of repeated falls from harmony more remote. Thus, Father Thames's prophecy imagines a future unstained by the bloodshed which followed the initial Age of Gold:

No more my Sons shall dye with *British* Blood
Red *Iber*'s Sands, or *Ister*'s foaming Flood.          (ll. 367–368)

Hunting—a pastime Pope did not admire but realistically admitted had "Authority and Custom to support it"[37]—still lingers as a "Trace" of war (l. 371), reminding man of his bloody past, just as Pope's reference to the tyranny of Spain (l. 409) emphasizes the imperfection of the present. But the commercial future, if not wholly utopian, still promises an immense improvement over the discord of the past, improvement epitomized by Pope's image of the "gasping Furies" who now "thirst for Blood in vain."

In *Windsor-Forest* the futile bleeding which characterizes discord is not merely stopped but transformed into a metaphor of man's new harmony with nature. The elevated diction of Father Thames's praise of commerce thus appropriately reflects a sense of heightened civility:

For me the Balm shall bleed, and Amber flow,
The Coral redden, and the Ruby glow.          (ll. 393–394)

Bleeding is now figure rather than fact. Blenheim and Saragossa are unstained with "*British* Blood," while coral and rubies redden naturally for man's delight. As the fruitful flowing of balm and amber replaces the futile bloodshed of war, gold, formerly a mark of human corruption, becomes both an image of natural process (l. 396) and an emblem of social regeneration, signaling the arrival of "*Albion*'s Golden Days." Individual nations enjoy freedom from tyranny, while commerce unites them in a circle of mutual self-interest. Even natural barriers are transformed, through art and labor, into connecting links, as "Seas but join the Regions they divide" (l. 400). The peace which Pope envisions in *Windsor-Forest* is not merely the conclusion to a specific war but the creation of a dynamic harmony that, like the circle of charity at its furthest extension, spreads "from Shore to Shore" (l. 407). While the godlike power of Queen Anne to still Discord accomplishes a crucial, if limited, political change, the promise of a "better" golden age also depends upon the civilizing art of the poet, whose corrective vision helps to counteract the internal violence of *furor* and whose invention discovers a poetic imagery reflecting the transformations by which mankind may advance and improve.

"Pope's life-work," G. Wilson Knight has observed, "is rooted in *Windsor-Forest*."[38] A corollary would also seem true. Virgil is far more than the poet of Pope's youth. No ancient poet is more important to his poetic development than Virgil, and Pope's life-work is rooted in the Virgilian attitudes expressed in *Windsor-Forest*. Although his methods later changed mainly to the satirical, he never swerved from the Virgilian goal of refining the uncivilized and warring down the proud (*debellare superbos*). Thus, in his role as civilized and civilizing poet, Pope, like Virgil, conceived of "correctness" in its largest and noblest sense. An early version of *Windsor-Forest*, for example, described the flags of England's commerical fleet by referring to their insignia as a "bloody Cross."[39] The later disappearance of the adjective *bloody* (l. 387) reveals more than Pope's ceaseless revising extended to a minor detail of imagery. The revision expresses his general attitude toward the relation between poetry and civilization. For Pope, as for Virgil, the refinement of the poem prefigures and advances the moral improvement of mankind. It is in such fundamental attitudes, rather than in specific verbal echoes and structural similarities, that we may locate Pope's most meaningful reliance upon Virgil. For Pope, Virgil was as much a sage as a poet, and what Pope learned from Virgil, above all else, involved an entire understanding of the nature of civilized man.

# V

## "The Visionary Maid": Tragic Passion and Redemptive Sympathy in "Eloisa to Abelard"

We open a Book of Devotion, and it touches us. We open a Book of Gallantry, and that too makes its impression. Shall I say it? 'Tis the Heart alone that reconciles Contrarieties, and admits of things incompatible.

—La Bruyère

SAMUEL JOHNSON dismissed with curt and undisguised contempt one of the most intensely erotic poems Pope ever wrote. "Poetry," he judged, "has not often been worse employed than in dignifying the amorous fury of a raving girl."[1] The remark, significantly, was not inspired by "Eloisa to Abelard" but by the equally impassioned "Elegy to the Memory of an Unfortunate Lady." Unlike many readers, who lump the two poems together as evidence that the heights of emotion were not entirely beyond Pope's reach, Johnson apparently found reason to discriminate carefully between them. He balanced his scorn for Pope's unfortunate lady, whose suicide in his view no passion could justify or excuse, with praise for "Eloisa to Abelard" excessive even by Johnsonian standards. "The *Epistle of Eloise to Abelard* is one of the most happy productions of human wit: the subject is so judiciously chosen that it would be difficult, in turning over the annals of the world, to find another which so many circumstances concur to recommend."[2] Certainly Johnson's grounds for approval, which include what he took to be Pope's reverent treatment of "religious hope and resignation," do not always coincide with those of later readers. Yet, with recent accounts generally agreeing that the poem has drastic flaws, Johnson's authority offers some comfort to admirers of "Eloisa to Abelard" and suggests the need for a detailed defense and explication—tasks Johnson does not undertake—stressing the principles or attitudes that seem to govern Pope's treatment of his subject. Such an inquiry has the special virtue of heeding the advice Pope himself thought fruitful in *An Essay on Criticism*:

> A perfect Judge will *read* each Work of Wit
> With the same Spirit that its Author *writ*,
> Survey the *Whole*, nor seek slight Faults to find,
> Where *Nature moves*, and *Rapture warms* the Mind;
> Nor lose, for that malignant dull Delight,
> The *gen'rous Pleasure* to be charm'd with Wit.   (ll. 233–238)

In addressing critics, Pope emphasized that emotion must accompany judgment—purifying and completing it—at times overruling or annulling the analytical perception of error. The value Pope gives in *An Essay on Criticism* to sympathetic insight, to emotional generosity, and to the reader's pleasure should raise at least the possibility that his retelling of Eloisa's "tender story" (l. 364) offers something other than a sermon against excess passion. As he explained about the time "Eloisa to Abelard" appeared, tenderness is the "very Emanation of Good Sense & Virtue." Then, in an unacknowledged paraphrase of Dryden, he added: "The finest minds like the finest metals, dissolve the easiest."[3]

## The Case against Eloisa

An effective defense of the poem requires our understanding the usual grounds for attack. Although individual writers sometimes combine arguments against "Eloisa to Abelard," the most common objections fall into three categories that have remained distinct since the eighteenth century, despite shifting theoretical and personal biases of individual critics. These general categories can be defined loosely as the aesthetic, the ethical, and the moral.

The aesthetic objection takes many shapes. In practice, the diverse complaints against Pope's artistry often reduce to the single claim that rhymed couplets and an artfully patterned rhetoric are inappropriate to Eloisa's impassioned meditations. If this claim were valid,

"Eloisa to Abelard" would fail by Pope's own standards: his idea of poetic wholeness, as we have seen, demands a harmony among subject, style, and form. At first glance, however, such aesthetic objections can seem justified, for "Eloisa to Abelard" hardly resembles a spontaneous passionate speech. Even Eloisa's most heartfelt cries incorporate a bookish and premeditated language with echoes of Milton and Dryden. Aesthetic objections, although finally inappropriate, call attention to an authentic and distinctive feature of the text. Elsewhere Pope imparted to his couplets a conversational ease and emotional immediacy that closely imitated actual speech, but in "Eloisa to Abelard" he chose instead a style that openly affirms its own literariness.

Pope understood, of course, that correspondents who write in the grip of passion do not normally compose in rhymed iambic pentameter. Nor do they express their feelings through the rhetorical intricacies of wit. For example, in his distress at the death of his father, Pope wrote to Lord Burlington with a spare directness that stands in vivid contrast to the intellectual and stylistic gamesmanship of his earlier letters. The entire text reads as follows:

> Chiswick: December 23
> I beg the favor of your Lordship to lend me a Servant of yours to send into the Country to a Relation of mine, with the ill news of my poor Fathers death—Your Lordship will believe I can never forget the obligations I owe You, when I remember them at this moment.
> I am always My Lord,/Entirely Yours/A. Pope
> I beg a few Hartshorn drops/of My Lady, for my Mother.[4]

If it seems unfair to compare a letter with a poem, that is exactly the point. "Eloisa to Abelard" reflects the proprieties of a verse epistle— particularly an Ovidian verse epistle modeled on the *Heroides*—not the patterns of speech or prose. Eloisa's stylized diction is a poetic hybrid, designed to emphasize her kinship with Ovid's literary heroines while it subtly blends her voice with Pope's. The style, if it fails by the standards of naive realism, serves the crucial purpose of interpreting and clarifying Eloisa's dilemma.

Pope's contrivances of diction, style, and form support his explicit announcement in the argument prefixed to the poem: "Eloisa to Abelard" is intended to offer a *"lively . . . picture of the struggles of grace and nature, virtue and passion."* One especially revealing aspect of the statement is its stylized balance and opposition. Although Eloisa might be imagined as subject to a multitude of conflicting pressures and confused emotions, Pope views her experience as a struggle of distinct opposites: grace and virtue compete with nature and passion for control of a psyche divided between the opposing claims of soul and body. These specific oppositions suggest an appropriateness in the rhetorical features analyzed by Jacob H. Adler. "Zeugma, chiasmus, and anaphora," he tells us, "are typical; but simple balance is more frequent, more typical. Eloisa's mind simply works—or is made to work—in pairs and in series. Almost everything is in conjunction with something else."[5]

Rhyme, like the balance of opposites, helps to represent the stylized conflict within Eloisa's mind. The poem, Adler reports, exhibits a greater proportion of off-rhymes than all but one of Pope's major works. In a poet who consistently labored to make the sound of his verse echo its sense, the jarring of imperfect rhymes emphasizes Eloisa's internal dissonance. Other pairs rhyme direct opposites: bloom/gloom, night/light, pray'r/despair, repose/glows, destroy/joy. Eloisa's internal division is even reflected in the contrast between passages of exaggerated rhetoric, such as "Ye grots and caverns shagg'd with horrid thorn!" (l. 20), and moments of quiet statement: "I have not yet forgot my self to stone" (l. 24). The manipulated contrasts may not please everyone, but they are certainly appropriate to a poem that defines Eloisa's struggle as the conflict of opposites.

Readers who may grant the propriety of Eloisa's language are liable to raise ethical objections, which, however, prove equally misleading. These ethical objections invariably raise questions about Eloisa's character and conduct. She is, her critics claim, an irrational creature, unhinged by love and sinfully obstinate in rejecting her duty to God. Literature, of course, is well supplied with fallen women, but Eloisa is uniquely notorious for her open defense of unwedded love:

> Love, free as air, at sight of human ties,
> Spreads his light wings, and in a moment flies.     (ll. 75–76)

Pope's early biographer Owen Ruffhead is not the last reader to discover a dangerous immorality in Eloisa's passion: "The glowing lines which express the extravagance of Eloisa's fondness, her contempt of connubial ties, and the unbounded freedom of her attachment, have been often repeated with too much success by artful libertines to forward the purposes of seduction, and have as often, perhaps, been remembered by the deluded fair, and deemed a sanction for illicit deviations from the paths of virtue."[6] Although the progress of sexual revolution now gives Ruffhead's warning a certain amusing charm, not even charm can redeem it as criticism. Eloisa's sensuality is linked with an equally strong love of God, and the Old Testament could be condemned by the same logic which Ruffhead employs to censure Eloisa.

Yet, it is still possible to claim, as has been claimed of the speaker in the "Elegy to the Memory of an Unfortunate Lady," that Pope portrays Eloisa's passion ultimately to discredit her.[7] Like Pope's explicitly satirical figures such as Atticus, Atossa, Sir Balaam, and Cibber, one can argue, Eloisa stands as a model of improper conduct: her passion and extravagance are self-incriminating. This argument should not be too hastily accepted, however, for "Eloisa to Abelard" is in many ways without parallel in Pope's career. Its spirit does not seem even obliquely satirical. If Pope designed her excess to be self-incriminating, why does he continually invite our compassion for his beleaguered heroine and conclude with a passage implying his direct sympathy? Recalling Johnson's careful discrimination between "Eloisa to Abelard" and the "Elegy to the Memory of an Unfortunate Lady," we must take Eloisa as we find her, I think, with her mixture of flaws and virtues, not judge her conduct against the standards of conventional morality. Understanding, not censure, is Pope's goal.

Unfortunately, ethical and aesthetic objections can seem strengthened or confirmed by the ease with which they support more general moral objections to the poem. While ethical judgments center on the character (ethos) of Eloisa, the broader moral objections usually consider the implications of poetic structure and development, what eighteenth-century critics of epic and drama usually included under the term *fable*. Fable referred to the unifying moral vision a work could be said to express. Homer's "fable" in the *Iliad*, according to Pope, concerned the relationship between personal anger and social discord. As he wrote of Achilles, "*Homer* proposes him not as a Pattern for Imitation; but the Moral of the Poem which he design'd the Reader should draw from it, is, that we should avoid Anger, since it is

ever pernicious in the Event" (note to *Iliad*, XX.541). "Eloisa to Abelard," falling outside the generic boundaries of epic and drama,
would not necessarily require a ponderous Homeric moral. But Pope
did require moral significance of all serious literature. ("No writing is
good that does not tend to better mankind some way or other.") He
would ask himself, and expect readers to ask of the poem, what general ameliorating purpose underlies his portrayal of Eloisa's intense
and disjointed struggle, from her first startled, hesitant questioning to
her final repose.

Pope's moral purpose is not to expose Eloisa as a woman justly af-
flicted for her uncontrolled passion and willful disobedience to God.
Like Achilles, she is hardly a pattern for imitation, but her virtues
and misfortunes make her equally inappropriate as merely an example of folly or misconduct. If Eloisa is neither wholly praiseworthy
nor entirely blamable, however, does the poem have a moral purpose?
Here opinion divides, and the division grows wider when readers
consider, in analyzing the development of the poem, the implications
of Eloisa's final state of mind. Some readers find her peaceful and
ready to die, fully accepting God's will, penitent for her sins and
trusting in the forgiveness of a merciful Redeemer. This reading has
the benefit of conforming with historical accounts of Eloisa's life. Its
defect, aside from a failure to convince readers for whom the *progress*
toward penitence seems haphazard or unclear, is that the poem appears to reward fornication and impiety with the solace of a blessed
end. Still other readers feel that Eloisa is not peaceful and composed
but merely exhausted, lapsed into quiescence: her passion is spent,
but her conflicts are unresolved. This view exposes Pope to attack for
daring to sympathize with a woman who never conclusively re-
nounces her life of sin. Either reading can lead to charges of moral
confusion.

At this point, waiving a lengthy theological explication of a poem
that seems more deeply concerned with Eloisa's mind than with her
soul, I cannot merely reply that Pope's ameliorating purpose in
"Eloisa to Abelard" has little to do with quotable, portable precepts
of morality. In understanding Pope's efforts "to better mankind," we
must temporarily put aside questions of morality and investigate instead such apparently nonmoral issues as human psychology, historical context, and literary form. Many of the most common
objections to the poem vanish completely when we view it as an ex-

ploration of the two closely related concepts of tragic passion and redemptive sympathy.

## Eloisa, Ovid, and Tragic Character

Pope modeled "Eloisa to Abelard" on the Ovidian heroic epistle. His
most valuable legacy from Ovid, however, like his legacy from Virgil
as expressed in *Windsor-Forest*, is not contained in direct borrowings
or explicit allusions but in a spirit, style, and series of poetic techniques. A too-detailed study of sources can obscure what Pope, and
also Dryden, found most important and most stimulating in Ovid's
work: its relation to drama. Dryden had called attention to the dramatic properties of Ovid in a passage quite relevant to "Eloisa to
Abelard": "Though I see many excellent thoughts in Seneca, yet he
of them [the ancients] who had a genius most proper for the stage,
was Ovid; he had a way of writing so fit to stir up a pleasing admiration and concernment, which are the objects of a tragedy, and to
show the various movements of a soul combating betwixt two different passions, that, had he lived in our age, or in his own could have
writ with our advantages, no man but must have yielded to him."[8]
What Pope discovered in Ovid was less the compendium of mythological imagery which Renaissance writers found than a way of in-
fusing poetry with the qualities of drama.

Pope's subject in "Eloisa to Abelard" is precisely what Dryden (in
praising Ovid) called "the various movements of a soul combating
betwixt two different passions." The poem might seem almost contrived to illustrate Dryden's analysis of Ovidian technique. Eloisa's
love for Abelard and her duty to God—like the opposing demands of
inclination and honor in Restoration heroic plays—provide the in-
gredients for dramatic tension. An understanding of this Ovidian
spirit, expressed in the poem's techniques and in its kinship with
tragedy, offers the best perspective from which to explore Pope's
treatment of Eloisa.

Pope's decision to cast Eloisa's story in the highly dramatic genre
of the Ovidian epistle, rather than as a play, was doubtless instinctive.
No amount of genuine interest in the theater could induce Pope to
turn dramatist. Early experience taught him "how much everybody
that did write for the stage was obliged to subject themselves to the
players and the town."[9] Critics too stood poised to hamper a play-

wright with their annoying and often barren controversies, among which a current dispute over the impropriety of love as a tragic passion would have assured Eloisa a stormy debut. It is also likely that Pope knew his own limitations at the sustained give-and-take of drama. There is substantial truth in Macaulay's jaundiced observation that "Pope writing dialogue resembled—to borrow Horace's imagery and his own—a wolf, which, instead of biting, should take to kicking, or a monkey which should try to sting."[10]

Yet, if Pope avoided formal drama except for collaborating on minor farces, he also employed various techniques for creating poems which are highly dramatic. *The Rape of the Lock* may owe its final shape to the influence of theatrical plotting in five acts, and Donald J. Greene is correct in stressing the "dramatic texture" that characterizes many of the later satirical poems. As poet, translator, editor, and critic, Pope reveals his lasting appreciation for the mixture of dramatic and nondramatic elements in a single composition, and this taste appears to have governed his treatment of Eloisa's story. In the rambling, sententious, original letters of the two lovers, he recognized the possibility of creating a highly concentrated dramatic episode. In effect, he isolates a moment of intense passion in a sequence of connected events and discards the shell of plot. Despite her role as a correspondent, Eloisa is essentially a tragic heroine.[11]

Eloisa's status as a tragic heroine undermines certain limited ethical and moral objections that critics such as Ruffhead make. In her tragic roles as both actor and victim—at once the willful agent of her own suffering and the prisoner of her fate—she joins the class of fictive protagonists whose histories are too tangled for simple moral judgment. *King Lear*, for example, can be forced to yield the lesson that discord follows the division of rule, although the play provides no assurance that not dividing the kingdom will preserve harmony. Few persons, however, would wish to extend such an allegorical reading to Lear himself or to Cordelia. It is not true that they get exactly what they deserve. That is one reason why Johnson found the conclusion of *King Lear* too painful for rereading, and why eighteenth-century audiences, attentive to the mechanics of poetic justice, enjoyed Nahum Tate's sweetened version, in which Cordelia marries the deserving Edgar. Although Shakespeare permits Lear and Cordelia to earn a measure of wisdom and self-knowledge at terrible cost, he does not permit the audience to indulge in a reassuring assessment of loss and gain. Pope restored Shakespeare's original ending in his edition of 1725, and he seems to have understood the force of Shakespeare's tragic vision. Like Lear, Eloisa both acts and suffers in ways too complex to summarize in an edifying maxim.

As a victim, Eloisa evokes the pathos that eighteenth-century readers admired in tragedy. Like Ovid's heroines, she is a remarkable woman abandoned by an apparently unfeeling male. Yet, her suffering never degenerates into fevered bombast, as sometimes happens to heroines in the rhetorical tragedies of Nicholas Rowe. The difference may involve Pope's care in establishing a depth of character and complexity of motive that locate the source of Eloisa's anguish in something beyond her own intense feeling and powers of speech. Certainly, like most tragic protagonists, she is in part the victim of her own impulsive and passionate nature—a point that recent criticism has rightly stressed. In addition, however, she is also beset by complicated forces essentially outside her control that include chance, historical circumstance, and the passions of those around her (a neoclassical version of fate). Especially because readers continue to see Eloisa as a woman too weak and foolish to control her own emotions, it is worth looking briefly at several of the forces that contribute to her misfortune.

"Eloisa to Abelard," like a history painting, presupposes a sequence of actions that generates the single moment depicted by the artist. It also presupposes an established idea of character to which the poet, no matter how he shades his interpretation, must pay homage. The legend of Eloisa—supplemented in Pope's day by John Hughes's *Letters of Abelard and Heloise* (1713), a translation of a romanticized French version of the original Latin correspondence—by no means pictured her as consistently weak and foolish, the witless agent of her own suffering. Whatever exaggerations have attended her legend, Hughes explained, she "may deservedly be placed in the Rank of Women of the greatest Learning."[12] Erudition certainly is no shield against folly; Pope delights in exposing the absurdities of pedantic learning. But Eloisa's accomplishments assure us that, however strong her passions, she possessed extremely well-developed powers of mind. Whatever her weaknesses, they are not the failures of a sinewless reason.

Nor is a love-sick or amorous temperament the source of Eloisa's anguish. She did not dizzily fling herself at Abelard, but succumbed only after a carefully plotted and relentlessly pursued seduction by the greatest philosopher of his day, abetted in his design by the stupidity and greed of her worthless guardian uncle. Even when deeply in love with Abelard—which surely is no crime—she resisted his demands for marriage, countering his passion with a rational and selflessly inspired argument emphasizing the irrevocable damage marriage would inflict upon Abelard's reputation and ability as a philosopher. All these facts of history (or legend) Pope works into his poem to support his depiction of a character whose inner life is divided by contradictions. We encounter a woman not only independent and strong-minded enough to argue persuasively for unmarried love but also so unselfish and loving that she rejects marriage, preferring to save Abelard's reputation at the cost of her own. Dido revealed no such regal dignity in love.

If Eloisa bears equal responsibility for the clandestine romance with her tutor, Abelard certainly did not distinguish himself for prudence. What can explain his blindness in anticipating no protest from Eloisa's outraged uncle and guardian, Fulbert? When revenge came, in the violent and humiliating castration, Abelard once more commanded her obedience, instructing her to take the veil at the convent of Argenteuil. Her friends dissented—sensibly thinking "the yoke of monastic rule intolerable for one of her youth"[13]—but she replied by quoting Cornelia, wife of Pompey, that she would gladly atone for causing the misery of her husband, an exceedingly generous idea of causation. Although it later pained her to learn that Abelard had cautiously delayed his vows until certain she was securely immured in the convent, she remained faithful to him while earning almost universal admiration as the efficient and devoted Abbess of the Paraclete. If Pope had wished to write about the dangerous propensity of amorous fury to overwhelm reason, Abelard would have made a better subject than Eloisa.

External pressures such as these might have bowed even a martyr, but Eloisa, although genuinely devout, was unluckily no saint. It is possible, however, that Pope wished us to consider an additional difficulty, for hers were not propitious times in which to reconcile the conflicting demands of reason and passion. In *An Essay on Man*, Pope chooses the lofty metaphor of friendship to describe the supporting and complementary relationship that reason and passion should hold. Their antagonism—so destructive in its consequences—

he traced directly to the false distinctions established by the scholastic philosophers of Eloisa's day:

> Let subtle schoolmen teach these friends to fight,
> More studious to divide than to unite,
> And Grace and Virtue, Sense and Reason split,
> With all the rash dexterity of Wit:
> Wits, just like fools, at war about a Name,
> Have full as oft no meaning, or the same. (ii.81–86)

Eloisa's struggle owes much to the historical split between reason and emotion that *An Essay on Man* was designed in part to heal. Ironically, Abelard's rashness as a philospher is at least indirectly related to the torment he causes Eloisa as a lover. Hughes tells us of Abelard: "He had a very subtle Wit, and was incessantly whetting it by Disputes, out of a restless Ambition to be a Master of his Weapons. So that in a short time he gain'd the Reputation of the greatest Philosopher of his Age; and has always been esteem'd the Founder of what we call the *Learning of the Schoolmen*."[14] Pope does not exploit the irony that Abelard, as the founder of scholastic philosophy, bears responsibility for the false philosophical antagonism between reason and passion that is a main source of Eloisa's dilemma. Yet, Hughes's description of Abelard certainly suggests an added reason for Pope's sympathetic attitude toward his heroine. Eloisa, though not blameless, is nevertheless a victim of forces far beyond her control. Nurtured by a pernicious guardian, seduced by an imprudent lover, virtually forced into marriage, wedded to a passionless castrate, shut away in a convent, and deceived by a philosophy that imagined reason and desire as eternal opposites, Eloisa inspires admiration simply by her power to endure.

What Eloisa *makes* of suffering is Pope's subject, and in this sense "Eloisa to Abelard" continues the studies of character which Pope pursued throughout his career. For Eloisa, suffering is not a passive process. Her pain is not something merely inflicted upon her, from outside, by forces beyond her control. She *adds* pain to pain. Suffering for Eloisa is an active, conscious, affirmative state. The Abbey of the Paraclete is for her no refuge, but a setting for struggle—often the projection or symbol of one portion of her mind—and she never retreats, despite her pain, into the madness or delusive solipsism that (as Freud wrote of neurosis) replaces the cloister in modern life.

# Alexander Pope

Eloisa offers a vivid instance of Pope's belief that character is open to extremes of internal discord or conflict. "No Prelate's Lawn with Hair-shirt lin'd, / Is half so incoherent as my Mind," he wrote in *The First Epistle of the First Book of Horace, Imitated* (ll. 165–166), and such inner contradictions seriously threaten the coherence and stability of human character. Suffering for Eloisa goes beyond endurance. It is a process by which character is expressed, developed, and affirmed in the face of contradictory desires that, in Eloisa's case, not even chance, error, and the pressures of history can render wholly self-destructive.

Among the various aspects of Eloisa's character Pope might have encountered in Hughes's translation or added from his own invention, two recur in the poem so frequently that they become almost defining traits. They are summarized in the phrase Eloisa once uses to describe herself—"the visionary maid" (l. 162)—for it is preeminently her distinctive powers of memory and of imagination that create her striking, singular, and even heroic identity. Many women have found themselves "Love's victim," as an appropriately nameless voice tells her from a nearby tomb (l. 312), but what raises Eloisa above this anonymous sisterhood are her extraordinary powers of remembering and imagining. These traits—which center the poem in the psychology of Pope's heroine—were not an inevitable choice for emphasis, however natural they appear.[15] The letters Hughes translated concern moral and ecclesiastical doctrine as much as Eloisa's mental processes, and the diffuse focus weakens even what psychological interest Hughes manages to convey. In creating from this hodgepodge source a unified, emphatic, and consistent idea of character, Pope achieves a remarkable revision, transforming a heterogeneous and digressive correspondence into the concentrated drama of Eloisa's mind.[16] The immediacy of the quasi-dramatic situation that Pope invents for Eloisa enhances his attention to psychological and interior processes. Hers is a drama not of action but of feelings, thoughts, and imagination that can find no outlet in events. This confinement to the inaction of a purely mental life resembles Pope's account of his own state, but she extends the poetic faculties of memory and imagination to self-tormenting extremes. Her remarkable powers magnify the conflict within her mind between Abelard and God. And such magnification of inner conflict is what helps Pope, in revising his source, to suggest the tragic dimensions of Eloisa's experience. Unlike

Addison's Cato, who simply asserts a prefabricated and unalterable character against external events that threaten him, Eloisa exhibits what Shakespearean tragedy offers at its best: character which is not fixed and immune from change but rather defined through the consciousness of internal as well as external conflict.

The importance of memory to Eloisa's character suggests how thoroughly Pope has modernized his medieval source. If in the Middle Ages and Renaissance memory could become a means of ordering the universe, as Frances A. Yates has shown, or a means of reconstituting through meditation the meaning of history, as Louis L. Martz has shown, memory in the Augustan Age holds the humbler but no less crucial function of ordering the individual.[17] Memory enables eighteenth-century man to assert a continuity with his own past, without which he might grow as fragmented and incoherent as Swift's impersonated modern author in *A Tale of a Tub*, who both laments and celebrates the "unhappy shortness" of his memory. Pope tells us in *The Dunciad* that "Wits have short Memories, and Dunces none" (IV.620)—which helps to explain why, despite the profusion of real names, Pope's mock-editor Martinus Scriblerus can insist that the dunces are merely inhuman "phantoms." Not to remember is to experience an attenuated, spectral existence. For Pope, memory is not only a source of inner coherence but provides the basis of all mental activity, all inwardness. As Johnson asserts: "Memory is the primary and fundamental power, without which there could be no other intellectual operation" (*The Idler* no. 44).

There are dangers, of course, in an undiscriminating or obsessive attention to the past, whether personal or historical. Pope observes in *An Essay on Criticism* that the predominance of memory inevitably restricts the force of understanding, just as the pictorial immediacy of imagination invariably overpowers the less vivid figures of memory (ll. 56–59). Pope's ideal, as always, is a harmonious balance among memory, imagination, and judgment, without which character faces potential dissolution, a lapse into stupor or meaningless contradiction. "Pope thinks of human character," Maynard Mack writes, "as a creative achievement, an artistic result, something built out of chaos as God built the world."[18] Man may be, as Pope calls him in *An Essay on Man*, a "Chaos of Thought and Passion, all confus'd" (ii.13), but he still retains the power of self-possession through an intelligent awareness of his condition, through connecting himself with the past by means of memory, and through sharing a charitable concern for the life around him. These activities—for they require active and continual exertion—help make Eloisa the deeply human, complex, and sympathetic character that Pope's satiric victims so clearly are not, and, greatly intensified, they help to raise her to tragic stature.

No illustration is needed to demonstrate Pope's emphasis upon Eloisa's powers of memory and of imagination. The entire poem fluctuates between her excursions into fantasy and her vivid recollections of the past. Although her understanding may seem to vary with each new image, the shifts occur because she never allows memory and imagination to overwhelm her perception of the actual state of things. Further, although the scenes unfolded in memory and in imagination certainly help inflame Eloisa's already kindled passions, her emotional fervor may be unphilosophical without being irrational or inappropriate to the occasion. In the situation which Pope invents, Eloisa, after many years of separation from Abelard, reacts with shock and confusion upon suddenly encountering his letter. The intensity of her passion is high tribute to the powers of human affection.

Unlike some later sentimentalists, Pope did not believe that emotional outbursts were necessarily good, but he also rejected the perpetual lukewarmness of an Atticus, locked in invariable restraint. Pope, like Fielding, argues implicitly for a direct correspondence between feeling and the occasions for feeling. When such a correspondence exists, as it does for Eloisa, the expression of strong emotion is a rational act—or at least consistent with reason. In another context Pope could exalt the unvarying temperance of Martha Blount, "Mistress of herself, tho' China fall."[19] But Eloisa's loss is not the breaking of a teacup—or a kingdom. Undiscriminating equanimity, after all, is no better than Belinda's undiscriminating passion in *The Rape of the Lock*. Eloisa, unlike Belinda, understands the difference between losing a lapdog and a lover. In far more difficult circumstances than befell Martha Blount, she remains truly mistress of herself, for she refuses to deny the uniquely developed powers of memory and of imagination that are fundamental to her character.

Probably the most effective way Pope stresses the remarkable extent of Eloisa's powers is through the simple but forceful device of contrast. Both Abelard and the Paraclete, linked imagistically throughout the poem, vividly represent the unimpassioned state of forgetfulness that is the opposite of Eloisa's condition. Memory for

Eloisa inspires feeling, and feeling signifies life, but the walls of religion and the dead calm inflicted upon Abelard unnaturally sever the knot uniting remembrance and desire. Addressing the walls which seem to oppress as they enclose her, Eloisa could also be accusing Abelard: "Tho' cold like you, unmov'd, and silent grown, / I have not yet forgot my self to stone" (ll. 23–24). Forgetting, Eloisa implies, is a means of denying oneself; it not only numbs the emotions but unravels the continuity between past and present. In truth, Eloisa is far from cold, despite the efforts of "stern religion" to quench the "unwilling flame" of Love (l. 39), and her inseparable warmth and pain become a measure of her sentient humanity. For Eloisa, not feeling, like not remembering, is virtually not to exist. The victory of reason over passion, whether won by confinement, by philosophy, by religion, or by mutilation, is pyrrhic, for it leads only to the lifeless self-denial of stoicism, an excess Pope rejected outright in *An Essay on Man*:

> In lazy Apathy let Stoics boast
> Their Virtue fix'd; 'tis fix'd as in a frost,
> Contracted all, retiring to the breast;
> But strength of mind is Exercise, not Rest:
> The rising tempest puts in act the soul,
> Parts it may ravage, but preserves the whole.　　(ii.101–106)

Passion is not for Pope the natural enemy of reason but a means of rousing the soul to action. It is astonishing how many modern readers assume that he would prefer Eloisa to encounter Abelard's unexpected letter with a cool and inexpressive self-control.

Stability of character—not static sameness or unflappable composure—is what Pope desired, a stability in which motion and change are consistent with a centered firmness, a dynamic equilibrium. His images of frost and of fixity in *An Essay on Man* recall the stony coldness repeatedly associated both with Abelard and with the Paraclete and remind us that Pope normally characterizes Eloisa through imagery of warmth, movement, and light. She will never achieve the serenity that she attributes to the vestal virgin whom she conjures up in imagination—"The world forgetting, by the world forgot" (l. 208)—because the price of such composure is oblivion, a denial of the individual character created and sustained through active remembering. Even though remembering for Eloisa is identical with suffering, she refuses to win release from pain through self-denial. Surrounded by various temptations to rest, to immobilize herself, and to forget, she exercises a virtue having nothing to do with chastity or religion. Her endurance is not a form of passive helplessness but an active refusal to contract into a stonelike fixity, a cold state of death in life.

Pope's ameliorating purpose in "Eloisa to Abelard" does not depend upon our ability to extract a moral from the poem but upon our willingness to experience through Eloisa the humanizing power of tragic passion and the potential dignity of human nature. In a mind wholly conscious of its division between mighty opposites, Eloisa's rising tempests of passion do indeed "put in act" her soul; and, although memory and imagination undeniably "ravage" her with the pain of conflict, her struggle affirms the value of consciousness: "strength of mind is Exercise, not Rest." Undoubtedly a distinction must be drawn between the "exercise" Pope recommends in *An Essay on Man* and the "struggles" he portrays in "Eloisa to Abelard." *An Essay on Man* offers a program for human happiness, and the disciplined strength suggested by the term *exercise* provides a means for overcoming misfortune and achieving personal contentment. "Eloisa to Abelard" in its tragic conflict of opposites cannot offer its heroine the consolation of individual happiness. Yet, while recognizing the finality of loss, the inevitability of error, and the perplexity born of chance, circumstance, and man's own nature, the poem also recognizes man's power to transform suffering into something beyond blank pain. If, in Addison's famous neoclassical tragedy, Cato's suicide is the logical extension of stoic rationality when confronted with the intolerable, Eloisa's struggle asserts the nobility of conscious endurance and the self-sustaining powers of remembrance. "It is, indeed, the faculty of remembrance," Johnson wrote, "which may be said to place us in the class of moral agents" (*The Rambler* no. 41). Not everyone will fall prey to the specific "sad variety of woe" (l. 36) which is Eloisa's fate. But everyone, in Pope's view, shares with her the same fundamental powers of mind, the same exposure to misfortune, the same capacity for self-torment, and the same necessity for struggle. If we can recognize ourselves—or aspects of ourselves—in Eloisa, then her experience permits both an increased knowledge of human nature and an improved self-understanding. Amelioration for Pope is not restricted to the influence of ethical precepts or of textbook morality, and "Eloisa to Abelard" illustrates one of the subtlest ways in which Augustan generality can be called didactic.

## "Well-sung woes": Love, Death, and Consolation

"The greater Part of those whose Souls I am most concerned for," Pope wrote to Swift in 1713, "were unfortunately Heretics, Schismatics, Poets, Painters, or Persons of such Lives and Manners as few or no Churches are willing to save."[20] Pope's effort "to better mankind" is not exhausted in the depiction of Eloisa's ennobling struggle. It extends to the attempt to evoke for his flawed, unsaintly heroine an answering sympathy in the reader. We have seen in *An Essay on Criticism* the knowledge that proceeds from sympathetic feeling in the critic. "Eloisa to Abelard," while depicting in Eloisa intense and painful emotion, also depends upon the understanding that sympathy makes possible. The relation between Eloisa's passion and the emotions the poem requests from its reader is close and complementary. Their interrelatedness is perhaps clearest in the poem's concluding passages, for there Eloisa composes herself for death and, blending her voice with the poet's, pleads for remembrance in generations to come.

The disagreement over Eloisa's final state of mind cannot be settled here. Both readers who view her as genuinely repentant and readers who find her merely lapsed into temporary quiet can find evidence to support their arguments. In my view, judgments concerning Eloisa's final state do not significantly affect the main focus of the poem. Pope centers attention not upon Eloisa's possible status in a life hereafter but upon her situation of conflict in the present. It might not be too extreme to suggest that the question of Eloisa's final state of mind is irrelevant to Pope's dramatization of tragic conflict, for her final composure results from her most compelling act of imagination: her vision of her own death. The new imminence of death changes utterly the nature of her conflict, for in preparing to die Eloisa virtually shifts the poem to a higher plane, a shift reflected in the changed tone of thoughtful resignation. (It was just such a shift that we witnessed in the final couplet of Pope's epitaph "On Himself.") Yet, although her imagined death brings "Eloisa to Abelard" abruptly to a conclusion, to regard Pope's ending as a true resolution seems imprecise. Death ends Eloisa's tragic struggle between her love for Abelard and her love for God, but it does not resolve the conflict. It simply terminates an opposition otherwise destined to continue indefinitely as long as both earthly and spiritual love assert their opposing claims on human character. Pope in effect shows Eloisa's conflict not resolved, but transcended.

One measure of the important shift at the conclusion of the poem is Eloisa's changed view of human affection. The once passionate lover of Abelard now imagines death so vividly present that she addresses it by name and is apparently untormented by the thought that even Abelard is "lov'd no more": "O death all-eloquent! you only prove / What dust we doat on, when 'tis man we love" (ll. 335–336). The meaning of Eloisa's apostrophe to death may be misunderstood if the word *only* is interpreted in a loose, colloquial sense, as if Eloisa were saying that death "just goes to show" the foolishness of loving. Actually, by using *only* in the strictly adjectival sense that follows Pope's normal usage (l. 173), Eloisa means that death *alone*—nothing but death—can deprive human love of its significance. For Eloisa, her love of God is powerful and genuine, but unable to drive out or diminish her feeling for Abelard. Death alone can accomplish that.

Occasion nowhere shows itself more crucial than in our interpretation of Eloisa's final words. The tradition of deathbed truth allows us to infer that her rejection of earthly love is sincere. Yet her words also point beyond her present situation. The apostrophe to death implies that for individuals *not* confronting imminent death or the vision of death, human affection necessarily remains strong and inextinguishable. Thus, although from Eloisa's final point of view love can seem suddenly insignificant, from Pope's vantage as poet it appears not only significant but essential in its power to redeem the waste which accompanies tragic passion. Because God alone can offer absolution of sin, sympathy remains the one redemptive gift within the range of human giving. Even Eloisa, caught up by the vision of her death, cannot resist a final exercise of her imaginative power:

> From the full quire when loud *Hosanna*'s rise,
> And swell the pomp of dreadful sacrifice,
> Amid that scene, if some relenting eye
> Glance on the stone where our cold reliques lie,
> Devotion's self shall steal a thought from heav'n,
> One human tear shall drop, and be forgiv'n.     (ll. 353–358)

Amid the celebration of the Eucharist, the major Christian sacrificial rite, which commemorates and perpetuates the mystery of Christ's redeeming love, Eloisa longs for a less exalted but complementary act of redemption. If in good times, as Pope asserts in the conclusion to *An Essay on Man*, the interpenetrating power of charity "Gives thee to make thy neighbour's blessing thine" (iv.354), in times of misfortune and tragedy it also breaks the potential isolation of suffering, redeeming man from that most dangerous (because most natural) form of solipsism.

Eloisa's prophetic wish for a "future Bard" to retell her story (l. 359), a desire—like her vision of the "relenting" worshiper—not found in Hughes's translation, emphasizes the value that she (like Pope) places on compassionate understanding as opposed to moralistic judgment:

> Such if there be, who loves so long, so well;
> Let him our sad, our tender story tell;
> The well-sung woes will sooth my pensive ghost;
> He best can paint 'em, who shall feel 'em most.   (ll. 363–366)

In sympathy Eloisa desires an attribute that, like reason, Pope identified as distinguishing man from the rest of animate creation: "he only knows, / And helps, another creature's wants and woes."[21] Further, she is correct, Pope would believe, in assuming that the poet is (or should be) the guardian of this high power. The walls of medieval religion enforce one kind of judgment; the art of the poet, while not openly disputing the judgments of religion, offers a different understanding of human experience. According to Eloisa, the poet's own resources of feeling are what allow him to offer the consolations of art. The generosity of spirit Pope expected of critics is no less essential for poets.

Eloisa, however, asks for more than sympathy. Earlier she had linked Fame with Love as the two "best of passions" (l. 40), and what she requests of the poet is not celebrity or renown but something close to simple remembrance. It is quite natural that the thought of being forgotten would disturb a woman who could never forget. Poets are also concerned with fame and remembrance, and throughout his life Pope engaged in his own version of the characteristically Romantic quest for permanence. In his view permanence could not be achieved within the natural world—as the early Words-worth thought it could—but only within the eternal order of Chris-tian redemption.[22] Eloisa's soul is the province of her Maker alone. The earthly permanence that concerns Pope belongs to the temporal realm of memory and language. On some occasions, the contrast be-tween time's power to destroy and the poet's limited preserving art could evoke a lament such as Pope's lines to the painter Charles Jervas: "Alas! how little from the grave we claim? / Thou but pre-serv'st a Face and I a Name."[23] Yet on other occasions this minimal power of overcoming death and time seemed the rock on which an ambitious theory of the poet's role could be built. If the poet can in-deed preserve a name, this power to memorialize human character gives the poet a vital purpose. It also helps to account for Pope's ex-tensive composition of epitaphs—which are usually ignored with the rest of his occasional verse. Whether in minor epitaphs or in major Horatian epistles, human character is, for Pope, the poet's special subject. With an appropriateness that betrays Pope's guiding hand, Eloisa wisely directs her final request toward the "future Bard" who, by his generous portrayal, will perpetuate her memory.

As the poet responsible for preserving Eloisa's memory in the fu-ture, Pope uses his substantial powers to win her a sympathetic hear-ing. "The Epistle of Eloise grows warm," he wrote to Martha Blount of the poem's development, "and begins to have some Breathings of the Heart in it, which may make posterity think I was in love."[24] Perhaps he was in love. The final couplets have traditionally been read as a private allusion to Pope's passion for the absent Lady Mary Wortley Montagu, whom he followed in her travels with an imagina-tion as active as Eloisa's. But the comment to Martha Blount contains a more important implication. Eloisa's "Breathings of the Heart" compress, in a single phrase, almost an entire poetics. For Pope, art overcomes its potential remoteness from life when it revitalizes the past and touches the present through the poet's quickening powers of memory and imagination. "It is my employment," Pope wrote con-cerning his Homeric translations, "to revive the old of past ages to the present."[25] In "Eloisa to Abelard," written while he was busy trans-lating Homer, Pope's efforts to reanimate the past allow a remarkable woman to live again as a complex and convincing character. It is not surprising that her special gifts of imagination and memory are a re-source she shares with the poet.

Eloisa's similarities to Pope extend to a point where their experience, rather than simply diverging, seems to point in opposite directions. Pope in many of his poems seeks to discover a resolution of
conflict which leads not simply to the restoration of harmony but to
the establishment of an improved and strengthened order, as when
commerce in *Windsor-Forest* creates the means for a heightened civility. In Eloisa, however, Pope creates a heroine for whom the resolution of her dilemma is impossible, short of death.[26] In Eloisa's
mind, where the drama of the poem is played out, there is no release
from conflict. Earthly love and spiritual love exert contrary, powerful, and equally valid claims upon her. Forgetfulness is not for Eloisa
the simple neglect of duty—as it was for Belinda, who carelessly forgot her prayers. To forget or to deny either form of love is to deny
herself. The choice offered her—Abelard *or* God—is clearly a choice
she cannot make. Nor should she. Her suffering is tragic at least in
part because it is unnecessary, because it traps her within the dilemma of a false choice.

The falseness of the opposition between Abelard and God is apparent when we recall the idea of love expressed in the conclusion to
*An Essay on Man*. There Pope envisions love expanding in concentric circles from an initial love of self, proceeding through the whole
range of familial and social relationships, then reaching further to
embrace all of animate nature, and culminating finally in the love of
God. The metaphor of concentric circles seems deliberately chosen to
replace the older metaphor of a ladder on which one climbs toward
God by *leaving behind* the lowly, fleshly, earthly, profane forms of
love. Human love for Pope is not something to be left behind, except
perhaps on one's deathbed. His conception of love is additive and inclusive. As individuals move from self-love to the love of God, they
do not reject or abandon the earlier stages of progress. Instead, the
final circle of divine love *encompasses* all the others. Eloisa, denied a
poet or philosopher to instruct her in reconciling human love with
divine, finds no release from her dilemma except in the sympathy of
readers who admire her willingness to live out the contradictions of a
solitary struggle that death alone could conclude.

# VI

## Rereading Pope:
## Language and Vision
## in *An Essay on Man*

The *Essay on Man* of Pope seems to me the most beautiful, most useful, most sublime didactic poem ever written in any language . . . Plato spoke as a poet in his not very intelligible prose, and Pope speaks as a philosopher in his admirable verses. He says that everything has been from the beginning as it has had to be, and as it is.

—Voltaire

N O ONE expected Pope to write *An Essay on Man*. Not his friends. (Swift confessed surprise to find Pope, as he put it, "so deep in Morals."[1]) And certainly not his enemies, who were trapped into praising him because he had published it anonymously. After secretly supplying his inveterate foe Leonard Welsted with a copy, Pope had the pleasure of hearing him reduced to self-incriminating rapture. "It is, indeed, above all commendation," Welsted wrote of *An Essay on Man*, "and ought to have been published in an age and country more worthy of it."[2] Welsted's rapture over the poem was not unusual. Pope's initial audience in the 1730s responded to *An Essay on Man* with an acclaim which was international. Even twenty years after its initial publication, the poem drew immoderate praise from Voltaire—not an easy reader to please—suggesting how deeply Pope had impressed his age. The controversy that soon enveloped the poem and occupied a small troop of metaphysicians and churchmen also attests to the power of *An Essay on Man* in commanding attention. It was considered both profound and dangerous—a work worth arguing about—and there is no sadder fate for such a challenging and controversial poem than its current status as a forlorn classic of ratiocination.

What made *An Essay on Man* worth arguing about—aside from the errors of a wildly garbled French translation by l'Abbé Jean-François du Resnel du Bellay—was its ambitious attempt to make sense of a world depicted as often senseless, splintered, and irrational. The poem's four epistles discuss the cosmos, human nature, social organization, and the ethics of happiness—a large order. Pope undertook this daunting task only after denying himself the use of the two major resources that had sustained the last great literary effort to explain the ways of God to man, *Paradise Lost*. First, Pope attempts to make sense of human experience without placing man in the context of Christian revelation. The Creation, the Fall, the Nativity, the Resurrection, and the Last Day—the definitive events of sacred history which, for Milton, impose meaning upon man's existence—Pope simply ignores. Second, Pope also chose to avoid the traditional explanations provided by myth and other narrative modes. *An Essay on Man* thus has no stories to tell, no legends to repeat. Pope offers instead a version of the figure who has grown increasingly familiar following the triumph of the Enlightenment: man alone, without church or priest, discovering through his reason the laws that bring order to a newly demythologized world—scientific, skeptical, secular.

It is Pope's language, however, not his doctrines, that I wish to emphasize and explore. The doctrines of *An Essay on Man* have been often discussed, and often misinterpreted, but they cannot be properly understood without a prior consideration of the distinctive language in which they are expressed. Yet, in considering Pope's language, I do not intend to focus on what is sometimes called the "poetry" of *An Essay on Man*—allusion or imagery or versification—which is all many critics find left when doctrine is subtracted from the poem. I focus instead on what happens to a theodicy, a work purporting to explain the ways of God, when it must accommodate itself to neoclassical ideas of language and to the literary purposes of Pope.

## Answerable Styles: Philosophy and Language

The language of *An Essay on Man* is far more rich, distinctive, and problematic than most modern expositors of Pope's doctrines believe. In style and in subject the poem seems very unlike the Horatian epistles and satires Pope was publishing simultaneously under his own name. As a theodicy, *An Essay on Man* encounters the inevitable dilemma of accommodating divine knowledge to earthly speech. For example, in another well-known theodicy, *Paradise Lost*, the archangel Raphael explains to Adam the unusual difficulties that attend his words:

> High matter thou injoin'st me, O prime of men,
> Sad task and hard, for how shall I relate
> To human sense th' invisible exploits
> Of warring Spirits . . . (V.563–566)

Milton's distinctive language, which seduced so many eighteenth-century imitators into seeking a shortcut to the sublime, was a direct response to the problem of finding what he calls in *Paradise Lost* an "answerable style" (IX.20): poetic expression appropriate to matters divine. In the final lines of *An Essay on Man*, Pope praised his philosophical companion, the semi-retired statesman Henry St. John, Viscount Bolingbroke, for inspiring a similar change. "Urg'd by thee," Pope tells Bolingbroke, "I turn'd the tuneful art / From sounds to things, from fancy to the heart" (iv.391–392). It is this poetic turning or modification that needs to be further explored, for Pope's changes involve far more than a shift in subject. Although his language is not Miltonic, like Milton (to whom the poem regularly alludes) Pope understood his highest challenge as nothing less than the reunion of poetry with truth. His task was to replace the "false mirror" of wit, deceptive and inauthentic, with "Nature's light" (iv.393). The task demanded not only a doctrine that was true but also a poetic language capable of expressing it truly. Pope's skill with this "turn'd" language helps to explain why even contemporaries who knew his work thoroughly, like Swift, did not guess his authorship.

Pope's need to discover an equivalent of Milton's answerable style was made more urgent by the campaigns for linguistic reform that intensified in the decades following publication of *Paradise Lost*. The proposals for reform varied, of course, but all agreed in their rejecting Renaissance theories of an original language in which words mysteriously contained or reflected a hidden knowledge. For the neoclassical theorist words do not descend from God to Adam as a form of spontaneous and intuitive wisdom bearing the imprint of their heavenly source, as Milton portrays them in *Paradise Lost*. Language is a man-made instrument. It contains a rich heritage of human usage— but no heavenly secrets. Words for Locke are not mysterious symbols but arbitrary signs; they do not refer to hidden essences but to our ideas of things. As Johnson in the preface to the *Dictionary* bluntly summarized this new demystifying tendency, "Words are the daughters of earth."

Language was not only made by man, according to most neoclassical writers, but its present corruption—in ways having nothing to do with Babel or the Fall—is also man's responsibility. The Baconian revolution in natural science, founded on a distrust of speculative thought and on a passion for observable facts, insisted on the necessity of a new philosophical language free from the jargon of medieval scholastic dispute, which the reformers characterized as a mere wrangling about words. Thomas Sprat in *The History of the Royal Society* (1667) praised the efforts of England's second-generation Baconians to "reject all the amplifications, digressions, and swellings of style." Their aim, as he described it, was "to return back to the primitive purity, and shortness, when men deliver'd so many *things,* almost in an equal number of *words.*"[3] The "Mathematical plainness" which the Royal Society demanded from the language of science found a parallel in the plain style increasingly recommended by poets, critics, churchmen, and philosophers.

Taste, Attic or Ciceronian, was not the main issue. Linguistic reform was instead intricately related to questions of knowledge and conduct. Hobbes had traced the origin of England's Civil Wars to the misuse of words, and Locke devoted an entire book of *An Essay Concerning Human Understanding* to abuses of language. The power of language to corrupt and to disorder human understanding had become a central problem for early modern philosophy and science, and Pope in *An Essay on Man* clearly allied himself with the reformers. In an introduction to the *Essay,* called "The Design," he openly promises to avoid scholastic jargon, "terms utterly unintelligible," and he twice observes the poem's lack of "poetical ornament." In fact, Pope directly echoed the credo of the reformers when he described himself as redirecting the art of poetry "From sounds to things" (iv. 392). Yet, it is not simply a commitment to linguistic reform that shapes the distinctive language of *An Essay on Man.* Its "turn'd" discourse is directly related to Pope's literary purposes in composing a philosophical poem.

There is good evidence that Pope's contemporaries understood *An Essay on Man* as belonging to the tradition of the philosophical poem.

His enemy Lord Hervey was penetrating, if ungenerous, when he described the poem as an incoherent *"Hodge-Podge Mess of Philosophy,"* and he specifically condemned Pope for his audacity in proposing "to turn *Philosopher*."[4] Swift, writing before he knew Pope was the author, complained that *An Essay on Man* was "too Philosophical for me," and Pope wrote to Swift, while the poem was still being published serially, "Do not laugh at my gravity, but permit me to wear the beard of a philosopher, till I pull it off, and make a jest of it myself."[5]

Self-deprecating humor, like anonymity, was a protective device Pope felt required to use because of the boldness of his new venture and because of his inexperience with philosophical writing. Indeed, his normal contempt for pedants vanished suddenly when Warburton's massy defense of *An Essay on Man* shielded him from attack. "I know I meant just what you explain," Pope assured his champion in a paroxysm of insincerity, "but I did not explain my own meaning so well as you."[6] It is true that readers who approach *An Essay on Man* in search of philosophical richness or infinitely subtle reasoning will be disappointed, because Pope was incapable of the sustained conceptual thinking that distinguishes Locke and Berkeley and Hume. Yet, philosophy in the eighteenth century was not yet a discipline restricted to professional philosophers or remote from practical questions of ethics. Furthermore, the works of prose philosophers are not a fair standard against which to judge *An Essay on Man*, as Voltaire recognized, for Pope is not a philosopher but a poet speaking "as" a philosopher in verse. In this literary office he had one great predecessor who in *An Essay on Man* is never far from view.

Because Pope insisted that proper generic identification is crucial for judging poetry, the most helpful development of recent scholarship is the demonstration that Pope's primary model for *An Essay on Man* was undoubtedly Lucretius. Lucretius, as the classical prototype of the philosophical poet, supplied Pope with both specific patterns of organization and a general rhetorical tone. The occasional stridency and sustained imperiousness of Pope's style in *An Essay on Man*, unmatched in his other works, are directly related to his imitation of Lucretius. Here is how Dryden described the Lucretian manner:

> If I am not mistaken, the distinguishing character of Lucretius (I mean of his soul and genius) is a certain kind of

noble pride, and positive assertion of his opinions. He is everywhere confident of his own reason, and assuming an absolute command, not only over his vulgar reader, but even his patron Memmius. For he is always bidding him attend, as if he had the rod over him; and using a magisterial authority, while he instructs him . . . He seems to disdain all manner of replies and is so confident of his cause, that he is beforehand with his antagonists; urging for them whatever he imagined they could say, and leaving them, as he supposes, without an objection for the future. All this, too, with so much scorn and indignation, as if he were assured of the triumph, before he entered into the lists.[7]

Because imitation for Pope is always a means of emphasizing change, the similar style and tone of *An Essay on Man* also point to major differences between Pope and Lucretius. It had long been a goal of Christian apologetics to provide a "reply" to the antireligious author of *De Rerum Natura*, and Pope's ultimate purpose in imitating Lucretius is to reclaim the philosophical poem for godliness. Arthur Murphy in 1762 surely alludes to this purpose when he refers to the author of *An Essay on Man* as "a CHRISTIAN LUCRETIUS."[8] Similarity of titles sometimes suggests that *An Essay on Man* is a didactic poem belonging to the same genre as *An Essay on Criticism*. Pope's poem on criticism, however, takes as its model the *ars poetica* of Horace and Boileau. *An Essay on Man*, in deriving its main characteristics from Lucretius, locates itself within an entirely different tradition.

The influence of philosophy upon the language of *An Essay on Man* commences even before the poem itself begins. The frontispiece Pope designed—first appearing in the editions of 1745—sets the scene for philosophy by surrounding us with the standard icons of *vanitas* (see figure 1). Broken columns, shattered busts, cobwebs, skulls: these images of mutability and emptiness articulate the occasion for thought. Although Pope's opening paragraph also invokes the traditions of philosophical dialogue, especially as revived in eighteenth-century treatises as a conversation among gentlemen of leisure, the melancholy vision of death and vanity is what in *An Essay on Man* adds an unusual urgency to Pope's philosophic meditations. Montaigne had devoted an entire essay to the proposition that "to study philosophy is to learn to die," and philosophy for eighteenth-

1 Frontispiece to *An Essay on Man* (1745 edition), from a drawing by Pope.

century readers often implied, as its ultimate subject, the contemplation of death, even as dying well was considered a practical demonstration of philosophy.

The world Pope describes in *An Essay on Man* is controlled, like his frontispiece, by the presence of death and vanity. Life, Pope tells us at the outset, "can little more supply / Than just to look about us and to die" (i.3). It is in this pressing context of human mortality that the Augustan philosopher loses his normal status as a satirical figure, Man Abstracted, a creature who wanders in a fog through the alien world of matter, banging into posts, plunging into ditches, betrayed by his own body and consumed in self-destructive fantasies of arid speculation. In passages such as the elegiac description of the ages of man (ii.275–282) Pope reinforces the vision established in the frontispiece where disorder and dissolution seem the prevailing state: the past is in fragments, the present hanging on the air like a bubble, the future impenetrable. Such a setting, both visually and verbally portrayed, calls out for a central figure—a philosopher or sage—whose thought will discover the coherence so vividly absent. It invites us to contemplate, against a background of fragmentation and decay, what ideal, enduring, invisible orders may lie concealed both within and—like Pope's absent sun—beyond the margins of sight.

Philosophy not only controls the mood and setting of *An Essay on Man* but, with Pope's very first words, invites us along with the poet's companion, Bolingbroke, to enter an altered state of language and of understanding:

> Awake, my St. John! leave all meaner things
> To low ambition, and the pride of Kings.

It is clearly not the case that Bolingbroke has momentarily dozed off. Rather, awakening is a metaphor for the philosophical passage from a state of deception (however pleasant) to a knowledge of realities. Philosophy reveals a counter-world in which things disclose their true natures. From the awakened and elevated perspective of philosophy, ambition looks "low"; kingly pride is a species of meanness. It is almost as if *An Essay on Man* had opened with a formal leave-taking, a departure from the ordinary world of politics, money, and fame. We must adjust rapidly to this sudden inversion of values and to a language in which truth will often appear paradoxical. Awake, we must awaken. Confronted with these adjustments, the reader, if not schooled to expect from the poem a primer of commonplace ideas, is likely to encounter significant difficulties understanding it.


## Four Readers: A Brief Experiment

The experience of Pope's earliest readers is well worth recovering for what it can tell us about the poem and its language. Such sparse evidence is too important to ignore, especially because the first readers of *An Essay on Man* were uninfluenced by knowing who the author was or by Johnson's damaging criticism. ("Never were penury of knowledge and vulgarity of sentiment so happily disguised."[9]) Clarity—the supreme Augustan virtue—was not what contemporary readers found to praise in *An Essay on Man*. One educated reader reported, on the contrary, that the second epistle proved in many places "too hard to be understood." Swift later softened a similar observation with politeness when confessing to Pope that "in some few places I was forced to read twice." The crucial word here is *forced:* Swift doubled back not for pleasure but because the meaning had been incomplete or interrupted. A third reader, although "much pleased" with the poem, complained that he found some lines "a little dark." The poet and bookseller Robert Dodsley described his experience more bluntly. On his initial encounter with *An Essay on Man* he was, he tells us, simply "Bewilder'd."[10]

All four of these early readers described a relationship between text and reader impeded by darkness, uncertainty, incomprehension. This is puzzling evidence from the audience often claimed to have regarded *An Essay on Man* as a mirror of their deepest beliefs. The language of the poem, as Johnson also observed in his colorful denunciations, somehow created a resistance to understanding—an impediment unusual enough to draw comment from Pope's early admirers, as if an implicit contract between poet and reader had been violated. This strange reserve or darkness of *An Essay on Man* is directly related, I believe, to its character as a philosophical poem. The poem's difficulties do not resemble the problems of understanding that Pope anticipated in gentlemanly readers of *An Essay on Criticism*, who had never considered criticism a form of coherent knowledge. It is a different *kind* of resistance which *An Essay on Man* offers, a resistance having as much to do with Pope's language as with his ideas.

## Toward Defining an Aphoristic Style

*An Essay on Man*, in its density and compression, speaks in a language of aphorisms, maxims, epigrams, axioms, adages, and sententiae. Any description of the verbal surface of the poem will find these terms and concepts, hard as they sometimes are to define, indispensable. What they share is more important than their slightly different shades of meaning, which eighteenth-century usage did not always observe. All refer to a form of language very distinct from the loose, verbose, imprecise, minute, over-modified, pointless, anecdotal speech that passes for normal communication. They are forms, we might say, reserved for the expression of truth—or, more precisely, forms in which wisdom is preserved, recorded, and passed on. Their history associates them with the earliest traditions of gnomic literature, where truth identifies itself by its spareness, by its simplicity, by is elemental, unadorned purity of form. Their power lies in complete and unqualified assurance, since truth, like the fiat of Genesis, was presumed to need no assistance from ornament or persuasion. "God said, *Let Newton be!* and All was *Light.*"

In its compression, assurance, and generality, the maxim is a convenient model or symbol of the aphoristic style. It is also a literary form which Pope examined closely about the time he began composing *An Essay on Man*. In fact, the poem very likely originated in what Pope called a "Set of Maximes" written to oppose the principles of La Rochefoucauld.[11] Just as Pope turned Lucretian forms against Lucretius, he used his opponent's celebrated weapon, the maxim, in combatting La Rochefoucauld's worldly cynicism. It is true that the aphoristic style of *An Essay on Man* bears some resemblance to the pointed, witty couplets of Pope's other works. But we should also recall his intention in *An Essay on Man* to turn poetry away from "wit's false mirror." The phrase is significant: he is not simply rejecting *false* wit—as he did in *An Essay on Criticism*—but implying that *all* wit is false and deceptive. If *An Essay on Man* cannot possibly invent a completely new style, one utterly unlike the language of any other poem by Pope, it offers nonetheless a significant modification or turning—in which certain stylistic features of Pope's earlier works recede and in which others receive new prominence and new purpose. For example, paradox, which in *The Rape of the Lock* is simply one of many stylistic figures contributing to the poem's witty exposure of the beau monde, serves in *An Essay on Man* as a means of expressing an entire world-view. Such changes are easy to ignore if we concentrate on the presence of familiar Popean techniques—balance, repetition, metaphor—but fail to ask how they are employed. Pope's anonymity in publishing *An Essay on Man* was effective only because most contemporary readers could *not* identify him by his language. To appreciate the distinctiveness of the poem we must consider four specific features of what (for the sake of brevity) I will continue to call its aphoristic style.

*Pointed language.* An aphorism or maxim or epigram is always a feat of verbal dexterity. It must speak with mysterious rightness: words so perfectly chosen that they seem not chosen but found, as if we had recovered an original truth long buried in language or in human consciousness. An aphorism gives us language arranged so exactly that nothing can be altered without damaging its truth. "A meaning changes," wrote the practiced aphorist Pascal, "with the words that express it."[12] The way to destroy an aphorism is simply to rephrase it. An aphorism is language at the point where it cannot be revised—hence its irresistible fascination for such a dedicated reviser as Pope. Aphorisms are refined or modified not by revision but by the invention of new aphorisms. This imperviousness to revision is especially crucial because the linguistic exactness and unrevisable perfection of the aphorism are closely linked to its power over memory. Consider the famous line "Hope springs eternal in the human breast" (i.95). The words are more than memorable; they are apparently unforgettable. The durability of Pope's line cannot lie in meaning alone, since a paraphrase holds no such claim upon the mind; nor does it help to observe that the phrase "springs eternal" neatly reverses and plays upon the edenic formula of "eternal springs"—a phrase Pope used some fifty lines later (i.153). The fact remains that Pope's arrangement of words has achieved something like permanence in English speech, and no one can tell us why.

The memorability of aphoristic language matters to Pope because lines possessing the mysterious power to imprint themselves upon the mind also possess a rich moral utility. "We frequently fall into error and folly," wrote Samuel Johnson, "not because the true principles of action are not known, but because, for a time, they are not remembered; and he may therefore be justly numbered among the benefactors of mankind, who contracts the great rules of life into short sentences, that may be easily impressed on the memory, and taught by frequent recollection to recur habitually to the mind" (*The Rambler* no. 175). For eighteenth-century writers memory, like philosophy, was instrumental in guiding a moral life, and an aphoristic style was thus particularly appropriate for a philosophical poem. Pope, in fact, explained in "The Design" that he wrote *An Essay on Man* in verse rather than in prose because "principles, maxims, or precepts so written, both strike the reader more strongly at first, and are more easily retained by him afterwards." Notice again that, as in *An Essay on Criticism*, *Windsor-Forest*, and "Eloisa to Abelard," Pope was continually concerned with the effects of his works upon the reader. He therefore built into *An Essay on Man* a mechanism for its eventual disassembly. Pope wanted the reader to carry away fragments of *An Essay on Man* embedded unforgettably within the mind, where they could offer ready insight, guidance, and consolation. Today slivers of his language lodge themselves in the speech of people who have never read—or heard of—Pope.

*Rhetorical completeness.* The aphoristic style also has an uncanny power of closure. It specializes in statements offering a convincing intellectual and linguistic finality, as if they represent the last word, all that need be said. The aphorism is an early form of minimal art: reduced any further, its content disappears; expanded, it ceases to be aphoristic. The apparent closure of its language gives the aphorism a powerful authority, simplicity, and finality that ordinary speech and other literary styles almost never attain. Indeed, the dream of silencing, with a curt truth, the endless palaver about human complexity is doubtless one strong attraction of the aphoristic style.

Yet at the heart of almost every successful aphorism, maxim, or epigram lies a potent contradiction. The aphoristic style convinces us of a completeness it cannot ultimately deliver. Its rhetorical finality is in conflict with a logical or intellectual openness. For instance, it is deeply satisfying to encounter the great dilemmas of human life contracted into the wisdom of a pithy remark: "The proper study of Mankind is Man" (ii.2). When we analyze this statement, however, our satisfaction may decrease. Like similar aphoristic formulas in law or politics ("All men are created equal") it opens itself, by virtue of its unmodified generality, to countless legitimate questions of interpretation. Is man the *only* proper study of mankind? (What about astronomy? mathematics? economics? alchemy?) Are *all* aspects of man equally proper for study? (The narrator of *A Tale of a Tub* celebrates himself for a treatise entitled *A general History of Ears.*) Such questions cannot always be settled by an appeal to the context. In context, Pope's phrase "the proper study of mankind" is not employed to define a well-mapped field of inquiry but to create a vivid contrast between two activities: the useful pursuit of moral knowledge and the futile curiosity of metaphysics. The aphoristic style, in closing one subject, opens another.

But unanswered questions are not the only effect of rhetorical closure. Certain aphorisms tease us with questions which are, in all likelihood, unanswerable. If not unanswerable, they are surely unresolvable. For example, once we have understood the meaning of the line "Hope springs eternal in the human breast," we are no longer confronted with questions of interpretation (what do these words mean?) but with questions of philosophy (why is this so?). Why is man never content with his present state? Why, despite the dissatisfactions of the present, does man always imagine an improved future? What is the role of hope in man's moral life? The aphoristic style, rather than closing off inquiry, often raises innumerable questions it cannot possibly answer. It can offer us only the attraction of reading on—in our eternal hope of finding an aphorism to resolve our questions. Yet in most cases we analyze the text in vain. The rhetorical finality of the aphoristic style necessarily incorporates a silent incompleteness at the heart of what seem wholly comprehensive, unqualified, and conclusive statements. This brings us to a third feature.

*Inexactness and inexplicitness.* "In all pointed sentences," Johnson observes, "some degree of accuracy must be sacrificed to conciseness."[13] As a master aphorist as well as lexicographer, Johnson speaks with authority. Not only their rhetorical closure but also their conciseness opens aphorisms to additional discourse. An inexactness, according to Johnson, is inherent in the aphoristic form itself, like a tiny crack or flaw in an otherwise perfect sphere. This description of an inherently flawed perfection seems confirmed from other sources. As several great aphorists have remarked, almost every wise saying has an opposite, equally wise, to balance and to refute it, so that aphorisms generate new aphorisms in response, much as sonnets generate sonnets. Yet Johnson's observation concerning the inexactness of the aphoristic style should be slightly amended. Inexactness is a less important product of brevity than inexplicitness, although both have much the same effect. The economy of the aphorism is precisely that so little contains so much: there is a great deal more to be understood than is expressed.

Their rich inexplicitness explains in part why aphorisms are so repeatable. They never decline into clichés. A truism or cliché is utterly explicit and gives up all of its sense at a single glance. A successful aphorism, by contrast, contains an undisclosed reservoir of sense that a single reading cannot exhaust. It can withstand repetition and searching reflection in ways that a truism cannot. Here perhaps is a source of its hold on human memory. It remains an *active* agent in the life of the mind, always capable of endless renewal, like hope itself. "An aphorism that has been honestly struck off," declares Nietzsche, "cannot be deciphered simply by reading it; this is only the beginning of the work of interpretation proper, which requires a whole science of hermeneutics."[14]

*Fragmentation.* "I have many fragments which I am beginning to put together": so Pope wrote some three years before the composition of *An Essay on Man* was finally complete.[15] Unlike other poems which begin in such a piecemeal fashion, *An Essay on Man* never completely loses the fragmentary nature of its origin. As Pope's frontispiece reminds us, fragments are the natural setting of the philosophic mind. Indeed, the fragmentary character of the aphorism—isolated, compact, self-contained—had recommended it to a thinker Pope called "the greatest genius that England, or perhaps any other country, ever produced."[16] He was speaking of Francis Bacon. Bacon not only practiced the aphoristic style in his essays, which are famous for their pithiness, but he also recommended and practiced the aphorism (in a related but different form) in his scientific writing, where he directly associated it with his revolutionary program for an empirical, inductive, and progressive model of knowledge. The scientific aphorism, dating at least to the time of Hippocrates, became both instrument and symbol of the new natural philosophy.

"Aphorisms," Bacon wrote, "representing a knowledge broken, do invite men to enquire farther."[17] Two separate claims are made here for the aphorism. Not only does its fragmentation advance the progress of science by stressing the need for further inquiry (hence additional aphorisms). As a symbol of "knowledge broken," the aphorism also represents or depicts the discontinuous state of human understanding. Its incompleteness, awaiting additions and future corrections, offers an image of the everyday world, a "mighty maze" (i.6) as Pope describes it, whose pattern is too vast for ordinary understanding. Bacon, writing a century before Pope, had used much the same image for describing man's environment. "The universe to the eye of the human understanding," he observed, "is framed like a labyrinth."[18] For both Pope and Bacon, the aphorism is a form of language well suited to a world of labyrinthine perplexities, confusion, misunderstanding, fragmentation, and deception.

Pope is no pure Baconian philosopher, despite his (sometimes broken) rule of reasoning only "from what we know" (i.18). In fact, the first epistle of *An Essay on Man* proceeds to explain the divine scheme of things through an entirely un-Baconian method of deductive reasoning in which Pope simply grants or asserts the three great truths whose implications he thereafter develops: (1) that God has created the best system possible; (2) that this system is abundant and coherent; and (3) that gradation by "degree" is the specific form natural order takes (i.43–46). Pope does not attempt to "prove" these three original propositions, as many readers mistakenly believe, but only, as Warburton observes, "to illustrate and inforce" them.[19]

Pope's opening lines inform us unambiguously that the mighty maze is not without a plan. Yet, too often we overemphasize the presence of order and system in *An Essay on Man* and ignore the poem's equal interest in fragmentation. Earlier generations of critics were inclined to believe that incoherence, rather than system, was the defining feature of Pope's thought. Thomas De Quincey, for example, argued that "the *Essay on Man* sins chiefly by want of central principle, and by want therefore of all coherency amongst the separate thoughts." He is incorrect, of course, but not unobservant, for his judgment recognizes the fragmentation inherent in the poem. This judiciousness is also reflected in De Quincey's additional comments on *An Essay on Man*. "But," he continued, "taken *as* separate thoughts, viewed in the light of fragments and brilliant aphorisms, the majority of the passages have a mode of truth; not of truth central and coherent, but of truth angular and splintered."[20]

The coherence of Pope's vision in *An Essay on Man* is inseparable from a language that expresses its insights in an extremely angular and splintered style. The language of the poem reflects Pope's belief that mankind encounters moral and ethical truths much as the Baconian scientist encounters the laws of nature: in bits and pieces. For generations of moralists from Solomon to Erasmus, the aphorism provided a means for reassembling the components of a unified moral vision now lost and scattered. It is this same dismemberment of truth that Milton in *Areopagitica* (1644) expressed through the myth of Osiris, whose body was hacked and scattered by the Egyptian Typhon: "From that time ever since, the sad friends of Truth, such as durst appear, imitating the carefull search that *Isis* made for the mangl'd body of *Osiris*, went up and down gathering up limb by limb still as they could find them."[21] The reader's task in *An Essay on Man* resembles the mission of Isis, slowly assembling the pieces of a dispersed and disjointed completeness. Pope assures us that the cosmic order we seek truly exists, and his poem (in ways De Quincey did not perceive) certainly guides us toward a vision of truth central and coherent. But, at least for some representative eighteenth-century readers, the language of the poem seemed to delay or to resist the satisfactions of order. Nor was such resistance simply a feature of Pope's aphoristic style. It extended as well to the paradoxical vision of the poem.

## The Language of Paradox

In correcting De Quincey's one-sided account, modern scholars have rightly emphasized the presence of order and coherence in *An Essay on Man*. It is also becoming clear, however, that in Pope's outlook order is consistent with and inseparable from the fragmentation of its parts. As Dustin H. Griffin summarizes this view, "The vision of the *Essay on Man* is double: the world is both pattern and puzzle, both accessible to our understanding and inaccessible."[22] Like the vision it describes, this statement is deeply paradoxical, and paradox is the poem's governing trope, not merely a stylistic feature. Pope moves beyond the position of the Royal Society that figurative language is necessarily deceptive. For Pope, paradox is his way not of recommending or embellishing truth but of recognizing and expressing it. *An Essay on Man* simply cannot express its central principles if denied access to the figure of paradox.

"Paradoxes," John Dunton asserts on the first page of *Athenian Sport: or, Two Thousand Paradoxes Merrily Argued, To Amuse and Divert the Age* (1707), "are Things which seem strange, absurd, and contrary to the Common Opinion."[23] This definition follows earlier usage in emphasizing the etymological contrast between paradox and orthodoxy (from the Greek: *ortho*, right, and *doxa*, opinion). Dunton's subtitle, however, mentions a crucial feature of paradox that his prose definition omits: the presence of reason or argument. Eighteenth-century paradoxes were not simply freaks of thought, alien and unconventional, but wrapped their strangeness in the prestige of rationality. Thus some of Dunton's more frivolous paradoxes require enormous investments of perverse ingenuity to make the absurd appear perfectly reasonable. For example: "In Praise of a COW's TAIL"; "That Content is the greatest Misery"; or—a proposition worthy of *The Dunciad*—"That Nature is our Worst Guide." This level of frivolity is characteristic of Dunton, but not all paradoxes can be dismissed as jokes or exercises in rhetorical ingenuity. Paradox—sometimes comically, sometimes seriously—challenges the systems which ordinarily regulate human understanding, especially the informal systems of language and common sense. Its challenge is aimed not at destroying the orthodox system but at identifying its loopholes, flaws, and blindspots. (This is what Hugh Kenner means in writing that paradox might be considered "the science of gaps."[24]) When we recognize the gaps and blindspots as locating truths an orthodox system simply cannot contain without self-contradiction, we are prepared to acknowledge what the modern philosopher W. V. Quine calls "veridical" (or truth-telling) paradoxes.[25] Veridical paradoxes, unlike Dunton's exercises in perverse rationality, are never merely frivolous, shocking, deceptive, or nonsensical, because, despite their strangeness, they express contradictions inherent in the nature of things.

The clearest example of veridical paradox in *An Essay on Man* is man himself. The proper study of mankind turns out to be a creature whose native element is apparent self-contradiction:

> Created half to rise, and half to fall;
> Great lord of all things, yet a prey to all;
> Sole judge of Truth, in endless Error hurl'd:
> The glory, jest, and riddle of the world! (ii.15–18)

It is the final term *riddle*—the common eighteenth-century synonym for paradox—which sums up the nature of man. This famous passage employs the language of paradox not to create pleasing verbal patterns or "poetical ornament" but to describe a being compounded of puzzling internal oppositions: rising/falling, lord/prey, error/truth, glory/jest. Each term of the opposition profoundly modifies its counterpart, and paradox is the only figure of speech flexible enough to encompass such radical disjunction. Yet man is subject not just to the paradox of his own nature. His internal oppositions—as he hangs in constant doubt whether "to deem himself a God, or Beast" (ii.9) —also reflect man's intermediate position within the vast extremes of the divine creation:

> Natures aethereal, human, angel, man,
> Beast, bird, fish, insect! what no eye can see,
> No glass can reach! from Infinite to thee,
> From thee to Nothing!                    (i.238–241)

Johnson later argued vigorously that the age-old Great Chain of Being, which Pope describes here, could not possibly exist. ("The highest being not infinite, must be, as has been often observed, at an infinite distance below infinity."[26]) Pope, though, does not deny but rather exploits the paradoxical nature of a gradation extending from infinity to nothingness. Man's middle state is difficult, in Pope's account, precisely because he occupies a position between unknown opposites, surrounded by darkness, subject to the contradictions of his own nature. For such a creature, the laws of paradox are purely descriptive.

In *An Essay on Man* paradox does not just help to illuminate man's position in the world; it also provides a cosmic principle of order— the central unifying force—that imparts coherence to Pope's universe. This unifying force is the classical principle of world harmony known as *concordia discors*, and in expounding it Pope's ultimate and controlling argument is that order prevails where disorder would seem to achieve its masterpiece: in the heart of ceaseless conflict.[27] A more paradoxical claim would be hard to construct, yet this is the foundation of Pope's argument in *An Essay on Man*. Undermine this foundation and the poem collapses. It would be possible, in fact, to find in almost every major proposition of *An Essay on Man* an illustration or extension of its underlying paradoxical doctrine: "ALL subsists by elemental strife" (i.169).

The function of paradox in *An Essay on Man* is not limited to expressing or representing doctrine. Equally important is the affective function of paradox in shaping the reader's experience. Thus John Dunton explains that the function of paradox is "to rouze and awaken the Reason of Men asleep, into a *Thinking and Philosophical Temper*."[28] Dunton's metaphor recalls Pope's opening exclamation to

## Alexander Pope

Bolingbroke and suggests why paradox would be particularly appropriate to a philosophical poem. As many philosophers have attested, paradoxes seem to mesmerize us, as if they have a unique power over our attention. A paradox is a maze or labyrinth in which the mind can wander ceaselessly, and a poem whose governing trope is paradox makes unusual demands on the reader. An attentive reader simply cannot read *An Essay on Man* as Swift apparently wished to read it—once straight through, as if reading and understanding were equivalent. For Pope, a philosophical poem forces the reader to pause for thought, to wonder what could be meant, to ponder undisclosed reserves of sense, at times to double back for reassurance and correction.

Paradox, in compelling such rereading and reflection, perfectly complements the inexplicitness and brevity of the aphoristic style. Indeed, the English translator of La Rochefoucauld explained at some length that the "close stile" of maxims depends upon a compactness that does not often yield to immediate understanding: "For this Reason it is, that the Reader ought to take time to penetrate into the full sense and force of the Words, and in his Mind to run over the whole extent of their Signification, before he proceeds to judgment."[29] Pope calculates that *An Essay on Man* will elicit from readers a twofold response: first, surprise at the striking initial impact of its splintered aphoristic truths, and second, thoughtfulness from the subsequent reflection and rereading necessary to transform obscurity, compression, incompleteness—and, above all, paradox—into sense and knowledge.

How might the poem's paradoxical, aphoristic style be related to the process of rereading and reflection? The following four lines appear as the conclusion to the first epistle and summarize its general argument:

> All Nature is but Art, unknown to thee;
> All Chance, Direction, which thou canst not see;
> All Discord, Harmony, not understood;
> All partial Evil, universal Good.                    (i.289–292)

In this passage Pope uses the most basic instrument of philosophical language, the definition. All $x$ is $y$. The absence of any "poetical ornament" brings the style close to what Thomas Sprat might have admired as "Mathematical plainness." Pope's equations, however, conceal in their plainness an obvious paradox. Traditional opposites are somehow transformed into identities: Nature is Art, Chance is Direction, Discord is Harmony. This paradox is not resolved by the modifications Pope attaches to it, for we are still confronted with the enigmatic concepts of an Unknown Art, an Invisible Direction, an Unintelligible Harmony. The effect of Pope's modifying phrases is to edge his statements from total contradiction (black is white) to apparent nonsense (black is an unknown shade of white). The statements are not wholly meaningless but rather, as John Dunton might describe them, strange, absurd, or contrary to the general opinion. They offer the puzzling resistance to understanding that invites us to question them further.

Focus on a single line: "All Discord, Harmony, not understood." What does this simple statement mean? The elusiveness of Pope's meaning may be judged by the differing interpretations the line has occasioned. The words allow for at least three different ways of understanding it. The first and most familiar interpretation posits a dualistic model of appearance and reality. A. R. Humphreys is unhesitating: "Pope's phrase—'All Discord, Harmony, not understood'—means . . . that discord is only apparent, harmony is the reality."[30] A second model for interpretation, however, is offered in the very next line of *An Essay on Man:* the relation of part to whole. Discord in this reading is not a mere appearance or illusion—something *not* real—but is instead an actual, present, enduring *component* of reality. Discord is the part, Harmony the whole. The third sense can be understood as the literal or musical model. It does not propose divisions—between appearance and reality, between part and whole—but reads the line to mean exactly what it says: that Discord and Harmony are identical. Harmony in this version is entirely made up of discord, just as music is composed of its differing sounds. Discord subtracted from Harmony leaves nothing.

Which explanation is correct? This is not among the occasions when criticism can congratulate itself for the rich multiplication of possible readings. Each of the three explanations considerably alters our understanding of the poem's central doctrine. Choice is necessary. The apparent lucidity, explicitness, and maximlike assurance of Pope's language have brought us, as Nietzsche had predicted, to an impasse where interpretation must summon all of its science.

Alexander Pope

## A Digression on Syntax

*An Essay on Man* is full not only of puzzling statements but also of questions and exclamations. These two syntactic forms, which govern not just the punctuation of the poem but the experience of the reader as well, can be considered inverse relations: a question is an inverted exclamation, an exclamation is an inverted question. One asks, one tells; one doubts, one commands. Given the uncertainties of eighteenth-century punctuation, we may not always be sure whether a particular statement is questioning or exclaiming or doing both at once—the question mark for Pope sometimes serves as a mild exclamation. It is Folly who asks many of the questions in *An Essay on Man* and who often receives short, scornful statements in response: "Why has not Man a microscopic eye?/For this plain reason, Man is not a Fly" (i.193–194). But plain reasons are not always available when the questions get harder, and sometimes it is Wisdom who must take up questioning in the manner of Jehovah to Job: "All this dread ORDER break—for whom? for thee?" (i.257). The continual movement from question to exclamation to question encourages a process of reading punctuated by disruption and discontinuities, much as in "Eloisa to Abelard" the abrupt movement between questions and exclamations reflects the disjointedness of Eloisa's thought. New voices—or at least radically new inflections—seem constantly breaking into *An Essay on Man*, disrupting a smooth development of ideas. Like aphorisms and paradox, Pope's syntax works to undermine a passive or stable relation between reader and text. Pope asks for readers who are always checking themselves against what they read, pausing for thought and for second thoughts, searching the text and subjecting it to scrutiny. The unreflective habit of mind is what the poem seeks to disrupt from the moment of its opening exclamation. How are we to decide the meaning of a line which can be interpreted in three different ways?

## The Two Discords: Paradox into Sense

The paradoxical statement "All Discord, Harmony, not understood" must be puzzled out through a process in which our sense of the whole poem, not merely the surrounding lines, comes into play. The statement's meaning is determined by its place within an entire vision—a vision to which it decisively contributes. This paradoxical situation is a variant of the well-known hermeneutic circle: the part is dependent for its full meaning upon its place within the whole, the whole presupposes a prior understanding of the parts. Such potential circularity may explain why Pope spurns the tradition in philosophy which insisted on beginning by defining terms. (In 1651 Hobbes had recommended and practiced this Euclidian method in his *Leviathan.*) The circular interdependence of part and whole belongs not only to the doctrine but also to the poetics of *An Essay on Man.* The word *discord*, it turns out, appears only once in the poem. Uncertainty simply increases when we turn to eighteenth-century dictionaries for assistance, because, unfortunately, they provide for *discord* two widely different meanings.

The two meanings can be traced back at least as far as Hesiod, who tells the story of two sisters both named Eris, or Strife. The younger sister is savage and warlike, representing all that is violent, uncivilized, and bloodthirsty in human nature. It is this younger Discord whom Pope includes among the destructive powers exiled by Peace at the conclusion of *Windsor-Forest* (ll. 413–414). The exile, as it happens, is brief, since it is the nature of exiles to return, and *An Essay on Man* devotes ample space to describing the violence, superstition, and tyranny which have disfigured human history. Yet, while the younger Discord is filling the world with violence, her sister, also named Discord, is offering what Hesiod calls "a blessing to mortals."[31] In Hesiod's account the elder Discord is something like a principle of friendly competition, a creative strife, like commerce in *Windsor-Forest*. *An Essay on Man* openly celebrates the harmonizing power of commerce, which transforms foes into friends (ii.205–206), and Pope finds in such harmonizing discord a description of political order as well. The strife of competing self-interests contributes to a more general concord:

'Till jarring int'rests of themselves create
Th'according music of a well-mix'd State.
Such is the World's great harmony, that springs
From Order, Union, full Consent of Things!     (iii.293–296)

Like Hesiod's myth, *An Essay on Man* offers us two images of discord. There is the warlike Discord, which expresses man's worst possibilities for violence. And there is the benevolent Discord, which, in its reconciliation of "jarring int'rests," is identical with "the World's great harmony." Discord both is and is not harmony.

The line "All Discord, Harmony, not understood" is engaged in reconciling two perspectives, two modes of vision, in a single phrase. Viewed from man's ordinary perspective, the world reveals nothing but fragmentation and discord. Viewed from the awakening perspective of philosophy, the fragments contribute to an awesome harmony and wholeness. Although it has been fashionable since the heyday of Victorian doubt to ridicule Pope's belief in a universal order, his vision of cosmic unity now finds unexpected support from the idea of relativity in physics. The truth or falsity of Pope's doctrine, however, is not the issue here. What matters is how he expresses his vision and beliefs with a language that makes unusual demands on the reader. It is a language that seeks to awaken us with its strangeness and to reconcile—even within a single phrase—opposing perspectives.

These purposes alone account for a certain difficulty or darkness. Yet, one further aspect of Pope's language needs to be explored, for the darkness of *An Essay on Man* undergoes an unusual change as one rereads the poem. In the case of veridical or truth-telling paradoxes—in contrast to merely ingenious riddles or entertaining nonsense—the better we understand them, the less paradoxical they seem. That is, much of the reader's initial estrangement in *An Essay on Man* depends on the clash of opposing perspectives. Once these opposing perspectives have been reconciled, the strangeness of Pope's assertions begins to diminish. What starts as paradox concludes as sense.

In the third epistle of *An Essay on Man* is a stirring description of the world as it appears to the "awakened" eye of philosophy:

> Look round our World; behold the chain of Love
> Combining all below and all above.
> See plastic Nature working to this end,
> The single atoms each to other tend,
> Attract, attracted to, the next in place
> Form'd and impell'd its neighbour to embrace.
> See Matter next, with various life endu'd,
> Press to one centre still, the gen'ral Good.
> See dying vegetables life sustain,
> See life dissolving vegetate again:

All forms that perish other forms supply,
(By turns we catch the vital breath, and die)
Like bubbles on the sea of Matter born,
They rise, they break, and to that sea return.
Nothing is foreign: Parts relate to whole;
One all-extending, all-preserving Soul
Connects each being, greatest with the least;
Made Beast in aid of Man, and Man of Beast;
All serv'd, all serving! nothing stands alone;
The chain holds on, and where it ends, unknown.     (iii.7–26)

This sublime vision of cosmic unity resembles the prospect view of descriptive poetry, which it perhaps imitates with its injunctions to "look" and "see." It is instructive, however, to compare this awakened vision with the picture of fragmentation and ruin which Pope provides in his frontispiece. Both, we must recognize, describe the same world. Indeed, what Pope exhorts us to "see" from the heightened perspective of philosophy is invisible to our normal sight. We see the world anew in the sense that we understand it differently. But, in understanding the world differently, of course, we also see it in a new way: its fragments are no longer random facts or Baconian splinters of experience but parts which "relate to" and refer to a magnificent whole. Our vision of the whole, in short, decisively transforms our perception and understanding of the individual parts. The broken and disorderly world we inhabit cannot look the same. In one sense, nothing has changed: wars, plagues, earthquakes, tyranny, injustice, crime, and impiety all continue to disfigure the scene of man with suffering. Yet, to the awakened vision of philosophy, such discord has been suddenly transformed. The transformation of a world in which nothing has changed—the great intellectual feat of *An Essay on Man*—returns us unavoidably to the subject of paradox.

Paradox contains a fascinating power of self-transformation. Like certain chemical compounds that tend to break down into simpler forms, paradoxes sometimes undo themselves, lose their strangeness, and pass into the opposing state of orthodoxy. For many years, for example, men referred to the extravagant notion of a sun-centered universe as the "Copernican paradox"—until the paradox was transformed into truth. Hamlet, meditating upon the bitter reflection that beauty makes a bawd of honesty, says: "This was sometime [formerly] a paradox, but now the time gives it proof" (III.i.114–115).

# Alexander Pope

Paradox in such instances ages into orthodoxy, as time transforms strangeness into sense. Such unstable paradoxes represent a situation not where the truth *is* and *remains* paradoxical—but where *formerly* or *apparently* paradoxical statements become orthodox truths.

In its vision and argument, *An Essay on Man* is characterized by the constant transformation or breakdown of paradox into sense. We come to accept as plain statements of fact assertions which, in most other contexts, would shock us by their oddity or falsehood. Pope's final lines well illustrate this transformation, for they restate doctrine with such axiomatic assurance that we must work to remind ourselves that the statements are not self-evident. To the contrary, the poem has exposed us to a continual persuasion designed to *convince* us of their validity. Here, from the final lines, is the summary of Pope's argument. He claims to have done the following:

> Shew'd erring Pride, WHATEVER IS, IS RIGHT;
> That REASON, PASSION, answer one great aim;
> That true SELF-LOVE and SOCIAL are the same;
> That VIRTUE only makes our Bliss below;
> And all our Knowledge is, OURSELVES TO KNOW.

(iv.394–398)

This is surely a poetry of statement—but what *kind* of statements are they? The history of the maxim "WHATEVER IS, IS RIGHT" shows that many people find it not only not self-evident but self-evidently false.

We can prove, of course, that such people do not understand the theology of *An Essay on Man*—or at least they reject Pope's arguments. But the demonstration is a pointless victory for scholarship, since it ignores what is most remarkable about Pope's language. He has somehow brought his "awakened" readers to accept as plain maxims and simple truths statements whose literal meaning is false to general human experience. George Barnwell in *The London Merchant* (1731) did not find that reason and passion "answer one great aim." His passion for the satanic Mrs. Millwood led directly to the gallows. Is it true that virtue alone makes us happy? No economic system this side of Houyhnhnm-land could survive such an assumption. Are private interest and public good always "the same"? The Opposition to Walpole thought otherwise. There is, in fact, a wonderful wrongness about Pope's entire conclusion if the statements are read without the awakened vision of philosophy. Who, unawakened, would not regard them as strange, absurd, or contrary to the general opinion? The awakened reader, however, understands Pope's language in a way which deprives it of its potentially paradoxical status. "It was said of *Socrates*," wrote Addison in *The Spectator*, "that he brought Philosophy down from Heaven, to inhabit among Men; and I shall be ambitious to have it said of me, that I have brought Philosophy out of Closets and Libraries, Schools and Colleges, to dwell in Clubs and Assemblies, at Tea-Tables, and in Coffee-Houses" (no. 10). *An Essay on Man* might be said to have attempted the great Augustan miracle of reconciling philosophy to the language of sense. It is a process which did not leave Pope's earliest readers unchanged.

Tributes from Pope's immediate contemporaries stressed the emotional and intellectual changes that accompanied their process of reading *An Essay on Man*. One contemporary reader addressed the anonymous author of the poem in the following style:

> Hail, then, instructing bard (whoe'er thou art)
> That *opens thus our eyes* and *clears our heart!*[32]

This imagery of opening the eyes and clearing the heart reports internal changes in the reader that are particularly appropriate to Pope's awakening efforts in the poem. Such a transformation of feeling and vision cannot be achieved merely by versified doctrines, and other contemporary readers have attested to the poem's power. Robert Dodsley offers a vivid account of the access to new vision that *An Essay on Man* provides. First he describes his experience of utter bewilderment—then continues his address to the poet:

> But reading more attentive, soon I found,
> The Diction nervous, and the Doctrine sound.
> Saw Man, a Part of that stupendous Whole,
> *Whose Body Nature is, and God the Soul.*
> Saw in the Scale of Things his middle State,
> And all his Powers adapted just to That.
> Saw Reason, Passion, Weakness, how of use,
> How all to Good, to Happiness conduce.
> Saw my own Weakness, thy superior Power,
> And still the more I read, admire the more.[33]

For Dodsley the poem is far more than a compendium of versified doctrine. It is the source of an experience which leads from darkness and confusion to total comprehension. His account, in which a "more attentive" rereading leads to a final certainty, is oddly similar to the experience of an Irish reader of *An Essay on Man* that Swift recounted to Pope. Wrote Swift: "On the first reading those Essays, he was much pleased, but found some lines a little dark; On the second most of them cleared up, & his pleasure increased; On the third he had no doubt remained, & then he admired the whole."[34] Here, repeated reading is not potentially endless, a source of perpetually new insights, but it leads one to attain a state of transformation after which understanding remains constant. Once the vision has been attained, it seems, everything suddenly makes complete sense.

There is no way now to test or recreate the experiences of Pope's earliest readers. Yet the surviving reports offer us a way to understand *An Essay on Man* that should not be automatically rejected simply because it conflicts with modern traditions of reading. Pope's early readers were in much the same condition as the central figure of his frontispiece, surrounded by the fragments, vanity, and disorder of ordinary understanding. It is the initial function of Pope's language not only to inform but also to awaken us. Indeed, no other poem in Pope's canon keeps us so continuously off balance. Its array of truths angular and splintered, paradoxes stable and unstable, aphorisms, exclamations, questions, arguments, satire, homily, sarcasm, commands, sublimity, and jokes all work to stimulate us into hard thinking. The poem is only more strange for accomplishing all this in an unexotic, plain diction that seems to promise immediate understanding.

To read the poem is to work toward a vision elevated and comprehensive enough to recognize the existence of God's vast, intricate, and harmonious order—not only beyond but *within* the fragments of a broken world. Once that vision has been achieved, through the work of rereading and reflection, neither Pope's earliest readers nor the poem they read could remain unaltered. If we can recover and understand that moment in the history of reading, we not only help to account for the impact of *An Essay on Man* on Pope's contemporaries but also create a fresh perspective from which to examine the poem's language. We will certainly be prepared to understand in Pope's request to his friend John Caryll, concerning a recently published, anonymous poem entitled *An Essay on Man*, something more than normal vanity and deviousness. "I want to know your opinion of it," he explained, adding the unusual proviso, "after twice or thrice reading."[35]

# ❧ VII

## Property, Character, and Money in the *Moral Essays*

There is nothing which so generally strikes the imagination, and engages the affections of mankind, as the right of property; or that sole and despotic dominion which one man claims and exercises over the external things of the world, in total exclusion of the right of any other individual in the universe.

—Blackstone

"HERE AM I, like Socrates, distributing my morality among my friends, just as I am dying."[1] Pope spoke these words—consciously ironic and gently self-deprecating, yet not wholly innocent of pride—several weeks before his death, in reference to a private edition of the *Moral Essays*, which he was distributing as a gift to friends.[2] The gift was well chosen. Pope's small volume, which now survives in only a few rare copies, is among the treasures of writings on ethics and morals. Morality for Pope did not refer to the tiresome business of telling other people how to behave. For him, as for Socrates, it involved the widest possible reference to what we might call the ethical life. In exploring the varieties of virtue and folly in the *Moral Essays*, Pope offers clear indications that his moral vision is based not on religious dogma or on social theory, but on the perception that certain ways of living are ultimately self-destructive. Immorality for Pope is the process by which character participates in its own undoing. Moral conduct is quite simply the art of living well.

The art of living well is for Pope inseparable from a steady commitment to self-knowledge. "Know then thyself," advises the speaker of *An Essay on Man* (ii.1), repeating the Delphic commandment to which Socrates had dedicated his life. Socratic or classical self-knowledge, of course, differs greatly from modern introspection. It does not command that we scrutinize our social background, family ties, sexual experience, or psychic conflicts. Classical self-knowledge begins not with the individual but with mankind. It assumes that to know ourselves we must first know what it means to be human.

Knowing what it means to be human is not for Pope a prelude to understanding and appreciating personal idiosyncrasies. Self-knowledge is instead a precondition of the ethical life, whose enemy so often lies within. Notice how often in Pope's work vice appears not only destructive and egocentric but also unconscious of its own nature, unable to "know" itself. For Pope, therefore, the quest for self-knowledge is necessarily directed outward, toward the shared features of human nature that underlie all moral action, rather than focused inward upon personal eccentricities. The mysterious and puzzling individuality of specific characters is not something Pope ignores. To the contrary, he delights in describing the unique combination of traits that makes every character distinctive. Yet, such distinctiveness for Pope always illustrates or confirms certain general laws that, in his view, govern human behavior. The great aim of classical moralists like Pope is not to promulgate rules of behavior—the wise will govern their own conduct—but to discover the principles of ethics and of human nature that make intelligent self-mastery possible. Pope's "morality," concentrated in the four remarkable poems making up the posthumously titled *Moral Essays*, belongs to this ancient and inexhaustible project of humanistic thought.

I consider the *Moral Essays* a single, cohesive work which, much like Blake's *Songs Of Innocence and Of Experience*, achieves a significance and power beyond the scope of its individual poems alone. The private edition Pope distributed among his friends certainly implies that he regarded the four verse epistles—each first published separately—as creating together a single, complete work. (*An Essay on Man* is similarly constructed of four separately published epistles.) Pope was referring specifically to the *Moral Essays* when he declared that his individual poems were not self-contained but—"like the works of Nature"—belong to a larger system: "much more to be liked and understood when consider'd in the relation they bear with each other, than when ignorantly look'd upon one by one."[3] Modern scholars have tended to disregard Pope's admonition and usually discuss the four epistles separately. Undoubtedly this procedure has advantages, for the *Moral Essays* (like *An Essay on Criticism*) can easily seem disconnected or unorganized. Pope adds to our sense of discontinuity in the *Moral Essays* by extending the practice initiated in *The Dunciad* of supplying long, interruptive footnotes packed with contemporary details. He teases our curiosity (or tries our patience) by mixing satiric descriptions of living people with more general, composite, fictive portraits. Finally, the poems contain some of the most difficult lines Pope ever wrote, as well as extensive passages that approach the clarity and directness of painting. It is not enough to explain these mixtures by observing that *satura* (the Latin root of *satire*) refers to a farrago or medley. In understanding the *Moral Essays*, we must confront the question of what "relation" draws together Pope's four separate studies of character and riches into a profound and cohesive vision of human moral life.

## Character and Capital

The fundamental connection among the four epistles of the *Moral Essays* is complex but clear. The originality of the composite poem derives from Pope's implicit insistence that human character and the art of living well must henceforth be understood within the boundaries of an economic system. This understanding represents a major change of emphasis in Pope's work—a perspective which considerably differs from his previous treatment of character and wealth. Avarice and prodigality, the central vices attacked in the *Moral Essays*, of course boast a timeless ancestry. Yet, Pope's unusual emphasis in his late epistles and satires on the subject of riches—"Why all this of Av'rice?" asks one of his adversarial voices[4]—is not merely the reworking of familiar literary themes. In the *Moral Essays* Pope depicts man as prey to the immemorial temptations of riches within a setting that bears little resemblance to earlier feudal or precapitalistic economies. Extravagance is no longer an eternal vice of courts, nor avarice the sin of misers in all ages. The dangers of wealth and the presence of folly are not what is new in the *Moral Essays*, but Pope's representation of the changed economic system within which money circulates and character is corrupted.

Mankind in the *Moral Essays* exists within a new world of property and finance that had developed with astonishing speed in the years after Pope's birth. The precariousness of this new financial world became obvious only following the South Sea Bubble in 1720, but the systemic changes reflected in the South Sea scheme had their origin decades earlier. The subject of finance, in fact, occupied some of the greatest thinkers of the age. Sir Isaac Newton had served as Surveyor of the Mint. Locke and Hume wrote lengthy discourses on the theory of trade and money. "The feeling that a science of economics existed apparently began to come upon Englishmen," writes a modern scholar, "during the first decade or two of the eighteenth century."[5] The long-established Tudor "moral economy"—in which landlord and tenant were bound together in reciprocal assistance, with charity a tenant's right and landlord's duty that eased the hardship resulting from poor harvests—was rapidly being displaced by the new bourgeois commercial order for which London was both center and symbol. So vast were the alterations in English economic life between 1688 and 1756—a period beginning with the year of Pope's birth—that they have been characterized as constituting nothing less than a "financial revolution."[6]

The financial revolution was less visible in rural areas than in London. London in 1700—with a population over half a million, with an appalling death rate, and with its dying replaced daily by fresh recruits from the countryside—was some fifteen times larger than its nearest rival in size, Bristol. It was also the financial capital. For Pope the voice of London uttered a single and repetitious cry: "Get Mony, Mony still!"[7] The creation and acquisition of wealth through unprecedented developments in public credit was at the heart of the new economic order that Augustan writers such as Swift, Gay, and Pope observe with growing dismay. This explosion of credit can be marked by the founding of the Bank of England in 1694. The bank provided better security and services than did the goldsmiths who previously handled most financial transactions; but convenience was not why it was founded. It was created mainly for the purpose of lending its assets to the Whig government of William III, which badly needed funds. Continual warfare with France for almost a quarter of a century between 1689 and 1714 left an unpayable debt that mounted yearly. In 1695 the national debt stood at the then awesome amount of £8.4 million. By 1715 it had increased more than fourfold, to £37.4 million, owed not only to the bank but to the East India Company and to the recently chartered South Sea Company. The sudden growth of these giant joint-stock companies found its parallel in the development of markets for trading the paper securities. A writer in 1749 noted that an entire financial subculture seemed to have developed during the past fifty years: "agents, factors, brokers, insurers, bankers, negotiators, discounters, subscribers, contractors, remitters, ticket-mongers, stock-jobbers, and . . . a great variety of other dealers in money, the names of whose employments were wholly unknown to our forefathers."[8]  Stock-jobbers and money-men (as they were called) were such regular targets in the satire of Swift and Pope that they can seem merely fictional. Yet, although no professional market for stocks existed in England before the 1690s, by 1697 stock-jobbers had grown troublesome enough to provoke a statute limiting the profession, on the grounds that "their number had very much increased during the few preceding years and were daily multiplying."[9] Such regulations had little effect.

The decline of the Tudor "moral economy" and its replacement by the cash nexus of England's new financial revolution is the indirect subject of the "Cotta" episode in Pope's *Moral Essays*. The elder Cotta's estate stands as in violation of the moral and social community celebrated by Ben Jonson, Thomas Carew, and Robert Herrick in their well-known "country-house" poems. Cotta's estate reflects more than its owner's avarice. It describes an entire economic order in transition—Pope would call it "decay"—where former rights and duties are being neglected:

> No rafter'd roofs with dance and tabor sound,
> No noontide-bell invites the country round;
> Tenants with sighs the smoakless tow'rs survey,
> And turn th' unwilling steeds another way.     (iii.191–194)

This picture of the absence of traditional economic and social relations is succeeded by the image of Old Cotta's heir, who is wasting his father's hoarded wealth on senseless extravagances. Ancestral property is transformed into cash as woods are cut and lands sold. The moral economy Old Cotta had neglected, his son now wholly disavows. In short, a way of life has vanished—but not *completely*. Pope can still find, in his friend Lord Bathurst or in the Man of Ross, exemplars of the old order who merit praise. But such exemplary figures are isolated and scarce, and their isolation only emphasizes the social and economic change they cannot successfully oppose. In such figures Pope contemplates not so much the hardiness of tradition as the acceleration of loss. They represent the painful moment when we can still see what we are losing:

> There, English Bounty yet a-while may stand,
> And Honour linger ere it leaves the land. (iii.247–248)

The new science of economics had as its first task the description of an economy in rapid transition.

Besides London, a symbol for Pope of the new economic order represented by stock-jobbers and money-men was the catastrophic South Sea Bubble (1720). Even some ten years later, when the first epistle of the *Moral Essays* was published, the South Sea Bubble still proved a lively subject for political skirmishing, since it was not only an unforgettable disaster but also the immediate occasion of Robert Walpole's rise to power.[10] Pope's direct and indirect references to the Bubble in the *Moral Essays* may have contributed something to the ongoing attempts of the Opposition to maneuver against Walpole, but the references belong mainly to his sustained attack upon the new economic order—so skillfully and corruptly manipulated by Walpole as First Lord of the Treasury. This attack was carried not by Pope's verse alone, but spilled over into his lengthy footnotes. These annotations are an integral part of the poem, because there contemporary names and facts take on a moral force. For example, in rejecting the Puritan doctrine that riches are a token of divine favor, Pope documents the indiscriminateness of wealth in a Spenserian catalogue of resonant names. Money, he points out, shows no particular respect for virtue:

> Giv'n to the Fool, the Mad, the Vain, the Evil,
> To Ward, to Waters, Chartres, and the Devil. (iii.19–20)

It is in his annotations that Pope begins to develop the significance of these once-notorious and now-obscure names.

In Pope's descent from general to particular, the names John Ward, Francis Chartres, and Peter Waters (or, in its interchangeable spelling, Peter Walter) are not specific examples of the mad, the foolish, and the vain, as if the couplet observed an exact parallelism. Corruption is not so tidy; it cannot be neatly summarized or contained in a single noun, and thus Pope's verse branches out into a vast annotation which extends far beyond the identifying purposes of a biographical footnote. John Ward, Pope informs us, was a member of Parliament suspected of "joining in a conveyance with Sir John Blunt, to secrete fifty thousand pounds of that Director's Estate, forfeited to the South Sea Company by Act of Parliament." Blunt, of course, was the former director of the South Sea Company—penalized for his misdeeds by the seizure of his estate—who enters the poem one hundred lines later, where he too receives detailed annotation (iii.135). As in his description of Blunt, Pope uses numbers as well as names to lend weight to his moral judgments, and he spares us few details of the financial odyssey of John Ward: "At his standing in the Pillory he was *worth above two hundred thousand pounds;* at his commitment to Prison, he was *worth one hundred and fifty thousand,* but has been since so far diminished in his reputation, as to be thought a *worse man* by *fifty or sixty thousand.*" The irony is somewhat oppressively managed, but Pope succeeds in transforming the names of Ward and Blunt into ciphers that call into question the entire concept of worth, as did the new financial order that they represented. In a social world where money and credit could purchase land and status, the shifting value of shares in the South Sea Company suggests a corresponding instability in reputations and individual lives. In January 1720 the price of South Sea stock stood at £128; in May it was £500; in August £1000 per share. One month later a share of South Sea stock had crashed to a price of £190.

The South Sea Bubble is an irresistible symbol of the new monied order for Pope because he is attacking not wealth itself but certain specific *sources* and *uses* of wealth. The South Sea project represents an economy in which land had been replaced by speculation and by public opinion as the measure of value. "Our estate is an imaginary one only," Pope wrote in a letter of 1720 referring to the modest investment he made with Martha and Theresa Blount in South Sea stock: "One day we were worth two or three thousand, and the next not above 3 parts of the sum."[11] The source of such fluctuating wealth, Pope correctly implies, is illusion, passion, rumor, and credit. A similar interest in the sources or origin of wealth underlies Pope's recurrent attacks upon Francis Chartres. Chartres, like John Ward, merits extensive annotation in the *Moral Essays* not merely because he combined moral worthlessness with great wealth (he was "infamous," Pope relates, for "all manner of vices"). What Pope emphasizes is not the gambling that established Chartres' fortune but the *subsequent* sources of his wealth: "After a hundred tricks at the gaming-tables, he took to lending of money at exorbitant interest and on great penalties, accumulating premium, interest, and capital into a new capital, and seizing to a minute when the payments became due." This is the career of an archetypal money-man. We should notice especially Pope's awareness of the process by which Chartres converted premium, interest, and capital "into a new capital." The changed economic context of Pope's satire no longer allows him simply to condemn greed, because greed now employs the methods of a vast new financial system.

The transformation of capital "into a new capital" is what unites Ward to Waters to Chartres in an unholy trinity for which the Devil supplies a natural fourth. Peter Waters (or when the rhyme serves, Peter Walter) had gained his fortune in the office of a scrivener, the original occupation of Sir John Blunt (Pope reports). A scrivener, as defined in Johnson's *Dictionary,* is "one whose business is to place money at interest"—a description which gains impact from the quotation Johnson supplies from Pope's friend Dr. John Arbuthnot: "I am reduced to beg and borrow from *scriveners* and usurers, that suck the heart and blood." The despised Peter Waters reappears so frequently in Pope's work as a personification of new-monied corruption that Pope even refers to the frequency of his appearances: "What, always *Peter?*"[12] Yet, although Waters, Ward, and Chartres personify the vile methods and vulgar origins of monied corruption, they are static figures, invoked like Miltonic demons, who tell us little about how the *process* of corruption weakens and destroys human character. Character is always, for Pope, capable of transformations both harmful and beneficent. ("Nero reigns a Titus, if he will."[13]) In the *Moral Essays* his most thorough analysis of new-monied corruption occurs in the tale of Sir Balaam, where we witness character in the process of self-destruction.

The tale of Sir Balaam is often misinterpreted as the parable of a man ruined by achieving riches. This conventional moralism equates wealth with evil, thus ignoring a distinction crucial to the *Moral Essays.* For Pope, although riches (like poverty) can supply an occasion for evil, they are morally neutral. Wealth for Pope is good or evil not in its own nature but in its use. Sir Balaam's experience is also incorrectly interpreted as the cautionary tale of a weak man who yields to temptation. Until the sudden conclusion, his long history has no fateful instant in which a specific failure or transgression propels him unmistakably toward disaster. Instead of such a clear, dramatic reversal, corruption, as Pope depicts it, simulates the progress of a slowly spreading stain or mist (iii.140). This slow, stainlike spreading of evil, with its suggestions of blurred outlines, loss of clarity, and amorphous movement too indistinct for effective opposition, becomes a powerful image repeated throughout Pope's work.

As with mists or stains, which we usually notice only after they have begun to spread, the exact origin of monied corruption is difficult to locate; Sir Balaam's London beginnings are thus appropriately obscure. His constancy at the Exchange (iii.347) suggests a background in trade, but we know with assurance only that he owns land in Cornwall. His fortune is certainly not untainted. He profits by the death of his father, by plunder from ships wrecked against his Cornish lands, and by sharp practices, such as outwitting an agent who deposits a stolen diamond as security. This is not exactly honest toil. But—up to this point in the story—it is important that Pope withholds clear proof of Sir Balaam's criminality or vice. What Pope depicts (as Sir Balaam's fortune accumulates) is a stiff, sanctimonious, frugal, businesslike citizen whom money improves into genial mediocrity: "Sir Balaam now, he lives like other folks, / He takes his chirping pint, and cracks his jokes" (iii.357–358). Even his self-deceptions are the sophistries of a thoroughly average mind: "I'll now give six-pence where I gave a groat, / Where once I went to church, I'll now go twice" (iii.366–367). Sir Balaam has his failings—so do we all—but they hardly merit the grim fate which befalls him.

The tale of Sir Balaam, far from recounting a dramatic surrender to evil, describes the career of an entrepreneur whose fall is an almost imperceptible and steady sinking, deeper and deeper, into a system which leads fatally toward corruption. The toneless, matter-of-fact phrases describing his ultimate demise suggest something predictable and ordinary in his fate: "My Lady falls to play; so bad her chance, / He must repair it; takes a bribe from France; / The House impeach him; Coningsby harangues; / The Court forsake him, and Sir Balaam hangs" (iii.395–398). It all happens so quickly, recounted in a relentless march of semicolons, as if foretold by a previous chain of events. Yet, what had Sir Balaam done to precipitate this inexorable, ignoble end?

The closest we come to a decisive turning-point in the history of

Sir Balaam is the moment when his first fortune begins to breed a second, when capital is transformed "into a new capital":

> The Tempter saw his time; the work he ply'd;
> Stocks and Subscriptions pour on ev'ry side,
> 'Till all the Daemon makes his full descent,
> In one abundant show'r of Cent. per Cent.,
> Sinks deep within him, and possesses whole,
> Then dubs Director, and secures his soul.       (iii.369–374)

This is no common temptation scene. Sir Balaam remains wholly innocent of any diabolic pact, unconscious of his complicity. The Devil simply operates through the normal mechanisms of the new economic order. From the time when Sir Balaam enters fully into the unsteady financial subculture of stocks, subscriptions, and directorships, he is fatally changed. His "manners turn" (iii.379); his character corrodes. It is as if once individuals sink into the system of modern finance, they cannot get free again. Like Danaë raped by Jove in a shower of gold, they are possessed.

## The Melodrama of Corruption

Possession—the ownership of property—assumed a meaning in the eighteenth-century far beyond its restrictive application within the old "moral economy," where property most often signified the right to receive revenues from land.[14] In the agrarian past, property did not refer directly to things but to rights "in" things, especially in land. By Pope's time linguistic usage and the social system it reflected were changing. Even the Devil—who carefully "secures" the soul of the man whom he "possesses whole"—now acts like a modern financier protecting his investments. Johnson's *Dictionary* defines *property* and *possession* as synonyms referring not specifically to land but to any material object: "the thing possessed." It is worth recalling that *Of The Use of Things* was Pope's original title for *Moral Essays* and that he began early to immerse his readers in a contemporary world cluttered with property, objects, possessions, knick-knacks—things. *The Rape of the Lock* is innovative in part because it imbeds in its polished surface something like a shopper's catalogue of fashionable gadgets—buckles, whistles, watches, canes, playing cards, china teacups, ivory combs, puffs, garters, nosegays, petticoats, sword-knots, snuff, bodkins, scissors, ribbons, bottles, tweezer-cases, wax candles, coffee-mills, fans, parrots. The extraordinary list goes on and on. In a sense the eighteenth century reinvented property. More goods than ever before were available through commerce and manufacture, and ownership itself became a subject for contemplation. Property was newly wrapped with theory and armed with law. In analyzing the relationship between possession and character in the *Moral Essays*, we must briefly reenter this transitional landscape where property received its modern formulations.

The new importance of property finds its clearest theoretical statement in the political philosophy of John Locke. "The great and *chief end* ... of Mens uniting into Commonwealths, and putting themselves under Government," wrote Locke, "*is the Preservation of their Property.*"[15] Locke's claim that all government—in effect, all civil society—derives from the institution of property is no mere exercise in speculative history. In Pope's day, the study of origins was usually a program for action. Origins had an almost holy status as expressing principles in their initial purity, free from the accumulated corruptions of time. In uncovering the origins of government, Locke implied that the preservation of property remains the principle upon which modern English politics should be established. The *London Journal*, cranking out propaganda for the Walpole ministry, needed to take only modest license in reformulating Locke's ideas as a maxim it presumed indisputable: "*Civil Liberty* consists in the Security of Property" (no. 605). The statement appeared in 1731, the year in which Pope published the first epistle of what eventually became his *Moral Essays*.

Theory had its counterpart in practice. The new importance of property as an idea was mirrored in down-to-earth details of crime and law. Every age, Pat Rogers suggests, has its special, self-defining crime. For the Elizabethans it was treason; for the Victorians, murder; for our age, perhaps espionage. "The archetypal Augustan crime, rather oddly," Rogers observes, "was theft."[16] Theft is doubtless as old as property. Yet, in the eighteenth century, theft also generated the glamorous fantasies, the morbid curiosity, and the brutal, legalized repression associated with subversive activities.

Theft, of course, does not destroy but simply redistributes property, hence it was the calculated, subversive *destruction* of property which accounted for the most infamous new legislation of the century. The Black Act of 1723—following the South Sea Bubble and a sudden increase in crime—created by a single statute some fifty new capital offenses. Directed specifically at a suspected group of rural extremists, the penalty of death now awaited any disguised, armed criminal found guilty of hunting, wounding, destroying, or stealing red or fallow deer; killing or maiming cattle; poaching hares, conies, or fish; cutting down trees in any garden or orchard; or setting fire to any house, barn, out-house, haystack, or woodpile. Such attacks on property were seen as endangering an entire social order, and thus we cannot dismiss the Black Act as simply another piece of barbarous, unenforceable legislation, with no conceivable relations to literature. It was indeed enforced. More important, it was symptomatic of other changes in attitudes toward law and property as reflected in literature, even in such fundamental economic issues as copyright. (The Copyright Act of 1709, for example, enabled authors for the first time to acquire the copyright of their works—which had previously been held by booksellers—and the history of Pope's publication of his works shows he shrewdly exploited copyright provisions to protect what was now his own property.) Property is in Walpole's era almost its own law. As E. P. Thompson concluded in his study of the Black Act: "Property and the privileged status of the propertied were assuming, every year, a greater weight in the scales of justice, until justice itself was seen as no more than the outworks and defenses of property and of its attendant status."[17] In Pope's *Moral Essays*, as well as in his imitations of Horace (written throughout the 1730s), property and its relation to human character became a recurrent concern.

Although Pope might seem to have been insulated from the violence against property and persons represented by the Black Act, it is very probable that he was intimately acquainted with its costs. His brother-in-law Charles Rackett and Rackett's son Michael were both accused of crimes under provisions of the Black Act. (Michael soon disappeared from England and lived abroad, his whereabouts mysterious; the case against Charles Rackett never—for reasons unknown—proceeded to trial.) Pope was also directly involved in the theoretical arguments concerning property and liberty through his support of the anti-Walpole group known as the Opposition. Pope's friend Bolingbroke, philosopher and propagandist for the Opposition, made property (meaning "real" property, or land) the corner-stone of his long campaign against Walpole. Bolingbroke was a master of expediency, and some historians find his sole principle to be self-interest; but, like Pope, in opposing Walpole, he gave consistent and eloquent support to the traditional, property-based ideal that scholars today call "civic humanism":

> It was a tradition which upheld the ideal of a society composed of citizens in arms, of men who regarded property not as the basis for productive [economic] life, but as a safeguard or guarantee of material autonomy or independence, who attached therefore special significance to real property, or property in land, which alone provided the conditions which permitted a man to realize his potential for citizenship. For the landed citizen possessed the means to bear arms in defence of the republic; he had sufficient leisure to cultivate the virtues requisite for a life of public debate and action; he enjoyed liberty, and could be relied upon to insist that governments must be so constituted that the spirit of liberty might animate the conduct of its public men; and . . . the participation of the patriotic citizen was stabilized by his attachment to the land, with its indissoluble connection with the country and its traditions of public and private life.[18]

Pope's poetry of solitude, retirement, landscape, and property is closely associated with this tradition of civic humanism and its open celebration of the landed estate. It is this tradition which Old Cotta and his son—as well as Timon and other landed aristocrats in Pope's satire—so deeply and fully violate. Further, the ideal of civic humanism, based on the significance of real property, offered a basis for the Opposition's understanding of recent English history during the unprecedented twenty years—from 1721 to 1742—that Walpole served as virtual "prime minister." (Walpole in effect created the position of "prime minister," which did not yet exist as a distinct office.) The Opposition reduced the recent past to simple and useful melodrama. In their reading of English history, a once independent Parliament had been subverted by Walpole's so-called "place-men," who were bought with lucrative appointments; the old landed families had been subverted in the ruling oligarchy by upstart stock-jobbers and corrupt ministerial hirelings; property had lost both its status and its privileges. As Bolingbroke summarized: "The power of money, as the world is now constituted, is real power."[19]

The increased power of money in eighteenth-century culture does not rest on the suspect testimony of Bolingbroke. Macheath in *The Beggar's Opera*, advising Lucy in the ways of the world, formulates as a maxim the open secret of Walpole's era: "Money well timed and properly applied will do anything" (II.xii). For Pope, however, bribery was an ancient technique that interested him less than the new modes of corruption made possible by the financial revolution. He observes that money was changing its nature, growing more pliant and insidious, less distinct and accountable than the hard currency of gold and silver coins that previously gave a real weight and substance to corruption. As Hume wrote: "No merchant thinks it necessary to keep by him any considerable cash. Bank-stock, or India-bonds, especially the latter, serve the same purposes." Or again: "Public securities are with us become a kind of money, and pass as readily at the current price as gold or silver."[20]

Such innovation, in Pope's view, simply accelerated the corrupting tendencies of modern life. Riches now assumed a formlessness impossible in the old world where real property was the basis for wealth:

> Blest paper-credit! last and best supply!
> That lends Corruption lighter wings to fly!
> . . . . .
> Pregnant with thousands flits the Scrap unseen,
> And silent sells a King, or buys a Queen.     (iii.69–78)

Corruption is an imageless, shapeless flying creature—silent, shifty, almost infinitely reproducible—whose "flitting" perfectly expresses its nature. As usual, Pope carefully considered the significance of verbs expressing motion. "Flitting," for example, is the action performed by the gnome Umbriel in *The Rape of the Lock*, who sinks to the Cave of Spleen in a parody of graceful flight, descending perhaps as a scrap of paper lurches down. The irregular motion of flitting ("to be flux or unstable," according to Johnson) exactly corresponds to the instability that the civic humanist tradition attributes to money as opposed to land. It also aptly describes the new world of finance, within which, as Sir Balaam demonstrated, human character proved radically unstable. In the Opposition melodrama, money is a magic potion or Circean drug that holds the power to transform men into whatever shape the wizard pleases. Pope actually depicts such a scene in the fourth book of *The Dunciad*. The wizard of corruption, of course, is always Walpole.

The term *corruption* occurs so often in the anti-Walpole writings of Pope, Swift, Gay, Bolingbroke, and Fielding that we should not neglect its special meaning. Corruption, of course, indicates at its most general level the fallen state to which man is always subject: "But Man corrupt, perverse in all his ways, / In search of Vanities from Nature strays" (*Sober Advice from Horace*, ll. 98–99). In eighteenth-century political writing, however, corruption has a more specific meaning. It refers beyond moral perversity or willful wrong-doing to the political and economic policy or Walpole's administration. It denotes Walpole's tacit programs for destroying the original balance between Parliament—whose independence was secured by property—and the Crown.[21] The most effective instrument in corrupting Parliament's independence was, of course, invariably identified as money, including its indirect forms as patronage and credit. Pope's image of paper credit as providing "Corruption lighter wings to fly" was certainly indebted to the Opposition's campaign against Walpole. Especially through its journal, *The Craftsman*, the Opposition generated a steady flow of anti-Walpole writing, from which Pope did not hesitate to draw. Yet, the Opposition press inevitably simplified and exaggerated its charges against Walpole. Although Pope sometimes accepted and used the melodramatic contrast of land versus money, he also recognized its limitation. As a satirist he needed to attack political and social corruption with whatever weapons proved most effective; as a moralist, he needed to reveal how even such useful weapons as the contrast between land and money might pose dangers to the ethical life.

Pope, my argument will run, both employs and exposes the Opposition melodrama of money versus land. There was great literary advantage in concentrating his attacks on Walpole in the effective theme of corruption, with its imagery of dispossessed landowners and grasping money-men. Yet, Pope could not wholeheartedly share the perspective of Bolingbroke and the landed tradition. His experience as the son of a Roman Catholic merchant placed him outside the circle of landed aristocrats whose friendship he shared. As a Catholic, he suffered various penalties (such as double taxation) and exclusions (such as the law forbidding residence within ten miles of London). Ownership of land for Catholics could be difficult and insecure. The improvements Pope made to his small estate at Twickenham concerned property he rented, not owned, and his attack on stock-jobbers and money-men did not prevent him from investing (modestly) in South Sea stock and in such nonspeculative securities as shares in the Sun Fire Office. Despite his affection for the great land-owners Lord Burlington and Lord Bathurst, Pope lived in a different world, made his living by his pen, cherished his independence. Only by considerable distortion, therefore, can Pope be transformed into the spokesman for civic humanism. In effect, his moral vision and his interest in character, no less than his family background and entre-preneurial spirit, led him beyond the ideology of Opposition politics. Although he attacked Walpole and the new financial system, he also recognized both the usefulness of money and the dangers of prop-erty—themes on which Bolingbroke was silent. For Pope, questions of politics and of economics finally become questions of morality. Thus, while *The Craftsman* shielded its attacks on Walpole behind the fraudulent slogan that "Measures, not Men" were its target, Pope preferred to focus his satire openly and directly upon men. Land and money assume their significance in his work not according to a politi-cal program but as they express and affect human character.

## Two Images of Riches

Character, one could say, is where, for Pope, politics, property, and money necessarily intersect. The complex interrelations of character and riches can be suggested by two extended images that help situate the *Moral Essays* in wider eighteenth-century contexts. The first extended image comes from William Hogarth's brilliant series of en-gravings *The Rake's Progress*, which appeared in 1735, the same year as Pope's first collected version of the *Moral Essays*. Questions of in-fluence are not at issue: although Swift had high praise for Hogarth, Pope maintained a steady silence, probably because he saw himself satirized in two of Hogarth's prints. Like Pope in the *Moral Essays*, Hogarth in *The Rake's Progress* makes the relationship of character to money a principal theme, and images of money dominate the entire sequence. Gold coins fall from the ceiling in the first scene, as Tom Rakewell attempts to buy off his pregnant ex-sweetheart, and, completing the frame, in the final scene the sketch of a huge halfpenny (added by Hogarth in 1763) seems to hang over Tom's head in Bedlam like an ominous moon. Within these imagistic bounds, Tom's relentless decline from folly to madness occurs in a landscape where money—as motive and object—shadows him almost like a parallel character or doppelgänger.

More important than the mere presence of money is the background it creates for tracing the strange fluctuations in Tom's appearance. From scene to scene his face and figure change, sometimes vastly. This representation of change or inconstancy was surely deliberate, because Hogarth was famous for his ability to catch a likeness. Rakewell does not simply change expression or alter with age and experience, but his whole being seems transformed, as if in each scene he were a different person. Hogarth, in effect, depicts character in the process of disintegration—corrupting or decomposing—until nothing is left but the mindless, unrecognizable shape of a man. Money seems able to deprive Tom Rakewell of any stable identity, fashioning him to its own changing features.

Pope's close association with Burlington and with Burlington's protégé (the painter and landscape designer) William Kent apparently earned him Hogarth's disfavor, but Pope and Hogarth both share an understanding of how money can erode human character. But, as artists born without wealth or title, determined to win their independence from the prevailing system of aristocratic and political patronage, they also understood that there are other relations possible between money and character. That is, if money could signify corruption and enslavement and disintegration, it also held for Pope the opposite promise of independence and self-possession. By "independence" Pope did not mean vast riches but an income sufficient to free him from the obligations due a patron, and in an age when patronage deeply influenced literary production Pope's independence had direct consequences for his writing. "He never exchanged praise for money," Johnson wrote, "nor opened a shop of condolence or congratulation."[22] Thus it is worth pausing to reflect on the situation of Pope and his family. In 1688, at the age of forty-two, his father had retired to rural Binfield with his wife and young son after a successful career as a London merchant. As a Roman Catholic, the elder Pope could expect no favors from the new reign of William III but suffered instead from automatic penalties. He was barred from owning land or from investing in land, and his sympathies for the exiled James II (Johnson tells us) kept him from lending to the government. What in 1688 would a retired Catholic merchant do with some twenty thousand pounds, the sole support for himself and his family? Pope's father, according to Johnson, locked the money in a chest.[23] The image of the elder Pope securing his independence with a locked chest of money may be apocryphal, but it also accurately reflects Pope's knowledge that his small inheritance was dwindling each year. According to Johnson, as expenses required, the chest was unlocked and money paid out bit by bit, so that when the elder Pope died in 1717 only about two thousand pounds remained. Pope was twenty-eight when his father died. His health was poor, his education was informal, his religion excluded him from public employment. He could not afford the luxury of imagining that human character—as reflected in how we act and in what we choose—might remain somehow untouched or uninfluenced by the power of money. Money can be the instrument of corruption, but—as Pope had seen in his father's retirement and as he foresaw in embarking on ten years of translating Homer—money can also provide the independence that permits human character to achieve a measure of stable, secure self-possession.

## Inconsistency and Inconstancy

Pope's theory of character in the *Moral Essays* seems to contain inconsistencies serious enough to reach the point of paradox or self-contradiction. We may wish to attribute these difficulties to Pope's attempt at reconciling contradictory theories, to the period's transitional understanding of character, or to his weaknesses as a theorist. Yet, before assigning causes, we should understand Pope's central assertions about character in the *Moral Essays*. These can be reduced to three propositions: (1) human nature is too various and inconsistent, human motives too cunningly hidden, and human observers too fallible and subjective ever to permit an accurate analysis of individual character; (2) nevertheless, once we penetrate to the concealed "ruling passion," then even the most puzzling individuals are suddenly and entirely comprehensible; (3) we can never be completely *certain* that we understand the "ruling passion" of a living person until the person dies. (Like the dying declaration or deathbed confession, which in law held the status of fact, a person's dying words or actions Pope considered an authentic, unimpeachable expression of character.) If there is a fourth proposition, it is that the first and third propositions do not apply to women. Women for Pope exhibit only two main ruling passions—the love of pleasure and the love of power— hence they do not reveal the multiplicity of character which Pope attributes to men. This unfortunate theory he expressed in a line cannily assigned to a female speaker: "Most women have no Characters at all" (ii.2). The fact is that Pope's theory of character is snarled in difficulties.

The difficulties surrounding Pope's theory of character certainly reflect his attempt to complicate a subject remarkable chiefly for its previous history of simplification. The immediate past offered Pope little help in understanding the nature of character. The theory of the four humors of the body, borrowed from the medicine of Galen and from Renaissance drama, identified character with a single, consistent, determining temperament. The theory of manners, which defined the figures popular on the Restoration stage, similarly reduced character—to a series of fixed social roles: the wit, the coquette, the fop, the lusty widow, and so on. Even the classical tradition of character-sketches from Theophrastus to Samuel Butler is based upon the assumption that character is free from internal contradiction, fully accessible to observation, and readily definable according to type.[24] Like the literary principle of decorum as formulated by Horace, this tradition insists that characters never violate the expectations of their fixed patterns. Old men must act like old men, youths like youths, and fops like fops. Pope, in the manner of Defoe and Richardson, attempted to move the study of character much closer to what we would recognize as the analysis of individual behavior.

Pope's emphasis upon individuality rather than typicality does not derive from the traditions of humors, manners, or character-sketches. Homer, Shakespeare, and Montaigne seem instead to be the most important influences on his work. As Pope writes of Homer's heroes, "Every one has something so singularly his own, that no Painter could have distinguish'd them more by their Features, than the Poet has by their Manners."[25] By "manners" here Pope refers not to social roles but to the passions, traits, and temperaments that define individuals. He observes that Homer explores the shades of individual differences that allow us to distinguish, for example, the courage of Achilles from the varieties of courage in Diomede, Hector, Menelaus, or Ajax. In addition, Pope praises the *mixture* of traits that contributes toward the individuation of Homer's characters. Pope's similar praise of Shakespeare's characterizations is well known: "Every single character in Shakespeare is as much an individual as those in life itself: it is impossible to find any two alike."[26] Pope, however, did not restrict this emphasis on individuation to his critical writing. The years 1715 to 1726, which he devoted to translating Homer and to editing Shakespeare, were among other things an apprenticeship in the study of character. The *Moral Essays,* even in its use of typical figures of satire, always seeks to discover in them the singular detail or personal trait which expresses their uniqueness. Patritio, the brilliant statesman, prides himself on parlor games (i.145); Rufa, the coquette, studies Locke (ii.23).

Rufa and Patritio not only violate our expectations of the stock figures coquette and statesman. Pope also seems to combine in each figure two *opposing* types. In Rufa, philosopher joins flirt; in Patritio, the trifler and the master strategist unite. Such extreme opposition within single figures suggests that the most instructive influence upon Pope's idea of character was not Homer or Shakespeare, but Montaigne. Montaigne added the fundamental concept that distinguishes Pope's theory of character from those of his predecessors and contemporaries: the idea of inconsistency. "Whoever will look narrowly into his own Bosom," wrote Montaigne, "will hardly find himself twice in the same Condition." Again: "We fluctuate betwixt various inclinations; we Will nothing freely, nothing absolutely, nothing constantly."[27] Montaigne views inconsistency not as a random attribute or freakish aberration but as the definitive quality of human nature. We cannot know what people truly are, he believes, only that they are truly inconsistent. Man for Montaigne is a creature of continual internal changes. Although Pope rejects the extreme skepticism of Montaigne's position, he also believes inconsistency a regulating feature of human character. In his occasional verse, he represents himself as subject to the influence of continually altering dispositions, which range from grave to playful, from pious to bawdy. Nor is such internal variance merely Pope's idiosyncrasy. "Show me one," he challenges, "who has it in his pow'r / To act consistent with himself an hour."[28]

The central importance of inconsistency in Pope's theory of character becomes clearer if we consider the marginal position that earlier theories assign to human variance. For example, the long tradition of character-sketches offered, in its gallery of type figures, a portrait known as the "Inconstant Man." In Dryden's famous portrait of Zimri in *Absalom and Achitophel* (1681) this traditional character was applied to the Duke of Buckingham and created a literary model so powerful that it seems never far from Pope's thoughts. The Inconstant Man, however, is only one type of character among many stereotypical figures—the Puritan, the Miser, the Virtuoso, the Quack, and so on. Pope departs from tradition by making continual variation not the attribute of one type only but the central feature of *all* people. Inconsistency and individuality together become the twin principles upon which he constructs his entire theory of character, and the *Moral Essays* asserts these principles as its founding doctrine:

> That each from other differs, first confess;
> Next, that he varies from himself no less. (i.19–20)

This is a theory of character for which the established poetic genres, with their usually self-consistent heroes and heroines, offered little encouragement, and thus it is not surprising that Pope would find himself returning to the freedoms of occasional verse, where opportunities for self-contradication and individual variance are implicit in the concept of occasion. But the occasional poems were not the only place where Pope's two principles contributed to a crucial change in the understanding of human character.

Pope's most innovative contribution to English theories of character is his effort, following Montaigne, to shift the locus of character from external actions or social roles or physiological humors to the mind. He explicitly rejects the Aristotelian doctrine that character is equivalent with action. For Pope, on the contrary, it is often impossible to understand character by studying actions—to "Infer the Motive from the Deed" (i.53). He moves close to the Lockean position that would equate identity with consciousness, except he also insists that consciousness is often unaware of its own "dim" sources and motives (i.45–50). Pope never adequately explored or described this inward relocation of character, but its significance was not lost upon Samuel Johnson. Character, as Johnson enumerated its accepted senses in the *Dictionary*, now included one highly untraditional definition: the "particular constitution of mind." Johnson borrowed his illustration for this meaning directly from the *Moral Essays*.

Pope's relocation of character so that it coincides with what Johnson called the "particular constitution of mind" was not without danger. The dangers to human character that Pope depicts in the *Moral Essays* extend beyond inconsistency to full self-contradiction. The mind, as Pope describes it, is such an abundant, dynamic, and unregimented space that character always contains the possibility of its own negation. This movement beyond inconsistency is evident when we compare Pope's theory of character with Dryden's. For Dryden, human character is mixed and various, but never self-contradictory. As he wrote: "A character, or that which distinguishes one man from all others, cannot be supposed to consist of one particular virtue, or vice, or passion only; but 't is a composition of qualities which are not contrary to one another in the same person; thus, the same man may be liberal and valiant, but not liberal and covetous."[29] For Pope, the ethical life is perilous and difficult not merely because of external temptations to wrong-doing but because human nature includes the possibility of radical self-contradiction. It is entirely possible, he shows, that the same person will be both liberal and covetous, both foolish and wise.

The dangers of self-negation will be clearer if we distinguish between inconsistency and its more extreme counterpart, inconstancy. For Pope, as we have seen, all individuals are characterized by inconsistency, but such variation necessarily implies the existence of a central, stable character against which variation may be measured. Man, as Pope puts it, varies "from himself": that is, we recognize what is inconsistent in human character by first recognizing what is consistent. In *An Essay on Man* Pope explains: "The rogue and fool by fits is fair and wise, / And ev'n the best, by fits, what they despise" (ii.233–234). Such individuals are inconsistent, but their fitful changes do not call in question their underlying nature as fools, rogues, or persons of virtue. Inconstancy, by contrast, involves a much more radical kind of change. It does not imply variation from or within a firm, centered, consistent character. Inconstancy suggests the absence of any center. Character becomes the focus of oppositions so extreme and changes so unceasing that there is a real question whether character still exists. In effect, persons who in their inconstancy are diverse enough to contain such radical opposition necessarily encounter within themselves a dangerous series of potential antiselves. There is nothing constant, nothing centered, nothing consistent. In extreme instances of such self-negation, nothing is all that remains.

Pope's studies of character in the *Moral Essays* might be understood as reflecting a version of Aristotle's schema for identifying virtue as a midpoint between opposite extremes. Inconsistency is Pope's midpoint of virtue, bordered on opposite extremes by inconstancy (which has no center) and by inertia or contraction or immobility (which is all center). Not only are individuals threatened by their own interior self-contradiction and radical inconstancy but also by its opposite—by the rigid, mechanical, obsessive sameness that fixes character in an unchanging inertia. Static, rigid immobility of character accounts for many of the comic failures satirized in the *Moral Essays*. Pope's dying courtier, for example, is always and unchangeably and eternally a courtier, extending his fixed servility even to the hereafter: "If—where I'm going—I could serve you, Sir?" (i.255). Self-parodic immobility here expunges all trace of individual uniqueness. Papillia, in an amusing variation, shows how even the virtue of a flexible inconsistency can be hardened and contracted into an inert vacillation:

> Papillia, wedded to her doating spark,
> Sighs for the shades—"How charming is a Park!"
> A Park is purchas'd, but the Fair he sees
> All bath'd in tears—"Oh odious, odious Trees!"     (ii.37–40)

Comic characters drawn with such rapid strokes necessarily resemble the old, one-dimensional characters of humors or manners—yet there are important differences. The one-dimensional portraits in the *Moral Essays* make sense within a theory of character that allows for much fuller representations of human individuality. (Contemporaries were forever trying to identify Pope's portraits with living people.) In addition, one-dimensional character such as we find in Papillia or the dying courtier is no longer a normal state but the sign of ethical failure. It testifies to mismanagements in the art of living.

Pope's portraits of Wharton and Atossa—the central studies of the

# Alexander Pope

first two epistles of the *Moral Essays*—are what instruct us unmistakably how the failure to stabilize human character leads to self-contradiction, sterility, and waste that is nearly tragic. Inconstancy is their defining attribute. The Duke of Wharton, blessed with "each gift of nature and of art," manages almost to erase or to annihilate his own character by a process of self-cancellation in which every trait or attribute seems linked with its opposite:

> A constant Bounty which no friend has made;
> An angel Tongue, which no man can persuade;
> A Fool, with more of Wit than half mankind,
> Too quick for Thought, for Action too refin'd:
> A Tyrant to the wife his heart approves;
> A Rebel to the very King he loves;
> He dies, sad out-cast of each church and state,
> And (harder still) flagitious, yet not great!           (i.198–205)

Wharton is a fabric of unresolved paradox and self-destructive contradictions. His female counterpart is "great Atossa"—a composite figure based mainly on Katherine Darnley, Duchess of Buckinghamshire—whose character proves as chaotic and unstable as her "Eddy Brain":

> Full sixty years the World has been her Trade,
> The wisest Fool much Time has ever made.
> From loveless youth to unrespected age,
> No Passion gratify'd except her Rage.
> So much the Fury still out-ran the Wit,
> The Pleasure miss'd her, and the Scandal hit.
>                 . . . . .
> Strange! by the Means defeated of the Ends,
> By Spirit robb'd of Pow'r, by Warmth of Friends,
> By Wealth of Follow'rs! without one distress
> Sick of herself thro' very selfishness!
> Atossa, curs'd with ev'ry granted pray'r,
> Childless with all her Children, wants an Heir.   (ii.123–148)

Wharton and Atossa are studies of internal contradiction. In a perverse mechanism of character, all innate or acquired powers are rendered futile or tormenting, every virtue mimics its opposite vice, and each achievement proves the reverse of what is desired. In Wharton generosity is as isolating as avarice; in Atossa health is as distressing as sickness. A malign process of self-negation seems uncontrollably at work. Wharton and Atossa are striking but sadly empty creatures, as if the intersection of opposing forces and desires nullified all coherence. Their incoherent lives are represented as forms of living death.

Death in Pope's work is represented in several different ways. Often it is simply accepted as a natural fact, a part of the human condition, as portrayed in the epitaphs "On Himself" and "On Mrs. *Corbet.*" Especially in his earlier poems, such as *The Rape of The Lock*, death evokes a consistent elegiac tone reminiscent of Elizabethan contemplations of mutability. In such poems, death becomes a sign of our shared humanity, a bond which unites us despite our faults and follies, an inevitable fate which adds a poignancy to all acts and achievements. In *An Essay on Man*, as we have seen, death is the occasion for philosophical meditations on human nature and divine order. The *Moral Essays*, however, presents death as a metaphorical equivalent of failures in the art of living. The earlier consoling, elegiac tone disappears as the epistles fill with images of madness, obsession, coldness, self-hatred, inertia, and futility:

> Still round and round the Ghosts of Beauty glide,
> And haunt the places where their Honour dy'd.   (ii.241–242)

Such mechanical death-in-life is Pope's recurrent metaphor for the failures of character that doom mankind to the wasted existences exemplified by Wharton and Atossa.

The self-negation or nullification at work in Wharton and Atossa strangely resembles the familiar Popean process of refinement run in reverse. Whereas refinement is a creative, progressive process in which opposing virtues combine and opposing weaknesses disappear, Wharton and Atossa attain a state in which virtues disappear and weaknesses combine. They demonstrate how character may be uncreated, and thus they provide a striking contrast with Martha Blount and with Colonel Cobham, whose portraits in the *Moral Essays* stand as climactic examples of how character might be truly created and sustained. This creative and sustaining process is also well illustrated in Pope's portrait of his friend Bolingbroke:

> Great without Title, without Fortune bless'd;
> Rich ev'n when plunder'd, honour'd while oppress'd,

> Lov'd without youth, and follow'd without power,
> At home tho' exil'd, free, tho' in the Tower.[30]

Bolingbroke stands as the model—paradoxically, but appropriately, in exile—of Pope's conviction that man's essential business is to be truly "at home." The same intersection of opposites which destroyed Wharton and Atossa—which earlier doomed Eloisa to an unresolvable pain—now transforms misfortune into blessings. Untitled, Bolingbroke retains his greatness; plundered, he remains rich; powerless, he retains followers. How is this rare accomplishment in the art of living possible?

Pope defined the ideal state of human character in a letter that described Bolingbroke as a man "who tho tost all his life by so many Whirls of Fortune, still possesses all in possessing himself."[31] The self-possession which allows man not merely to survive but to transform all worldly disadvantages is not just the singular achievement of Pope's philosopher-hero, Bolingbroke. It can be discovered in his portraits of Martha Blount and Colonel Cobham in the *Moral Essays*, or in the "Epitaph. On Mrs. *Corbet*." It is also eloquently recommended in what Pope considered the best study of human character ever written, the *Essays* of Montaigne. "The greatest thing in the world," wrote Montaigne, "is for a man to know that he is his own."[32] To attain a self-possession that would secure one's character against radical inconstancy and self-contradiction—dangers mirrored in the "Whirls" of fortune and in the shifting financial mechanisms of capital and credit—was the goal of all Pope's ethical writing. Such self-possession is possible, although enormously difficult, Pope believed, only if we understand two forces that exert an inescapable influence over human character: property and virtue.

## Property and Self-Possession

Although the relation of property to character is a theme continuously explored throughout the *Moral Essays*, Pope's most explicit and prolonged meditation on property appears in his *Second Epistle of the Second Book of Horace, Imitated*, published in 1737, two years after the first collected version of the *Moral Essays*. The occasion for the *Second Epistle* is both melancholy and ironic, for Bolingbroke (despairing of an effective Opposition to Walpole) had put his estate, Dawley Farm, up for sale, preparing once again to leave England—this time to settle permanently in France. The event has an almost allegorical quality: aristocratic virtue, in the person of Bolingbroke, has been forced off its land by the power of monied corruption, personified by Walpole. The Opposition melodrama of money versus land helps to explain Pope's poetical insult to the prospective purchaser of Dawley Farm—one Joshua Vanneck—whom Pope converts into a villain he calls "vile Van-muck" (l. 229). Muck, like dirt and excrement, is one of Pope's repeated, charged images for money; in a letter written about the same time, he refers to Vanneck as a "Child of Dirt, or Corruption," "Money-headed & Money-hearted."[33] Yet, though Pope predictably sides with landed virtue against the forces of monied corruption, he also creates from a few hints in Horace a vivid metaphor that, unexpectedly, links the supposed stability of land with the acknowledged capriciousness of money and credit:

> Estates have wings, and hang in Fortune's pow'r
> Loose on the point of ev'ry wav'ring Hour;
> Ready, by force, or of your own accord,
> By sale, at least by death, to change their Lord.   (ll. 248–251)

It was commonplace in Augustan writing on economics to associate credit with an unnatural instability, as when Pope described paper securities as giving "wings" to corruption. J. G. A. Pocock explains the general belief among theorists of civic humanism: "Only the individual whose personality was founded on real property could perceive himself as real and virtuous; the creature of the credit mechanism must be a creature of passion, fantasy, and other directedness."[34] Now, however, Pope imagines land itself as winged for flight. In effect, he profoundly modifies the argument of civic humanism, by suggesting that all claims of property or ownership are equally vacuous:

> All vast Possessions (just the same the case
> Whether you call them Villa, Park, or Chace)
> Alas, my BATHURST! what will they avail?
> Join Cotswold Hills to Saperton's fair Dale,
> Let rising Granaries and Temples here,
> There mingled Farms and Pyramids appear,
> Link Towns to Towns with Avenues of Oak,
> Enclose whole Downs in Walls, 'tis all a joke!
> Inexorable Death shall level all,
> And Trees, and Stones, and Farms, and Farmer fall.
>
> (ll. 254–263)

Death reenters the poem here both as a natural fact and as a metaphor for the futility of ownership. There is no steadfastness in the world of property. Falling is the common fate shared by man and by everything he appropriates. Pope's final line may also imply that it is the nature of possessions to reduce mankind, as the Circean wizard of *The Dunciad* reduces men, to the status of the material property they possess. The farmer loses his human distinctness in a motion that rolls him indiscriminately and incongruously along in the ruin of trees and stones and farms.

We should not attribute this view of property to the specific occasion of Bolingbroke's misfortune. *The Second Satire of the Second Book of Horace, Paraphrased* (1734) includes a short dialogue, not in Horace, in which Swift expresses his wish that Pope possessed the title to his rented house at Twickenham: "I wish to God this house had been your own" (l. 162). Pope's reply expands considerably upon Horace's simple doctrine that nature makes no man "lord of the soil as his own" (*propriae telluris erum*). What is truly "your own" for Pope cannot be held by titles:

> What's *Property?* dear Swift! you see it alter
> From you to me, from me to Peter Walter.      (ll. 167–168)

Walter/alter is among Pope's more successful conceptual rhymes, for Peter Walter is the personification of slippery dealings in finance, and Pope's paragraph goes on to explore the slipperiness of property for an additional ten lines, before the poem concludes with a couplet that also departs from Horace. In Horace's conclusion, the inconstancies of fortune lead to a recommendation that we should live as brave men (*fortes*) opposing adversity with brave hearts (*fortiaque pectora*). Pope ignores Horace's emphasis upon fortitude and instead returns to the personal context of Swift's desire to see the Twickenham estate Pope's "own." Neither Horatian fortitude nor Swiftian property offers Pope a truly sustaining permanence:

> Let Lands and Houses have what Lords they will,
> Let Us be fix'd, and our own Masters still.      (ll. 179–180)

Self-mastery and self-possession are what Pope proposes to replace the shifting world of property, where lands and houses are no less variable than credit and money. The sole point of fixity he contem-

206

plates is the centering of the individual in virtue, which, as he argues in *An Essay on Man*, is the "only point where human bliss stands still" (iv.311). Dislodged from the center that is virtue, human character enters into a fluctuating state that resembles the fluid world of property and finance. Composure and stability belong only to the virtuous few who are truly their "own."

Like money, like the financial mechanisms of credit, property in Pope's work has a way of dispossessing those who embrace it. Yet, this position is also subject to modification. In rejecting the idea that property is a source of human stability, Pope does not necessarily imply a total rejection of property. Property, like money, takes its value from the use we make of it, and the use we make of property depends, in large part, upon our character. This close, almost circular, relationship between property and character is what allows Pope to employ objects and possessions in his satire as the reflection of moral states. His famous description of Timon's villa provides a clear example of how wealth in the *Moral Essays* functions as an image of character, almost an alter ego or double which reflects its owner. His estate, in its vast absurdity and vulgar display, is more than a monument to Timon's bad taste. Pope carefully places its owner in comic relation to the property he owns, as if Timon (like Sir Plume) had somehow distributed himself throughout the world of objects. The sham library expresses his ignorance and his pretension to knowledge; the rich chapel expresses his confusion of luxury with piety; his costly dinner expresses his addiction to spectacle and to pomp. Timon's bad taste is not merely an aesthetic failing. Like the "mighty pleasure" (iv.128) he takes in being seen, like the rich bindings of his unread books, like the "Pride of Pray'r" (iv.142) which passes for devotion in his chapel, like the elaborately staged meal where (as Pope's note informs us) "pride destroys the ease" of entertainment, Timon's entire estate is an expression of his vanity. Money and property, in Timon, have become means of transforming his internal defects of character, as in a masque or allegory, into visible and outward signs.

The capacity of our possessions to express and to represent character finds innumerable comic uses in the *Moral Essays* when Pope exposes the varieties of bad taste. Yet, if Timon's tasteless possessions express his moral failures, other objects offer a means of representing virtuous character. Thus architecture and gardening, as Pope describes them, are not merely aesthetic activities but a means by which artists and patrons inscribe their virtue upon the landscape. Buildings and gardens thus correlate directly with internal states. What Pope told his friend Ralph Allen about the selection of paintings for Allen's estate, Prior Park, also holds for the other arts: "A Man not only shews his Taste but his Virtue, in the Choice of such Ornaments."[35]

The function of property in expressing and in representing character provides a way of understanding Pope's "improvements" to his rented house and grounds at Twickenham (figure 2). The house "expressed its owner" (in Maynard Mack's phrase) especially through the more than one hundred portraits of friends that crowded Pope's walls. "There is nothing that is meritorious," Pope said after having received the last rites, "but Virtue, & Friendship, and Friendship indeed is only a part of Virtue."[36] The paintings not only express his devotion to his friends and to the ideal of friendship but also reflect the importance he attributed to virtue in stabilizing human character. Another aspect of Pope's character was revealed in his carefully designed garden, where an obelisk to his mother aesthetically and emotionally ordered the landscape, expressing at the same time his extraordinary filial devotion. (Swift once described Pope as "the most dutifull son that I have ever known or heard of."[37]) Even the famous grotto—with its flashing bits of mirror and glittering ore—was expressive of his character. Johnson unfairly considered it a monument to Pope's vanity, but the long association of grottos with the Muse made it what Pope called a "Scene for contemplation."[38] The unrefined crystal, minerals, and gems, and the resulting play of light and reflections, suggest something like a Cave of Fancy where the poet could find the perfect setting for his natural inventiveness. A contemporary drawing (figure 3), embellished with grotesques appropriate both to grottos and to creative fancy, shows Pope at work in his subterranean cell, pensive and solitary, engaged in the imaginative labor that is inseparable from his character as a poet.

Pope's home at Twickenham becomes his material image for the self-possession that he equates with the art of living. "If there be truth in Law, and *Use* can give / A *Property*," he wrote, "that's yours on which you live."[39] The persons who live well appropriate whatever they turn to virtuous use, whereas Timon, by contrast, demonstrates how possessions revenge themselves upon their foolish proprietors. Property and money are dangerous, in Pope's view, be-

2   Pope's house at Twickenham on the Thames, after Augustin Heckell.

3　Pope in his grotto, by William Kent.

cause possessions have a way of possessing people. Objects, no less than passions, may run away with us, like Sir Morgan astride his cheese, and the master of vast wealth becomes too often the "Slave" (iii.110) of what he owns.

The power of objects and property to dispossess and to enslave their owners has a final extension in the *Moral Essays* that is crucial to an understanding of Pope's work. For Pope, ideas and ideologies may prove as dispossessing as objects—capable of seizing possession of the mind which holds them—inducing a kind of rigor mortis as they turn into obsessions and thus deny the inconsistency and fluid movement native to human character. Pope's ideal is moderation, but that does not imply a fixed or restrictive middle state from which he never varies. When such an unvarying moderation was once described in Pope's work, he carefully attributed it to his friend Hugh Bethel, whom Pope says he loved more than he resembled.[40] Pope's ideal of moderation is not fixed or restricted to a middle state but moves and flows between extremes:

> Sworn to no Master, of no Sect am I:
> As drives the storm, at any door I knock,
> And house with Montagne now, or now with Lock.
> Sometimes a Patriot, active in debate,
> Mix with the World, and battle for the State,
> Free as young Lyttelton, her cause pursue,
> Still true to Virtue, and as warm as true:
> Sometimes, with Aristippus, or St. Paul,
> Indulge my Candor, and grow all to all;
> Back to my native Moderation slide,
> And win my way by yielding to the tyde.[41]

The view of human character expressed in these lines allows for a perpetual self-modifying movement ("I plant, root up, I build, and then confound"[42]) that is nonetheless stabilized and centered in virtue. In his correspondence Pope recognized how difficult this ideal of self-possession is to sustain. "Indeed of late a number of tiresome businesses of many kinds have taken me even from myself as well as from my friends in general," he wrote in a typical complaint. "I am hoping still, but still disappointed, that I shall live composedly again and be as much my own as I was."[43] The desire to be one's "own"— self-possessed and composed—is a theme Pope could not let go of.

"Hurry, noise, and the observances of the world," he lamented on another occasion, "take away the power of just thinking or natural acting. A man that lives so much in the world does but translate other men; he is nothing of his own."[44] Then the greatest translator of the age quoted a passage from Seneca:

> Infelix!
> Qui notus nimis omnibus,
> Ignotus moritur sibi.

The man who dies "to himself unknown" is for Pope an archetype of misery, and the *Moral Essays* provides a continuous spectacle of igno- rant and miserable deaths. The deathbed occupies such a prominent place in the *Moral Essays* not simply because Pope believed that death always exposes the hidden truth about character. It also offers—in the composure of virtuous dying and in the foolish, erratic, lonely, tormented, or obsessive deaths of those who fail to achieve self-possession—a final, irrefutable argument for the ethical life.

## Whose Dog Are You?

Virtue and self-possession have a tendency to become oppressively solemn topics. Thus Pope often shifts the burden of unmodified vir- tue onto minor characters—such as Martha Blount, Mrs. Corbet, the Man of Ross—wisely reserving for himself as poet the advantages of humor and imperfection. Although he professes to admire the equa- nimity of his friend Hugh Bethel—"His equal mind I copy what I can, / And as I love, would imitate the Man"[45]—such composure proves far easier to admire than to imitate. Human character, as Pope represents it in himself, has a way of losing track, forgetting its good intentions, going on holiday. In large part because of man's innate in- consistency, self-possession is not something that is attained once and for all, but remains an ideal from which most individuals continually fall away. Even Bolingbroke, Pope's philosopher-hero, cannot secure himself against an occasional "Fit of Vapours."[46] Self-possession is at best always interruptive, punctuated by moments when our compo- sure deserts us. Thus, the ethical life cannot for Pope be a uniformly solemn, intense, continuous struggle. It is, rather, a mixed state, that recognizes human imperfection and that finds in humor (the lan- guage of fallibility) a power to refine and to renew us.

The infusion of humor into morality might be considered the indirect purpose of Pope's two-line occasional poem entitled "Epigram. Engraved on the Collar of a *Dog* which I gave to his Royal Highness" (1738). Here is the entire poem:

> I am his Highness' Dog at *Kew;*
> Pray tell me Sir, whose Dog are you?

Perhaps we are meant to imagine a stiff, self-important courtier, attached to the Prince of Wales, bending with infinite dignity, to ingratiate himself with the royal pet. An elegant gesture brings him smoothly toward the engraved silver collar-plate. What he discovers, of course, is a witty sermon about self-knowledge and self-possession. His Highness' dog, it turns out, knows exactly who he is—and knows also that it is an honor (among dogs) to be the property of a great prince. The courtier, however, is not the only presence the epigram invites us to imagine. Who could have written these lines? Only a poet who is self-possessed and independent. As Pope wrote to Spence, "There is one thing I value myself upon and which can scarce be said of any of our good poets—and that is, that 'I have never flattered any man.' "[47] The comic focus of the "Epigram" keeps Pope offstage—but reminds us of his character nonetheless. Courtiers of every century and profession, meanwhile, must straighten hastily, hoping they were unobserved, and resume whatever dignified business it is that possesses them.

# VIII

## The Muse of Pain:
## *An Epistle to Dr. Arbuthnot*
## and Satiric Reprisal

*Satyre.* Girding, biting, snarling, scourging, jerking, lashing, smarting, sharp, tart, rough, invective, censorious, currish, snappish, captious, barking, brawling, carping, fanged, sharptooth'd, quipping, jeering, flouting, sullen, rigid, impartial, whipping, thorny, pricking, stinging, sharp-fanged, injurious, reproachful, libellous, harsh, rough-hewne, odious, opprobrious, contumelious, defaming, calumnious.

—Poole

“IF THE MODERNS have excelled the Ancients in any species of writing," declared Joseph Warton in 1756, "it seems to be in satire." Yet the flowering of satire in the Augustan Age, if such a thorny species can be said to flower, was quickly followed by decline, neglect, and misunderstanding. The new heroes and heroines of sentiment in the later eighteenth century had hearts too tender for satire. Hobbes's theory that laughter signifies "sudden glory" in our superiority over what causes us to laugh gave way to theories which emphasized the healing, communicative, and consoling powers of mirth. The concern of satire with politics and history found no outlet in the new meditative or expressive lyric. Satire, cut off from its former resources, came to seem almost antipoetic: transitory, local, limited, inessential, and eventually unintelligible. "Gulliver in the next century," Warton predicted, "will be as obscure as Gargantua."[1] Like Rabelais, Augustan satirists often fill their works with contemporary references, making later readings difficult. Difficulty, in fact, was in Dryden's view intrinsic to satire—"which is not written to vulgar readers."[2] But our distance from the literary and social tradi-

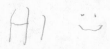

tions underlying Augustan satire is what creates the most considerable barrier to our understanding it. Pope's achievement as a satirist depends at least partly on our ability to recover the context in which it was possible to compose a work so particular, so abusive, and so personal as *An Epistle from Mr. Pope to Dr. Arbuthnot* (1734/5).

The modern recovery of Augustan satire owes a great deal to Maynard Mack, who in a famous essay urged that readers shift their attention from the personality or temperament of the satirist to the varieties of literary artifice that characterize satire as a genre. Today few scholars would disagree with Mack's fundamental argument that the contours of a formal verse satire, such as Pope's *Epistle to Dr. Arbuthnot*, are not established "entirely or even principally by a poet's rancorous sensibility; they are part of a fiction."[3] Mack's emphasis upon the fictions of satire opened a fruitful field for study, where much investigation still remains to be done.

Although it is certain that satire depends upon literary techniques and tactics properly described as fictions, the fictionality of satire nevertheless seems distinctive in ways that ultimately undermine its status as fiction. Augustan satire often pushes fiction over an indefinite border where historical people and contemporary facts take precedence over the general truths of human nature so dear to eighteenth-century theorists of literature. In satire, the power of language to represent or to refer to ideas, images, and objects is linked with more primitive forms of speech. Pope's friend the philosopher (and later bishop) George Berkeley observed in *A Treatise Concerning the Principles of Human Knowledge* (1710) that "it is a received opinion that language has no other end but the communicating [of] ideas, and that every significant name stands for an idea." Yet, the general assent to a representational theory of language, in which words "stand for" ideas, could not in Berkeley's view survive the evidence of ordinary usage. He continued: "The communicating of ideas marked by words is not the chief and only end of language, as is commonly supposed. There are other ends, as the raising of some passion, the exciting to or deterring from an action, the putting the mind in some particular disposition." Berkeley even supposes that certain passions—he names fear, love, hatred, admiration, and disdain—may arise immediately in the mind upon the perception of specific words "without any ideas coming between."[4] Although he is not offering a theory of satire, Berkeley touches upon something satirists have known ever since their legendary Greek forerunner Archilochus discovered that poetic language could drive his enemies to suicide.

Satire for Pope, as it was for Archilochus, is a special kind of fiction that insists upon its distance from traditional literary forms, which it frequently appropriates for its own purposes, much as *Gulliver's Travels* appropriates the form of travel narratives. In *The Dunciad,* when tragedy and comedy sink beneath the opiate of Dulness, it is the nontraditional "Sister" (IV.42) arts of history and satire that sustain them, acting as their substitutes in a debased age. The alliance Pope proposed between satire and history suggests that the satirist's art, like the historian's narrative, seeks a truth which is immediate, exemplary, and factual, distinct from the conventions of literary or fictive "truth." In *An Epistle to Dr. Arbuthnot* the historical and nonfictional perspective required by satire forces Pope to reject even his own best early work:

> Soft were my Numbers, who could take offence
> While pure Description held the place of Sense?
> Like gentle *Fanny's* was my flow'ry Theme,
> A painted Mistress, or a purling Stream.     (ll. 147–150)

Self-censure for Pope could not penetrate deeper than a comparison likening him to gentle Fanny, his sexually indefinite nickname for Lord Hervey. In rejecting the conventions of descriptive verse and literary pleasure, he implicitly affirms the satirist's passion for breaking through the maze of words, for making contact—sometimes forcefully—with the world outside satire. Sporus—Pope's other name for gentle Fanny in *An Epistle to Dr. Arbuthnot*—in some sense *is* Lord Hervey, in ways that extend the normal powers of mimesis, and Hervey's father, Lord Bristol, seems perfectly justified in referring to the poet as "that little poysonous adder Pope."[5] Satire conceals a real snake in an artificial garden. Pope as satirist had created, in his portrait of Sporus, a uniquely venomous fiction capable of inflicting severe wounds upon living contemporaries. Satire in his hands is a dangerous form of language. Its pleasures are almost always mixed with pain.

## Curse, Lash, and Apology

It is the association between satire and pain that I propose to explore in an effort to understand the distinctive, strange, and compelling language of satirical fictions. As Pope implied in rejecting his earlier descriptive verse, satire is an art which relies on its power to offend. Offensiveness was so natural to satire that its absence became for Dryden grounds for ridiculing Thomas Shadwell in *Mac Flecknoe:* "With whate'er gall thou sett'st thyself to write," Dryden taunts, "Thy inoffensive satires never bite" (ll. 199–200). Inoffensive satire, for Dryden and for Pope, is a contradiction in terms. Satire—which Dryden called "almost as old as verse"—had maintained its ancient alliance with various primal, violent, and uncivilized uses of language.[6] Its direct, if often unacknowledged, ancestor is the curse or spell, where words possess a magical power to inflict harm. "One great thing I know," boasts Archilochus, the legendary founder of satire: "how to recompense with evil reproaches him that doeth me evil."[7] The legend of Archilochus was still active in Pope's day, and Pope's ally Walter Harte ironically lamented that time had deprived satire of its original power to slay:

> More fierce, *Archilochus!* thy vengeful flame:
> Fools read and *dy'd:* for Blockheads then had *Shame.*[8]

Even if no longer lethal, even if civilized and refined through its accommodations with art, satire in Pope's age still remembered its archaic power to inflict injury upon its victims, and the Augustan satirist, though capable of infinite politeness and Horatian good humor, always had ready the forgotten or unspoken language of violence, rooted in a timeless past. Access to such knowledge is sufficient to render the satirist feared and even despised. Wrote Addison: "I cannot but look upon the finest Strokes of Satyr which are aimed at particular Persons, and which are supported even with the Appearances of Truth, to be the Marks of an evil Mind, and highly Criminal in themselves" (*The Spectator* no. 451). Satire, with its power to inflict pain, seemed associated with human impulses and purposes now outlawed by polite society. Nor do only the abuses of satire—personal lampoon, libel or slander, and malicious lies—retain a trace of primitive dread. Even in its most smiling and toothless versions, Augustan satire makes us conscious of a power that is perhaps being withheld only temporarily, or is simply disguised, as Addison once implied: "*Satyr* had Smiles in her Look, and a Dagger under her Garment" (*The Spectator* no. 63). The rage of Archilochus may give way to smiling civility, but Augustan satire never wholly relinquishes its access to pain. It is polite yet unsociable, untrustworthy, unsafe. As Addison put it, "There is nothing so difficult to tame, as a Satyrical Author" (*The Spectator* no. 451).

The domestication of satire, of course, was a major project of the neoclassical mind. Dryden in English and Boileau in French provided models for transforming the cankered, rough, licentious, openly violent satire of the Renaissance into a form of civil discourse. Learned ironies and elegant wit began to supplant railling and abuse. This transformation of satire was timely, because wit and ridicule in late seventeenth-century England were under fierce attack as the instruments of irreligion, immorality, and personal spite.[9] Thus Richard Steele, in what became the standard eighteenth-century defense, was moved to assert that there was nothing in satire to outrage virtue and that "Good-Nature was an essential Quality in a Satyrist" (*The Tatler* no. 242). Libel laws proved more effective than such dubious assertions in taming the satirical spirit. As Pope wrote in very free imitation of Horace:

> At length, by wholesom dread of statutes bound,
> The Poets learn'd to please, and not to wound.[10]

Yet, eighteenth-century libel laws were not sufficient to prevent the wounds of satire, both because such laws were easily evaded and because libel was a useful instrument of political power. For example, after the Licensing Act (which granted the government effective powers of censorship) was allowed to lapse in 1694, succeeding ministries employed the statutes prohibiting libel as a tool for suppressing antigovernmental opinion, even while they hired political journalists such as Swift and Defoe to circulate libelous, anonymous attacks.

Strange as it sounds, literary scholarship, not libel laws, did most to promote the ideal of the satirist as a good citizen and honest teacher. Chief among the scholarly apologists for satire were the editors and critics of an earlier generation—Isaac Casaubon, Nicolas Rigault, Daniel Heinsius, Sir Robert Stapylton—whose learned prefaces and treatises strongly asserted the satirist's high moral purpose. Dryden in his famous "Discourse concerning the Original and Progress of Satire" (1693) echoes this pious tradition when he elevates satirical writing to a pinnacle of respectability. "Satire," he asserts, "is of the nature of moral philosophy, as being instructive."[11]

The wounding satirist is reborn as a moral philosopher, and satire is redeemed by the proclamation of a didactic purpose so worthy that it gets repeated with the regularity of a creed: "The principal end of *Satyr*, is to instruct the People by discrediting Vice," wrote René Rapin. "The true end of *Satyre*, is the amendment of Vices by correction," said Dryden. "The End of Satyr is Reformation," claimed Defoe.[12]

Instruction, amendment, reformation: such edifying purposes take us far from the "one great thing" Archilochus knew, as satire in the Augustan Age is drawn, like so many other literary forms, into a poetics of refinement, improvement, and correction. Yet, there is more to the Augustan discussion of satire than pious assurances that satirists are men of good nature who write with high moral purpose. We must listen also to less official voices. We must consider by what *means* morality attains its ends. We must ask if instruction, amendment, and reformation are the *only* purposes which animate the muse of satire.

"When you think of the World," Swift wrote Pope in 1725, "give it one lash the more at my Request."[13] The lash of satire is such a common figure of speech that it often appears simply a dead or exhausted metaphor. "A Lash like mine no honest man shall dread," Pope writes in *Arbuthnot* (l. 303), and his metaphor seems merely conventional. Again in *Arbuthnot* Pope employs the same figure—"He lash'd him not" (l. 377)—and again the metaphor does not attract attention. Yet, for Augustan writers the lash of satire is an image containing a powerful reserve of implication and meaning. The distinguished French scholar-critic André Dacier could thus employ the lash as providing a full and sufficient definition of satirical writing. "Satyr," he writes in Charles Gildon's translation, "with us, signifies the same thing, as exposing, or lashing of some-thing or Person."[14] As a teacher, the satirist simply exchanges the lash for the rod, without yielding his right to distribute pain. Indeed, in that age of flogging pedagogues, like Westminster's notorious headmaster Dr. Richard Busby, whipping was a standard form of academic correction. Dr. Busby's appearance in *The Dunciad* is a moment of sublime mock-terror:

When lo! a Spectre rose, whose index-hand
Held forth the Virtue of the dreadful wand;
His beaver'd brow a birchen garland wears,
Dropping with Infant's blood, and Mother's tears.
O'er ev'ry vein a shudd'ring horror runs.     (IV.139–143)

219

Pope had personal experience with the "dreadful wand" of correction. His half-sister reports that he was "whipped and ill-used" at Twyford School—for the offense (appropriately) of composing a satire on his master. Satire and pain, as with Dr. Busby's appearance in *The Dunciad,* seem never far apart.

For Swift, the bond linking satire, pain, and schoolroom discipline provided a source of ready images. Imagining himself in collaboration with Caleb D'Anvers, who was a satirical character invented by Opposition writers in *The Craftsman,* Swift describes with some relish the corrective measures awaiting their foes:

> Let me, tho' the Smell be Noisom,
> Strip their Bums; let CALEB hoyse 'em;
> Then, apply ALECTO's Whip,
> Till they wriggle, howl, and skip.[15]

Swift's lines do nothing to allay the suspicion that some satirists, like certain infamous English schoolmasters, found a perverse pleasure in the act of correction. Even the courtly Boileau confessed that his muse took pleasure in administering lashes and grew bolder with each successive stroke. As Swift elaborates in the preface to *A Tale of a Tub:* "I have observ'd some Satyrists to use the Publick much at the Rate that Pedants do a naughty Boy ready Hors'd for Discipline: First expostulate the Case, then plead the Necessity of the Rod, from great Provocations, and conclude every Period with a Lash."[16] The lash of satire is an important image to recover. It allows us to recognize that the noble Augustan purposes of instruction, amendment, and reformation often prove inseparable from the process of inflicting and of receiving pain.

I will return to the subject of satirical punishment, but first we should ask whether the purposes of satire are always as noble and edifying as the apologists profess. Swift's letter to Pope is again instructive: "The chief end I propose to my self in all my labors is to vex the world rather then [sic] divert it." Vexation as the "chief end" of Swift's labors cannot be easily reconciled with the dominant literary program of instruction, amendment, and correction. (It is Gulliver—not Swift—who claims to write for the "amendment" of mankind and who notes unhappily that after six months his book had improved, corrected, or reformed no one at all.) In addition to such

official apologists as Dryden, we must take into account the unofficial
voices throughout Swift's work claiming that satire is perfectly use-
less, that it is a mirror in which we see everyone's face but our own, a
ball which we constantly strike from us, and that we are so insulated
by self-protective egotism and folly that we are, like the Yahoos, virtually unteachable. Our knowledge of satirical fictions, of course,
makes us wary of interpreting these voices as Swift's, yet wary too of
dismissing them outright. The means of education in the eighteenth
century were not always gentle, and we too easily forget that claims
about the "instructive" nature of satire may conceal vexation, pain,
and punitive force not usually associated with moral philosophy.
Alecto's whip is, in any case, slightly different from the schoolroom
rod of discipline. Alecto is one of the Furies, the demons of vengeance, and her name means unceasing-in-anger.

The punitive pain of satire sometimes extends far beyond a desire
to instruct or mildly vex. Swift confessed to Esther Johnson
("Stella") in the privacy of his journal that he had composed a popular and anonymous lampoon on a great man who had received him
coldly. "But say nothing," Swift cautions, "'twas only a little revenge."[17] Revenge, of course, cannot be limited to lampoon, which
Samuel Johnson defined in his *Dictionary* as "a personal satire;
abuse; censure written not to reform but to vex." The distinction between satire and lampoon, while evident at the extremes, continually
blurs when examined closely, and, although most writers agreed that
lampoons were unlawful, Dryden, like Swift, was unwilling to renounce so useful a weapon. In his "Discourse concerning Satire"
Dryden identified two occasions when he believed lampoons were
justifiable: first, when the person attacked had become a "public nui-
sance"—an exemption that would therefore protect only the obscure
and innocuous; and second, when the writer composes for purposes
of personal "revenge."[18]

This sanction of vengeance caused Dryden great uneasiness, for he
acknowledges at length that revenge is incompatible with Christian
forgiveness. Revenge, nevertheless, remained in his view an acceptable or unavoidable motive, as it did for Pope. Once Pope sought re-
prisal for numerous small injuries by slipping an emetic into the
drink of the unscrupulous bookseller Edmund Curll. But literary revenge held subtler powers of torment, and within days Pope had
published the story of Curll's misfortune as *A Full and true Account*

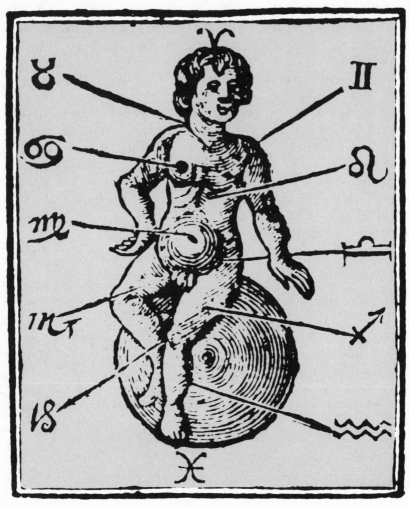

4   Zodiac Man, from *The Ladies' Almanac* (1725).

*of a Horrid and Barbarous Revenge by Poison on the Body of Mr. Edmund Curll* (1716). Writing for Pope extends and refines mere bodily pain. For example, he explained to Joseph Spence that various literary maneuvers preliminary to final publication of *The Dunciad* were meant to distract and torment its real-life antihero, Colley Cibber. "He will be stuck, like the man in the almanac," Pope exults, "not deep, but all over. He won't know which way to turn himself to. [He will be] exhausted at the first stroke, and reduced to passion and calling names, so that he won't be able to write more, and won't be able to bear living without writing."[19] Here is truly diabolical artifice. Pope's galling fictions will not only torment Cibber but deprive him of the power to retaliate. The man in the almanac to whom Pope refers is a chubby figure pierced with diagrammatic lines like a smiling Saint Sebastian (figure 4). Yet there is more than comedy in the picture of Cibber "stuck all over." It suggests that satire, for Pope, differs from other genres not in its artfulness but in the violence its fictions hold, often tenuously, under control.

The violence of Augustan satire is usually held in reserve, not roughly displayed from beginning to end in ways which would erode its effectiveness. This *reserved* violence—so different from the open and sustained abusiveness of much Renaissance satire—extends not just to actual people like Cibber. The violation of polite standards and decorous manners is equally provoking, especially when performed with an air of politeness. Yet, in its sometimes coarse diction and unsavory images, Pope's satire will also abandon politeness, risking a direct assault on the normal Augustan virtues of moderation, good taste, and restraint. "This filthy Simile, this beastly Line, / Quite turns my Stomach," one of Pope's impersonated opponents complains, referring to a comparison in which Pope described court wits as a circle of hogs, with each hog eating its neighbor's excrement.[20] Satire, even when on its best behavior, threatens to cross the borders of taboo, to shock and outrage "decent" people. Think of the responses to part four of *Gulliver's Travels,* where Gulliver identifies mankind with the beastly and degraded Yahoos, a vision which Thackeray censured as "furious, raging, obscene." Transgression—passing from decency to the obscene—is a characteristic resource of Augustan satire and never fails to draw a pained reproof. As Johnson observed in condemnation: "Pope and Swift had an unnatural delight in ideas physically impure, such as every other tongue utters with unwillingness, and of which every ear shrinks from the mention."[21] Johnson here clearly sees the power of the greatest Augustan satirists to push beyond what he considers *universally* accepted standards of decorum. Satire, in this sense, may be said to repossess areas of experience outlawed by the civilized psyche and polite community. It reminds us of what is unmentionable and speaks what we are unwilling to hear. Such violations help explain why Addison, as representative of the new gentility, could protest so vehemently against the satirist's art. It is no accident that Pope included a portrait of Addison in *An Epistle to Dr. Arbuthnot.* "Atticus" has not purified himself of satirical, violent impulses; he is instead timid and hypocritical: "Willing to wound, but yet afraid to strike" (l. 203). The satirist's uncivilized willingness to strike not only distinguishes Pope from Atticus but also suggests why Addison would declare all personal strokes of satire "Criminal." Addison's metaphor expresses far more than simply his antagonism to certain kinds of wit. Criminality is a concept that regularly appears throughout the voluminous eighteenth-century discussions of satire. What does it mean, we must ask, when satirists so often find in crime a cluster of images and ideas that somehow describes their activities? What is the relationship that binds satirists to criminals, as if (like modern doctors and patients) they are locked in an intimacy perhaps neither truly desires?

## Crime and Punishment

Criminality provides Augustan satirists with a rich store of abusive images and epithets for denigrating their enemies. Abuse, however, can tap much more eloquent sources of denigration. The relation between satire and crime goes deeper than name-calling. Their buried connection is at least partly visible in the etymology linking pain (Latin *poena*) with punishment. Punishment in the eighteenth century usually implied the infliction of pain, and satire was widely regarded as an art of punishment. Renaissance theory and practice, of course, had recognized a punitive element in satire, most notably in the satirical figures of the railler and scourge, who whip and punish their enemies, sometimes punishing themselves in the process. The scourge and railler, however, even if viewed as administering divine justice, are outside the legal and social systems within which Augustan satire operates, and their wholly unrefined language—like the scurrilous, ribald, and obscene verses which Pope condemned in "beastly Skelton"—was exactly what Augustan satirists wished to avoid.[22] A more acceptable acknowledgment of pain was available from Renaissance theories that compare satire to medicine, and Pope once referred to this medical tradition when he defended satire as an art which "heals with Morals what it hurts with Wit."[23] Here again we should notice his open acknowledgment of the pain satire can cause. Yet, Pope seldom mentions the medical theory of satire. Surgery until 1745 was still the trade of barbers—hardly a group that Augustan writers would wish to resemble—and healing was not a purpose Pope generally assigned to satire. What he preserves from Renaissance theories of satire is an interest in punishment and pain, but he changes the theoretical framework within which pain and punishment are understood. The pain of Augustan satire is neither divine affliction nor surgical healing but the social, deterrent pain of the law.

In exploring the legal or judicial basis of Pope's satire, we must be aware of several facts about the eighteenth-century system of justice.[24] One crucial difference from our own system is that in Pope's day imprisonment was not the normal social response to crime. Prisons—our supposedly painless response—were reserved primarily for pretrial detention. They were also employed for debtors, who could leave when the debt was paid, and for vagrants. In most other cases, once a trial was over, once a sentence was pronounced, the criminal's body was the locus of punishment. Loss of liberty was rare. Instead, branding, confinement in a pillory, whipping, hard labor, and other afflictions of the flesh were among the most common instruments of justice. Hanging was the standard penalty for most crimes where damages exceeded forty shillings, and, through the Black Act and similar new legislation, the crimes for which people could be hanged multiplied dramatically in Pope's lifetime. The gallows now awaited numerous criminals convicted of what we would consider clearly noncapital offenses, such as horse stealing, picking pockets, arson, receiving stolen goods, forgery, impersonation with intent to defraud, blackmail, or burglary. Often local judges and juries contrived to avoid sentencing a criminal to death, reducing the penalty to one less harsh, such as whipping or transportation to the colonies. But, in contrast to the modern goal of correction or "rehabilitation" through imprisonment, the goal of eighteenth-century justice was deterrence. No matter whether sentences were reduced or executed with full severity, the deterrent function of pain was unquestioned. Punishment was public; it was directed in most cases at the body of the criminal; and it was meant not to reform or to correct the offender but to deter everyone, culprit and crowd alike, from criminal activity.

The theory of deterrence was eventually swept aside in the great humanitarian reforms initiated in the late eighteenth century, but in Pope's day its primacy was secure. Pain thus had a legal function that extended throughout the system of justice, even in punishments we might consider relatively mild. For example, standing in the pillory would seem more embarrassing than painful, but a foreign visitor to England in the eighteenth century reported otherwise: "This position is so uncomfortable *as to become gradually unbearable.* The low populace, to make this punishment worse, pelts the prisoner with mud, rotten apples, dead cats and dogs."[25] Such suffering had to be public, for how else could punishment deter? Hangings thus sometimes resembled public carnivals. Criminals were flogged through the streets. Mutilated corpses were left hanging in irons, and the heads of traitors grinned atop long poles or pikes. Instead of being hidden away, most eighteenth-century criminals suffered in ways which transformed the body into a visual sign carrying a clear message to the assembled spectators.

The fictions of satire may strike modern readers as cruel, but they are often no match for the reality of the law. Most students of literature, for example, know the name Titus Oates mainly because Oates appears as the figure Corah in Dryden's *Absalom and Achitophel.* His two indictments for perjury in the trials associated with the Popish Plot, however, drew Oates far milder treatment from Dryden than from Lord Chief Justice Sir George Jeffreys. Jeffreys' sentence included the requirement that on two successive days Oates would stand in the pillory, first at the gate to Westminster Hall ("with a paper over your head declaring your crime, which you must first walk with round about to all the courts in Westminster hall"), then at the Royal Exchange in London. On the third day Oates was to be whipped from Aldgate to Newgate and next, after a day's rest, whipped from Newgate to Tyburn. Jeffreys' sentence did not stop with provisions for public punishment on those five days but continued with an extraordinary provision for Oates's "annual punishment." Every year as long as he lived Oates was ordered—on appropriately commemorative dates—to stand in the pillory: on April 24 at Tyburn, on August 9 at the Westminster Hall gate, on August

10 at Charing Cross, on August 11 at Temple Gate, and on September 2 at the Royal Exchange.[26] What is most unusual about the annual progress through these stations of pain is the clarity with which it reveals how public punishment resembled a violent form of street theater. Like the paper over his head ("declaring your crime"), Oates's body was meant to be read as a cautionary text. Jeffreys' ingenious punishment succeeded in transforming Oates into something like a living satire.

The relation between law and satire has evident limits, for folly in its milder shapes is often wisely left to constitute its own punishment, as it is in *The Rape of the Lock*. Yet, elsewhere Pope openly endorsed the relation between satire and jurisprudence when he announced his subject as "Crimes that scape, or triumph o'er the Law."[27] In effect, law establishes a context for justifying the pain that satire causes. The satirical victim has quasi-legal status as a malefactor; his arraignment is a form of poetic justice; and the satirist, after serving first as judge and jury, steps forward to carry out the necessary punishment, all for the public good. The reader, like the crowd at eighteenth-century executions, holds the uneasy and sometimes alarming role of witness, for whom the spectacle of someone else's punishment cannot be entirely undisturbing. (James Boswell, in his role as spectator, passed nights of stark terror after witnessing the executions he could not prevent himself from attending.) Here is how the rough Restoration satirist John Oldham addressed himself to an offending printer:

> Perhaps thou hop'dst that thy obscurity
> Should be thy Safeguard, and secure thee free.
> No, Wretch, I mean from thence to fetch thee out,
> Like sentenc'd Felons, to be drag'd about:
> Torn, mangled and expos'd to Scorn, and Shame,
> I mean to hang, and Gibbet up thy Name.[28]

The gibbet extended legal punishment even beyond death, subjecting the corpse (hung in irons) to the final injuries of mutilation, exposure, and lingering decay, much as the bodies of notorious criminals were sent to the dissecting theater as a last humiliation. Oldham's violent invective is an example of exactly what Augustan satirists wished to reform, but in refining the language of satire they nonetheless retained the metaphors of crime and punishment that govern Oldham's rant. To the extent that a name or reputation is an extension of a person, the Augustan satirist often proceeds—in a much more refined manner—with the same process of execution that Oldham describes.

Even the classic Augustan defense of satire as an art of "fine raillery" cannot remove all traces of judicial violence. In a passage more often quoted than analyzed, Dryden in his "Discourse concerning Satire" concludes his defense of artful raillery with a memorable comparison: "There is still a vast difference betwixt the slovenly butchering of a man, and the fineness of a stroke that separates the head from the body, and leaves it standing in its place. A man may be capable, as Jack Ketch's wife said of his servant, of a plain piece of work, a bare hanging; but to make a malefactor die sweetly was only belonging to her husband."[29] Dryden's analogy is so witty that its implications are usually ignored. It is possible that a Shakespearean bawdiness associated with the ideas of dying and hanging imparts an undercurrent of sexual innuendo to Dryden's comparison. But far more striking is the metaphor of execution which dominates his description of satire. Dryden, in contrasting rough invective with fine raillery, offers simply two versions of dismemberment, two types of hanging. The question at issue wholly concerns the aesthetics of injury.

The aesthetics of injury is not a trivial issue, for the annals of early modern capital punishment contain frightful accounts of hangmen whose miscalculations concerning weights and distances resulted in grisly, unplanned decapitations. The "slovenly butchering" of a man was not a fanciful image but a brutal fact of the gallows and the block. When Captain Kidd was hanged in 1701 the rope broke and he had to be hauled up and hanged a second time. There was good reason why the condemned often presented the executioner with a gift—half of which might be entrusted to friends or family until the job had been decently and swiftly accomplished. Yet, an improved or refined execution is still an execution. The satirist who leaves the severed head standing in place has demonstrated great skill and art, but we must not entirely neglect what this art has accomplished. Of course, Dryden is only writing in metaphor. His choice of metaphor, however, is not entirely casual or innocent.

As it is in Dryden's influential defense of fine raillery, the relationship between satire and legal or quasi-legal punishment is intrinsic to much of the greatest Augustan satire. The crucial and necessary qualification, in any case, is that satirical and judicial deterrence are linked not merely through punishment but—as the punishment of Titus Oates demonstrates—through what might be called the stylization of pain. Satirical pain requires art. Thus Lady Mary Wortley Montagu understood that the surest way to injure Pope was to malign his skill as an artful stylist. In *Verses Address'd to the Imitator of Horace* (1733) she abuses him with a deftly calculated thrust:

> *Satire* shou'd, like a polish'd Razor keen,
> Wound with a Touch, that's scarcely felt or seen.
> Thine is an Oyster-Knife, that hacks and hews.  (p. 4)

We should notice that Lady Mary affirms, even celebrates, the premise that satire exists to inflict wounds, but just as important is her Augustan proviso that the wounds of satire be so refined that the victim scarcely will recognize them. The satirist, Dryden and Lady Mary both agree, is a refined assailant, someone who wounds softly and sweetly, before we know what has happened.

It is a peculiar wound which the victim scarcely sees or feels. What elegant refinement of pain shall we call it when we are injured without our knowledge? On a question so delicate Augustan theories of satire are in deep disagreement. For example, Dryden distinguishes between the responses of two different classes of satirical victims. "A witty man is tickled while he is hurt in this manner," he claims, "and a fool feels it not."[30] In describing the experience of witty men, Dryden does not deny their pain but argues that it is mixed with pleasure. His related claim that fools feel no injury is equally significant because it repeats a standard argument among satirists. "You think this cruel?" Pope asks in *An Epistle to Dr. Arbuthnot*, adding: "Take it for rule, / No creature smarts so little as a Fool" (ll. 83–84). Yet, in apparent self-contradiction, Pope elsewhere defended the use of fictionalized portraits in satire by arguing that generality multiplies pain: "A hundred smart in *Timon* and in *Balaam*."[31] Perhaps he means a hundred men of wit, but, in truth, the pro forma disclaimer that victims of satire feel no pain is almost always hedged with loopholes—such as Lady Mary's complacent adverb "scarcely." Even Dryden's unfeeling fools will come to know their wound, he allows, when the "malicious world" informs them. Is delayed pain less painful? Did Lady Mary honestly believe that Pope would experience a tickling pleasure when she compared his satire to an oyster knife?

The fiction of an almost painless wound is at best an official equivocation that obscures the awkward truth that satirists, unlike judges, punish without lawful authority. Finally, the pain not felt by certain insensitive victims is often reserved for the reader, for without at least the perception that someone is being punished, there is no deterrence.

As Pope in his late satires moves toward openly admitting his intention to deter rather than to reform, his satirical characters are increasingly associated with criminality. Sometimes they are real criminals, such as the aptly named Japhet Crook, who, in addition to his treatment in Pope's satire, was sentenced to stand in the pillory, to have both his ears cut off close to his head, to have both his nostrils slit and seared with a hot iron, and to be imprisoned for life.[32] The pain of satire was no doubt the least of his troubles. Outnumbering actual criminals, however, are culprits who, in Pope's words, "scape" the law or, worse, "triumph" over it. (Like so much else in Walpole's England, justice was frequently up for sale.) Even the minor dunces, whose crimes are literary rather than civil, receive from Pope the punishment commonly reserved for felons. The Advertisement prefatory to *The Dunciad* explains the poem's copious annotation with the following remark: "*If a word or two more are added upon the chief Offenders; 'tis only as a paper pinn'd upon the breast, to mark the Enormities for which they suffer'd; lest the Correction only should be remember'd, and the Crime forgotten.*" This is comic exaggeration, surely, but the metaphor of legal punishment and public execution is not randomly selected. As Pope wrote explicitly in a letter to Dr. Arbuthnot on the subject of satire: "To reform and not to chastise, I am afraid is impossible." Or again: "If some are hung up, or pilloryed, it may prevent others." Or, lastly, in what is an unmistakable illustration of how theories of satire and theories of justice coincide: "I hope to deter, if not to reform."[33] Reformation depended ultimately upon the self-improvement of the culprit. Deterrence required only that the culprit suffer—and that the spectator or reader bear witness.

## Sporus and Indignation

"Let *Sporus* tremble . . ." *An Epistle to Dr. Arbuthnot* is advertised as a "Bill of Complaint"—a formal list of legal charges—but it is more like the execution of a sentence, especially upon Lord Hervey as

represented by the character Sporus. The poem's ostensible subject is
Pope himself, the man and the poet, but the subject is developed primarily through a series of contrasting portraits that surround him
with the images of his contemporaries. It is the appearance of Sporus,
however, which generates the poem's intensest passion—loathing,
anger, outrage—and no discussion of the poem really makes sense
until we confront the astonishing energy of destructiveness centered
in the portrait of Sporus. Pope deftly employs Dryden's trick of
granting the good qualities which his enemy possesses—beauty, talent, wit, birth—and then turning them to contempt. He allows us to
say of Sporus that even his virtues are repulsive:

> Beauty that shocks you, Parts that none will trust,
> Wit that can creep, and Pride that licks the dust. (ll. 332–333)

It is the power of beauty, Pope insists in *The Rape of the Lock*, to
attract us, to master us, to draw us with a single hair, like Hercules
enchained by eloquence (ii.28). In Sporus we encounter a paradoxical beauty that does not attract but appalls and repels, thus achieving
the effect usually attributed to its opposite, ugliness, just as pride in
Sporus stoops to the basest servility. Like the process of self-negation
at work in Wharton and Atossa, there is a radical incoherence to
Sporus which links every trait with its opposite, so that character
seems nullified in self-contradiction. Sporus, as Pope depicts him, is a
personified antithesis—"now Master up, now Miss" (l. 324)—in
whom stable identity seesaws in a continual undoing. Amorphous,
plaint, he is a man of "Parts" or abilities whose accomplishments
arouse only mistrust. He is a man of wit whose intelligence lowers
rather than exalts him. We dissipate the power of Pope's satirical
portrait if we too quickly observe that, as Sporus, Lord Hervey has
been transformed into an image of evil incarnate: "*Eve's* Tempter
thus the Rabbins have exprest, / A Cherub's face, a Reptile all the
rest" (ll. 330–31). Pope's point is that evil incarnate looks different
than we had imagined. Incarnate evil in the modern world is no Miltonic Satan commanding a mighty legion of devils. We must learn to
recognize it instead in an effete, smiling, dimpled, witty, duplicitous
court fop, for whom no act of corruption is too vile. The portrait of
Sporus is not an example of what Dryden praised as "fine raillery."
Pope's withering contempt rises above coarse invective, but rarely
has finesse been wedded to such destructive force. As Joseph War-

231

ton puts it accurately: "He has armed his muse with a scalping knife."[34]

How are we to understand the violence contained in the portrait of Sporus? Such violence does engender the satirical pain guaranteed by the theory of deterrence, but it also obviously and simply expresses anger. As a normal human emotion, anger is easy to recognize on the street, but its role in literary discourse is more problematic. We are eloquent in describing the minutest gradations of eros, but tend to fall silent before anger. Undoubtedly, recent emphasis on the fictive qualities of satire has discouraged analysis of the motives or impulses or passions that animate the satirist. Yet, anger is not only an emotion that often impels the satirist; it is also an energy contained and expressed by the satire; and, in some cases, it is transmitted directly to the reader, although in passing from satirist to work to reader it undergoes various transformations. The genesis of satire is as tangled as the origins of most literary works. But the importance of anger in satire goes beyond questions of origins. Perhaps it is time to reappraise, with proper caution, what place anger holds in the character of the satirist, in the experience of the reader, and in the satirical text.

When Pope praised Swift for defending Irish interests in his satires, Swift had nothing to say about the literary artifice and satirical fictions which modern critics admire. "What I do," he responded, "is owing to perfect rage and resentment, and the mortifying sight of slavery, folly, and baseness about me, among which I am forced to live."[35] The fictiveness of Swift's satires, in short, draws upon and transforms energies for which the word *anger* seems tame. "The essence of satire, we have suggested, is generally the symbol of an author's disappointment in, or even annoyance with, his world and its inhabitants," wrote two modern scholars who labor to assert the regenerative and redemptive powers of Augustan satire.[36] Unfortunately, such understatement and restraint simply cannot do justice to the violence of much great satire. In the thirty-second canto of the *Inferno* Dante—in a gesture which links satire with its primitive origins—kicks one of the immobilized sinners in the head. "You advise me right, not to trouble myself about the world," Swift wrote to Pope: "But, Oppression *tortures* me."[37] Swift's savage indignation is, by his own confession, the response to an intolerable pain, a torture, and the lash of satire—with which Swift inflicts pain and vexation in return—allows him in some sense to redistribute emotion. The differences in age, temperament, and philosophy separating Swift from

Pope make it especially significant to hear Pope in 1725 describe his literary plans in language that reflects a wholly Swiftian stance toward the world: "I'll sooner write something to anger it, than to please it."[38]

Anger, as a resource for writers and a response of readers, held a secure (even if subordinate) place in eighteenth-century discussions of satire. For example, it provided the basis for Dryden's praise of Juvenal, which is by modern standards an altogether disconcerting piece of literary criticism. Juvenal, as Dryden wrote in a revealing confession, "gives me as much pleasure as I can bear; he fully satisfies my expectation; he treats his subject home: his spleen is raised, and he raises mine."[39] Spleen, the seat of anger, seems a curious source of pleasure. In *The Rape of the Lock* Pope portrayed the Cave of Spleen as a region of pain and disfigurement where self-torment is characteristic. Classical and Christian moralists were united in their condemnation of anger. Seneca in his *De Ira* argued unyieldingly that anger cannot coexist with virtue, and Montaigne (among many others) advanced the argument. "There is no Passion that so much transports men from their right Judgments," he affirms, "as Anger."[40] Yet, Pope distinguished one occasion on which anger might be useful, even indispensable, and he described this occasion in *An Essay on Criticism*, written long before he expressed his plans to anger the world rather than please it. He imagined a critic whose temper could not be entirely reconciled with the principle of generosity:

> But if in Noble Minds some Dregs remain,
> Not yet purg'd off, of Spleen and sow'r Disdain,
> Discharge that Rage on more Provoking Crimes,
> Nor fear a Dearth in these Flagitious Times.     (ll. 526–529)

Like fame for Milton, anger here is a final infirmity of the magnanimous soul. Its counterpart in the technical vocabulary of eighteenth-century criticism was *indignation*—which Johnson defined as "the anger of a superior" (*Dictionary*). As a technical term, *indignation* has a history dating back at least as far as Quintilian, and its relevance to eighteenth-century satire should be clear from Dryden's entirely conventional description of Juvenal: "Juvenal always intends to move your indignation, and he always brings about his purpose."[41] Juvenal was in fact the writer who almost single-handedly established the validity and power of satirical anger.

The indignation concentrated in the portrait of Sporus has long perplexed readers of Pope, some of whom find its violence morally and aesthetically unintelligible. "The portrait is certainly *overcharged*," Joseph Warton observed, adding: "the strokes of satire in many parts of this epistle, have such an extraordinary energy and poignancy, that our author's want of temper has been much censured."[42] Pope's overcharged emotion seems singularly out of place, uncalled for, even self-contradictory, since the poem labors to create a contrary impression that Pope is forgiving and inoffensive. In this vein, the portraits of Atticus and Bufo, which precede that of Sporus, seem written more in sorrow than in anger. Nothing prepares us for the sudden violence of Pope's response to Sporus. It breaks out unexpectedly. Even Pope's interlocutor is surprised by the passion which the name of Sporus evokes:

> —"What? that Thing of silk,
> *Sporus*, that mere white Curd of Ass's milk?      (ll. 305–306)

Several readers have correctly sensed that Sporus functions in the poem as an antitype of the poet. The true and manly satirist meets in Sporus his opposite—the sycophant, the hypocrite, the liar, the hermaphrodite—and Pope's indignation thus expresses the antagonism of an eternal loathing.

Yet, the problem remains that the passionate anger aroused by Sporus seems to undermine Pope's self-portrait as a mild, forgiving, harmless man. "Whom have I hurt?" he earlier asks (l. 95). Thus, in attempting to calm or dissuade him, Pope's interlocutor reminds him of the tradition that fools are insensible to injury: " 'Satire or Sense alas! can *Sporus* feel? / Who breaks a Butterfly upon a Wheel' " (ll. 307–308). The engines of satirical pain, he implies, should be reserved for more substantial offenders. Yet, as we know, Pope cannot or will not be stopped but rushes on to the attack: "Yet let me flap this Bug . . ." (l. 309). Theories of satire here seem distant abstractions, for Pope depicts himself as possessed by the immediate and enigmatic violence with which a mild, patient man will suddenly crush an insect. The "imitator of Horace" (as Pope was addressed by Lady Mary) now reveals an un-Horatian capacity for anger which entirely revises our understanding of his character.

Pope's outburst of intemperate, indignant anger in *An Epistle to Dr. Arbuthnot* is not an aesthetic or ethical lapse—in the sense of being undesigned or inappropriate—but part of a deliberate strategy. It is his purpose to reveal in the "imitator of Horace" a capacity for Juvenalian indignation that will surprise his readers—and deter his enemies. Yet, the indignation dramatized in Pope's portrait of Sporus, even if justified, must also be revealed as temporary. In addition to demonstrating his capacity for indignant anger, Pope must also demonstrate that indignation is not his permanent state of mind or an uncontrollable passion, as it sometimes seems in Juvenal. Indeed, the Angry Man is a stock figure of comedy, as Pistol is in Shakespeare or Kastril is in Jonson, and his lesson to a talented satirist is clear. "Did you never mind what your angry critics published against you?" Spence asked Pope. "Never much," he replied: "only one or two things at first. When I heard for the first time that Dennis had writ against me, it gave me some pain, but it was quite over as soon as I came to look into his book and found he was in such a passion."[43] Pope surely exaggerates his tranquillity, but we should not discount his awareness that impassioned anger may neutralize the pain it wishes to inflict. As opposed to mere rage or anger, the controlled, rational, stylized violence of indignation is what permits satire to inflict a truly lasting pain. Such lingering, almost permanent punishment is what Samuel Johnson had in mind when he described satire as equipped with a quiver of poisoned arrows—"which, where they once drew blood, could by no skill ever be extracted" (*The Rambler* no. 22).

It is not merely the protraction of injury that Pope accomplishes by deliberately circumscribing his anger. While he endows his character as poet with a passion and candor that Atticus so sadly lacks, he also emphasizes a self-possession that even his anger cannot—for long—destroy. Thus, after the explosive passion of the Sporus episode, Pope contrives to end the poem in a spirit of quiet reverence, centered in virtue, as he resumes his character as the self-possessed imitator of Horace. The concluding portrait of his own father may be Pope's implicit signal that Horace is again his model, for Dryden had conspicuously praised Horace for creating "the best character of a father I ever read."[44] This Horatian ending, however, is not meant to erase our recollection of Pope's capacity for indignant anger, which Horace never revealed. The combination of Horatian and Juvenalian modes is itself doubtless another deliberate tactic in Pope's self-portrayal as a satirist. Everything we know of Pope assures us that, confronted

235

with the traditional contrast between Juvenal and Horace, he would not identify himself as a satirist with either extreme—violent indignation or smiling good humor—but would instead follow a strategy of refinement, as he does in *Arbuthnot*, that would allow him to combine the strengths of both.

## "No Names": The Individuation of Pain

*An Epistle to Dr. Arbuthnot* continues an argument—both within Pope's works and within the journals of the day—concerning the merits of general versus individual satire. Satire, according to the pro-Walpole *London Journal*, is just only when it is concerned with general vice and folly: the satirist who attacks specific persons is guilty of libel (no. 5). Arbuthnot, in a letter written a few months before his death, had also seemed to urge Pope to restrict himself to such general satire, not for fear of libel but because satire that aims at specific persons is exceedingly dangerous. (Dryden, as was well known, had been beaten in Rose Alley because of a satire.) In *An Epistle to Dr. Arbuthnot* Pope's interlocutor voices a similar caution:

> —"Hold! for God-sake—you'll offend:
> No Names—be calm—learn Prudence of a Friend:
> I too could write, and I am twice as tall,
> But Foes like these!" (ll. 101–104)

The passage returns us to the question of satire's inherent offensiveness. Although the policy of "No Names" seems a straightforward counsel of safety, yet, as Pope knew, the issue of general versus individual satire was less easily solved. Not naming names contained its own danger. "Ev'n those you touch not, hate you," an anonymous adviser warns him.[45] (To touch, according to Johnson, means to censure.) General portraits create the risk that Pope's enemies would misapply them to his friends and allies, thus embroiling him in endless difficulties. This once happened. In fact, the violence of Pope's attack on Lord Hervey as Sporus owes much to a damaging rumor Pope blamed on Hervey: that Pope's generalized portrait of Timon—from the epistle *To Burlington*—actually satirized Pope's ally the Duke of Chandos. (Hervey's mischievous rumor proves truly satanic if, as some scholars believe, the portrait of Timon was meant as a veiled attack on Hervey's patron, Walpole.) In the devious and counterplotting world of political satire, individual, named portraits would at least limit the damage possible from hostile misattributions. We underestimate both the dangers and the attractions of Augustan satire if we ignore the sense in which general and individual portraits could be equally damaging. Yet, while Pope as satirist took pains to avoid legal entanglements because of his satire, he apparently dismissed such concern as Arbuthnot's for his personal safety. "My brother," Pope's half-sister reported, "does not seem to know what fear is."[46]

For Pope, the argument concerning general versus individual satire must be decided not on grounds of safety but on ethical and literary grounds, as his reply to Arbuthnot's dying request makes explicit: "To attack Vices in the abstract, without touching Persons, may be safe fighting indeed, but it is fighting with Shadows . . . The only sign by which I found my writings ever did any good, or had any weight, has been that they rais'd the anger of bad men."[47] This statement is fascinating in suggesting how satire differs from other literary forms. Against postmodern preoccupations with literary works as self-referential systems of language, Pope writes of satire as a direct engagement with the "Persons" who make up what we call the real (nonfictional) world. His satire is a form of "attack" on vice as it manifests itself in specific individuals, and the "anger" of his opponents is Pope's assurance that his language has indeed made contact with the world outside fiction. There was nothing fictitious about the pistols he carried for protection on his walks between Twickenham and Richmond. His engagement through satire with the world outside fiction Pope considered the most important change in his career, which he described in a famous couplet from *Arbuthnot:*

> That not in Fancy's Maze he wander'd long,
> But stoop'd to Truth, and moraliz'd his song.     (ll. 340–341)

Pope's development as a satirist, from the first version of *The Rape of the Lock* in 1712 to the final version of *The Dunciad* in 1743, is shaped by his recognition that evil cannot be effectively opposed unless individuals are held responsible, publicly, for their misdeeds. There is nothing but scorn in his ironic praise of generalized satirical portraits that he finally rejects as ineffectual: "Come harmless *Char-*

*acters* that no one hit."[48] To be effective, satire cannot be innocent or
inoffensive, restricted to fictive "types" and general "characters." It
must "hit" individuals. It must take what risks are necessary to make
bad men angry. *An Epistle to Dr. Arbuthnot*, with its recognizable
portraits of contemporary figures, is a decisive step toward the explicitness of Pope's boldest satirical writings of the late 1730s. ("Yet
none but you by Name the Guilty lash."[49]) Satire, Pope came to believe, must inflict its pain and punishment upon specific living persons. "Nothing can be *Just* that is not *Personal*," he wrote, almost as
if responding to the *London Journal:* "I am afraid that all such Writings and Discourses as touch no Man, will mend no Man."[50]

The injuriousness of satire is part of its history and part of its nature, no matter how offensive such stylized violence appears to readers for whom deterrence is an obsolete and barbarous theory. Pain
and pleasure were for Pope, as for Aristotle, not simple sensations but
moral categories, intrinsic to ethical life. In *An Essay on Man* Pope
took the extreme position that pleasure, depending on how it is understood, constitutes either "Our greatest evil, or our greatest good"
(ii.92). Like pleasure, pain may prove beneficial or harmful, depending on how it is understood. The literary uses of pain cannot
possibly be understood, however, if criticism systematically ignores,
denies, or deplores satire's power to inflict injury. Thus we should
resist the attempts to detoxify Augustan satire through assurances—
from Pope's contemporaries or from modern scholars—that satirical
attacks are ultimately redemptive and regenerative, that satirists are
always good-natured and humane. Despite Pope's self-serving argument that satire is a "sacred" weapon reserved for the defense of
truth, denied to all but "Heav'n-directed" hands, the fact seems
rather that satire, like other weapons, can also be skillfully used by
absolute villains.[51] Some satirists write with uplifting moral purpose,
some do not.

More fruitful than inquiries into the morality of satire is the recognition that satire, as a weapon, constitutes a form of literary discourse uniquely concerned with power. Satire is a resource that writers of any persuasion may use whenever anger and indignation
and the less violent tensions of wit demand a strong language. Perhaps the aggressive and potent energies of Augustan satire, especially
the anger and indignation Pope demonstrates in *An Espistle to Dr.
Arbuthnot*, are best visible by contrast. Compare the poet of *Arbuth-*

*not*, for example, with a figure who comes to dominate nineteenth-century literature: the kindly author. This serene, wise, compassionate, humane individual—who so often narrates the Victorian novel—personifies the central values of a fiction that turns away from contemporary strife. As James R. Kincaid explains: "The recurrent lessons of many nineteenth-century novels are of pessimistic tolerance, realized in withdrawal. The object is not truth but kindness, even, sometimes, the simple ability not to cause pain."[52] The willingness to cause pain is, as I have argued, fundamental to Augustan satire. The Augustan satirist is often far from tolerant—as in Swift's version of Catholicism in *A Tale of a Tub*—while pessimism leads not to withdrawal but to strenuous engagement. In his satire Pope comes *out* from retirement. His object is not kindness or inoffensiveness but truth, however painful to individuals. Swift, who more than once announced his hatred for mankind, wrote of Pope: "I will swear you have fifty times more Charity for mankind than I could ever pretend to."[53] From a contemporary who knew Pope well, this is reliable evidence, which finds support in the emphasis on charity, sympathy, generosity, and benevolence throughout Pope's work. Yet, Pope also observed a careful distinction. "I hate no man as a man," he wrote, "but I hate vice in any man; I hate no sect, but I hate uncharitableness in any sect."[54] The emotional energy of hatred—so closely akin to pain and anger—is inseparable from the greatest Augustan satire. Pope's satire often seeks to imprint its fictions upon the world which receives it much as a lash imprints itself upon the flesh, transforming words into weapons. Satire is the revenge of sense upon men and women who seemed so often incorrigible—foolish, corrupt, greedy, vicious, stupid, and dangerous—unwilling to listen to reason.

The functions of pain in satire to punish and deter the unreasonable are linked with a biblical question that Pope had pondered directly: *Wherefore doth the way of the wicked prosper?* (note to *Iliad* XIII.779). In the 1730s Pope approached this question from two directions. First, in *An Essay on Man* he argued that the wicked only *seem* to prosper. Despite their wealth or fame, they are always secretly miserable or self-deceived, since happiness resides in virtue alone. This philosophical account equating true prosperity with virtue did not entirely satisfy Pope, however, perhaps because only a philosopher could believe it consistently. Were Hervey and Walpole and Chartres truly miserable? If so, their lack of self-knowledge prevented them from always understanding or feeling the extent of their misery. Thus Pope allowed himself a second approach to the question of why evil prospers. The pain of satire, as Pope employs it, deprives wickedness of its self-insulating complacency. It forces the villainous to experience both the reality of their unhappy state and the unhappiness they cause others. In this office, the satirist is merely the agent for awakening vice to its own nature. In the satirist's hands, pain reestablishes its traditional association with wickedness, so that vice is denied even the illusion of happiness. Prosperity, for criminals who escape the law, will not be unmixed with torment, for the satirist ensures that knaves will feel a pain which is not merely the punishment of vice but also its natural condition.

# ❧ IX

## Politics, Time, and Deformity:
## *Epilogue to the Satires*

It is remarkable that the expletive Mr. Pope generally used by
way of oath, was, "God mend me!"

—*The World*, 50 (Dec. 13, 1753)

"THERE'S NO fooling with Life, when it is once turn'd
beyond Forty," wrote the seventeenth-century poet
and essayist Abraham Cowley, whom Pope admired for his heartfelt
truths even though Cowley's labored pindarics and metaphysical
style had passed from favor.[1] Pope had turned forty in 1728, the year
that signaled his transition to satire with the appearance of *The Dunciad* in its initial three-book format. Pope was fifty when he published the equally transitional *Epilogue to the Satires* (1738), which
closed a decade of ethical writing unparalleled in English poetry.
Pope was acutely conscious of the sense of closure. He concluded the
epistolary satire that had occupied him steadily during the 1730s with
a firm resolution—later printed as a final annotation to the *Epilogue*—"to publish no more." We should understand Pope's five-year
silence after publishing the *Epilogue* not as an evasion or disclaimer
of his responsibilities as satirist, but as a steadfast refusal. He called it
"a sort of PROTEST." The corruption of the times had grown so insuperable, he explained, that satire was now both "unsafe" and "ineffectual."[2] Yet, the decade of Pope's forties was also a time of personal
changes which in some sense predicted his refusal to publish.
Repeatedly his letters express versions of his statement to Bolingbroke, after a period of severe illness, that he had left behind a former
stage of life: "I am already arriv'd to an Age which more awakens my
diligence to live Satisfactorily, than to write unsatisfactorily."[3] Art

for Pope in the 1730s finds its justification almost wholly as an instrument of the ethical life.

His forties especially sharpened Pope's sense of change by forcing upon him an intensified experience of illness and loss. At age thirty-nine he could write, in reference to his own weakness and the condition of friends: "I see and hear of nothing but sickness and death."[4] Six years later the death of his elderly mother, whom he had tended devoutly during her long years of decline, initiated what Pope called a "new AEra" in his life. Yet, while freeing him from the pleasing melancholy of his constant attention to her needs, the loss of his mother (with whom he felt a deep companionship) also served as a reminder of other recent losses. These Pope recorded in his Elzevir edition of Virgil. Beginning when Pope was thirty-five, they include the death of John Gay in 1723, the same year in which Pope lost Bishop Atterbury to exile; the death of Robert Harley in 1724; in 1726 the death of Pope's lesser-known friends Robert Digby and Edward Blount; in 1728 the death of Congreve and Swift's permanent return to Ireland. Soon after Pope's mother died in 1733, Bolingbroke left for voluntary exile in France, while in 1735 death claimed both Lord Peterborough and Dr. Arbuthnot. "I am a man of desperate fortunes," Pope wrote in his late forties, "that is, a man whose friends are dead: for I never aimed at any other fortune than in friends."[5]

The changes around him were inevitably accompanied by internal changes. With the steady loss of friends Pope also grew more conscious of the toll time exacted from his own character. In imitating a passage from Horace, he altered the meaning slightly but decisively in describing the loss of his companions as a form of self-diminishment:

> Years foll'wing Years, steal something ev'ry day,
> At last they steal us from our selves away;
> In one our Frolicks, one Amusements end,
> In one a Mistress drops, in one a Friend:
> This subtle Thief of Life, this paltry Time,
> What will it leave me, if it snatch my Rhime?
> If ev'ry Wheel of that unweary'd Mill
> That turn'd ten thousand Verses, now stands still.[6]

The tone of this passage is so mixed—compounded of meditative pathos, irony, and self-deprecating humor—that we cannot know quite how to understand Pope's attitude toward his art, which seems all that stands between self and nothingness, all that (in its unwearied motion) remains constant amid his growing sense of departure and change. The farewell or leave-taking is a repeated gesture in his later verse. Pope had once described the poet's life as leaving father and mother to cleave unto the Muse. Now even the Muses are included in a half-joking, half-serious valediction. As he tells his old friend John Caryll: "It is high time after the fumbling age of forty is past, to abandon those ladies, who else will quickly abandon us."[7]

## From the Golden Age to History

Pope is among the first English poets who considered poetry his vocation, his life's work, and who understood his literary acts as constituting a developing career or oeuvre. The *Epilogue to the Satires*, closing the decade of his forties and his series of Horatian imitations, thus offers an appropriate occasion for examining several important changes in Pope's career. He began, of course, committed to the Virgilian paradigm of poetic development, leading from pastoral to georgic to epic. After *Windsor-Forest*, the Virgilian schema began to wobble and finally collapsed. Instead of the original epic he had planned—on the subject of Brutus, legendary founder of Britain—Pope turned to the mock-heroic, to translations of Homer, and to Horatian epistles and satires. One reason for his failure or refusal to create an original epic poem was doubtless Pope's unshakable distrust of heroism. *An Essay on Man* casts a cold eye on traditions of heroic conduct, present and past:

> Heroes are much the same, the point's agreed,
> From Macedonia's madman to the Swede;
> The whole strange purpose of their lives, to find
> Or make, an enemy of all mankind! (iv.219–222)

From Alexander to Charles XII, Pope saw only a procession of lunatics and bullies, and even Homer's world, where poetry made large amends for a chronicle of bloodshed, clearly began to exhaust and to disspirit him. Achilles and Brutus were simply too ponderous, despite their virtues, to carry Pope's concern for the quality of individual lives. After Homer, he longed for a change. "I mean no more

243

Translations," he wrote, "but something domestic, fit for my own country, and for my own time."[8] The immediate present, in his occasional poems, had always offered Pope an appealing diversion from the demands of timeless themes and historical significance. In his forties, with each day stealing something irreplaceable, Pope made his "own time"—including his character as poet and the events of each new year—the explicit subject of his works.

The original titles of the two related "dialogues" which comprise the *Epilogue to the Satires* offer a vivid illustration of how he uses temporality as a theme in his later poetry. The full titles are *One Thousand Seven Hundred and Thirty Eight. A Dialogue Something like Horace* and *One Thousand Seven Hundred and Thirty Eight. Dialogue II.* A title consisting almost entirely of digits is more than a curiosity, more than a deliberate violation of strictures against numbering the streaks of the tulip. It represents a complete reversal of the course of Pope's poetic career. Just as *An Epistle to Dr. Arbuthnot* contains an explicit critique of his own early writings, the *Epilogue to the Satires* insists on its corrective relation to other aspects of Pope's oeuvre. As "epilogue" to the imitations of Horace which Pope published throughout the 1730s, it continues and comments upon the work which it implies is now at an end, much as the epilogue to a neoclassical play serves as both commentary and coda. But the numerical explicitness of the original titles also looks back to the very beginning of Pope's career and in a sense brings it full circle. The power of Pope's speech in the *Epilogue* depends in part on our recognition of how much has changed in his life and art.

Pope's changing attitudes toward time and literary form are most evident if we compare the *Epilogue* with his first published poems, known today under the collective name of the Pastorals. They were published originally in 1709, when Pope was little more than twenty, and appeared under the individual titles "Spring," "Summer," "Autumn," and "Winter." Such self-explanatory titles invite little commentary, but it is significant (in marking the change from Renaissance to neoclassical poetics) that Pope has reduced and simplified Spenser's twelve monthly pastorals in *The Shepheardes Calender* (1579)—a work to which Pope openly alludes—to the trim symmetry of four seasons. Significant, too, is the (limited) choice of sequence, because a series beginning in winter and ending in fall, for example, would convey quite different impressions. Pope chooses to begin the Pastorals in "Spring," which he depicts as a dewy and dawn-filled space, where there is no chronology, no history, only (as in Milton's Eden) an endless cycle of delight. Change in "Spring" exists simply to add the pleasures of variety to what is already perfect. Such changeless variety is appropriate, because a pastoral, according to Pope, is by definition uninvolved with time. It presents a picture of the *"Golden Age"* (*The Guardian* no. 40). Loving and singing are its chief actions, leisure pursuits devoid of genuine conflict; and, where conflict does not exist, coyness is welcome and seduction unnecessary. Like the bowl Daphnis proposes for a prize, embossed with images of the four seasons bound "in beauteous Order" (l. 40), "Spring" describes a world in which change is always harmonious and benign. The succeeding pastorals—"Summer," "Autumn," and "Winter"—introduce increasingly disharmonious elements. Love changes from erotic play to anxiety, betrayal, and loss. The songs grow strained. The final poem, "Winter," closes with the first of Pope's literary farewells, as Thyrsis stands at the point where pastoral dissolves irrevocably into the landscape of time:

> Sharp *Boreas* blows, and Nature feels Decay,
> Time conquers All, and We must Time obey.
> Adieu ye *Vales*, ye *Mountains*, *Streams* and *Groves*,
> Adieu ye Shepherd's rural *Lays* and *Loves*,
> Adieu my Flocks, farewell ye *Sylvan* Crew,
> *Daphne* farewell, and all the World adieu!

The change that converts the Virgilian *omnia vincit amor* into Pope's elegiac and pessimistic "Time conquers All" suggests how thoroughly pastoral is being left behind. Pope would write no more eclogues. Despite its finality, however, there is nothing hasty or haphazard about Thyrsis' departure, for his valediction is highly stylized and recapitulates in the final four lines the distinctive subjects and scenes of each of the preceding poems. Pope's Pastorals, even in acknowledging the nonpastoral world of time and loss, manages to contain it within the composing and consoling patterns of art.

Art in the *Epilogue to the Satires* has renounced its power to oppose change with aesthetic order. Change has darkened to corruption, and form too decomposes as we plunge into the unpatterned disorder brought on by history. Damon, Thyrsis, Lycidas, and Strephon— names timeless and euphonic—give way to the cacophonous register of modern knavery: Selkirk, Bond, Walter, Wild, Chartres, Walpole. The luxuriousness of pastoral lament yields to the abruptness and sharpness of satirical innuendo mingled with humiliating abuse. The couplet, which begins as an artificial language that calls attention to its own fictive contrivances, now yields its balance to asymmetry, violation, and disfigurement. Aesthetic order now seems so minimal and makeshift that it is always on the edge of a collapse into formlessness. Interruption and confusion are among the most conspicuous features in Pope's later poems. Here, for example, are the opening three lines from Dialogue II of the *Epilogue:*

> *Fr.*  Tis all a Libel—*Paxton* (Sir) will say.
> *P.*  Not yet, my Friend! to-morrow 'faith it may;
>   And for that very cause I print to day.

No other poem by Pope—no other English poem, so far as I know— *begins* with a triplet rhyme. Indeed, Pope normally avoided triplet rhymes. The effect of this beginning is thus to interrupt or to violate the expectations his practice had helped to establish. The disruptive beginning also creates potential confusion by introducing the name Paxton. Swift had protested vigorously that Pope's allusions to specific people and events were too obscure. "Twenty miles from London," Swift insisted, from personal experience, "no body understands hints, initial letters, or town-facts and passages; and in a few years not even those who live in London."[9] Nicholas Paxton, Walpole's private watchdog for antiministerial publications, was hardly a household word. (Pope's only other reference to him occurs in this same dialogue.) Yet, Paxton and the triplet rhyme are symptomatic of a deepening confusion. *What* is all a libel? (Using a strategy borrowed from Donne, Pope plunges the reader instantly into a conversation that precedes the poem, making the text merely a fragment of a longer discourse.) And what *is* libel if it can change its meaning from day to day?

The confusion, fragmentation, and disruption Pope embraces in the *Epilogue* reflect not simply the inevitable differences between a satire and a pastoral but the changed perspective of the poet. In his Pastorals Pope had assigned himself, as poet, a place outside of history. He arranged time in the poem as if he were immune to it, ordering Spenser's bulky calendar so that each of the four seasonal pastorals has its distinguishing location and time of day. Like the contrived symmetries which characterize his revisions of *The Rape of the Lock*, such aesthetic ordering implies a theory of art in which form represents the poet's attempt to resist or control time and the disorder it brings. In the *Epilogue* Pope, as speaker and as author, no longer stands apart from the disorders that surround him. Unlike the poet of the Pastorals, he speaks from *inside* history.

This new position within history is noticeable in all of the Horatian satires and epistles Pope imitated during the 1730s, but, like Horace, Pope nevertheless maintained some distance from the disorders he was attacking—a distance he emphasized by printing Horace's Latin text directly opposite his imitation. Indeed, Pope found it convenient to suggest at times that he was merely modernizing Horace's examples, illustrating in resemblances between Rome and England the timelessness of folly. In the *Epilogue*, however, Pope takes pains to dissociate himself from Horace. His words are no longer shadowed by a Latin text across the page, and English corruption no longer takes its model from Rome. In establishing such distance, the *Epilogue* does not repudiate its debt to Horace, but the most immediate influence upon the form and technique of the poem is Pope's immersion in a temporal world of conflict where the imitative and composing harmonies of art are inappropriate—and perhaps unavailable. Conflict is not merely the subject of the poem but its shaping force as well.

A poet writing within history has no alternative but to open his verse to the disordering interruptions of time. Unlike the decorous antiphonal speeches in the Pastorals in which each shepherd completely finishes speaking before his partner responds in (most often) an equal number of lines, the principal exchanges in the *Epilogue* are hasty, unbalanced, and incomplete:

> *P.* Ye Rev'rend Atheists!—*F.* Scandal! name them, Who?
> *P.* Why that's the thing you bid me not to do.
> Who starv'd a Sister, who forswore a Debt,
> I never nam'd—the Town's enquiring yet.
> The pois'ning Dame—*Fr.* You mean—*P.* I don't.—*Fr.*
> You do.
> *P.* See! now I keep the Secret, and not you. (ii.17–23)

Secrecy and innuendo are to meaning what interruption is to form. Although Pope had labored to make his Pastorals "musical" (as he said) to a degree unprecedented in English, especially by maintaining the caesura at what he considered the natural pause after the fourth, fifth, or sixth syllable, he seemed to abandon this goal in the *Epilogue*, where caesuras fall almost anywhere—once, incredibly, before the very last syllable of the line: "Scandal! ‖ name them, ‖ Who?" The meter returns to its iambic base only to depart from it, repeatedly and eccentrically, making regular scansion impossible. Immersed with history, the poet cannot use his leisure for corrections and cannot afford the time to deliberate over revisions. Writing at high speed, he rushes to publish—"I print to day"—before vice can transform today's truths into tomorrow's lies.

A sense of Pope's developing career helps us to recognize how far he has moved toward a purposeful disfigurement of his art. The "Freedom" he granted to epistolary verse cannot alone account for the conscious deformities of the *Epilogue to the Satires*.[10] The *Epilogue* is extreme even among Pope's earlier Horatian imitations. In the *Epilogue* points of debate are not resolved or developed but hastily put aside to explore adjacent (but not necessarily related) topics. No subtle design holds the various parts together in a pleasing unity. Instead, we experience an *illusory* movement which leads nowhere. Neither speaker truly responds to the other but simply asserts a position. Pope, of course, contrived such a fruitless exchange to emphasize the inflexible knavery of his temporizing, self-serving opponents. No true dialogue is possible, it seems, when virtuous poet and worldly courtier enter into conversation. Yet, the contrivance also attributes to virtue an unfortunately strained and inflexible self-righteousness, creating a curiously static poem, as if it were meant to dramatize a state of impasse, a condition in which poetry, as we normally understand it, cannot be written.

The two dialogues could be said to exist mainly for the sake of their conclusions, which abruptly shift the poems to a new level of discourse, elevated and visionary (in its Augustan sense). We enter something like an allegorical moment in which time, in all its particularity, is both acknowledged and abruptly transcended. Dialogue I closes with the vivid picture of the Triumph of Vice, while Dialogue II shows us the Muse, as Priestess of Virtue, opening the Temple of Eternity. These concluding passages resemble nothing that has preceded them and are certainly among the most noble lines Pope ever wrote. I will return to them after another brief look at the changes in Pope's poetic career.

## From Solitude to Isolation

Pope's poetic career began with a poem he claimed to have written (even before the Pastorals) about age twelve: the "Ode on Solitude." Like so many of his works, it continued to receive minor refinements throughout his life. The "Ode" is remarkable not only because it is an attempt by a twelve-year-old to imitate in English verse the classical form called Sapphic stanza but also because it succeeds in evoking a genuinely classical spirit. Although it has no single, specific source, the poem reads like the translation of a familiar Latin text:

> Happy the man, whose wish and care
> A few paternal acres bound,
> Content to breathe his native air,
> > In his own ground.
>
> Whose herds with milk, whose fields with bread,
> Whose flocks supply him with attire,
> Whose trees in summer yield him shade,
> > In winter fire.
>
> Blest! who can unconcern'dly find
> Hours, days, and years slide soft away,
> In health of body, peace of mind,
> > Quiet by day,
>
> Sound sleep by night; study and ease
> Together mix'd; sweet recreation,
> And innocence, which most does please,
> > With meditation.
>
> Thus let me live, unseen, unknown;
> Thus unlamented let me dye;
> Steal from the world, and not a stone
> > Tell where I lye.

This is far more than a precocious, academic exercise, with its echoes of Horace and Cowley. Pope seemed to pass directly from infancy to middle age or its literary equivalent. As a boy, he found his companions not among children but among aging writers and rural men of

leisure, and he never lost his early affection for a life of study and retirement. The "Ode" thus accurately reflects an enduring aspect of
Pope's character. It also describes a mode of life that helps us to understand the changed form of solitude we encounter in the *Epilogue*.

The benign solitude invoked in Pope's "Ode" is not a state of privation, but a full and satisfying happiness created by the acceptance
of limitation. It bespeaks the contentment that flows from reducing
our claims upon the world. The happy man, in Pope's ode, is someone who has "bound" his desires to the limited sphere of what is
enough to meet his basic needs. His estate is itself limited—"A few
paternal acres"—land that directly relates him to his own past. This
limiting of desire also creates a harmonious relationship with nature,
which in turn supplies the necessities of food, clothing, shelter and
warmth. Limitation proves to be a state in which circumscribing one
virtue makes room for another. Thus study is enhanced by periods of
ease, recreation by meditation. Like the self-modifying union of con-
traries in Mrs. Corbet, who joins masculine firmness to feminine softness, the limitation Pope celebrates in the "Ode" makes possible a
fullness otherwise unattainable. Time, if not excluded, is almost suspended in a slow movement of stealing and sliding, verbs that acknowledge change but deny its abrupt discontinuities. As in the rest
of Pope's occasional poetry, history in the "Ode" is meant to be
obliquely visible by its absence. In the "Ode," solitude affirms the
withdrawal from *polis* and from politics. Solitude, as Pope represents
it, is an ideal condition, akin to life in a pastoral, where individuals by
limiting their desires live free from the intervention of government or
state.

Solitude remained a powerful attraction for Pope throughout his
life, especially in his times of retirement at Twickenham. Though his
immediate source is a passage from Horace, the details come directly
from Pope's experience and infuse the lines with his distinctive character:

> Content with little, I can piddle here
> On Broccoli and mutton, round the year;
> But ancient friends, (tho' poor, or out of play)
> That touch my Bell, I cannot turn away.
> 'Tis true, no Turbots dignify my boards,
> But gudgeons, flounders, what my Thames affords.
> To Hounslow-heath I point, and Bansted-down,

Thence comes your mutton, and these chicks my own:
From yon old wallnut-tree a show'r shall fall;
And grapes, long-lingring on my only wall.[11]

The social aspect of Augustan solitude is, of course, vastly different from the spiritual communion with nature and melancholic loneliness emphasized by Romantic writers on solitude. By shutting out both crowd and state, Pope opens himself to "ancient friends," just as by rejecting artificial and excessive luxury he receives a "show'r" of natural, healthy abundance. Further, the freedom he gains by spurning worldly distractions is not purchased at the expense of stoic self-denial or rigorous self-mastery but rather flows from a secure self-possession that takes its origin in virtue. For Pope, it is only in solitude and in retirement that human character achieves its maximum stability and coherence. Yet, what is especially significant about solitude and moderation for Pope is that they are unsustainable ideals. When growing up in rural Binfield, Pope devoted himself to study with such zeal that he suffered a complete breakdown at seventeen. (As his half-sister reported: "He did nothing but write and read."[12]) A similar violation of ideal solitude marks his retired life at Twickenham, where instead of ignoring state and crowd, he wrote Horatian satires that increasingly turned their lash upon the politics and ethics of Walpole's ministry. Whether by choice or by compulsion, he found himself continually drawn from solitude into an engagement with vice and folly that threatened both his self-possession and his personal safety and impelled him, continually, to seek again a life of solitude. Solitude and engagement—the retired life of contemplation and the distracted life of action—balanced each other in a kind of systole and diastole, a dynamic equilibrium whose interchanging rhythm, for Pope, became inseparable from existence itself.

In the *Epilogue to the Satires* the ideal state of solitude seems completely inaccessible. The poet speaks from a position of isolation within the sordid contemporary world from which retirement is psychologically and politically impossible. There is no breaking free from history. Twickenham had been unable to shield him from literary pests—"They pierce my Thickets, thro' my Grot they glide" (*Arbuthnot*, l. 8)—and it cannot shield him from more serious forms of public vice and corruption. "I envy you this Distance from a Town of Knaves & Politicians," Pope in 1742 wrote to the Earl of Orrery, then in Somersetshire. "It is in vain I sequester myself from the Action, when the Riot & the Ruin spread around me."[13] In the worst of all possible worlds, man is both psychologically isolated and politically embroiled. Such a condition is not far from the stance Pope assumes in the *Epilogue*.

Early in his career, in his prologue to Addison's tragedy, *Cato*, Pope had referred to Cato as Rome's "last good man" (l. 35). Now Pope depicts himself as the final, lone champion of virtue in a falling land. This militant and melodramatic stance is inconceivable within the retired world of solitude, where the acceptance of limitation assures health, wisdom, and abundance, where man lives in harmony with an environment that nurtures him, where the state is invisible, where time slides and steals in an almost imperceptible motion. Pope's correspondence of the 1730s, like his poetry, expresses a sense of his immersion in a world of crowds, enemies, politics, and pressing time from which retirement was less and less possible: "My own health is breaking more ways than one," he wrote to his friend William Fortescue; "and I begin to be so great a fool, as to be concerned for the Publick weal, which I think breaking too."[14] The fragmentation of the social order and the breakdown of his own health are changes which solitude cannot prevent and which his poems cannot exclude. When concern for the state and lack of concern are equally foolish, folly is no longer the exclusive province of fools. The poet, caught up by the history he would record, cannot free himself from error. He cannot step aside and separate himself cleanly from the world he opposes. In such changed circumstances, literary form and technique are also implicated in the very disorder they seek to resist.

The *Epilogue*, in its concern for the "Publick weal," continues the political satire of Pope's preceding Horatian imitations, yet here too changes are evident. In 1738 the long campaign by the Opposition against Walpole now seemed in disarray, although modern historians argue, with the benefit of hindsight, that Walpole's power was eroding. Erosion was not so easy to detect at the time. In May 1738 Walpole's victory in the House of Commons in breaking the Opposition's attack upon his policy toward Spain seemed to the antiministerial forces a crushing, final defeat. Several days before Dialogue I of the *Epilogue* appeared, Pope's correspondent Lord Marchmont wrote to his fellow peer Montrose, "I look, as several others do, upon the Opposition as at an end."[15]

Pope's earlier imitations of Horace had expressed a struggle against

Walpole which, however uneven, never seemed futile or quixotic. Dialogue I of the *Epilogue,* by contrast, describes corruption in utter triumph. Now the poet can merely bear witness to an evil that appears unstoppable. As Bolingbroke was to write in a manuscript he entrusted to Pope: "The utmost that private men can do, who remain untainted by the general contagion, is to keep the spirit of liberty alive in a few breasts; to protest against what they cannot hinder, and to claim on every occasion what they cannot by their own strength recover."[16] Such a program imposes an especially unusual and difficult dilemma on the satirist. How does the satirist, in entering history, remain "untainted" by general contagion? How can satire lash a situation or a group? What happens when lashing is not only unsafe but (as Pope lamented) "ineffectual"? Whom does the satirist deter from crime when the public now holds criminals in "reverential Awe"?

## Two Senses of an Ending

The questions Pope as a satirist faced in the last years of Walpole's administration are reflected in the conclusions to Dialogue I and Dialogue II of the *Epilogue to the Satires.* In several ways the two conclusions affirm and continue Pope's earlier practices. Composed of two separately published Dialogues, the *Epilogue* owes its final form to Pope's normal process of development through addition, which significantly changes emphasis and meaning. The two conclusions do not simply reinforce or repeat each other but are instead mutually modifying. Following his general practice of refinement, Pope provides in the conclusion to Dialogue II an ending not simply changed but strengthened and improved, an ending that supersedes its predecessor without cancelling or denying it. In effect, the second conclusion would be weakened if it had appeared alone, without requiring the reader to pass through a previously incomplete ending. The poet who created two versions of *The Rape of the Lock* and two versions of *The Dunciad* should not surprise us by creating for the *Epilogue to the Satires* two very different conclusions.

The endings of Pope's poems usually follow one of several basic patterns. The simplest could be called the reiterative ending, in that it summarizes or recapitulates what came before. Thus, for example, Thyrsis in the final lines of "Winter" reiterates the subjects and scenes of the preceding four pastorals, much as the conclusion to *An*

# Alexander Pope

*Essay on Man* recalls and summarizes that poem's fundamental arguments. A second pattern of ending does not reiterate an earlier development but decisively advances and eventually resolves it, as commerce resolves conflict in *Windsor-Forest* or as elegiac consolation appropriately concludes *The Rape of the Lock*. A third pattern Pope employs is starkly interruptive, as when a preceding development or argument is suddenly broken off. The arrival of Chaos and Night simply interrupts the slumbering multitudes in *The Dunciad*, concluding the poem by breaking it off, much as Eloisa's vision of her own death concludes "Eloisa to Abelard" with its abrupt consolation.

Death, in fact, frequently serves Pope as a concluding motif, but not only by being interruptive. Pope portrays death as interruptive when it catches people unaware and unprepared, as in the case of Sir Balaam, but it also serves a reiterative function when it stands as a metaphor for wasted lives. The superannuated "Ghosts of Beauty" in the *Moral Essays*—who spend their nights in endless, circular, repetitious imitations of pleasure—offer a poignant example of how wasted existences are represented in Pope's work as forms of living death. The metaphorical, summarizing function of death loses any poignancy, however, when in the *Moral Essays* Pope turned to describe the profligate George Villiers, Duke of Buckingham:

> In the worst inn's worst room, with mat half-hung,
> The floors of plaister, and the walls of dung,
> On once a flock-bed, but repair'd with straw,
> With tape-typ'd curtains, never meant to draw,
> The George and Garter dangling from that bed
> Where tawdry yellow strove with dirty red,
> Great Villers lies.           (iii.299–305)

Despite the shocking contrast with his former life of riches and pleasure, Villiers' deathbed accurately sums up—exposes the reality of— a debased existence. Yet, death is not restricted to satirical uses. Like conclusions which advance or resolve an earlier pattern of development, death in Pope's poems also finds a place in the natural sequence of life, completing it, fulfilling it, especially when virtuous individuals attain the solace of a peaceful and settled dying. The deaths of Pope's father and mother, which he reflects upon in the conclusion of *An Epistle to Dr. Arbuthnot*, offer perhaps the best example in all his works of dying understood as a natural, sequential fulfillment, not a desperate interruption or metaphoric repetition.

254

In addition to endings that reiterate, interrupt, or resolve an earlier development, Pope sometimes closes with a fourth pattern that is explicitly self-reflexive, in which the poem concludes by reminding us of the poem and of the poet himself, of his character, values, and compositions. The two conclusions to the *Epilogue to the Satires* are unusual in that they draw upon all four of these patterns. The conclusion to Dialogue I—described by Joseph Warton as "perhaps the noblest . . . in all his works"—is also unusual in its extensiveness.[17] Pope's concluding paragraphs are often quite brief, even though readers will disagree about where, exactly, a conclusion may be said to begin. The conclusion to Dialogue I, however, continues without pause for over thirty lines and has the cohesiveness of a formal oration. In a poem which develops through a series of conversational exchanges and interruptions, Pope's conclusion shifts suddenly to sustained declamation—in effect, interrupting interruption. The decisive shift occurs with the introduction of Virtue, who quickly yields to a vividly personified portrait of Vice. The ending simply resists all attempts to break in:

> *Virtue* may chuse the high or low Degree,
> 'Tis just alike to Virtue, and to me;
> Dwell in a Monk, or light upon a King,
> She's still the same, belov'd, contented thing.
> *Vice* is undone, if she forgets her Birth,
> And stoops from Angels to the Dregs of Earth:
> But 'tis the *Fall* degrades her to a Whore;
> Let *Greatness* own her, and she's mean no more:
> Her Birth, her Beauty, Crowds and Courts confess,
> Chaste Matrons praise her, and grave Bishops bless:
> In golden Chains the willing World she draws,
> And hers the Gospel is, and hers the Laws:
> Mounts the Tribunal, lifts her scarlet head,
> And sees pale Virtue carted in her stead!
> Lo! at the Wheels of her Triumphal Car,
> Old *England*'s Genius, rough with many a Scar,
> Dragg'd in the Dust! his Arms hang idly round,
> His Flag inverted trails along the ground!
> Our Youth, all liv'ry'd o'er with foreign Gold,
> Before her dance; behind her crawl the Old!
> See thronging Millions to the Pagod run,
> And offer Country, Parent, Wife, or Son!
> Hear her black Trumpet thro' the Land proclaim,

That "Not to be corrupted is the Shame."
In Soldier, Churchman, Patriot, Man in Pow'r,
'Tis Av'rice all, Ambition is no more!
See, all our Nobles begging to be Slaves!
See, all our Fools aspiring to be Knaves!
The Wit of Cheats, the Courage of a Whore,
Are what ten thousand envy and adore.
All, all look up, with reverential Awe,
On Crimes that scape, or triumph o'er the Law:
While Truth, Worth, Wisdom, daily they decry—
"Nothing is Sacred now but Villany."


Yet may this Verse (if such a Verse remain)
Show there was one who held it in disdain.


This vision of "thronging Millions" who run to sacrifice country and family before the towering idol of Vice is Pope's most sweeping condemnation of England under Walpole. (The entire population of England and Wales in the 1730s was little more than six million.) The passage builds to a gathering crescendo of incrimination—"All, all look up." The conclusion, aspiring to the sublimity often associated with Juvenal, would seem to press toward silence as the only possible sequel, and the text suggests such pressure with the blank space before its final couplet. Never in Pope's work has the principle of modifying contrasts operated with greater daring or effectiveness. The self-reflexive final couplet returns us from Juvenalian sublimity to the honest, simple speech of a single unamplified voice in which virtue still asserts its determined, if futile, opposition to vice.

Despite the firm protest of Pope's concluding words, the poet's role in the conclusion to Dialogue I is ambivalent, even paradoxical. The Triumph of Vice is among the most powerful denunciations of contemporary manners and morals in the history of satire, yet Pope represents himself finally as a mere witness. Powerless to deter or to reform, the satirist in his attacks on vice has become more than ineffectual. He appears almost ludicrous in his futility. Lashing out is now an absurd mission, like sweeping back the tide. Even his status as witness is contingent upon the survival of his verse, which he represents as uncertain. In effect, the satirist seems doomed to a life of contradiction. He continues to lash out at individuals, though under the cover of innuendo. (As James M. Osborn has shown, Pope's depiction of Vice alludes to Walpole's recent marriage to his long-time mistress, Molly Skerrett.[18]) Yet, his attack, at its moment of intensest rhetorical power, has also betrayed his weakness, his inefficacy, his isolated absurdity. Further, by exaggerating the satirist's isolation and defiance, Pope risks transforming him into an unwitting self-parody—a Jeremiah, whose prophetic gloom would be too weighty for a modern man of sense, however virtuous. Pope's outlook, as expressed in his correspondence and occasional verse, never came to rest in such unrelieved pessimism. His private life afforded him a continuing source of consolation and pleasure despite the inroads of vice; and even corruption had its limits. "Public Calamaties touch me," Pope wrote in 1741; "but when I read of Past Times, I am somewhat comforted as to the present, upon the Comparison."[19] His judgment would not allow Pope to conclude his poem with the satirist's unambiguous passivity and pessimism as the last word on the universal ruin he witnessed. In Dialogue II Pope thus complicates and modifies his earlier conclusion with a second, less solitary, less ambiguous version of the poet's role.

In the conclusion to Dialogue II the poet turns from passive witness to active guardian. Instead of ambiguous attack or solitary disdain, he celebrates the constructive power of communal praise. Although still isolated within the world of history and politics, he relieves his solitude by including the satirist within the larger, timeless circle of virtuous men. No longer is the survival of his protest conditional—"*if* such a verse remain"—but the poet is instead assured, defiant, and resolved to assert his lapsed powers:

> Let Envy howl while Heav'n's whole Chorus sings,
> And bark at Honour not confer'd by Kings;
> Let Flatt'ry sickening see the Incense rise,
> Sweet to the World, and grateful to the Skies:
> Truth guards the Poet, sanctifies the line,
> And makes Immortal, Verse as mean as mine.    (ll. 242–247)

This bold claim of immortality for verse so choked with the debris of time and history is linked directly with a defense of satire as a "sacred Weapon" (l. 211). If literary force proves ineffective in attacking Vice, it is still useful in defending Virtue. As an active guardian of Virtue, the poet can work constructively despite the howls of envy or triumph of corruption. In the first of three successively shorter concluding paragraphs, Pope imagines the Muse as the "Priestess" of Virtue, crowned with "divine" rays, admitting the virtuous into the "Temple of Eternity" (l. 235). Walpole and Molly Skerrett and the disfigured world of history have been transcended, left behind, in a concluding vision of timelessness.

Pope's vision of the Temple of Eternity does not magically transform the time-bound world. Vice still rules; the poet is still embattled and solitary. "Yes, the last Pen for Freedom let me draw," he affirms in the next to last paragraph, but, despite his isolation, he speaks now with a confident authority that conceals no passiveness or resignation. The new qualities of affirmation and confidence in Dialogue II were evident to Pope's perhaps most tiresome correspondent, the indefatigable Aaron Hill. "I find in this satire," he wrote, "something inexpressibly daring and generous . . . It places the *Poet* in a light for which *nature* and *reason* designed him; and attones all the pitiful *sins* of the *trade*, for to a *trade*, and a *vile* one, poetry is irrecoverably sunk in this kingdom."[20] This is intelligent commentary that Pope would appreciate. Poetry as a trade implies none of the rich exchange between present and past that Pope evoked in his metaphors of commerce. Trade is mere day-labor, common journeyman's work, like the hack writing and Grub Street propaganda which Walpole so heavily subsidized. In restoring to the poet an ancient alliance with truth and virtue, Pope thus also implicitly insists that poetry can serve an elevated and affirmative purpose *within* the corrupt world of politics and time, even if it will surely be deformed in the process. Pope's renunciation of satire at the conclusion of the *Epilogue to the Satires* depends for its full significance on our sense that it is one change in a poetic career that continues to unfold. The tradesmen-poets of Pope's day could have ceased to publish for five years without anyone's noticing. Only Pope could transform even silence into an eloquent and continuing, if desperate, speech.

The most reassuring sign of Pope's new confidence at the conclusion to Dialogue II is the return of humor. Unlike Dialogue I, which reserved the ominous last words for Pope, Dialogue II concludes with the words of the *adversarius*, who in exasperation offers the poet some brief advice:

> *Fr.* Alas! alas! pray end what you began,
> And write next winter more *Essays on Man*.

258

Such a self-reflexive ending not only relieves Pope of the burdensome solemnity of prophecy but also provides, at his expense, a moment of comedy that both admirers and critics of *An Essay on Man* can relish. Philosophy, like satire, is not for all occasions. While exposing for a last time the unawakened reason of his adversary, Pope good-humoredly also acknowledges that his masterly philosophical poem could serve as a synonym for any long, dull, harmless piece of writing. (Johnson could say of *Paradise Lost* that no man wished it longer.) Pope's comic ending, however, is important for more than just the stabilizing influences of the humor it provides. Like Flavia in "A Standish and Two Pens," Pope's solicitous *adversarius* seeks to deflect him from purposeful satire into writing that seems an innocuous and potentially endless distraction. In effect, the *adversarius* wishes to interrupt what Pope means to conclude.

Pope intends the *Epilogue to the Satires* to bring to completion his long series of imitations of Horace. More accurately, the completion does not so much resolve or fulfill as it cancels or terminates a project that might have continued much longer. The series concludes not because of any internal or aesthetic compulsion but because, for various reasons, Pope chooses to announce its termination. An arbitrary termination differs radically from the formal conclusions of Pope's Pastorals or *The Rape of the Lock*. With its fragmentary exchanges and two different endings, the *Epilogue* is not a richly satisfying study in harmonious composition; yet, its internal differences—as reflected in the two conclusions—stand in sharp contrast to the potentially endless, pointless duplication suggested by the *adversarius* in recommending "more *Essays on Man*." One of the most remarkable aspects of Pope's poetic career is its record of change. Unlike many fine poets, in composing new poems he almost never repeats himself. The comic termination of the *Epilogue to the Satires* is one more gesture of leave-taking, one more sign of Pope's ability to move on in his career. He would write no more *Essays on Man*, no more imitations of Horace.

## Virtue and Defect of Form

"When in doubt," wrote Robert Frost, "there is always form for us to go on with."[21] Form itself, for Frost, is an unmitigated good, a stay against confusion, a reassuring figure of order and concentration opposed to the utter chaos and blackness which surround it. In its clarity and precision, the Frostian poem, like Pope's pastoral poem "Spring," is an alternative to the temporal disorder in which we live. Pope's elaborate care in creating individual couplets indicates that he was always a formalist, and few poets of any era have created artifacts of such exquisitely beautiful form as *The Rape of Lock*. Yet, when we look beyond the construction of individual couplets, what may strike us about Pope's later verse is not the clarity, intricacy, and precision of its form but its almost calculated disregard of logical or architectonic principles. For example, Pope could write his imitations of Horace so quickly and freely (as he reported) because the Latin original provided a ready-made structure. Imagery, theme, characterization: these had always given coherence to Pope's work, and their importance in the later poems expands because other aspects of formal design seem conspicuously absent. In *An Essay on Man*, couplets or paragraphs sometimes prove interchangeable. *To Cobham* exists in two vastly different arrangements, the second version produced after Warburton found the original "without order, connexion, or dependence."[22] *The New Dunciad* (1742)—which became book IV of the finished poem—is so notably lacking in form that scholars have professed to find its underlying pattern in such odd sources as theatrical farce or academic degree ceremonies. Once Pope passed the fumbling age of forty, among the toys of youth to which he bid farewell was the Virgilian fascination with intricate, internal correlations of form.

One measure of Pope's changing attitude toward literary form is his new emphasis, in the later satires and epistles, on the facts of his personal appearance. He was "about four feet six high," reported Sir Joshua Reynolds, "very humpbacked and deformed."[23] Tuberculosis of the bone had curved his spine and contracted one side—as two rare contemporary drawings show (figure 5). These visible deformities were reflected in his early writings in two ways. First, in his letters Pope openly turned his physical disadvantage into comedy—a self-protective measure to deprive ridicule of its sting. Second, as Maynard Mack has argued, Pope's awareness of his deformities manifested itself in poems that dramatized the pathos of exclusion from love. The excluded figures, such as the giant Polyphemus, all suffer a grotesque defect or malformation.[24] Pathos and comedy, however, have little to do with Pope's self-portraits in his later poems. Especially after publication of *The Dunciad* in 1728, Pope's enemies in-

5  Pope, by William Hoare
(left)  and  William  Kent.

creasingly attacked him and ridiculed him for his physical deformities (figure 6). Self-ridicule no longer provided any defense. At the same time, however, Pope also began to think of his physical appearance as a resource he could use without apology or pathos, as symbolic in its way as his garden or grotto.

Pope intensified the public curiosity about his appearance by several means. He was the willing subject of many paintings, which, in engraved or oil copies, circulated his likeness throughout England. That Pope's portraits carefully avoided any reference to his physical deformity did not suppress people's curiosity about it. He also carefully limited their opportunity to view him firsthand. "Pope was seldom seen in public," Sir Joshua Reynolds tells us, "so it was a great sight to see him."[25] It was surely with deliberation that Pope in the last decade of his life began a series of explicit references to his appearance. In *An Epistle to Dr. Arbuthnot* the tone is playful but complex:

> There are, who to my Person pay their court,
> I cough like *Horace*, and tho' lean, am short,
> *Ammon*'s great Son one shoulder had too high,
> Such *Ovid*'s nose, and "Sir! you have an *Eye*—"
> Go on, obliging Creatures, make me see
> All that disgrac'd my Betters, met in me.          (ll. 115–120)

Here any comic effect comes at the expense of flatterers who attempt to gild the plain facts: he is short, lean, sickly, malformed, with a long nose and myopic eye. Three years later—in the same year in which the *Epilogue* appeared—Pope continued the process of self-description in *The First Epistle of The First Book of Horace, Imitated*, addressing his philosophical companion, Bolingbroke:

> You laugh, half Beau half Sloven if I stand,
> My Wig all powder, and all snuff my Band;
> You laugh, if Coat and Breeches strangely vary,
> White Gloves, and Linnen worthy Lady Mary!     (ll. 161–164)

Clearly Horace's original says nothing of wig, band, gloves, or ill-matched coat and breeches. These details—like the phrase "half Beau half Sloven"—are wholly Pope's addition, and we must suppose them accurate. His weakness meant that he required assistance in

6  Frontispiece to *Pope Alexander's Supremacy and Infallibility Examin'd* (1729).

even the most common acts of dressing, so that in private his costume was doubtless inelegant. Indeed, the later portrait by Jean Baptiste Van Loo (figure 13, p. 311) shows an unusual modification of Pope's normal pose; his fingers are thrust *underneath* the wig, which sits oddly askew. In subsequent engravings the effect of slightly rumpled finery is more exaggerated. Defect of form was no longer something Pope concealed or made light of. It became, instead, one of the signs by which Pope associated himself with honesty and virtue.

Two changed conditions help account for Pope's new uses of deformity in his later verse. First, traditional forms of all kinds began to seem subverted or corrupted by the progress of vice. Pope's philosopher-friend Bolingbroke in his *Letters on the Study and Use of History* (written between 1735 and 1738) offered the following analysis of English political life. "The state," he wrote, "is become, under ancient and known forms, a new and undefinable monster; composed of a king without monarchial splendor, a senate of nobles without aristocratical independency, and a senate of commons without democratical freedom."[26] The situation is somewhat analogous to Pope's vision of the Triumph of Vice, which in outward form retains all the traditional elements of a triumphal procession, complete with trumpets, proclamations, captives, and adoring multitudes. The traditional form remains, but the content has been wholly subverted and corrupted, even to the detail Bolingbroke could have provided of England's entire free-born aristocracy "begging to be Slaves." Defect of form, especially through such techniques of satire as parody, caricature, and grotesque exaggeration, became in Pope's later verse a way of exposing the corruption that had subverted traditional literary and cultural modes. Yet, when the subversion of traditional forms is extensive enough, parody may become impotent, since to distinguish the parody from the original is impossible. Further, and equally perplexing, vice had not only corrupted the traditional forms of virtue but had also discovered ways to make the monstrous pleasing. As Pope observed in *An Essay on Man:*

> Vice is a monster of so frightful mien,
> As, to be hated, needs but to be seen;
> Yet seen too oft, familiar with her face,
> We first endure, then pity, then embrace.          (ii.217–220)

Pope does not dispute that Vice is intrinsically hateful. Rather, he insists that if, by degrees, Vice surrounds us with its images, we may come to *love* what is monstrous and vicious and hateful. There is no longer any possibility of retaining the neoplatonic correlation between virtue and beauty proposed in *An Essay on Criticism* (ll. 76–79). Where the monstrous now seems pleasing and where traditional forms have been corrupted by vice, the virtuous poet faces a difficult dilemma. While avoiding what is truly monstrous, truth must somehow disorder its appearances. Virtue, in the landscape of 1738, would be recognized by its deviations from the line of beauty.

The deformities or defects of form in Pope's later works are calculated violations, as remote from the monstrous as from the beautiful. Violation is certainly the charge his adversarial voices never tire of repeating. Because they are corrupt, they wish to confine the poet within (the subverted) forms of politeness that will disarm and emasculate him, and his task increasingly must be redefined as the violation of polite forms. Excremental imagery that was evident only sparingly in Pope's early work is now used fully and openly to offend those who speak the language of official lies, flattery, and evasions. "All your Courtly Civet-Cats can vent," Pope tells his accusers, "Perfume to you, to me is Excrement" (ii.183–184). Such offensiveness, in a world of refined falsehood, becomes a way of calling things by their right names. Where vice has corrupted the forms of virtue, Pope's enemies speak like moralists, leaving Pope no choice but to redefine virtue as impudence, eccentricity, and pride:

> *Fr.*  You're strangely proud:
> > *P.*  So proud, I am no Slave:
> So impudent, I own myself no Knave:
> So odd, my Country's Ruin makes me grave.
> Yes, I am proud; I must be proud to see
> Men not afraid of God, afraid of me.        (ii.204–209)

Surrounded by self-confessed knaves and slaves, the satirist boasts of a pride which is not sin or weakness but the sign of moral strength. The violation of polite forms extends not only to such immoderate and eccentric boasting. It also encompasses an indirect rejection of Horace—indirect because Pope's adversary is praising Horace:

> His sly, polite, insinuating stile
> Could please at Court, and make AUGUSTUS smile:
> An artful Manager, that crept between
> His Friend and Shame, and was a kind of *Screen*.        (i.19–22)

Although Dryden shared Pope's genuine admiration for Horace's virtues, he had not refrained from criticizing the same qualities Pope exposes here. Horace, he wrote, was "a temporising poet, a well-mannered court-slave . . . who is ever decent, because he is naturally servile."[27] Pope goes even further, slyly transforming Horace into a surrogate Walpole, alluding to Walpole's notoriety as Screenmaster General and Artful Manager of Commons. It is a significant expression of change that Pope would conclude a series of Horatian imitations with this firm, even if indirect, rejection of Horace.

Like his new emphasis on the facts of his personal appearance, like his exploration of deformity and defect of form in art, Pope's ironic rejection of Horace is directly related to the self-portrait he develops in his later verse as the friend and champion of virtue. Virtue has explicit political meaning in Pope's later poems, as Paul Gabriner has shown.[28] Bolingbroke and the Opposition to Walpole had consistently appropriated the term *Virtue* as something of a party slogan or label, just as their rhetorical campaign consistently attacked the Walpole ministry through the idea of corruption. Like the term *corruption*, virtue had specific, political associations inside the tradition of civic humanism, which identified virtue with free citizens whose freedom was guaranteed by an independent Parliament and by the ownership of land. Yet, while virtue sometimes holds this specific, political meaning in Pope's later satire, we must also recognize that even early in his career Pope saw in private virtue the only alternative to the futility of public, political life. It is hard to imagine anyone weeping over Addison's *Cato*, yet Pope reported that the play "drew tears" from him in several places.[29] What was it that so moved Pope? His prologue, in commending Addison, repeats the explanation he offered in his correspondence:

> Virtue confess'd in human shape he draws,
> What *Plato* thought, and godlike *Cato* was.     (ll. 17–18)

Pope viewed Addison's hero as an embodiment of godlike and intangible Virtue. Virtue here is not a limited political concept but an antidote to politics. Pope's emotion is less a tribute to Addison, one could say, than to his feeling for the ethical life. Well before he entertained in the *Epilogue* apocalyptic visions of England as a falling state, the life of virtue seemed to him the only sane course for mankind. This is the implicit argument of the "Ode on Solitude."

We have seen in the *Moral Essays* how virtue serves as the force that stabilizes and centers the potentially self-destructive contradictions of human character. Virtue, Pope insists in *An Essay on Man*, is the only true source of happiness, the "only point where human bliss stands still" (iv.311). Without virtue, individuals simply disfigure themselves, creating rigid or incoherent parodies of human nature, as we see in the fate of Pope's satirical victims from *The Rape of the Lock* through *The Dunciad*. Mankind, for Pope, cannot upset the order of God's universe, which contains provision for human discord. We can only disorder ourselves and the equally precarious equilibrium of social relations. Yet, this dark vision also offers a significant place for hope, and hope is in Pope's view an indispensable component of the ethical life. What in our blindness we may disfigure and disorder we may also, by our insight, improve and correct. It is virtue, for Pope, which makes all the difference.

The enormous importance Pope gives to virtue no doubt reflects a wide-spread effort in the Enlightenment to discover new grounds for justifying morality. Such justification was an urgent requirement, according to Alasdair MacIntyre, because the authority of Christian and classical moral argument was decisively breaking down. It was the task of Enlightenment philosophers, he argues, to discover a new and convincing rationale for an ethical life bereft of its old supports.[30] Pope's contribution to this rethinking of morality is the poetic demonstration that virtue represents the only alternative to social and to human disintegration. Human history, as Pope surveys it, passes relentlessly from periods of civility to barbarism, just as human character (in the absence of a unifying, ethical life) faces potential self-destruction. Whereas knowledge recedes from man like a horizon of Alps upon Alps, virtue for Pope remains a possible human achievement. "We cannot be knowing," he wrote in an early letter, "but we can be virtuous."[31] In 1738 virtue was no less necessary, but Pope's confidence in the possibility of achieving virtue—both beyond and within the sphere of private life—was considerably shaken.

Pope's concern for virtue and for the ethical life had not changed, but the poet of the *Epilogue to the Satires* (and after) faced a world in which the progress of vice and corruption seemed greatly accelerated, creating added dangers for human character and social order. "My Mind," Pope wrote to his friend Ralph Allen in 1741, "at present is as dejected as possible, for I love my Country, & I love Mankind, and I see a dismal Scene Opening for our own & other

Nations."[32] Swift might have shared and thus relieved somewhat Pope's dejection—although he could not have expressed Pope's love for mankind—but Swift was fast becoming senile, according to reports Pope was receiving from Ireland. (A year later Swift would be formally declared "of unsound mind and memory"—finishing his last years in madness.) Other members of the early Scriblerus Club (Gay, Harley, Bolingbroke, Arbuthnot, Atterbury, Congreve, and Thomas Parnell) had all died or scattered, and Pope was left to find solace in less talented and less congenial souls: Ralph Allen, William Warburton, Hugh Bethel, William Fortescue. His gift for attracting new friends could not stop or soften the dispossessions of time.

Yet, change in the late 1730s was not restricted to the literary form of Pope's works or to his declining health and shrinking circle of friends. Bolingbroke had grounded his philosophy of history and his political opposition to Walpole in a study of English social and economic structures. It is a sign of Bolingbroke's dismay—and perhaps of Pope's influence upon Bolingbroke—that in his last and most famous work, *The Idea of a Patriot King*, Bolingbroke abandoned his former social and economic diagnosis of historical change and emphasized instead, as a chief cause of political stability or decline, the "spirit and character" of the people. In *The Idea of a Patriot King* Bolingbroke in effect accepted Pope's conviction that an active pursuit of the ethical life was the prerequisite for political well-being. Now he viewed Walpole's most serious crime as "the constant endeavor he has employed to corrupt the morals of men."[33] Indeed, Bolingbroke regarded the decay of virtue to have proceeded so far that the only hope for the restoration of a just kingdom lay in the accession of a monarch unprecedented in his wisdom and goodness, a true Patriot King. "He, and he alone," wrote Bolingbroke, "can save a country whose ruin is so far advanced."[34] Pope, to whom Bolingbroke entrusted the manuscript of the *Patriot King*, tried out this idea in an unfinished sequel to the *Epilogue* entitled *One Thousand Seven Hundred and Forty. A Poem:*

> Whatever his religion or his blood,
> His public virtue makes his title good.
> Europe's just balance and our own may stand,
> And one man's honesty redeem the land.

But here the fragmentary draft breaks off. The fantasy of a patriot king, with only the weak and pathetic Prince Frederick available as a royal candidate, held only temporary appeal; "one man's honesty" was not a sufficient power for national redemption. Pope wrote to the Earl of Marchmont in 1741: "I am determined to publish no more in my life time, for many reasons; but principally thro' the Zeal I have to speak the *Whole Truth*, & neither to praise or dispraise by halves, or with worldly managements." Then he added a thought that was often in his mind, although the exact age kept being pushed ahead: "I think fifty an age at which to write no longer for Amusement, but for some Use, and with design to do some good."[35] Two years later his silence was interrupted when he published his revised, four-book version of *The Dunciad*—a work in which time, deformity, and the poet are once again central figures.

# X

## The Kinship of Madness in *The Dunciad*

Behold, my desire is, that mine adversary should write a book.

—Job

WHEN THE playwright and poet laureate Colley Cibber in 1743 first appears as the hero of Pope's revised version of *The Dunciad*, with him appear two related figures: "Great Cibber's brazen, brainless brothers" (I.32).[1] Pope refers, of course, to the two stone statues of raving and melancholy madness above the gates of Bethlehem Royal Hospital, "Bedlam," and he uses the term "brothers" justifiably, because the statues were carved by Caius-Gabriel Cibber, father of the laureate (figure 7). Pope might have seemed to sleep or nod, however, in employing "brazen" (made of brass) to describe stonework. Thus a note explains: "Mr. Cibber remonstrated that his Brothers at Bedlam ... were not *Brazen*, but *Blocks;* yet our author let it pass unaltered, as a trifle, that no way lessened the Relationship" (note to II.3).

Pope's apparent error, of course, is deliberate and satirical. The epithet "brazen" not only adds an appropriately dull alliterative emphasis to the line but also perfectly suits the character of Cibber himself, whose impudence was renowned. In addition, the reference to Cibber's "brazen" brothers supplies the earliest hint that Cibber is closely related to another antihero of dullness, Sir Robert Walpole, whose name was regularly associated with brass. Pope's mention of the famous statues above the gates of Bedlam was equally appropriate, however, in a more general sense. The "Relationship" linking madmen and dunces expands and deepens throughout the poem, and Pope means to imply that the association between Cibber and his

7 Raving Madness (above) and Melancholy Madness, by Caius-Gabriel Cibber.

stone brothers extends their common paternity to a darker connection: the kinship of madness. In exploring this relationship, Pope
moves *The Dunciad* far beyond its origin as a satire of incompetent
writing. Pope's attack on hack writers has expanded—like Dulness
itself—to encompass a powerful moral and psychological and literary
study of the irrational.

The addition of Cibber's stone kin, then, was more than a lucky,
passing stroke of wit. It opened the poem to Pope's pervasive thematic explorations of the complex relationship between folly and
madness. Significantly, in revising the original version of *The Dunciad,* Pope moved the "sacred Dome" of Dulness from a location near
the Tower of London to a "Cave" near the walls of Bedlam, "where
Folly holds her throne" (I.29). The action of the revised poem thus
originates close to England's most famous scene of madness, and on
several occasions Pope directly links his hero to the madmen confined
in Bedlam, so that the poem continually returns to its source in the
irrational. (Turning in circles is the characteristic motion of Dulness.) Cibber's stone brothers, although mentioned only twice, in ret-
rospect assume an almost symbolic power as haunting figures whose
petrifaction seems a kind of cruel Ovidian change, epitomizing the
death-in-life of madness. To Pope's age the lunatic was a comic as
well as a pathetic sight, but the comedy or farce of irrationalism was a
spectacle, like a public execution, that never completely lost its power
to unnerve. The madman was always a frightening reminder of how
tenuous man's grip on sense and reason is. For Pope's age, madness
concealed no redeeming glimpse of divine truth or human genius. Beyond madness there was nothing.

## Irrationality in the Age of Reason

The early eighteenth-century view of madness was so different from
ours that, unless we account for cultural change, Pope's punishment
of Cibber and the dunces seems merely sadistic, far exceeding the
cruelty licensed by satire's efforts to deter. Madness to Pope and his
age was not considered a form of mental "illness." (Doctors were
sometimes consulted and medicines prescribed, but hospitals such as
Bedlam were places mainly for confinement, not treatment.) It was
certainly not considered an inevitable or appropriate response to an
irrational world, as some modern writers describe it. Nor did mad-

ness then include the religious meaning it assumed in the Middle Ages, when the mad might be respected as "Christ's fools," or the spiritual and artistic meaning that the Renaissance and the Romantic era attributed to it as a sign of inspired genius. Instead, the Augustan view was twofold: the madman was at once a natural curiosity and a moral exemplum. His fate in both capacities was confinement and display. Like the two-headed calves and freakish specimens collected at Gresham College, the lunatic fascinated an age in which—as a corollary of the interest in "general nature"—aberrant forms aroused a special curiosity. Bedlam, in fact, was a regular stop on a circuit of London's bizarre sights, which included visits to the lions kept at the Tower, the anomalies collected at Gresham, and—as Swift reported of his own tour—the puppet show. Before admission was restricted in 1770, as many as ninety-six thousand spectators in a single year passed through the gates of Bedlam to observe the chained or strolling inmates.[2]

Display, exposure, and confinement, of course, were also normal forms of civil punishment, and the madman suffered his fate at Bedlam partly because the age believed that irrationality implied moral failure, a weakness of will that should be penalized and, if possible, corrected. Physicians and moralists both insisted that reason involved conscious volition, that, in effect, people *chose* to be rational or mad.[3] Needless to say, these attitudes, however mistaken, did not drain the age of all human sympathy for the mad. Swift, in a gesture not free from irony, left them what little wealth he had. "*Babylon* in Ruins," wrote Addison of the distracted man, "is not so melancholly [sic] a Spectacle" (*The Spectator* no. 421). But spectacle it was, despite sympathy, a pageant for which Bedlam provided both stage and symbol. Reconstructed at Moorfields in 1675, Bethlehem Royal Hospital was perhaps the most triumphantly ambiguous monument of the neoclassical period (figure 8): a magnificent and mathematically regular edifice which housed, behind an exterior one observer compared to the Louvre, all the casualties of rationalism.

The cultural history of madness is important in helping to illuminate the general form and texture of *The Dunciad*, which have puzzled even Pope's greatest admirers.[4] Almost everyone reports that the poem seems opaque, dense, intractable. Yet it seems unlikely that Pope failed for lack of skill to achieve (if he meant to achieve) the clarity and coherence that are his trademark. Some of the obscurity of

273

8  Bethlehem Hospital ("Bedlam"), where the figures of Raving and Melancholy Madness appear above the central gate.

the poem is doubtless an effect of time. Swift's view of *The Dunciad* was quite different from that of most modern readers: "I never in my opinion saw so much good satire, or more good sense, in so many lines."[5] Yet, the evident obscurity, density, and confusion of *The Dunciad* are, even if the product of time, highly appropriate to a mock encomium of Dulness and to an anatomy of the irrational. The duncelike modern poets had been earlier described in the Scriblerian parody of Longinus—*Peri Bathous* (1728)—as proponents of dark composition, melee, and the grotesque. Pope's deliberate violations of polite form and his ironic representation of the monstrous in *The Dunciad* are techniques of satirical parody. As William Kinsley observes: "The Dunces produce bathos by accident, Pope by design. They produce poetic chaos, he reproduces their chaos in a way that transforms it into an unusually rich and complex poetic order."[6]

Although some complain that its deformities and contemporary detail make *The Dunciad* unreadable today, it is certain that Pope anticipated this criticism and recognized the thematic uses of obscurity. He intended his poem to darken with age. As an amateur painter, he understood how time obscures the brightest canvas, and in *An Essay on Criticism* he explicitly compared the painter's fading colors with the mutability of language (ll. 484–493). He predicted that time would inevitably render his diction obscure, his allusions uncertain, his topical references impenetrable, and *The Dunciad* accelerates these effects of mutability to complement Pope's treatment of intellectual decay. He made sure that a poem celebrating dunces would resemble the condition of a Gothic ruin, full of dark corners and mysterious passages. We are meant to encounter it with a sense of awe mingled with confusion, as characters such as Settle, Heidegger, Oldmixon, Dennis, Ozell, and Curll slip through the gloom with the impersonality of ghosts, identified only by the long biographical notes which Pope plants like tombstones at the foot of the page. *The Dunciad*, in effect, would achieve its maximum impact only when time had robbed the dunces—"ev'ry nameless name" (III.157)—of everything except their names. Pope expected them to fade until they met their proper fate in his poem—surviving their own identities, transformed into faceless embodiments of their own perverse aesthetics.

The weird landscape in which Pope exhibits the dunces bears some resemblance to their more appropriate place of confinement at Bedlam. Writing of form in the *Peri Bathous,* Pope recommended that the poet's design "ought to be like a Labyrinth, out of which no body can get you clear but himself."[7] Pope's mock-labyrinth is, like Bedlam, a dark place of confinement where the friends of unreason chatter, play, befoul themselves—all supervised by the *magna mater* of madness and folly, the goddess Dulness. Pope was fond of using impressionistic metaphors to characterize authors and works—Homer is a wild paradise, Shakespeare an irregular Gothic building—and, though individual episodes in *The Dunciad* have specific models in literary tradition or in public ceremony, the atmosphere conveyed by so many species of folly collected in such array could well remind an eighteenth-century reader of Bedlam.

This supposition agrees with Pope's use of another curious, submerged image that unites reason and unreason, form and antiform. The Lord Mayor's Day, which Pope specifies as the "time" of the action, also implies the uneasy conjunction of high life and low life, of popular culture and official culture, characteristic of the entire poem. On each Lord Mayor's Day, the formal parade and splendid ceremonies inspired an unofficial, parodic antiparade: grotesque pageants staged by the rabble, who thronged the streets, flinging dead cats and mud, howling with drink.[8] Just as Bedlam unites in one image an imposing classical edifice and the madman inside, the Lord Mayor's Day is a ready-made paradox in which order and disorder—reason and unreason—share a single image. The poem's calculated disharmonies reflect the strain of such paradoxical imagery. Pope's purpose in *The Dunciad* is nothing less than to construct, with all his art and skill, a satirical imitation of the irrational.

Criticism of *The Dunciad* usually labors in the coils of a further paradox. The subtlety of Pope's art and the ultimate seriousness of his themes are contained within a comic work whose broad humor sometimes descends to slapstick. The poem is not only a rich, allusive, learned satire on contemporary culture but also a low burlesque that provides a stage for simple pranks, such as when Queen Dulness (after deceiving Curll with a prize that vanishes) proves her title by simply repeating the same joke, or when Curll wins the urination contest with a stream that smokes and flourishes above his head. The "heroic" games in book II are probably the best instance of Pope's ability to mix crude lampoon with a more subtle comic spirit. Here is Emrys Jones's account, which succeeds in conveying a feeling for the comedy of *The Dunciad:*

Wilson Knight has remarked on the absence of cruelty in this narrative of the games. On the contrary, every one is having a wonderful time, for within the imaginative world of the poem no one is conscious of humiliation. These dunces are, in fact, like unabashed small children—but children viewed with the distance and distaste of the Augustan adult. The world they inhabit is, like that of early infancy, wholly given to feeling and sensation, and so all the activities are of a simple physical nature: they run races, have urinating, tickling, shouting, and diving competitions, and finally vie with each other in keeping awake . . . "Here strip, my children!" cries their mother Dulness at one point, and they strut about naked, play games, quarrel, and shout, as free of inhibition and shame as any small infant.[9]

Yet, even such broad humor makes a contribution to significant themes that the poem develops. The folly of the dunces, no matter how exuberant and amusing, is linked always with more serious forms of irrationality.

The games celebrated in book II of *The Dunciad* offer an especially fine example of Pope's ability to combine comic nonsense with serious sense. For Virgil, Pope's immediate source, epic games were far from childish. In memorializing the death of Anchises in the *Aeneid*, they express the filial piety and ceremonial reverence that mark Aeneas as a civilized hero. Further, in adapting to peaceful uses the military skills required of conquerors, they blend natural energy with rational form—a combination which for Virgil, as for Pope, is the precondition of culture. Thus the debased ceremonial rites in *The Dunciad*, like the bankrupt rituals of the beau monde in *The Rape of the Lock*, are more than parodies of epic form; they debase the meaning which ceremonial forms can express. The behavior of Pope's infantile dunces as they tickle and shout and dabble in excrement is not meant as a celebration of childhood. The dunces are not simply parodies of adults. They are creatures who unite the outward form of adults with what Pope's age considered the prerational or subrational mindlessness of infancy.

Children in eighteenth-century paintings seem a particularly humorless species, perhaps because they were expected to pose as adults, and adults who act like children in *The Dunciad*, giving themselves over to infantile play, achieve their humor at great cost.

Such images throughout *The Dunciad* combine broad comedy with satirical pain. The meaningless diversion of the heroic games conforms to wider patterns of cultural error and absurdity. In the playful dunces we see how natural energy has assumed an irrational shape, how the normal development of the individual is reversed. In fact, everything in *The Dunciad* seems in the process of reverting to its earliest, unformed, embryonic, or preconscious state. Just as the power of Dulness—"turning topsy-turvy the Understanding, and inducing an Anarchy or confused State of Mind" (note to I.15)—subverts the right growth and government of the intellect, the topsy-turvy antics of the dunces are more than a farcical inversion of heroic standards. They reflect a general breakdown or collapse, a letting go, a failure of will. Pope observed in the *Peri Bathous* that "when a Man is set with his Head downward, and his Breech upright, his Degradation is compleat."[10] Although there is much to enjoy in the infantile games of folly in book II, we may at last grow uneasy as the spectacle of degradation spreads beyond the subculture of Grub Street.

The comic postures of Pope's individual dunces, then, are more than isolated configurations of folly. As Locke wrote: "There are *degrees* of Madness, as of Folly."[11] Without abandoning humor, Pope allows us to glimpse serious implications in the degrading comedy of Dulness as we experience the various degrees which characterize the irrational. When such implications accumulate, as the fragmentary acts of folly themselves accumulate and cohere, ideas, images, allusions, and sallies of wit begin to assume added significance. Mankind, as represented by the ubiquitous dunces, increasingly comes to resemble animated versions of the stone brothers atop the gates of Bedlam, especially because characters who represent the standard of rational humanity are excluded from their company. Although the serious implications of Pope's satire have long occupied critics, his exploration of the irrational—through its manifestations in the psyche of his hero—deserves special attention. The study of irrationality in *The Dunciad* introduces a number of related topics—dreams, solipsism, sleep, exhibitionism, pride, night journeys, charity, and nonbeing—that may seem strangely incompatible with a satire on hack writers. Before we can begin to explore their importance, however, it is necessary to consider briefly the eighteenth-century psychology of madness.

## Cibber: The Moral Psychology of Madness

Madness in the eighteenth century was not the opposite of reason—
necessarily apart from reason or defined by its absence. Total absence
of reason implied to eighteenth-century writers either annihilation or
brutality. As Pascal wrote: "I cannot conceive of a man without
thought; that would be a stone or a brute."[12] Madness is created not
by the disappearance of reason but by the dominance of another
mental power: the imagination, or fancy. Paradoxically, madness *requires* the presence of reason, just as it requires that reason be enveloped within the images generated by fancy. Fancy, or imagination
(the terms in the early eighteenth century were interchangeable) is
always defined as the pictorial, image-making faculty of the mind,
and madness occurs when the relation between image and reason
grows disordered. As Michel Foucault explains: "The ultimate language of madness is that of reason, but the language of reason enveloped in the prestige of the image, limited to the locus of appearance
which the image defines. It forms . . . an abusive, singular organization whose insistent quality constitutes madness. Madness, then, is
not altogether in the image, which of itself is neither true nor false,
neither reasonable nor mad; nor is it, further, in the reasoning which
is mere form, revealing nothing but the indubitable figures of logic.
And yet madness is in one and in the other: in a special version or figure of their relationship."[13]

The figures of logic, in the presence of an obsessive image, create a
counter-world of the mind that replaces—or threatens to replace—
the everyday world of the senses. Reason is thus not the pure opposite of madness, as common usage sometimes implies, but madness is
*inseparable* from the capacity to reason. This crucial distinction emphasized by Foucault finds clear expression in Locke's description of
madmen in *An Essay Concerning Human Understanding:*

> They do not appear to me to have lost the Faculty of Rea-
> soning: but having joined together some *Ideas* very
> wrongly, they mistake them for Truths; and they err as
> Men do, that argue right from wrong Principles. For by
> the violence of their Imaginations, having taken their Fan-
> cies for Realities, they make right deductions from them.
> Thus you shall find a distracted Man fancying himself a

279

> King, with a right inference, require suitable Attendance,
> Respect, and Obedience: Others who have thought them-
> selves made of Glass, have used the caution necessary to
> preserve such brittle Bodies. Hence it comes to pass, that a
> Man, who is very sober, and of a right Understanding in
> all other things, may in one particular be as frantick, as
> any in *Bedlam*.[14]

It is not the loss of reason that distinguishes the mad from the sane.
Madness, rather, involves a special configuration of reason and
nonreason—not absolute thoughtlessness but a topsy-turvy mental
life where reason works separately from sense and nature, where an
unbounded imagination (in Pope's cautionary phrase from *An Essay
on Man*) "plies her dang'rous art" (ii.143).

It is the necessary conjuction of reason and imagination that creates
the Augustan moral psychology of madness wherein people are held
responsible for their own mental aberrations. "All power of fancy
over reason," declared the philosopher Imlac in *Rasselas,* "is a degree
of insanity; but while this power is such as we can controul and re-
press, it is not visible to others, nor considered as any depravation of
the mental faculties: it is not pronounced madness but when it comes
ungovernable, and apparently influences speech or action."[15] Pope's
dunces are, in this sense, legitimate objects of satire, because they
have given an ungovernable credence to images of reality that are
more than normally fractured and incongruent, to the point that
speech and action are visibly disordered. The episode in which Dulness awards the victorious Curll a plump (but vanishing) poet for a
prize typifies the close relationship between comic folly and madness.
The greedy bookseller simply cannot seem to grasp what he sees:

> And now the victor stretch'd his eager hand
> Where the tall Nothing stood, or seem'd to stand;
> A shapeless shade, it melted from his sight,
> Like forms in clouds, or visions of the night.     (II.109–112)

This is not simple deception. All of the dunces chase personal versions of Curll's "tall Nothing," attributing reality to images as insubstantial as they are deceptive. The dunces inhabit a world which they
have remade to the specifications of their uncontrolled fancies.

In associating Curll's daytime delusion with "visions of the night,"

Pope suggests a link between the waking action of book II and the sleeping inaction of book III. "Then take a Hero," Pope advised the poets of bathos, "whom you may chuse for the Sound of his Name."[16] Cibber's name almost plays a more active role in the poem than he does. There is one indispensable, thematic quasi-action, however, that occupies the hero in book III. He spends the entire book sleeping. In his annotations to the *Iliad* Pope often comments on sleep—which he defines as a "Cessation of Thought and Action" (note to XIV.281). Like another favorite pastime of the dunces, eating, sleep in Homer's world of epic belongs to the ritualized cycles of heroic labor. Sleep intervenes so than action may begin anew. It is thus intrinsic to epic action, and its function is renovating and restorative, as in the episode from the *Odyssey* in which Minerva uses sleep as the medium for renewing the faded loveliness of Penelope:

> O'er all her senses, as the couch she prest,
> She pours a pleasing, deep, and deathlike rest,
> With ev'ry beauty ev'ry feature arms,
> Bids her cheeks glow, and lights up all her charms.
> (XVIII.221–224)

The drowsy spirit that Dulness "pour'd" over the frenetic, torpid world of dunces serves to deform and to obliterate the past, not revitalize it. Sleep in *The Dunciad* is not a natural, ritualized pause from labor, part of a cycle in which activity is renewed, but a denial of meaningful action, a state of deathlike negation in which almost nothing happens. Yet, there is one event (or active nonevent) that accompanies Cibber's sleeping in *The Dunciad*. Like various heroes before him, he passes by means of sleep into the prophetic and visionary realm of dream:

> Then raptures high the seat of Sense o'erflow,
> Which only heads refin'd from Reason know.
> Hence, from the straw where Bedlam's Prophet nods,
> He hears loud Oracles, and talks with Gods.      (III.5–8)

In pursuing a version of refinement that attenuates—rather than strengthens or complements—reason, Cibber as usual manages to approach truth exactly backward.

Book III is, in effect, a panorama of Cibber's imagination, a prospect of the inner world revealed when fancy overwhelms the conscious powers of sensation and reflection. The "dream-work" which the sleeping hero undertakes is certainly unlike conventional epic actions—that is the point—but Pope also refuses to let us associate Cibber's dreaming with the prophetic or supernatural dreams which in biblical narrative or classical epic or medieval romance give the hero a privileged access to the future. Pope's contemporary Lord Shaftesbury had insisted on the basic Augustan distinction between true inspiration (a genuine communication with the divine) and mere enthusiasm.[17] Cibber's vision allies him not with any of the Old Testament figures whom God visits in dreams but with the Bedlamite enthusiast raving in his straw. Having refined his reason almost, but not quite, out of existence, Cibber in book III actually does hear oracles and talk with (mock) gods: the creatures of his own mad brain.

Dreams, of course, are not themselves mad. In the eighteenth century, they frequently served a rational and literary purpose as moral commentaries or descriptive visions. For example, the dream-vision so effectively employed by Addison in *The Spectator* is in effect a disguised form of reason, in which dreaming explicates or clarifies waking reality. Yet, because dreams normally occur when reason is suspended, they also enter into a close relationship with madness. Dreams in the Augustan Age are the sane man's glimpse into the disordered world that madmen inhabit full time, and madness is understood as a dreamlike irrationality that carries over to man's waking state. The complete sameness of his dreaming and waking states is what makes Cibber so complacent: he perceives no difference between the appealing deformities he sees in his dream and the objects of his normal consciousness. Thus Settle assures him:

> "Son; what thou seek'st is in thee! Look, and find
> Each Monster meets his likeness in thy mind."  (III.251–252)

This total congruence of Cibber's waking and dreaming states is what distinguishes his experience from the temporary dreams or rational dream-visions of the sane. For Cibber, the irrational and the monstrous in his own psyche are affirmed by his waking consciousness. Imagination and reason, in their entanglement, convert the dream into a component of madness.

The monstrous scenes that Cibber witnesses in book III offer a good example of the mad conjunction, within the privacy of his mind, of dream, reason, and reality:

> All sudden, Gorgons hiss, and Dragons glare,
> And ten-horn'd fiends and Giants rush to war.
> Hell rises, Heav'n descends, and dance on Earth:
> Gods, imps, and monsters, music, rage, and mirth,
> A fire, a jigg, a battle, and a ball,
> 'Till one wide conflagration swallows all.          (ll. 235–240)

Pope's lines are such an extravagant description of nonsense that we may miss his reference to historical fact. The prodigies, Pope assures us, actually appeared on the English stage between 1726 and 1727, when "both Play-houses strove to outdo each other" in a competition of farces (note to III.233). Cibber, as co-manager of the Drury Lane Theater, was in part responsible for this competitive folly: "I see my Cibber there!" Settle cries out (l. 266). That Cibber's grotesque dream coincides exactly with historical fact does not indicate his sanity but rather the dangerous "expansion" of Dulness that Pope takes for his subject. In *The Dunciad* irrationality is spreading outward from the privacy of individual minds to the public world of art and politics. Through his hero, Pope records the passage of folly and madness as they successfully infiltrate the highest domains of power, reason, and history, carrying "Smithfield Muses to the ear of Kings" (I.2). Meanwhile, the conjunction of historical fact and grotesque fancy so essential to Cibber's dream-vision in book III parallels a similar confusion of reality and irrationality that further traces the laureate's derangement.

In a stroke worthy of Dryden's invisible decapitation, Pope fills his footnotes with quotations of Cibber's prose, allowing Cibber to convict himself with his own words. The waking voice of the hero thus transfuses his dream with self-incriminating commentary. In describing the theatrical war of farces, for example, Pope adds a footnote that quotes directly from the autobiographical *Apology for the Life of Mr. Colley Cibber* (1740), in which Cibber explains his reason for agreeing to stage performances that he frankly admits were "monstrous" medleys. "If I am asked why I assented?" Pope quotes him as saying, "I have no better excuse for my error than to confess I did it against my conscience." His daylight reason assures us that Cibber's dream is more than a harmless, temporary flight of fancy.

Foucault stresses that the dream-images, no matter how grotesque or irrational, do not in themselves create madness. "Madness occurs," he explains, "when the images, which are so close to the dream, receive the affirmation or negation that constitutes error."[18] Thus, while Pope's verse presents directly the grotesque images of Cibber's dream and madness, the quotation from the *Apology* confirms it. Verse and prose, then, Cibber's imagination and his reason, combine on the page to render the single verdict of irrationality. Pope does not need overtly to call Cibber mad—because the evidence Pope presents lets Cibber convict himself of a folly so deep as to be indistinguishable from madness.

Cibber is a genial madman, of course, who remains a comic, even sometimes sympathetic figure. His shameless admission of acting against his conscience is at least partly redeeming in its candor. But a modern fondness for antiheroes should not obscure Pope's thematic uses of Cibber's candid self-exposure. "Madness," according to Johnson, "frequently discovers itself merely by unnecessary deviation from the usual modes of the world."[19] Exhibitionism and self-exposure are the consistent signs of insanity in the eighteenth century, epitomized by the odd spectacles at Bedlam. In an age that considered social decorum an expression of communal wisdom, Cibber's zest for confession and self-exposure far exceeded the range of amiable eccentricity. In fact, as actor, theater manager, and author, Cibber could be said to have earned his living by exhibiting folly. Again quoting the *Apology*, Pope records his hero as boasting, "I look upon my Follies as the best part of my Fortune." Within the context of *The Dunciad*, Cibber's open embrace of foolishness does not appear an act of commercial good sense. It is one more evidence of irrationality.

Candid self-exposure, in Pope's treatment of his hero, is not represented as the product of honesty or virtue but rather as the expression of a flaw rooted deeply in Cibber's moral character: the sin of pride. His exhibitionism is simply a function of his narcissism. As Pope again quotes Cibber from the *Apology:* " 'Nature (saith he) hath amply supplied me in Vanity; a pleasure which neither the pertness of Wit, nor the gravity of Wisdom, will ever persuade me to part with.' " The words could come only from a genuine follower of Dulness, who instructs her children:

> All my commands are easy, short, and full:
> My Sons! be proud, be selfish, and be dull.      (IV.581–582)

It is apt that the commandments of Dulness are redundant. For Pope, pride, selfishness, and dullness are overlapping and intertwined failures—any one of which could serve as a synecdoche in summoning up the others.[20] Pope's view of the human condition, in fact, is dominated by the vision of a perpetual conflict between the two opposing forces of pride and charity. This conflict, developed at length in *An Essay on Man*, underlies his satiric treatment of Cibber and the minor dunces.

## Charity, Pride, and Solipsism

Counterfeiting, both literary and economic, was a problem of alarming new dimensions in the eighteenth century. The financial revolution, with its proliferation of paper currency and securities as well as the vastly increased trade in books and journals and (for the first time) daily newspapers, created a situation in which forgery and piracy were thriving enterprises. Curll and the Grub Street subculture of *The Dunciad* were directly linked with the world of counterfeit literature, but it was not only in literature and economics that Pope recognized a need to distinguish carefully between the genuine and its false resemblances. In *An Essay on Criticism* Pope challenged his readers to distinguish between true wit and false wit, between true ease in writing and false ease or carelessness. Such discriminations between true and false were especially important in the area of moral knowledge, where vice so often usurps the outward forms of virtue. Thus, in "The Universal Prayer" Pope insisted that, despite the limitations of human understanding and the confusions of "this dark Estate," God had bestowed on mankind the power "To see the Good from Ill" (ll. 9–10). The ability to discriminate carefully between similar but opposed values and ideas is crucial to an understanding of all of Pope's work, and no distinction is more fundamental to his thought than the difference between true and false self-love.

Earlier, *An Essay on Man* had explicitly and unambiguously asserted that self-love is one of the two elemental principles of human nature, driving us forward toward the goals of pleasure and happiness. Although it always requires the guidance of reason, self-love was understood as beneficial and productive, contributing to general harmony: "true SELF-LOVE and SOCIAL are the same" (iv.396). Yet, the concept of true self-love affirms that there are both productive and destructive (true and false) versions of self-love. Unless reason directs self-love outward, toward God and society, the ego swells in a morbid, all-consuming selfishness, and in his pride man imagines the whole universe created for him alone:

> "For me, the mine a thousand treasures brings;
> "For me, health gushes from a thousand springs;
> "Seas roll to waft me, suns to light me rise;
> "My foot-stool earth, my canopy the skies."     (i.137–140)

This mad, false gospel of egotism Pope contrasts with the right balance of self-love with reason that is expressed in charity—celebrated in the extended, penultimate paragraph of *An Essay on Man*. There, as we saw earlier, self-love was pictured working in the rational mind like a small pebble dropped into a peaceful lake. Succeeding circles radiate from the center of self to embrace a wider and wider world: first friend, parent, and neighbor, then country, and finally the whole range of animate nature, concluding in the love of God:

> Earth smiles around, with boundless bounty blest,
> And Heav'n beholds its image in his breast.     (iv.371–372)

The possibility of recreating a paradise within, an image of prelapsarian harmony, helps to explain the vehemence with which Pope denounced the egotism of false or irrational self-love: "oh Madness, Pride, Impiety!" (i.258). Pride and impiety, like all failures of charity, are for Pope a form of self-destructive madness.

The philosophical conflict between pride and charity in *An Essay on Man* extends as well to *The Dunciad*. Images of weight, emptiness, and constriction—as of things pressing in upon a center—serve to embody the idea of pride or selfishness. Charity, by contrast, is described in images of light, symmetry, and expansion—as of an energy radiating out from a center. The use of this pattern of imagery to characterize the solipsistic world of Dulness creates a thematic unity between passages that could otherwise seem merely offensive or "low." The conclusion of book II, for example, in which the reading contest finally overwhelms all of the dunces with sleep, describes the victory of fatigue with an unpleasant simile:

> As what a Dutchman plumps into the lakes,
> One circle first, and then a second makes;
> What Dulness dropt among her sons imprest

Like motion from one circle to the rest;
So from the mid-most the nutation spreads
Round and more round, o'er all the sea of heads. (ll. 405–410)

The padding of now-forgotten names that follows this passage emphasizes Pope's point. All here is heaviness and vanity, well symbolized by an excremental image. A constriction of the bowels initiates a process of mock-expansion which parodies the natural outward movement of charity. In its grotesque extension, far from creating a meaningful union of the individual with wider circles of society and nature, Dulness seals each of Pope's solitary and self-absorbed dunces in the psychic isolation of sleep.

A similar pattern of imagery emphasizing the opposition between Dulness and charity appears throughout *The Dunciad*. Although specific details of the imagery may change, its underlying geometrical and intellectual pattern remains consistent—as in book III, when Cibber hears from Settle the prediction that his house will thrive:

Happier thy fortunes! like a rolling stone,
Thy giddy dulness still shall lumber on,
Safe in its heaviness, shall never stray,
But lick up ev'ry blockhead in the way.     (ll. 293–296)

Though the movement of the stone is linear rather than circular, in its progress Dulness creates a huge, unwieldy, self-centered mass, layer upon layer. Its accumulating weight is the inversion of charity. Charity is the transformation of self-love as it radiates outward toward man and nature and God, while Dulness simply draws everything into itself. If it is right that Cibber should represent the center of Dulness in book III, the Goddess herself appropriately replaces him in book IV:

None need a guide, by sure Attraction led,
And strong impulsive gravity of Head:
None want a place, for all their Centre found,
Hung to the Goddess, and coher'd around.
Not closer, orb in orb, conglob'd are seen
The buzzing Bees about their dusky Queen.     (ll. 75–80)

The isolation of sleep in book II left the dunces possessing at least their own names—although little more—but Dulness here obliterates all identity: total service of the self, paradoxically, destroys individuality. Reduced to the impersonal and involuntary state of mere matter, the dunces, in their rejection of mind and spirit, now simply yield to the mechanical laws of motion:

> The gath'ring number, as it moves along,
> Involves a vast involuntary throng,
> Who gently drawn, and struggling less and less,
> Roll in her Vortex, and her pow'r confess.    (ll. 81–84)

Sheer mass eventually begins to exert a cumulative and oppressive force in *The Dunciad*, as the Goddess takes over the center for the huge, slowly-circling volume of mindlessness, which, in its lumbering expansion, threatens to overwhelm and obliterate all intelligence.

The perverse expansion of Dulness reaches its limit in book IV, where the yawn of Dulness, dropped among her children like a stone, spreads in expanding circles of sleep until the entire intellectual world—religion, education, government, art—is swallowed in darkness. As I argue later, Pope represents this condition of universal slumber as a form of madness—a new global irrationality in which the individual fragments of folly, like the dunces at the call of Dulness, finally cohere. Pope's concluding image of expanding circles, however, does more than provide thematic consistency for his apocalyptic ending. It also permits us to trace the expanding circles of irrationality to their source.

Pope's cultural Doomsday, like the catastrophe of a neoclassical play, originates in a single action expressing the character of the hero. All centers on Cibber's solipsistic answer to the riddle that he poses to himself as he contemplates the ruin of his fortune and career: "What then remains?" His answer constricts the world to his own dimensions, recreating reality in his image. It is a moment of sublime reductiveness:

> Ourself. Still, still remain
> Cibberian forehead, and Cibberian brain.    (I.217–218)

In a perfect harmony of sound and senselessness, Cibber's name consumes seventy-five percent of the slow-moving, repetitive alexandrine line. His invincible pride and egotism are the center from which radiates an ultimately annihilating cultural folly and madness. Like Belinda at her dressing table, but with more serious consequences, he worships his own reflection as a god, even as he serves as son and apostle of a divinity "Wrapt up in Self" (IV.485). Pope's religious imagery makes Cibber a parody of a messiah, a modern "Antichrist of wit" (II.16) who inverts Christ's roles as the embodiment of Charity and as the creative Logos, and who leads ultimately to the "uncreating word" (IV.654) of Dulness. Although the sin of solipsism assumes many names and shapes, some of them undeniably comic, it represents for Pope an always dangerous act of irrationality, extending beyond the self-centeredness of a single fool.

## Cibber's Night Journey

If Pope depicts Cibber's solipsism as a force capable of radiating outward into society, in ever-increasing circles of irrationality, he also traces an inward movement equally pertinent to the exploration of madness. This movement, as Cibber in book III dreams out beyond the fringes of reason, might be best described in Arthur Koestler's terminology as fitting the psychic and mythic pattern of the night journey. As Koestler describes this pattern,

> It is variously known as the Night Journey, or the Death-and-Rebirth motif; but one might as well call it the meeting of the Tragic and the Trivial Planes. It appears in countless guises; its basic pattern can be roughly described as follows. Under the effect of some overwhelming experience, the hero is made to realize the shallowness of his life, the futility and frivolity of the daily pursuits of man in the trivial routines of existence. This realization may come to him as a sudden shock caused by some catastrophic event, or as the cumulative effect of a slow inner development, or through the trigger action of some apparently banal experience which assumes an unexpected significance. The hero then suffers a crisis which involves the very foundations of his being; he embarks on the Night Journey, is suddenly transferred to the Tragic Plane—from which he emerges purified, enriched by new insight, regenerated on a higher level of integration.[21]

Only the language of Koestler's analysis might have puzzled Pope. The pattern of the experience it describes, far from being unfamiliar, closely follows the two main models Pope used for book III.

Cibber's dream is based on two literary sources: the final books of *Paradise Lost,* in which Adam ascends the Mount of Speculation, and book VI of the *Aeneid,* describing the hero's journey to the underworld. Both Aeneas and Adam return enriched and regenerated. Time, for both, is the focus of integration, just as in *The Dunciad* time is the focus of disintegration. Despite the effects of prevenient grace, for example, the present in which Adam is cursed to live can become meaningful only when history and destiny unite in his knowledge of the Savior. Likewise, although Aeneas intends only to visit his father, his underworld journey both reunites him with the past and unveils the future—equipping him to meet his destiny. Without this experience, Aeneas and Adam, however outwardly heroic their actions, would continue to function on the Trivial Plane. Beginning as individuals immersed in time, who view time as a progression of present moments, they develop an understanding of time as a coherent, meaningful relationship of past, present, and future. The temporary release into dream, vision, and an underworld of the unconscious establishes contact with dimensions beyond the self.

Although the night journey traditionally inspires in the hero a deepened knowledge and renewed purpose, Cibber remains untouched by his experience. Not only does he end as he began, a fool, but—in contrast to his heroic models—he never returns from his journey into night. Dream and reality are for Cibber identical; his folly and egotism protect him from the shock of spiritual crisis, and he never budges from the Trivial Plane. His métier is precisely what Koestler calls the "futility and frivolity of daily pursuits," a celebration of the meaningless, which Pope artfully represents in the "twisted Birth-day Ode" (I.162) that tops Cibber's sacrifice to Dulness. Since Dulness is an ahistorical force, collapsing distinctions among present, past, and future, Cibber has little to learn when Settle shows him—in a detailed historical survey—the progress of irrationality. This temporal survey, flattened (appropriately) to a series of pictures, introduces Settle's prophecy of a new era of Dulness: "All nonsense thus, of old or modern date, / Shall in thee centre," he instructs Cibber, "from thee circulate" (III.59–60). The familiar imagery of center and circumference depicts the laureate as a timeless figure, an anthology of the irrational, whose work compresses into a single bolus all the nonsense of the ages. Time no longer matters. Without relevance beyond the present or the self, his work, like that of the bathetic poets, is simply a form of "Poetical Evacuation"[22]—matter alone, in its crudest and most offensive state, the daily, undifferentiated product of all mankind. Sleep, then, timeless and unthinking, is indeed Cibber's proper function, for it allows him to make the temporary and potentially fruitful sojourn into dream a sterile, trivial, permanent condition of existence.

Although sleep is an action or inaction especially appropriate to Cibber, it has far wider thematic functions in *The Dunciad*. Book I begins with the poet's formal invocation, in which sleeping is identified as somehow central to his subject:

> Say how the Goddess bade Britannia sleep,
> And pour'd her Spirit o'er the land and deep.       (ll. 7–8)

The same book ends with Dulness describing to Cibber her wish to suckle and soothe the land like a "Nursing-mother":

> Till Senates nod to Lullabies divine,
> And all be sleep, as at an Ode of thine.       (ll. 317–318)

The three succeeding books continue this strange pattern. A reading competition that finishes with all the dunces dozing in a circle concludes book II, while book III recounts the dream of Cibber, who remains sleeping throughout. Finally, at the end of book IV, Dulness puts the entire world to sleep with her contagious and all-powerful yawn. This recurrent pattern creates what one critic has called "the most important prevailing paradox of the whole poem: that it is a poem about everyone going to sleep, which is nevertheless crowded with the most intense manic activity."[23]

The paradox is not inexplicable, however, for like much else in *The Dunciad* its meaning is related to Pope's treatment of irrationality. As Foucault explains: "The important thing . . . is that madness is not associated with dreams in their positive phenomena, but rather to the totality formed by sleep and dreams together: that is, to a complex which includes—besides the image—hallucination, memory, or prediction, the great void of sleep, the night of the senses, and all that negativity which wrests man from the waking state and its apparent truths. Whereas tradition compared the delirium of the madman to the vivacity of the dream images, the classical period identified delirium only with the complex of the image and the night of the mind,

against which background it assumed its liberty."[24] The framing episodes of Cibber's sleep, for example, transform book III from a static
display or series of grotesque fragments into a panoramic night of the
mind against which Cibber's distorted fantasies flit like shadows. The
great void of sleep combines with the images themselves to create a
complex which is madness—an emblem, in the little world of Cibber,
of the all-consuming irrationality which at the end of book IV
plunges the entire world into darkness.

Cibber's bodily presence, then, is essential to the meaning of book
III. But why, as Pope's critics often complain, does he disappear in
book IV? The disappearance surely marks a deliberate change in the
poem's intensity and scope. We leave the night of a particular mind to
encounter a more general, a more frightening realm of mental darkness. No longer simply the comic fate of individual dunces, the irrational now pervades the entire range of civilization. While Cibber
dozes on the lap of Dulness, oblivious to the force he has unleashed,
the poem itself performs the dunces' characteristic intellectual act
and, in effect, forgets him. (Wits have short memories, Pope tells us,
and dunces none.) Cibber simply vanishes, as if he were no longer
required to assist in the progress of irrationality. Nevertheless, although his hero's sudden disappearance helps Pope to expand the
scope and intensity of his satire, we are meant to notice Cibber's absence. He was, as fools often are, undeniably useful, a comic scape-
goat and a diverting spectacle. When he disappears, we are left alone
to face the effects of aggregate folly. Where has he gone? We are told
that he remains throughout book IV sleeping on the lap of the Goddess. But in another sense he has entered a frightening special realm
associated with sleep: the limbo of nonbeing.

Ezra Pound provides an oblique but helpful approach to understanding this limbo in his argument that the proliferation of minor
dunces creates an intolerable barrier to modern understanding of *The
Dunciad*. "Such reading is not even training for writers," he argues.
"It is a specialized form of archaeology."[25] Yet, Pope had heard such
criticism. He responded (in an appendix to *The Dunciad*) that he
would not have the reader "too much troubled or anxious" if unable
to decipher the names: "since when he shall have found them out, he
will probably know no more of the Persons than before" (p. 206). As
authors wholly committed to the present, who believed it "Chimerical to write for *Posterity*,"[26] the dunces receive an appropriate form of

punishment: they almost disappear. "Thou may'st depend on it," Scriblerus announces, "no such authors ever lived: All phantoms!" (note to II.126). Transformed to insubstantial "phantoms," the dunces are condemned to face posterity neither truly remembered nor wholly forgotten but loitering in a ghostly existence somewhere between memory and oblivion. They must not be confused with "real persons," another note insists (II.126), because nothing wholly committed to the vanishing present can be "real" for more than a moment. Pound's irritated criticism recognizes an important fact: the dunces are indeed like unknown figures disinterred from the past— shadowy, disconcerting creatures who neither exist nor do not exist.

As the prototype of dunces, Cibber retires early to the intermediate state of nonbeing—"the mild Limbo of our Father Tate" (I.238)—anticipating the fated disappearance of his entire race. If character is a function of consciousness, he stumbles upon truth in declaring (as Pope quotes him) that "he had it in his power *to be thought no body's son at all*" (p. 263). Like his brothers at Bedlam, he embodies the paradox of irrationality, which reduces man to something less than human. Humanity, for Pope, is by nature a "riddle," but the madman is a flat self-contradiction. "Joining vision and blindness, image and judgment, hallucination and language, sleep and waking, day and night," writes Foucault, "madness is ultimately nothing, for it unites in them all that is negative." Madness in the neoclassical age, he says, "ceased to be the sign of another world, and . . . became the paradoxical manifestation of non-being."[27]

Cibber's disappearance in book IV is thus entirely appropriate as a paradoxical manifestation of nonbeing. As an action or state, it could be said to bring to completion Pope's studies of human character, since disappearance or nonbeing serves even better than death to describe the condition of persons who fail to achieve the great blessing invoked in the *Moral Essays:* " 'while we live, to live' " (ii.90). Those who, living, fail to live well—despite the evidence of their bodily presence—always in Pope's work press toward the tautological state of nonbeing, a state especially apt for writers, who (as Pope lamented) necessarily resign much of their lives to the invisible activity of writing. Anything less than excellence, in Pope's view, was a literary equivalent of nothingness. "Middling poets," he once told Spence, "are no poets at all."[28] The limbo of nonbeing is not simply a fitting place of punishment for a writer of Cibber's submediocrity. It is also the logical consequence of his pride and folly, and it is prelude to the vaster spectacle of disappearance when the entire civilized world yields to the consuming shadow of irrationality: "*Art* after *Art* goes out, and all is Night."

*In describing the ultimate triumph of madness, Pope borrowed his metaphor from the idea of the Last Day—when the world would be consumed in* fire and God descend to judge the quick and the dead. A favorite subject among minor poets who turned to religion as a source of the sublime, the Last Day lends an aura of apocalyptic finality to Pope's description, as well as providing an appropriate instance of mock-sublimity, perfect for concluding a poem in praise of dunces. The Last Day, however, serves Pope as a metaphor only. Literal annihilation is not his theme. The real threat in *The Dunciad* is not individual death or worldly destruction but human irrationality: folly in its lighter guises, madness in its darkest shape. The irrational is especially dangerous, to society and to the individual, because in the limbo of nonbeing, moral action stops. Life dwindles from tragicomedy to farce; God's divine plan appears a jest without meaning. The face of madness, then, conceals an emptiness which comedy cannot entirely deprive of its terror.

Although Newton reassured mankind that the emptiness of space actually comprised the vast "sensorium of Deity," the interior vacuity of the madman was—to Augustan eyes—wholly without redeeming divinity. Madness, for Pope, meant ultimately the revelation of nothingness, and in the last lines of *The Dunciad* he forces his readers to imagine a world emptied of everything that gives it value. At the interruptive approach of Chaos and Night, even the narrative itself disappears, following its hero, Cibber, as if vanished into the lacuna symbolized by a row of asterisks across the text. As Martinus Scriblerus comments in his mock annotation: "It is impossible to lament sufficiently the loss of the rest of this Poem, just at the opening of so fair a scene as the Invocation seems to promise" (note to IV.626). The final hour now "Resistless falls" (l. 628), sealing the world of mind in a darkness far deeper than sleep:

> Lo! thy dread Empire, CHAOS! is restor'd;
> Light dies before thy uncreating word.          (ll. 653–654)

At the conclusion of *The Dunciad* Pope's satire on hack writers and pedants and miscellaneous fools has been superseded by a vision that associates the poem with the great world-myths of uncreation. The irrational has finally managed to restore a state so primitive that even madness, with its colorful hallucinations and perverse logic, is merely a metaphor—an inaccurate surrogate—for a negation even more intense.

# Conclusion:
# The Poet as Man of Sense

"You ought not to write verses," said George the Second, who had little taste, to Lord Hervey. " 'Tis beneath your rank. Leave such work to little Mr. Pope. It is his trade."

—Warton

"Lost was the Nation's Sense" (IV.611). This line from the conclusion of *The Dunciad* aptly summarizes the dimensions of collapse which Pope portrays in that poem. As a cliché borrowed from the current political vocabulary, "the Nation's Sense"—referring to a general consensus or widespread conviction—emphasizes that the breakdown Pope describes is social and civic as well as literary. The formulaic phrase was especially useful to Pope, however, because the cliché contained a potent metaphor waiting for rediscovery. What *The Dunciad* describes is far more than a loss of political consensus; it is something like the approach of mass lunacy. The irrationalism is not only widespread; it is concentrated, intensified, consolidated. Pope has perfectly understood how mindlessness tends to collect and multiply in groups: professions, disciplines, political parties, institutions, nations. All England is out of its senses. The loss of sense is an especially significant privation because sense was the fundamental, central value on which the Augustan ideal had been founded. Pope's trust in a renewal of English culture in many ways depended on sense. The coronation sermon for Queen Anne in 1710 had taken its text from Isaiah: "Kings shall be your foster fathers, and their queens your nursing-mothers" (49:23). When in 1743 Queen Dulness finally accomplishes her wish—"And, I, a Nursing-mother, rock the throne" (I.312)—Pope recorded the antithesis of cultural awakening. In the sleep of reason there is no access to sense. Philosophy, physics, mathematics, metaphysics: none survives the annihilating power of Dulness. "In vain! they gaze, turn giddy, rave, and die" (IV.648).

The Man of Sense—another Augustan cliché—may be considered the most important cultural invention of the early eighteenth century, personifying the central value whose loss impels *The Dunciad* toward its dark conclusion. As a representative figure, the Man of Sense is too seldom identified or discussed in scholarly accounts of the period, perhaps because he tends to disappear between his more colorful and durable rivals, the Restoration's Man of Wit and the Enlightenment's Man of Feeling. In fact, after a relatively brief struggle with his Restoration predecessor, the Man of Sense was rapidly shoved offstage by the new, tearful heroes of sensibility, such as Goethe's young Werther.

The triumph of sensibility and sentimentalism beginning in the 1760s prevents us from understanding the ideal of sense except through the history that displaced it. Indeed, the historical critique of sense is part of Jane Austen's subject in *Sense and Sensibility* (1811), where Elinor Dashwood—Austen's flawed but noble heroine who belongs to the old world of sense—is regarded by her more fashionable sister and mother as hopelessly eccentric, out of date, and emotionally disabled. It is symptomatic of Elinor's arrested growth (so her sister and mother believe) that she retains a taste for Pope. The tendency to view sense through the lenses of sentiment and sensibility, as Austen's characters show, brings inevitable distortions. In 1700 the Man of Feeling was a prodigy still unborn—although a few vigorous courtships were already in progress. For Pope's contemporaries, the ideal of sense assumed its meaning not in opposition to sensibility but as it was defined and defended as an improvement upon Restoration wit.

The new ideal of sense required both defense and definition especially because its opponents were so numerous and well-established. As Pope wrote in describing his age: "There are twenty men of Wit for one man of Sense."[1] What Pope describes in this statement is a culture in transition. Literature, he implies, is overrun with authors imitating the patterns of an exhausted style, wit-writing, which belonged to the court of Charles, to the Restoration stage, to the age of Dryden. It is the Man of Wit who represents for Pope the poetic sins of a previous generation—ribaldry, repartee, irreligion, nonsense, and elaborately artificial conceits—which the much-outnumbered Men of

Sense labor to correct. This antagonism between sense and wit may seem surprising, because wit is certainly a recognized feature of Pope's style. About the turn of the century, however, wit was also the subject of a bitter literary quarrel.[2] The dimensions of this quarrel are best reflected in a poem by Daniel Defoe called *The Pacificator* (1700), in which Defoe imagines the entire literary world divided into two hostile camps: "The Men of Sense against the Men of Wit."[3] A few years later Addison devoted six essays in *The Spectator* (nos. 58–63) to working out a careful distinction between true and false wit, and Pope in *An Essay on Criticism* undertook a similar process of discrimination. Through such efforts, Augustan wit was extensively redefined to distinguish it from its Restoration antecedents. In effect, when true wit reappears as a positive value in the work of Addison and of Pope, it has been purged of its former errors and emerges as something very close to a synonym for sense. The Restoration Man of Wit is officially declared an anachronism, as in Richard Steele's attack in *The Spectator* on Ethredge's great Restoration comedy *The Man of Mode:* "a Perfect Contradiction to good Manners, good Sense, and Common Honesty" (no. 65). Wit, to be preserved, must be chastened and corrected for a more polite age. Addison composed the manifesto for this quiet revolution in a sentence from *The Spectator* series on wit: "No Thought can be valuable," he sweepingly asserted, "of which good Sense is not the Ground-work" (no. 62).

Locating sense on an historical continuum between Restoration wit and Enlightenment sensibility is far easier than explaining what it is. In redefining sense, Pope and his contemporaries were describing a complex series of interlocking values for which the word *sense* was a metonym. Sense, as the "Ground-work" of all valuable thought, thus cannot be reduced to a convenient synonym or defining phrase precisely because it must cover so much territory. Johnson found it necessary to offer ten separate definitions—one of which is *reason*, a word he gives eleven entries of its own. (*The Oxford English Dictionary* offers twenty-nine separate definitions of *sense.*) The territory covered by sense was vast not simply because of the word's various uses but because it carried an enormous burden of tacit cultural assumptions. For example, the formula "man of sense" conveys an implicit suggestion that sense is specifically a masculine virtue. It is unusual when eighteenth-century writers praise women for their sense, which lends special importance to the occasion when Pope in the *Moral Essays* distinguishes Martha Blount from other women on account of her "Sense" (ii.292). What we need is not so much a definition as a social and intellectual history of sense—or at very least a description of the contexts in which sense was understood—because it is not simply as a word or abstract idea that sense functioned in Pope's time.

The function of sense in its social context is illustrated in a strange scene of courtship that took place in Birmingham about the time Pope was completing *An Essay on Man*. There a raw and very poor young man addressed himself to a widow almost twice his age. The widow's daughter later described the appearance of this odd suitor when he was first introduced to her mother. "He was then lean and lank, so that his immense structure of bones was hideously striking to the eye, and the scars of the scrophula were deeply visible." His hair was "stiff and straight"—not decorously hidden by a wig—and, to make matters worse, he was often seized by "convulsive starts and odd gesticulations, which tended to excite at once surprize and ridicule." It is hard to imagine a less winning appearance. This ungainly figure was, of course, Samuel Johnson, and his future wife found herself so engaged by his conversation that she overlooked all his disadvantages. As she said to her daughter: "This is the most sensible man that I ever saw in my life."[4]

Sense, as the widow Porter understood, is not merely a way of talking or of thinking; it is a mode of being. Courtship, relaxation, writing, dining—all aspects of life came under its power. Reports that Pope never laughed out loud, for example, suggest how the new ideal of sense deeply influenced behavior, sometimes at a level which extends (like the suppression of laughter) to the most tangled interrelations of body and mind.[5] Further, sense as an ideal was intimately associated with the acceptance of limitations, so that it always entails an awareness of restraints, denials, and outright refusals. Sense is much more complex than any analysis of its parts can convey, but without at least an introductory analysis we will not understand how Pope integrates into his character as poet both the virtues and limitations which he recognized in the eighteenth-century Man of Sense.

Sense, first, is a form of knowledge. It conveys the meaning of its Latin cognate, *sensus*, which implies firsthand experience, direct awareness of the world, including one's mental and emotional content.[6] It is an empirical and immediate kind of knowledge, emphasizing the role of the five senses in developing and in testing ideas. Thus the Royal Society, in describing the principles which should regulate scientific inquiry, announced that its purpose was "to bring knowledg back again to our very senses, from whence it was at first deriv'd."[7] In less technical contexts sense implies a wisdom which comes not through formal education but as if through the body or through the collective experience of mankind, tested and ready for use. Even though it is no science, Pope writes, sense is "fairly worth the sev'n"[8]—meaning that its value equals the sum of formal schooling: geometry, arithmetic, music, astronomy (the quadrivium), plus grammar, rhetoric, and logic (the trivium). Like Gulliver stranded in unfamiliar lands, measuring everything he can reach, the Man of Sense possesses a practical, adaptable, resourceful kind of knowing that allows him to survive by his wits. He can anticipate what needs to be done. He is truly "at home" in the same cosmos which terrified Pascal with thoughts of nothingness.

The elementary but invaluable knowledge which the Man of Sense carries in his bones gives him a confidence—a deep composure—that seems wholly undeserved. However, one of the amiable qualities of sense is to be self-evident. Sense often discloses its validity at a glance, like true wit: "*Something*, whose Truth convinc'd at Sight we find" (*An Essay on Criticism*, l. 299). The composure of the Man of Sense thus flows from his direct access to what is immediately and visibly true. He is someone who knows—because he sees at a glance—that witches, for example, are merely unfortunate old women, that ghosts are bugbears to frighten children. He lives at ease in a newly demystified universe because he can dismiss what is arcane or mysterious as therefore false or not worth knowing. Difficulties give him pause, even unsettle him, for sense is inconsistent with whatever must be laboriously constructed or unraveled, like the project of Swift's Universal Artist to breed a flock of naked sheep. Sense, again like wit, is recognized as a restatement of what we already know. It "gives us back the Image of our Mind" (*An Essay on Criticism*, l. 300). Sense can surprise us—if we have forgotten what we once knew, or never knew we knew it—but sense cannot shock us or thrill us with something wholly unknown or unimagined. As the satirical moralist Jean de La Bruyère summarized these attributes, "A man of sense has in him the seeds of all truth and opinions; nothing is new to him. He admires little, it being his province chiefly to approve."[9] Pope, of course, restated this proposition in *An Essay on Criticism* as he emphasized the judgment and experience which protect the true critic from ignorant wonder: "For Fools *Admire*, but Men of Sense *Approve*" (l. 391). The time for treading on the brink of nonsense had evidently passed.

Sense, however, is not only something one possesses, like traditional wisdom or literary taste, but also something one makes. Indeed, making sense—that is, creating statements of self-evident rightness—becomes an identifying feature of Augustan man. The Latin term *sententia*, referring to a maxim or aphorism in which truth may be recognized by its concise style, shares the same root as the English word *sense*, and it is wholly in character for the Man of Sense to express himself in a sententious style, especially in company. The Man of Sense is preoccupied, even obsessed, with style—style in speech, in dress, in writing, in conduct. This is in part because style is regarded as the natural counterpart of sense, its way of becoming visible. The style of a work, Pope urges, must seem an echo of its sense, appropriate not only to the content but also to the occasion. Because sense often restates what we already know, the form of its expression becomes especially crucial in commanding attention. In expressing himself well, therefore, the Man of Sense fits his language to the occasion and company, favoring the conciseness which adds force and reflects a concentration of thought. The young Sam Johnson's conversation, we should recall, was what led his future wife to declare him the most "sensible" man she had ever seen.

The natural marriage of conversation and sense—as if sense were invented to provide the appropriate substance for conversation, or as if the eighteenth century had rediscovered the art of conversation because so much good sense was suddenly available—introduces a further characteristic of the Man of Sense. Unlike reason, which may lock itself away in a chamber of pure thought, sense is aggressively and essentially social. The Man of Sense not only expresses himself in a sententious style, he is a native of the drawing room. Sense is above all a sociable virtue. It does not thrive in the mountains of the sublime or in the closets of learning. Mr. Spectator could therefore lay it down as a positive rule that "A General Trader of good Sense, is pleasanter Company than a general Scholar" (no. 2). Thus Pope reported that Dryden—the greatest poet of the last age, who was "intimate" with "none but poetical men"—was "not very conversible." Dryden, Pope adds, was "not a very genteel man."[10]

Gentility—meaning that one possessed the manners of a gentle-man—was an absolute prerequisite of sense, for gentlemen are by definition incapable of rude or senseless behavior. Fine manners are what allows sense to mix in the world of business and affairs, where it eschews the eccentric, the violent, the pedantic, the fanatic, and the dull, who are almost always bad company. The ideal of sense implied the existence of a middle ground even in the heart of conflict, where, as Johnson put it, a wise Tory and a wise Whig will agree. (Pope im-agined a similar basis—the practice of charity and resignation to God—in which all religious factions could agree.[11]) After more than a century of discord and open warfare, agreement seemed an alto-gether worthy goal. Sense, in short, would become the instrument of consensus, bringing mankind into the civil harmony and social un-derstanding for which conversation, when practiced as an art, is a model.

Because sense is so thoroughly social, conditions of enforced isola-tion or prolonged estrangement provided Augustan writers with a perfect laboratory for testing the resources and breaking-point of sense, when (as happens to Gulliver and to Crusoe) the familiar, companionable, conversible world abruptly disappears. The limita-tions of sense—its resolute refusals to pursue the siren songs of reli-gious, political, or literary excess—are what create its greatest strength, but its strength, therefore, is necessarily limited. An asocial environment or an unforeseen event, such as Crusoe's island or the appearance of a talking horse, may finally confront the Man of Sense with challenges that genteel self-composure cannot adequately con-trol. This inherently self-limiting quality of sense is among its most important features and demands further exploration. First, however, it will be helpful to examine several portraits of Pope, in which the imagery of sense is as significant as the depiction of Pope's appear-ance.

Pope was the subject of more paintings in his lifetime than any other writer, living or dead, and the multiplication of this personal imagery, through painted copies and engravings, created an unprece-dented situation. As Voltaire reported of a trip to England, with per-haps a touch of envy: "The portrait of the prime minister hangs above the fireplace in his office; but I have seen that of Mr. Pope in twenty houses."[12] These numerous formal portraits painted by some of the most prominent artists of the time hold a considerable value in showing us how Pope wished to be perceived. Both his fame and his firsthand knowledge of painting allow the safe assumption that it was Pope—not the painter alone—who determined the general design by which the poet made his appearance. What is especially evident from one of the earliest paintings—by Pope's friend Charles Jervas (figure 9)—is that Pope aspired to identify himself with the new ideal of sense. This identification was easy and natural in large part because good sense, as Johnson observed, was an essential and dominant quality of Pope's mind. ("Of his intellectual character the constituent and fundamental principle was Good Sense."[13]) The portrait by Jervas has special importance, however, because Pope used an engraved version of it as the frontispiece to the first volume of his collected *Works*, published in 1717. No longer the young author of separate poems appearing one by one, Pope, almost thirty years old, now faced the world as an established poet. We are meant to recognize the author as someone claiming his place among the worthy men of his times. His good sense is not simply a personal trait but a shared quality which allies the poet with all gentlemen of distinction.

One especially revealing feature of the Jervas frontispiece is how it complements Pope's preface to the *Works* in depicting the poet as a Man of Sense, a member of the clear-eyed community of gentlemen. Visually Pope makes this point by appearing in the pose and format identified with the famous series of Kit-Kat portraits painted by Sir Godfrey Kneller between 1702 and 1717. (Nineteenth-century editors were so thoroughly deceived that they attributed the Jervas portrait to Kneller himself.) Although doubtless mothers and mistresses of the Kit-Kat Club members could tell them apart, to a modern eye the Kit-Kat portraits are remarkable chiefly for their astonishing sameness, as suggested by the generic nickname "Whigs with Wigs." The interchangeable nature of the portraits is precisely the point. Poets, in their dedication to the ideal of sense, appear outwardly no different from statesmen, statesmen no different from publishers, publishers no different from courtiers, lawyers, or peers. Pope in the Jervas frontispiece and in his preface strains for acceptance in this worldly brotherhood. "I confess," he explains disingenuously, "it was want of consideration that made me an author; I writ because it amused me; I corrected because it was as pleasant to me to correct as to

9 Pope, by Charles Jervas, used as frontispiece to Pope's collected *Works* (1717).

write; and I publish'd because I was told I might please such as it was a credit to please." What could be more sensible? In this spirit of polite good sense, Pope explicitly dissociated himself from the extremists among contemporary poets and critics who misconstrued their limited function and importance: "I am afraid this extreme zeal on both sides is ill-plac'd," he remarked, adding in coy half-truth: "Poetry and Criticism being by no means the universal concern of the world, but only the affair of idle men who write in their closets, and of idle men who read there."[14] This is the speech of a man whom no one could call—as Pope called Dryden—ungenteel. It is also a pose that Pope soon began to modify or correct.

A second portrait of Pope also by Jervas represents a subtle but distinct modification of the pose of sense (figure 10). Between 1715 and 1726 Pope was absorbed in publishing his translation of Homer, which contemporary readers immediately acclaimed a masterpiece. Johnson, whose praise seldom reached such heights, declared the Homeric translations a "poetical wonder," "a performance which no age or nation can pretend to equal."[15] As such praise suggests, Pope's translations of Homer had decisively altered his status as poet, both in reputation and in wealth. He claimed that in his youth he had been too poor even to buy books. Now, thanks to Homer, he was prosperous and independent. This new affluence is conspicuous in Jervas' portrait, and it should be said at once that affluence was not something eighteenth-century poets desperately avoided as smacking of bourgeois complacency. In *The Dunciad* Pope located the residence of Dulness within the "Cave of Poverty and Poetry" (I.34), emphasizing the relationship between bad writing and the impoverishment of Grub Street, where literature was no more than a trade. Gentility was a way of life almost incompatible with poverty, and good sense (even if too polite to say so) recognized that no one who could avoid it would choose to be poor. We should not discount as meaningless, then, the comfortable setting and rich clothes in which Jervas depicts Pope. Yet, there is something more to his painting than an image of the Man of Sense as the genteel and newly affluent translator of Homer, whose bust broods over the scene.

Three features of the portrait complicate it: Pope's gaze, his posture, and the young woman whom Jervas represents in an oddly twisted pose as she removes a folio from the shelf—or perhaps replaces it. She is indeed a puzzle, a strange contrast to the poet. In a

305

10 Pope with a lady, by Charles Jervas.

subtle exchange of masculine and feminine traits, her stolid weight emphasizes the poet's delicacy, her submissive assistance emphasizes his independence, her activity emphasizes his contemplative musing. William Kurtz Wimsatt—the authority on portraits of Pope—reports simply that she acts as librarian and that her pose is "Titianesque."[16] But more needs to be said about this puzzling assistant.

Her extremely unusual pose is borrowed, in fact, not from Titian but from Michelangelo. Jervas has painted her, unmistakably, in the posture of the Libyan Sibyl from the ceiling of the Sistine Chapel (figure 11). According to Pausanias, the Libyan Sibyl was the daughter of Zeus and of the sorceress Lamia, but, like the other ancient sibyls, she was subsequently absorbed into traditions of Christian prophecy, which is why she appears in the Sistine Chapel. Her posture is reproduced so exactly in Jervas' painting that it constitutes a direct "quotation"—described by Horace Walpole as occurring "when a single posture is imitated from an historic picture and applied to a portrait in a different dress and with new attributes."[17] There seem to be no sources that attribute a specific importance to the Libyan Sibyl, to distinguish her from all other sibyls. Rather, her distinctive posture allows Jervas to create an allusion to sibylline prophecy in general. Yet, if the presence and purpose of an assistant in the portrait are already puzzling, how are we to understand the mysterious bond which links the eighteenth-century librarian with the legendary inspired seers of pre-Christian times?

Before we can resolve this question we need to look again at the figure of the poet, for several details require closer attention. The unfocused eyes and relaxed facial features, for example, support the claim by a nineteenth-century writer that Pope is depicted "as in a pleasing reverie."[18] The writer went on, unfortunately, to speculate that Pope was dreaming of the buxom librarian behind him. It is much more likely Homer—or the muse—who holds Pope's thoughts in poetic commerce. But other details help to focus the vague idea of reverie. The most prominent of these is the pose or gesture created as Pope inclines his head toward his shoulder, while his fingers rest lightly against his cheek and temple. This pose—first appearing in a portrait of Pope by Jonathan Richardson about 1718—soon became a standard feature in other portraits of Pope (figure 12). Pope's friendship with Richardson suggests that he certainly approved and perhaps specified the pose, which started to reappear almost like a personal

11  The Libyan Sibyl, by Michelangelo.

12  Pope, by Jonathan Richardson.

signature, as in the portrait of Pope by Jean Baptiste Van Loo (figure 13).[19] Why did Pope choose to be represented, again and again, in this unusual and distinctive posture?

As we might expect from a master of allusion, Pope's characteristic pose is connected with a long literary and iconographic tradition, for it recreates the conventional painterly representations of melancholy. Melancholy since the time of Dürer's famous engraving had assumed the same general posture which Pope adopted in his portraits. The pose appears, for example, at the top center of the frontispiece to Robert Burton's *Anatomy of Melancholy* (figure 14), and its relation to melancholy was well understood. We must still ask, however, why Pope would wish to associate himself with the figure of Melancholy. One explanation is simply that Pope recognized a strong element of melancholy in his character, just as he recognized a strong element of good sense. Yet, this biographical explanation is not sufficient to account for the other images that complement and accompany his melancholy posture. In searching further, we need to consult the ancient tradition which held that melancholy was the dominant humor or temperament of all great artists. This ancient tradition also emphasized the association between melancholy and inspired genius. As Robert Burton summarized in his encyclopedic account, melancholy "causeth many times divine ravishment, and a kind of *enthusiasmus*." It is this divine ravishment, he continues, which stirs the melancholic "to be excellent Philosophers, Poets, Prophets, &c."[20]

The association between melancholy and visionary or inspired genius—especially as these powers repose in the character of the poet—seems undeniably at work in Jervas' portrait of Pope. In signifying the presence of creative powers which can be explained only through the mysteries of genius or inspiration, the pose of melancholy perfectly complements Jervas' puzzling allusion to the sibyl, for it was the sibyl who "gathered into her person all the mystery and reverential awe which attach to a communication from an unknown and intangible world."[21] The poet depicted by Jervas is far more than a prosperous and talented Man of Sense. Without denying Pope's connections to the social world of sense, Jervas has also surrounded him with images that speak of his contact with the ancient mysteries of inspired genius. Sense has been infused with a power that seems almost the antithesis of sense.

The infusion of sense with an almost antithetical presence suggest-

13  Pope, by Jean Baptiste Van Loo.

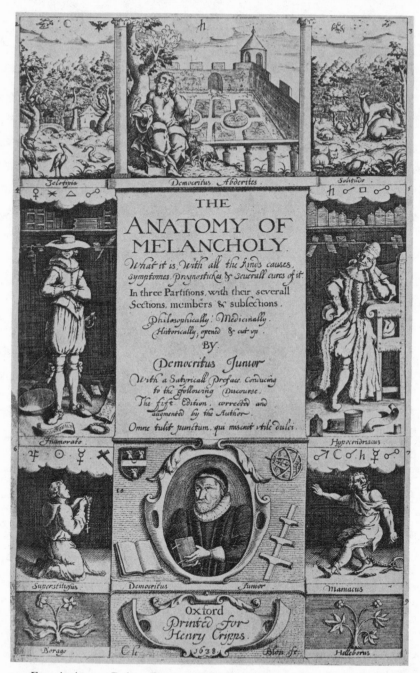

14 Frontispiece to Robert Burton's *The Anatomy of Melancholy* (1638 edition).

ing inspiration and creative genius seems the latent subject of another major portrait of Pope, by the celebrated painter Michael Dahl (figure 15). Dahl belonged to a circle which included several friends of Pope, and we may assume that the highly unusual pose in which he represented Pope had received Pope's approval. The portrait is so distinctive that it is clearly identified by the brief description in a nineteenth-century text: "startled look, pen in hand."[22] The reference to Pope's "startled look" is accurate (the wide-open eyes suggest a sudden, intense shift of attention) but the portrait requires further analysis. Pope is not simply startled. His eyes—not directed toward the paper on which he is writing, but raised, lifted well above the normal plane of vision—suggest that he is gazing upward, intently. This is a very strange posture. Its meaning becomes clearer, however, if we examine the long tradition of "evangelist" portraits. Caravaggio's (second) *Saint Matthew Composing His Gospel* is a well-known example of this genre, where the elevated gaze is directed toward a hovering angel who dictates the text (figure 16). Matthew, according to Saint Jerome, was the first evangelist to commit his memories of Christ to writing and thus (with angelic assistance) to create the first divinely inspired Christian text.[23] As in the many other portraits from this tradition, especially the portraits of Saint Jerome by Tintoretto and by Guido Reni, the essential elements are the text, the suspended pen, and the excited, intense, elevated gaze. Dahl reproduces all three identifying features in his portrait of Pope. There is, of course, no dictating angel. The secular fiction of an unseen muse or the rapt transport of genius are sufficient to explain the upward-gazing eyes and to associate Pope with a tradition of inspired writing. Here again, as in the pose of melancholy and in the allusion to sybilline prophecy, we find Pope depicted through an iconography almost wholly antithetical to the familiar social figure of sense and reason. The poet as Man of Sense, in correcting the past, has also maintained unmistakable, if indirect, contact with the legacy of inspired writing that, for Pope, united the great ancient poets with their modern heirs.

"Poetry," wrote the influential French critic Charles de Saint-Evremond in the last decades of the seventeenth century, "requires a particular genius that agrees not overmuch with good sense. It is sometimes the language of gods, sometimes of buffoons; rarely that of a gentleman."[24] We might take this statement as the challenge that Pope accepted in his lifework: to reconcile the antithetical or contrary

15 Pope, by Michael Dahl.

16 Saint Matthew Composing His Gospel, by Caravaggio.

languages of genius and of sense. Before we can trace this reconciliation further, however, we need to understand (as the portraits by
Jervas and Dahl suggest) the importance of genius to Pope's idea of
the poet. Indeed, Pope's emphasis upon genius as an essential element
in poetry has been generally neglected by historians of criticism and
aesthetics, who usually focus on events in the mid-eighteenth century, when a small avalanche of texts on genius suddenly appeared.[25]
This midcentury writing marked a considerable change from earlier
decades, when Addison began his essay on genius in *The Spectator*
by remarking on his choice of "so uncommon a Subject" (no. 160). A
dictionary of 1721 still defined genius in its normal meaning as "a
Man's Nature, Fancy, or Inclination," and Pope observed that "what
we call a Genius, is hard to be distinguish'd by a man himself, from
a strong inclination."[26] Quite clearly in Pope's day there was considerable confusion and disagreement about the nature of genius.
But, especially with the increasing popularity of Longinian ideas
of sublimity during the early decades of the century, there was also
a recognition that genius was essential to poetry. Pope would have
found his opinion stated quite openly by Dryden. "A happy genius,"
Dryden explained, "is the gift of nature: it depends on the influence of the stars, say the astrologers; on the organs of the body,
say the naturalists; it is the particular gift of Heaven, say the divines,
both Christians and heathens. How to improve it, many books can
teach us; how to obtain it, none; that nothing can be done without
it, all agree."[27]

The necessity of genius is a theme Pope repeats both in his correspondence and in his critical writing, although he tends to say much
more about the acquirements of art than about the endowments of
native genius. Still, he leaves no doubt that great writing cannot be
achieved by study alone. "A genius," he tells Swift, "has the intuitive
faculty."[28] In *An Epistle to Dr. Arbuthnot* he makes it clear that the
great writer—Addison is his example—is someone whom "True Genius kindles" (l. 196). "True Genius" is for Pope an absolute prerequisite of poetry that no amount of sense or art or conscious judgment
can supply. This insistence is present from Pope's earliest works to
his latest. The dunces, in showing their contempt for "A Newton's
genius, or a Milton's flame" (IV.216), characteristically neglect the
essential power of all genuine achievement—a power which Pope had
described at twenty-two in *An Essay on Criticism:*

In *Poets* as true *Genius* is but rare,
True *Taste* as seldom is the *Critick*'s Share;
Both must alike from Heav'n derive their Light,
These *born* to Judge, as well as those to Write.     (ll. 11–14)

True genius is a light from heaven, a divine spark, an innate power. Anyone with a little skill, Pope believed, could produce acceptable rhymed verse. Good judgment, although less common among poets, is also something that can be improved with experience. Genius, however, is not a power that can be acquired or explained. It is the mysterious presence that makes all the difference between a true poet and the mere man of rhymes. Sense, in its intrinsic limitations, thus cannot provide an entirely adequate description of the poet's role. The ideal of sense must itself be modified or refined, for Pope, by the addition of almost antithetical qualities for which *genius* and *inspiration* prove acceptable, traditional terms.

"We are indebted to Heaven for all things," Pope wrote, "& above all for our Sense & Genius."[29] The conjunction of sense and genius—both recognized as divine gifts—is characteristic of Pope's thought. In joining the two concepts, he not only recognized their potential harmony but also their considerable differences. It is certain that Pope recognized the inherent limitations of sense and its traditional antagonism with genius, as when he praised Voltaire as "not less a poet for being a Man of Sense."[30] Being a Man of Sense is an almost automatic disqualification for writing poetry, at least in the view expressed by Saint-Evremond. It is this awareness of the limits of sense which Johnson expressed in describing Pope's character. "Good sense alone," he wrote, "is a sedate and quiescent quality, which manages its possessions well, but does not increase them; it collects few materials for its own operations, and preserves safety, but never gains supremacy."[31]

The Man of Sense is sometimes openly parodied by eighteenth-century writers for his innate limitations. Yet, despite a recognition of the limits of sense, Pope never represents it as a deficient or untrustworthy power, something which will betray those who rely on it. Rather, the limitations of sense are simply the boundaries that distinguish it from other virtues—virtues an ambitious poet will also wish to possess. What is remarkable in Pope's work is his tendency to expand the traditional boundaries of sense, so that it encompasses or suggests far more than its normal, limited meaning. For Pope, sense becomes "the Soul" of "ev'ry Art" (*To Burlington*, l. 65). It sometimes constitutes a one-word definition of everything valuable in poetry. The economical phrase "Bacon's Sense" (III.218) thus serves in *The Dunciad* to summarize the achievement of the man Pope considered the greatest genius England had ever produced. We look in vain for contexts in which Pope implies that sense is somehow a quality of small minds or timid natures. On the contrary, his praise of it sometimes usurps the imagery reserved for religious inspiration or the most elevated flights of human invention. Here, for example, is the description of sense (originally intended for *An Essay on Criticism*) that Pope included in his epistle *To Burlington:*

> Something there is more needful than Expence,
> And something previous ev'n to Taste—'tis Sense:
> Good Sense, which only is the gift of Heav'n,
> And tho' no science, fairly worth the sev'n:
> A Light, which in yourself you must perceive;
> Jones and Le Nôtre have it not to give.          (ll. 41–46)

Although he does not use the exact phrase "inner light," Pope nevertheless brushes close to the old language of religious enthusiasm. His purpose seems identical with the purpose that moved Jervas to place just behind Pope's chair a figure alluding to the Libyan Sibyl. Sense is being redefined in such a way as to associate it with a higher—in many ways antithetical—power.

The reconciliation of sense with genius within the character of the poet can be considered the crowning ideal of Popean refinement. Refinement, as we have seen, is a process depending on revisions that add virtue to virtue, strength to strength, while eliminating the weaknesses and limitations of earlier, unmodified positions. All virtues, considered singly, are necessarily limited, in Pope's view, if only because they differ from other virtues equally desirable. The ideal, therefore, is always a compound form, in which two or more strengths are joined, like the "Reserve" and "Frankness" or like the "Modesty" and "Pride" which Martha Blount unites (*To a Lady*, ll. 277–278). As in the example of Martha Blount, the compound forms created by refinement are of greatest benefit when they unite qualities normally regarded as opposite, antagonistic, or incompatible. It was such a reconciliation of traditional opposites—wit and judgment in *An Essay on Criticism*, reason and passion in *An Essay on Man*—which remained Pope's goal, in art, in politics, in culture, and, above all, in human character. The model for this process in literature we have already examined in Dryden's poem "To my Dear Friend Mr. Congreve." For Dryden, Congreve's role was to unite the strength and genius of the great Elizabethan writers with the art and judgment of their Restoration successors, while simultaneously eliminating both Restoration weakness and Elizabethan irregularity. This was not a program for prudent compromise—resting weakly between opposed desires—but an attempt to create new and superior virtues which combine formerly incompatible strengths. For Pope, this process meant that the two formerly independent and incompatible virtues of sense and genius had to be brought into new relation. Just as Dulness in *The Dunciad* manages to unite nonsense with enthusiasm in an amalgamation of negatives, the true poet for Pope seeks to unite in sense and genius two positive forces charged with energies that resist fusion, that tend to thrust them apart, like mutually repellent particles. From the difficult fusion of genius and sense, so Pope believed, a power might be created superior to either alone. For Pope the challenge of the new age was to create a language in which good sense could at last find a poetic voice without allowing the infusion of sense to rob poetry of its ancient alliance with the mysteries of inspired genius. Sense must be added to genius, genius to sense, in ways which strengthen and redefine each concept, so that sense retains at least a metaphoric contact with the older concept of inspired writing, while genius remains free from the danger of enthusiastic follies. Free, to be sure. But it is also remarkable how far Pope is willing to edge toward the extremes he explicitly rejects.

It is not my purpose to decide whether Pope succeeded in the difficult compounding of sense and genius that, as he knew, would have to be achieved in his character as poet, where the equilibrium could never be stable or easy. We must recognize, at least, that the ideal he affirms is very different from either an unmodified poetry of sense or a pure poetry of genius. If Pope's commitment to genius is rarely acknowledged, however, it is also seldom understood that sense involved—at least for Pope—a considerable element of risk, which would distinguish it from the clichés and platitudes that counterfeit genuine sense. Sense is always at some peril in a world well content with self-deception, nonsense, and official lies. In a culture where heroic bombast and sentimental bathos held the stage, Pope saw himself compelled to speak out against the times. In his prologue to Addison's *Cato* he urged his countrymen to seek within themselves the means of reform: "Dare to have sense your selves" (l. 43).

Sense in 1713 did require some daring, not only on the stage. "I find by dear experience," Pope wrote, "we live in an age, where it is criminal to be moderate." The word *criminal* is a surprise. Pope implies that, where extremism is the rule, moderation and sense—in refusing to conform to the prevailing single-minded ideologies— necessarily stand opposed to the social norm, thus taking the criminal's established position. Equally surprising, especially to readers who associate Popean moderation with compromise and decorous neutrality, is his statement in the same early letter that "no man ever rose to any degree of perfection in writing, but through obstinacy and an inveterate resolution against the stream of mankind."[32] Sense, clearly, does not consist for Pope in telling readers only what they want to hear, in repeating what they already know. The poet who speaks sense must often utter unpalatable and unwelcome truths. A poetry of sense must risk inciting the anger of readers who oppose its implicit ethical stance:

> Soft were my Numbers, who could take offence
> While pure Description held the place of Sense?

Sense in Pope's work assumes the dangers that come with being understood. Its standing rebuke to pomposity, obfuscation, and to the infinite varieties of professional and literary posturing help to explain why, as Pope once put it simply, "Blockheads with Reason Men of Sense abhor."[33]

Sense makes enemies almost instantly. Unfortunately, blockheads are not its only natural foes. Nearly every spokesman for power and privilege argues that there are times when it is possible to see too sharply, to think too clearly, to speak too openly. Dull and inept writers are attacked in *The Dunciad* not merely because they are annoying or incompetent but also because they hire themselves to corrupt politicians who use them to spread corruption. Making sense challenges the enormous self-interest mankind invests in error, in nonsense, and in all forms of deception. Like friendship, like pain, like property, like character, sense is ultimately for Pope a moral category that attains its importance because—like "that dangerous weapon,

Poetry"—it helps to determine the quality of individual lives. Sense represents for Pope a deep and strenuous sanity, compatible with genius in the poet, which finds its most compelling expression not in Gulliver's mind-locked composure, not in the smiling reserve of Chesterfield's well-bred gentleman, but in the unsettled and unsettling engagement with one's own time that the poet, above all others, comes to see as his inescapable task. Ethical poetry for Pope was far more than the pursuit of reason. "Anybody can be reasonable," wrote Oscar Wilde, "but to be sane is not common; and sane poets are as rare as blue lillies, though they may not be quite so delightful."[34] It would be possible to turn this thought another way. A poetry of sense, especially when sense attains a rare confederation with genius, is something the world does not quickly forgive.

# ❧ Notes

## Abbreviations

*Correspondence*          *The Correspondence of Alexander Pope.* Ed.
                          George Sherburn. 5 vols. Oxford: Clarendon
                          Press, 1956.

*Essential Articles*      *Essential Articles for the Study of Alexander
                          Pope.* Ed. Maynard Mack. Revised edition.
                          Hamden, Conn.: Archon Books, 1968.

*PW*                      *The Prose Works of Alexander Pope.* Ed. Nor-
                          man Ault. Oxford: Basil Blackwell (for Shake-
                          speare Head Press), 1936.

*Recent Essays*           *Pope: Recent Essays by Several Hands.* Ed.
                          Maynard Mack and James A. Winn. Hamden,
                          Conn.: Archon Books, 1980.

Spence                    Joseph Spence. *Observations, Anecdotes, and
                          Characters of Books and Men* (1820). Ed. James
                          M. Osborn. 2 vols. Oxford: Clarendon Press,
                          1966.

Twickenham edition        *The Poems of Alexander Pope.* Ed. John Butt et
                          al. 11 vols. London: Methuen, 1939–1969.

## Introduction

Epigraph: *The George Eliot Letters,* ed. Gordon S. Haight, 7 vols.
(New Haven: Yale University Press, 1955), VII, 230.

1. Reuben A. Brower, *Alexander Pope: The Poetry of Allusion* (Oxford: Clarendon Press, 1959), p. viii. I do not mean to slight various introductory books which undertake the difficult task of reviewing, in a few
brief chapters, the life and art of a prolific, complex writer whose major
works span three decades; Pat Rogers' *An Introduction to Pope* (London:
Methuen, 1975) is a reliable guide. I should also express my debt to four

skillful studies which extend the analysis of a special topic or controlling theme throughout Pope's work: Thomas R. Edwards, Jr., *This Dark Estate: A Reading of Pope* (Berkeley: University of California Press, 1963); Patricia Meyer Spacks, *An Argument of Images: The Poetry of Alexander Pope* (Cambridge, Mass.: Harvard University Press, 1971); Frederick M. Keener, *An Essay on Pope* (New York: Columbia University Press, 1974); and Dustin H. Griffin, *Alexander Pope: The Poet in the Poems* (Princeton: Princeton University Press, 1978).

2. In Spence, I, 25. Pope's relation to Dryden is the subject of two essays by Reuben Brower: "An Allusion to Europe: Dryden and Poetic Tradition" (1952), reprinted in *Essential Articles*, pp. 132–145; "Dryden and the 'Invention' of Pope," in *Restoration and Eighteenth-Century Literature: Essays in Honor of Alan Dugald McKillop*, ed. Carroll Camden (Chicago: University of Chicago Press, 1963), pp. 211–233.

3. *Correspondence*, I, 2 (26 December 1704). On Pope's correspondence—especially its shifting voices and social strategies, which affect the meaning of nearly every statement—see James Anderson Winn, *A Window in the Bosom: The Letters of Alexander Pope* (Hamden, Conn.: Archon Press, 1977).

4. In Spence, I, 28. When Bloom describes Milton's Satan as a figure of the modern poet "because he shadows forth gigantically a trouble at the core of Milton and of Pope," I assume that he considers Pope among the writers "troubled" by their relation to the past; see Harold Bloom, *The Anxiety of Influence: A Theory of Poetry* (New York: Oxford University Press, 1973), p. 20. With good reason, Bloom draws most of his examples from post-Augustan writers.

5. "Preface" to the *Iliad* (1715), in *PW*, p. 251.

6. *An Essay on Criticism* (1711), l. 135.

7. "Dedication of the Aeneis" (1697), in *Essays of John Dryden*, ed. W. P. Ker, 2 vols. (1900; rpt. New York: Russell & Russell, 1961), II, 201.

8. Dryden, "A Parallel of Poetry and Painting" (1695), in *Essays*, II, 138. Pope maintains a similar view of invention: "It furnishes Art with all her Materials, and without it Judgment itself can at best but *steal wisely:* For Art is only like a prudent Steward that lives on managing the Riches of Nature. Whatever Praises may be given to Works of Judgment, there is not even a single Beauty in them but is owing to the Invention" ("Preface" to the *Iliad*, in *PW*, p. 223).

9. Dryden, "Dedication of the Aeneis," in *Essays*, II, 201.

10. In Spence, I, 24. In a similar spirit, Dryden describes the diction of his translation of the *Aeneid* by saying, "I must acknowledge that Virgil in Latin, and Spenser in English, have been my masters" (*Essays*, II, 218). Pope's apprenticeship to the great "masters" of the past is clear from the anecdote he told concerning his early attempt at an epic poem, as recounted by Spence: "I endeavoured (says he, smiling) in this poem to collect all the beauties of the great epic writers into one piece. There was Milton's style in one part and Cowley's in another, here the style of

Spenser imitated and there of Statius, here Homer and Virgil, and there Ovid and Claudian" (Spence, I, 18).

11. See Eli Heckscher, *Mercantilism* (1931), trans. Mendel Shapiro, rev. ed., 2 vols. (New York: Macmillan, 1955), and J. H. Parry, *Trade and Dominion: The European Overseas Empires in the Eighteenth Century* (New York: Praeger, 1971). A useful introduction to the literary uses of mercantile doctrine is Louis A. Landa, "Pope's Belinda, The General Emporie of the World, and the Wondrous Worm" (1971), reprinted in *Recent Essays*, pp. 177–200. See also James H. Bunn, "The Aesthetics of British Mercantilism," *New Literary History* 11 (1980), 303–321.

12. Dryden, "Dedication of the Aeneis," in *Essays*, II, 234. Addison in *The Spectator* (no. 69) provided one of the most glowing contemporary accounts of the benefits which flow from commerce: "Our Ships are laden with the Harvest of every Climate: Our Tables are stored with Spices, and Oils, and Wines: Our Rooms are filled with Pyramids of *China*, and adorned with the Workmanship of *Japan*: Our Morning's-Draught comes to us from the remotest Corners of the Earth: We repair our Bodies by the Drugs of *America*, and repose our selves under *Indian* Canopies. My friend Sir ANDREW calls the Vineyards of *France* our Gardens; the Spice-Islands our Hot-Beds; the *Persians* our Silk-Weavers, and the *Chinese* our Potters. Nature indeed furnishes us with the bare Necessaries of Life, but Traffick [commerce] gives us a great Variety of what is Useful, and at the same time supplies us with every thing that is Convenient and Ornamental." *The Spectator*, ed. Donald F. Bond, 5 vols. (Oxford: Clarendon Press, 1965).

13. Dryden, *Essays*, I, 88, 28, and 82.

14. *Correspondence*, I, 20 (2 July 1706). On the possibility of "mutual gain" from trade, see Richard C. Wiles, "Mercantilism and the Idea of Progress," *Eighteenth-Century Studies*, 8 (1974–75), 56–74. Also useful is John McVeagh's *Tradefull Merchants: The Portrayal of the Capitalist in Literature* (London: Routledge & Kegan Paul, 1981)—especially the chapter entitled "The merchant as hero: 1700–1750."

15. Samuel Johnson, *Lives of the English Poets* (1779–1781), ed. George Birkbeck Hill, 3 vols. (Oxford: Clarendon Press, 1905), I, 469. The best introduction to this subject is the brief essay by Susan Staves entitled "Refinement" (delivered at the forty-first session of The English Institute, 26 August 1982).

16. All quotations from Dryden's verse refer to the four-volume *Poems of John Dryden*, ed. James Kinsley (Oxford: Clarendon Press, 1968). For additional clarification of Dryden's views of the past, see Achsah Guibbory, "Dryden's Views of History," *Philological Quarterly*, 52 (1973), 187–204.

17. For Pope's comments on Dryden, see *The First Epistle of the Second Book of Horace, Imitated* (1737), ll. 213–214, 267–269, 280–281.

18. Johnson, *Lives of the Poets*, I, 460.

## I. The Occasional Self

Epigraph: *Essays of Michael Seigneur de Montaigne. In Three Books*, trans. Charles Cotton, 3 vols. (London, 1685–1686), II, 9–10. Inside the back cover of his copy of (Cotton's) Montaigne, Pope wrote: "This is (in my Opinion) the very best Book for Information of Manners [that is, character], that has been writ. This Author says nothing but what every one feels att the Heart," quoted in Maynard Mack, "Pope's Books: A Biographical Survey with a Finding List," in *English Literature in the Age of Disguise*, ed. Maximillian E. Novak (Los Angeles: University of California Press, 1977), p. 281.

1. *Correspondence*, I, 269 (24 November 1714).
2. On the new forms of autobiographical writing and of fictional autobiography, see John N. Morris, *Versions of the Self: Studies in English Autobiography from John Bunyan to John Stuart Mill* (New York: Basic Books, 1966); Joan Webber, *The Eloquent "I": Style and Self in Seventeenth-Century Prose* (Madison: University of Wisconsin Press, 1968); Elizabeth W. Bruss, *Autobiographical Acts: The Changing Situation of A Literary Genre* (Baltimore, Md.: The Johns Hopkins University Press, 1976); Patricia Meyer Spacks, *Imagining A Self: Autobiography and Novel in Eighteenth-Century England* (Cambridge, Mass.: Harvard University Press, 1976); *The Author in His Work: Essays on a Problem in Criticism*, ed. Louis L. Martz and Aubrey Williams (New Haven: Yale University Press, 1978).
3. See Christopher Fox, "Locke and the Scriblerians: The Discussion of Identity in Early Eighteenth Century England," *Eighteenth-Century Studies*, 16 (1982–83), 1–25. For other studies on the concepts of self or identity in eighteenth-century writers, see John O. Lyons, *The Invention of the Self: The Hinge of Consciousness in the Eighteenth Century* (Carbondale: Southern Illinois University Press, 1978); Baruch Brody, "Locke on the Identity of Persons," *American Philosophical Quarterly*, 9 (1972), 327–334; D. F. Pears, "Hume on Personal Identity," in *David Hume: A Symposium*, ed. D. F. Pears (London: Macmillan, 1963), pp. 43–54. A good introductory source is *Personal Identity*, ed. John Perry (Berkeley: University of California Press, 1975).
4. *Correspondence*, III, 156 (18 December 1730).
5. "Preface" to the *Iliad*, in *PW*, p. 252.
6. *The Art of Painting*, trans. anonymously (London, 1706), p. 52, italics added.
7. *Correspondence*, III, 347 (16 February 1732/3), italics added, punctuation slightly altered.
8. "Several Discourses by way of Essays, in Verse and Prose" (1668), in *The Complete Works in Verse and Prose of Abraham Cowley*, ed. Alexander B. Grosart, 2 vols. (1881; rpt. New York: AMS Press, 1967), II, 339.
9. Dryden, "A Discourse concerning the Original and Progress of Satire" (1693), in *Essays*, II, 80.

10. *Characteristics of Men, Manners, Opinions, Times* (1711), ed. John M. Robertson, 2 vols. in 1 (New York: Bobbs-Merrill, 1964), I, 109.

11. In Maynard Mack, "Pope's 1717 Preface with a Transcription of the Manuscript Text," in *Augustan Worlds: New Essays in Eighteenth-Century Literature*, ed. J. C. Hilson, M. M. B. Jones, and J. R. Watson (New York: Barnes & Noble, 1978), p. 103.

12. See Spence, I, 142.

13. *Correspondence*, II, 381 (3 July 1726).

14. Ibid., p. 386 (9 August 1726).

15. Ibid., I, 81 (10 April 1710).

16. Ibid., II, 433 (3 May 1727).

17. Matthew G. Lewis, *The Monk: A Romance* (1796), ed. Louis F. Peck (New York: Grove Press, 1952), p. 205.

18. In Spence, I, 168.

19. In this respect, Pope's occasional poems share features which Kingsley Amis finds characteristic of the "light-verse poem" ("Traditions of Light Verse," *Times Literary Supplement*, 2 June 1978, p. 615). They also exercise the same powers demanded by his major works. As he wrote of his practice in translating Homer: "I correct daily, and make them [the verses] seem less corrected, that is, more easy, more fluent, more natural"; *Correspondence*, II, 320 (14 September 1725).

20. Johnson, *Lives of the Poets*, III, 212.

21. *To Cobham* (1733), l. 30.

22. In James Boswell, *Life of Johnson* (1791), ed. R. W. Chapman, corrected by J. D. Fleeman (New York: Oxford University Press, 1970), p. 979.

23. The best source for studying how Pope's character had passed into the public domain is J. V. Guerinot's *Pamphlet Attacks on Alexander Pope, 1711–1744* (New York: New York University Press, 1969). Keener's *An Essay on Pope* (1974) and Griffin's *Alexander Pope: The Poet in the Poems* (1978), in exploring the relation between Pope's life and art, pursue a direction pointed by John Butt in his essay "Pope: The Man and the Poet," in *Of Books and Humankind: Essays and Poems Presented to Bonamy Dobrée*, ed. John Butt (London: Routledge, 1964), pp. 69–79. This direction has also been pursued in an excellent essay by S. L. Goldberg entitled "Integrity and Life in Pope's Poetry" (1973), reprinted in *Recent Essays*, pp. 15–44.

24. Spence, I, 259.

25. Johnson, *Lives of the Poets*, III, 211.

26. John Paul Russo, *Alexander Pope: Tradition and Identity* (Cambridge, Mass.: Harvard University Press, 1972), p. 171.

27. Johnson, *Lives of the Poets*, III, 188. "He pretends insensibility to censure and criticism, though it was observed by all who knew him that every pamphlet disturbed his quiet, and that his extreme irritability laid him open to perpetual vexation" (III, 209).

28. Punctuation and typography are altered slightly.

29. *Correspondence*, II, 227 (9 April 1724).

30. Ibid., IV, 199 (November 1739).

31. Dryden, "Preface to the Translation of Ovid's Epistles" (1680), in *Essays*, I, 241. A bibliography and discussion of major trends in stylistics is available in Morton W. Bloomfield, "Stylistics and the Theory of Literature," *New Literary History*, 7 (1976), 271–311.

32. In Spence, I, 171. Spence's protest directly follows Pope's statement.

33. *Correspondence*, III, 401 (6 January 1733/4). Swift's claim to recognize Pope by his style appears in a letter of 1 November 1734; see *The Correspondence of Jonathan Swift*, ed. Harold Williams, 5 vols. (Oxford: Clarendon Press, 1965), IV, 263. For modern studies of Pope's style, see Jacob H. Adler, *The Reach of Art: A Study in the Prosody of Pope* (Gainesville: University of Florida Press, 1964); John A. Jones, *Pope's Couplet Art* (Athens: Ohio University Press, 1969); William Bowman Piper, *The Heroic Couplet* (Cleveland: Press of Case Western Reserve University, 1969); two well-known essays by W. K. Wimsatt, Jr., reprinted (with slightly altered titles) in *The Verbal Icon: Studies in the Meaning of Poetry* (Lexington: University of Kentucky Press, 1954); and Hugh Kenner, "Pope's Reasonable Rhymes" (1974), reprinted in *Recent Essays*, pp. 63–79.

34. *Correspondence*, II, 426 (8 March 1726/7). As Berel Lang argues: "The repetition that adheres to style, that identifies it, is . . . not the *product* of a person or of that person's vision, something made by him, but the articulation of the person or vision itself"; see "Style as Instrument, Style as Person," *Critical Inquiry*, 4 (1978), 728. Psychology offers a similar understanding of style: "To the artist, of course, technique, style, is everything . . . it occupies the foreground of his awareness, perception, manipulation. The style is himself, it is what he exhibits and communicates . . . Surely it is not Cézanne's apples that are interesting—though they are by no means irrelevant—but his handling and what he makes of, precisely, apples"; see Frederick Perls, Ralph F. Hefferline, and Paul Goodman, *Gestalt Therapy: Excitement and Growth in the Human Personality* (New York: Julian Press, 1951), p. 395.

35. Johnson, *Lives of the Poets*, III, 262. For the arguments concerning the historical identity of the woman Pope celebrates, see Mack, "Pope's Books," p. 229. The epitaph is inscribed at St. Margaret's Church (Westminster) in remembrance of Mrs. Elizabeth Corbet, daughter of Sir Uvedale Corbett of Longnor; see *An Encyclopaedia of London*, ed. William Kent, rev. Godfrey Thompson (London: J. M. Dent, 1970), p. 259.

36. "Essays Upon Epitaphs" (1810), in *The Prose Works of William Wordsworth*, ed. W. J. B. Owen and Jane Worthington Smyser, 3 vols. (Oxford: Clarendon Press, 1974), II, 80.

37. For Locke, judgment consists in "separating carefully, one from another, *Ideas*, wherein can be found the least difference, thereby to avoid being misled by Similitude, and by affinity to take one thing for another"; see *An Essay Concerning Human Understanding* (1690), ed. Peter N. Nidditch (Oxford: Clarendon Press, 1975), p. 156.

38. *Correspondence*, I, 335 (20 March 1715/6).

39. Rachel Trickett, *The Honest Muse: A Study in Augustan Verse* (Oxford: Clarendon Press, 1967), p. 251. The simplicity and plainness of Pope's epitaphs "On Himself" and "On Mrs. *Corbet*" find a parallel in the simplification of wills and funerals beginning in the late seventeenth century; see Phillipe Ariès, *The Hour of Our Death* (1977), trans. Helen Weaver (New York: Random House, 1982), pp. 322–324.

40. Among ten defining features of an "Augustan mode" in poetry, Ralph Cohen lists the following: "The grammatical principle of modification in adjectival and adverbial words, phrases and clauses, implying a precise tradition improved by degree and by qualification" and "the gradual shifts toward greater syntactic qualification and intermingling of verse techniques, implying an increasing awareness of the unresolvably complicated world of man and nature"; see "The Augustan Mode in English Poetry," *Eighteenth-Century Studies*, 1 (1967–68), 32. Although Cohen links the use of modifying techniques to beliefs and to experiences widely shared by Augustan writers, I am concerned with the ways in which Pope develops the resources of a shared style for his individual purposes.

41. "Even of my darling Poetry I really make no other use, than Horses of the Bells that gingle about their ears (tho' now and then they toss their Heads as if they were proud of 'em) only to jogg on a little more merrily"; *Correspondence*, I, 330 (10 February 1715/6).

42. Ibid., I, 185 (14 August 1713). Pope encountered William Whiston and John Tidcombe at Will's Coffee House, where Whiston lectured after being deprived of his Cambridge professorship in 1710. Tidcombe was a Whig Major-General and member of the Kit-Kat Club.

43. *Correspondence*, III, 348 (16 February 1732/3).

44. Ibid., I, 353 (18 August 1716). In the preface to the 1737 quarto edition of his correspondence, Pope describes his letters as written "fresh from the occasion"—suggesting to what extent his letters and occasional verse share a similar poetics. Like his occasional verse, the letters also take character as a major, if indirect, subject. "Had he sate down with a design to draw his own Picture," Pope wrote of himself as correspondent, "he could not have done it so truly" (I, xxxviii–xxxix).

45. In Spence, I, 258.

## II. Civilized Reading

Epigraph: *An Essay on Criticism*, ll.574–575.

1. In *Alexander Pope: A Critical Anthology*, ed. F. W. Bateson and N. A. Joukovsky (Baltimore: Penguin Books, 1971), p. 216.

2. J. W. H. Atkins, *English Literary Criticism: Seventeenth and Eighteenth Centuries* (1951; rpt. London: Methuen, 1966), p. 167.

3. Ripley Hotch, "Pope Surveys His Kingdom: *An Essay on Criticism*," *Studies in English Literature*, 13 (1973), 474.

4. See William Empson, "Wit in the *Essay on Criticism*" (1950), in

*Essential Articles,* pp. 208–226; Edward Niles Hooker, "Pope on Wit: The *Essay on Criticism*" (1951), in *Essential Articles,* pp. 185–207; Patricia Meyer Spacks, "Imagery and Method in *An Essay on Criticism*" (1970), in *Recent Essays,* pp. 106–130.

5. Ed., *The Works of Alexander Pope,* 9 vols. (London, 1797), I, 173.

6. Johnson, *Lives of the Poets,* III, 228.

7. J. M. Cameron, "Mr Tillotson and Mr Pope," *Dublin Review,* 233 (1959), 158.

8. See Spence, I, 45.

9. See Paul Feyerabend, *Against Method: Outline of an Anarchistic Theory of Knowledge* (1975; rpt. London: Verso Edition, 1978). Feyerabend attributes to Galileo what he calls the "method of anamnesis" as a means of obtaining the acceptance of his new assertions about nature. Arguments are not enough. Galileo must insinuate "that the new results which emerge are known and conceded by all, and need only be called to our attention to appear as the most obvious expression of the truth" (p. 81). Classical physics, according to Feyerabend, adopts a "tendentious presentation of the *results* of research that hides their revolutionary origin and suggests that they arose from a stable and unchanging source. These methods of concealment start with Galileo's attempt to introduce new ideas under the cover of anamnesis, and they culminate in Newton" (pp. 89–90).

10. *Correspondence,* I, 128 (19 July 1711).

11. See J. E. Spingarn, ed., *Critical Essays of the Seventeenth Century,* 3 vols. (1908–1909; rpt. Bloomington: Indiana University Press, 1957), I, lxxxviii–cvi. For an unsimplified version of the critical traditions which Pope evokes, see William Edinger, *Samuel Johnson and Poetic Style* (Chicago: University of Chicago Press, 1977).

12. See John M. Aden, *The Critical Opinions of John Dryden: A Dictionary* (Nashville: Vanderbilt University Press, 1963), p. 145; H. James Jensen, *A Glossary of John Dryden's Critical Terms* (Minneapolis: University of Minnesota Press, 1969), pp. 68–70.

13. See *A Concordance to the Poems of Alexander Pope,* ed. Emmett G. Bedford and Robert J. Dilligan (Detroit: Gale Research Co., 1974).

14. Additional "outside" standards existed as well: "apparent solar time" (the interval between two successive passages of the sun across a fixed meridian), "mean solar time" (a measure of the rotation of the earth), and "sidereal time" (the interval between two successive passages of a star). "Mean solar time" was introduced in the seventeenth century.

15. Dryden, "A Discourse concerning Satire," *Essays,* II, 17.

16. In Spence, I, 45.

17. Hoyt Trowbridge, "Scattered Atoms of Probability," *Eighteenth-Century Studies,* 5 (1971–72), 37. Trowbridge demonstrates persuasively the influence of probabilistic thought in the language and methods of Johnson's "Preface to Shakespeare."

18. Edward Gibbon, *An Essay on the Study of Literature* (London, 1764), p. 51.

19. Locke, *An Essay Concerning Human Understanding*, p. 652.

20. Ibid., p. 653.

21. "The Preface of the Editor" to *The Works of Shakespeare* (1725), in *Eighteenth-Century Critical Essays*, ed. Scott Elledge, 2 vols. (Ithaca, N.Y.: Cornell University Press, 1961), I, 281.

22. *Correspondence*, II, 228 (9 April 1724). For Pope's denigration of editorial commentary, see his "Preface" to *The Works of Shakespeare* (in *Eighteenth-Century Critical Essays*, ed. Elledge, I, 289).

23. *The Second Epistle of the Second Book of Horace, Imitated* (1737), ll. 157–159 (italics added). This passage concludes with a self-quotation from *An Essay on Criticism*.

24. Quoted in Spence, I, 169. Swift could be equally laconic in declining specific rules for writing: "Proper Words in proper Places, makes the true Definition of a Stile"; see *A Letter to a Young Gentleman, lately enter'd into Holy Orders* (1721), in *The Prose Works of Jonathan Swift*, ed. Herbert Davis, 14 vols. (Oxford: Basil Blackwell, 1939–1968), IX, 65.

25. *Correspondence*, I, 110 (17 December 1710). My treatment here supplements the observations of Emerson R. Marks, "Pope on Poetry and the Poet," *Criticism*, 12 (1970), 271–281.

26. *Correspondence*, I, 110 (17 December 1710).

27. Spence, I, 251. For treatments of "variety" in Renaissance criticism, see Bernard Weinberg, *A History of Criticism in the Italian Renaissance*, 2 vols. (Chicago: University of Chicago Press, 1961).

28. "Preface" to the *Iliad*, in *PW*, p. 237.

29. In Spence, I, 151.

30. "Preface" to *The Works of Alexander Pope* (1717), in *PW*, p. 290.

31. *Correspondence*, I, 135 (12 November 1711).

32. *Correspondence*, IV, 145 (5 November 1738), and IV, 526 (19–29 May 1744). Sherburn notes: "Pope in his letters made almost a cult of friendship" (I, ix).

33. See Lawrence Stone, *The Family, Sex, and Marriage in England, 1550–1800* (New York: Harper & Row, 1977). As an illustration of the changing ideas of friendship, Stone quotes Samuel Johnson's description of the friend as someone who "supports you and comforts you while others do not," someone with whom you "compare minds and cherish private virtues" (p. 97).

34. Wentworth Dillon, Earl of Roscommon, *An Essay on Translated Verse* (1684), in *Critical Essays of the Seventeenth Century*, ed. Spingarn, II, 300. Pope gives the concept of critical sympathy a humorous twist in describing his role as Homeric translator and critic: "I am almost apt to flatter my self, that *Homer* secretly seems inclined to a correspondence with me, in letting me into a good part of his intentions"; *Correspondence*, I, 208 (30 January 1713/4). Critical sympathy was also implicit in the theory and practice of Longinus, who was celebrated (as was Roscommon) in the conclusion to *An Essay on Criticism*.

35. *An Epistle From Mr. Pope to Dr. Arbuthnot* (1734/5), l. 205.

36. Johnson, *The Rambler*, ed. W. J. Bate and Albrecht B. Strauss, *The*

*Works of Samuel Johnson*, IV (New Haven: Yale University Press, 1969), 122 (no. 92).

37. Johnson, *Lives of the Poets*, I, 410 (italics added).
38. Ibid., III, 200.
39. *To Cobham*, ll. 11–13.


## III. The Aesthetics of Revision in *The Rape of the Lock*

Epigraph: Samuel Johnson, *Lives of the Poets*, III, 218.

1. *Byron's Letters and Journals*, ed. Leslie A. Marchand, 12 vols. (Cambridge, Mass.: Harvard University Press, 1973–1982), VII, 229.
2. Johnson, *Lives of the Poets*, III, 219.
3. In *Pope: A Critical Anthology*, ed. Bateson and Joukovsky, pp. 186, 198. Byron dissented from this general Romantic view of Pope.
4. *Correspondence*, I, 110 (17 December 1710).
5. Ibid., I, 19 (2 July 1706).
6. In Spence, I, 41.
7. See John Butt, "Pope's Poetical Manuscripts" (1957), reprinted in *Essential Articles*, pp. 545–565. On the specific subject of Pope as revisionist, see R. H. Griffith, "Pope Editing Pope," *Studies in English* (Austin: University of Texas Press, 1944), pp. 5–108; George Sherburn, "Pope at Work," *Essays on the Eighteenth Century, Presented to David Nichol Smith* . . . (Oxford: Clarendon Press, 1945), pp. 49–64.
8. In Spence, I, 171.
9. Robert M. Schmitz, ed., *Pope's Windsor Forest, 1712: A Study of the Washington University Holograph*, Washington University Studies in Language and Literature, n.s. 21 (St. Louis: Washington University Press, 1952), p. 65.
10. See Martin C. Battestin, "The Transforming Power: Nature and Art in Pope's Pastorals" (1969), reprinted in *Recent Essays*, pp. 80–105. Pope's description of Addison is meant to illuminate the differences in their practice as revisionists: "Mr. Addison would never alter anything after a poem was once printed, and was ready to alter almost everything . . . that was found fault with before" (in Spence, I, 75).
11. Joseph Warton, *An Essay on the Genius and Writings of Pope*, 2 vols., I (London, 1756), 298. Volume 2 was first published in 1782, when Warton revised his original title (which had been *An Essay on the Writings and Genius of Pope*).
12. In Spence, I, 45. A collation of the major editions of the poem appears in Edward G. Fletcher, "The Rape of the Lock," *Studies in English* (Austin: University of Texas Press, 1944), pp. 109–173. For a critical discussion of Pope's changes, see Robin Grove, "Uniting Airy Sub-

stance: *The Rape of the Lock*, 1712–1736," in *The Art of Alexander Pope*, ed. Howard Erskine-Hill and Anne Smith (London: Vision Press, 1979), pp. 52–88.

13. Hugh Kenner and W. K. Wimsatt, Jr., have provided the best discussions of Pope's rhyming (see Chapter 1, note 36)—although in my view Wimsatt overemphasizes the frequency of Pope's "semantic" rhymes.

14. In Spence, I, 174.

15. Nelson Goodman, "The Status of Style," *Critical Inquiry*, 1 (1975), 803.

16. "The Morgan manuscript of the four epistles of the *Essay on Man* contains almost 250 lines which did not appear in versions printed by Pope" (Sherburn, "Pope at Work," in *Essays on the Eighteenth Century*, p. 63).

17. "Preface" to the *Iliad*, in *PW*, pp. 224–25.

18. A less-developed description of Pope's dramatic structure appears in James L. Jackson, "Pope's *The Rape of the Lock* Considered as a Five-Act Epic," *PMLA*, 65 (1950), 1283–87. I have divided Dryden's third stage, *catastasis*, into two parts: reversal (*peripetia*) and embroilment (*catastasis*). Dryden's account is as follows: "First, the *Protasis*, or entrance, which gives light only to the characters of the persons, and proceeds very little into any part of the action. Secondly, the *Epitasis*, or working up of the plot; where the play grows warmer, the design or action of it is drawing on, and you see something promising that it will come to pass. Thirdly, the *Catastasis*, or counterturn, which destroys that expectation, imbroils the action in new difficulties, and leaves you far distant from that hope in which it found you . . . Lastly, the *Catastrophe* . . . the discovery or unravelling of the plot" (Dryden, *Essays*, I, 45). Pope's interest in theater is studied by Malcolm Goldstein, *Pope and the Augustan Stage* (Stanford: Stanford University Press, 1958).

19. In Spence, I, 55.

20. "Repression" (1915), in *The Standard Edition of the Complete Psychological Works of Sigmund Freud*, trans. and ed. James Strachey et al., 24 vols., XIV (London: Hogarth Press, 1957), 146.

21. See Jeffrey Meyers, "The Personality of Belinda's Baron," *American Imago*, 26 (1969), 71–77.

22. "The importance of this type of woman for the erotic life of mankind is to be rated very high," Freud observes. "Such women have the greatest fascination for men, not only for aesthetic reasons, since as a rule they are the most beautiful, but also because of a combination of interesting psychological factors. For it seems very evident that another person's narcissism has a great attraction for those who have renounced part of their own narcissism and are in search of object-love"; see "On Narcissism: An Introduction" (1914), in Freud, *The Standard Edition*, XIV, 89. My purpose in citing Freud is not to transform the poem into a clinical history or to develop a full psychological reading of character. I cite Freud in the

way Pope might have appreciated him: as the greatest modern student of human nature.

23. *The Spectator* no. 281. The tiny image of a beau discovered in the coquette's heart does not contradict Addison's point that her heart is impervious to desire. The image signifies not a repressed or unacknowledged passion but a self-absorbed nullity: the beau and coquette are like vacuous partners in a set of matching dolls. Belinda's "Earthly Lover," by contrast, is a genuine threat, as Ariel perceives.

24. See "Epistle to Miss Blount, with the Works of Voiture," l. 31; and *To a Lady*, ll. 203, 213. George Sherburn writes of Pope's youth: "The truth is that he was during these years much thrown into the society of women, and thus came to sympathize with feminine sorrows"; see *The Early Career of Alexander Pope* (Oxford: Clarendon Press, 1934), p. 203. For a discussion of Belinda's delicate position in negotiating the claims of masculine and feminine expectation, see Ellen Pollak, "Rereading *The Rape of the Lock*: Pope and the Paradox of Female Power," *Studies in Eighteenth-Century Culture*, vol. 10, ed. Harry C. Payne (Madison: University of Wisconsin Press, 1981), pp. 429–444.

25. In Robert Halsband, *Lord Hervey: Eighteenth-Century Courtier* (New York: Oxford University Press, 1974), p. 100.

26. J. H. Plumb, *The Making of a Statesman* (1956; rpt. London: Allen Lane The Penguin Press, 1972), p. 74. This is volume 1 of Plumb's larger study *Sir Robert Walpole*.

27. See especially Martin Price, *To the Palace of Wisdom: Studies in Order and Energy from Dryden to Blake* (1964; rpt. New York: Anchor Books, 1965), pp. 151–152. Price, like later students of game, recognizes the important work of Johan Huizinga, *Homo Ludens: A Study of the Play Element in Culture* (1944), trans. anonymously (1950; rpt. Boston: Beacon Press, 1955).

28. Warton, *An Essay on the Genius and Writings of Pope*, I, 233. For a review of the play-by-play analysis, see W. K. Wimsatt, Jr., "The Game of Ombre in *The Rape of the Lock*," *Review of English Studies*, n.s. 1 (1950), 136–143; "Belinda Ludens: Strife and Play in *The Rape of the Lock*" (1973), reprinted in *Recent Essays*, pp. 201–223.

29. *Correspondence*, I, 42 (18 March 1707/8), punctuation altered slightly. In *The Court Gamester ...* (1719), Richard Seymour emphasizes the role of Chance or Fortune in ombre: "Now I have laid down all the Rules of the Game of *Hombre;* but notwithstanding all my Directions, yet, let a Person play with ever so much Judgment and Caution, he will often find himself Disappointed in his Game, for Fortune will have a Hand in small Things as well as Great, so that it is not to be expected that the best Gamesters shall always win; you may lose upon a very good Game, when all the Trumps that are against you, fall into one Hand; on the contrary, when they happen to be divided, you may win a very small Game" (pp. 42–43).

30. *Correspondence*, I, 233 (29 June 1714).

31. Huizinga, *Homo Ludens*, p. 10. J. S. Cunningham offers an excellent description of the way in which Popean irony allows both an appreciation of beauty and an exposure of folly—sometimes simultaneously: "There are many times when one feels not so much that Belinda's world is disparagingly contrasted with a more 'considerable,' incomparably wider one, as that the world of Homer and Virgil has been scaled down, wittily and affectionately, to admit the *boudoir* and the coffee-table. In other words, the gap between the two worlds can in this poem be ironically exploited to favour either side, or even both sides at once; it can remain more or less neutral, simply funny; and it can be closed, whether ludicrously . . . or seriously." *Pope: The Rape of the Lock*, Studies in English Literature, no. 2 (London: Edward Arnold, 1961), pp. 11–12.

32. For such standard views, see Hugo M. Reichard, "The Love Affair in Pope's *Rape of the Lock*," *PMLA*, 69 (1954), 887–902; Murray Krieger, "The 'Frail China Jar' and the Rude Hand of Chaos" (1961), reprinted in *Essential Articles*, pp. 301–319.

33. In Spence, I, 43–44.

34. "Preface" to *The Works of Alexander Pope*, in *PW*, p. 292.

35. *Correspondence*, I, 211 (28 February 1713/14).

## IV. Virgilian Attitudes in *Windsor-Forest*

Epigraph: Virgil, *Aeneid*, trans. John Dryden, VI. 1168–77.

1. Earl R. Wasserman, *The Subtler Language: Critical Readings of Neoclassic and Romantic Poems* (Baltimore: Johns Hopkins University Press, 1959), pp. 101–168.

2. *Correspondence*, I, 179 (23 June 1713). Pope is recalling Dryden's preface to *Absalom and Achitophel* (1681), and he explicitly quotes Dryden, with slight variation, in a letter of 17 October 1713 (I, 194). Pope's veiled attack on William III (through allusive descriptions of William the Conqueror) is discussed by John Robert Moore, "*Windsor-Forest* and William III" (1951), reprinted in *Essential Articles*, pp. 242–246.

3. Swift, *Journal to Stella*, ed. Harold Williams, 2 vols. (Oxford: Clarendon Press, 1948), II, 635.

4. Pamela Poynter Schwandt, "Pope's Transformations of Homer's Similes," *Studies in Philology*, 76 (1979), 388. See also Robert Crossley, "Pope's *Iliad:* The Commentary and the Translation," *Philological Quarterly*, 56 (1977), 339–357.

5. *The Guardian* no. 40 (1713), in *PW*, p. 98.

6. In Spence, I, 229.

7. From an early version of Pope's "Epistle to Mr. Jervas," quoted by Norman Ault, *New Light on Pope* (1949; rpt. Hamden, Conn.: Archon Books, 1967), p. 73.

8. Johnson, *Lives of the Poets*, III, 224.

9. E. Audra and Aubrey Williams, eds., *Pastoral Poetry and An Essay*

*on Criticism,* Twickenham edition, p. 132. The best general account is in John Chalker's *The English Georgic: A Study in the Development of a Form* (Baltimore: Johns Hopkins University Press, 1969). Recent work on the *Georgics* includes: L. P. Wilkinson, *The "Georgics" of Virgil: A Critical Survey* (Cambridge: Cambridge University Press, 1969); Michael C. J. Putnam, *Virgil's Poem of the Earth: Studies in the "Georgics"* (Princeton: Princeton University Press, 1979); Gary B. Miles, *Virgil's "Georgics": A New Interpretation* (Berkeley: University of California Press, 1980).

10. Brower, *The Poetry of Allusion,* pp. 61–62.

11. Roscommon, *An Essay on Translated Verse* (1684), in *Critical Essays of the Seventeenth Century,* ed. Spingarn, II, 300. Longinus' recommendation, in chapter 11 of Boileau's translation, is quoted by Dryden in his preface to *Troilus and Cressida* (*Essays,* I, 206).

12. Ovid, *Metamorphoses,* II.328. No English version available to Pope translates the Latin phrase in the exact words "greatly-daring died"—but Pope's allusion does not depend upon the wording of a specific translator. A literal reading of Ovid makes the bilingual pun unmistakable. Thus Mary M. Innes in her literal Penguin Classics translation of the *Metamorphoses* offers the version: "Here Phaethon lies: his father's car he tried—/ Though proved too weak, he greatly daring died." Pope encountered a similar version of Ovid's famous epitaph on Phaethon when he edited *The Works of John Sheffield* (1723). Sheffield's works included a poem laboriously entitled "On *Don Alonzo*'s being killed in *Portugal* upon Account of the *Infanta,* in the Year *1683.*" This celebration of a Phaethon-like youth destroyed by his own boldness concludes with the lines: "If from the glorious Height he falls, / He greatly daring dies." Pope seemed attracted to the figure of Phaethon, a rash but courageous overreacher. Once he playfully compared himself to Phaethon as someone "knockd down" by his extensive travels (*Correspondence,* IV, 192).

13. Thomas M. Greene, "Petrarch and the Humanist Hermeneutic," in *Italian Literature: Roots and Branches,* ed. Giose Rimanelli and Kenneth John Atchity (New Haven: Yale University Press, 1976), p. 213. The debate concerning the range and significance of Popean allusion is carried on—at the extremes of polysemy and explicitness—by Earl R. Wasserman and Irvin Ehrenpreis. See Wasserman, "The Limits of Allusion in *The Rape of the Lock*" (1966), reprinted in *Recent Essays,* pp. 224–246; Ehrenpreis, "Meaning: Implicit and Explicit," in *New Approaches to Eighteenth-Century Literature: Selected Papers from the English Institute,* ed. Phillip Harth (New York: Columbia University Press, 1974), pp. 117–155.

14. Quoted by Greene, "Petrarch and the Humanist Hermeneutic," pp. 211–212.

15. *The Guardian* no. 12 (1713), in *PW,* p. 91.

16. Patricia Meyer Spacks, *The Insistence of Horror: Aspects of the Supernatural in Eighteenth-Century Poetry* (Cambridge, Mass.: Harvard University Press, 1962), p. 142.

17. See, for example, Thomas Otway's "Windsor Castle" (1685), in *Minor English Poets, 1660–1780*, comp. David P. French (New York: Benjamin Blom, 1967), I, 520.

18. "The conflict of *pietas* and *furor* is one of the most important motifs in the *Aeneid* and permeates the entire poem"; A. J. Boyle, "The Meaning of the *Aeneid:* A Critical Inquiry," *Ramus*, 1 (1972), 64. The range of meaning associated with the concept of *furor* can be sampled from book V of Pope's translation of the *Iliad*—a book almost wholly devoted to violent and frenzied warfare—in which Pope uses the word *fury* at least twelve times and the adjective *furious* at least ten. The following description and explication of a standard pictorial emblem of Furor is also pertinent: "A Man shewing Madness in his Looks, his Eyes tied with a Fillet, in a Posture as if he had a Mind to throw a Bundle of Arms bound up, in a short Habit. The Fillet denotes the Understanding *lost*, when Madness has Dominion, for Madness is the *Blindness* of the Mind. The Arms signifie that Fury is ever *arm'd* for Revenge. The short Garment shews that he respects neither *Decency* nor *good Manners.*" Caesar Ripa, *Iconologia: or, Moral Emblems* (London, 1709), p. 30—an adaptation of Ripa's original text published in 1595.

19. In Schmitz, ed., *Pope's Windsor Forest, 1712*, p. 32.

20. In Schmitz, ed., *Pope's Windsor Forest, 1712*, p. 40.

21. Addison, "An Essay on Virgil's *Georgics*" (1697), in *Eighteenth-Century Critical Essays*, ed. Elledge, I, 3.

22. T. S. Eliot, "Isolated Superiority," review of *Personae: The Collected Poems of Ezra Pound*, *The Dial*, 84 (January 1928), 5.

23. In Spence, I, 545.

24. "Preface" to the *Iliad*, in *PW*, p. 231. Pope may have recalled Dryden's discussion of Virgilian subjectivity in the preface (1667) to *Annus Mirabilis* (*Essays*, I, 15–16). Pat Rogers has argued persuasively that *Annus Mirabilis* is a major source for *Windsor-Forest*; see "Trade and Dominion: *Annus Mirabilis* and *Windsor-Forest*," *Durham University Journal*, 38 (1976), 14–20.

25. Brooks Otis, *Virgil: A Study in Civilized Poetry* (1964; corrected ed. Oxford: Clarendon Press, 1966), pp. 49–50. Kenneth Quinn discusses specific techniques which contribute to Virgil's distinctive style in *Virgil's "Aeneid": A Critical Description* (Ann Arbor: University of Michigan Press, 1968), pp. 77–83.

26. Wasserman, *The Subtler Language*, p. 131.

27. See J. Roger Dunkle, "The Hunter and Hunting in the *Aeneid*," *Ramus*, 2 (1973), 127–142. The only unambiguously positive version of the hunt occurs in book I, when Aeneas kills seven stags immediately upon arrival on the coast of Africa. (The aim of his hunting, however, is not sport but food.) It is possible here, as elsewhere, that Pope may think of Virgil and Dryden simultaneously. See Rachel A. Miller, "Regal Hunting: Dryden's Influence on *Windsor-Forest*," *Eighteenth-Century Studies*, 13 (1979–80), 169–188.

28. Rebecca Price Parkin, *The Poetic Workmanship of Alexander Pope* (Minneapolis: University of Minnesota Press, 1955), p. 173.

29. From a poem by Francis Knapp prefixed to the 1717 edition of Pope's *Works*. The Longinian discussion of *enargeia* appears in chapter 13 of Boileau's translation—a chapter Boileau entitled *"Des Images."* Pope also employs the phrase "flames with Gold" (which describes the dying pheasant) in a passage where Homer describes spears, helmets, and shields that are the "Pillage" of war (*Iliad* XIII.346).

30. See Thomas R. Edwards, Jr., "The Colors of Fancy: An Image Cluster in Pope," *Modern Language Notes*, 73 (1958), 485–489.

31. Gilbert Wakefield, *Observations on Pope* (London, 1796), p. 39.

32. Michael C. J. Putnam, *The Poetry of the "Aeneid": Four Studies in Imaginative Unity and Design* (Cambridge, Mass.: Harvard University Press, 1965), p. 192. For a discussion of Dryden's responsiveness to Virgilian ambivalence concerning the costs of empire, see Robert H. Bell, "Dryden's 'Aeneid' as English Augustan Epic," *Criticism*, 19 (1977), 34–50. T. W. Harrison documents the tendency toward political readings of Virgil among seventeenth- and eighteenth-century commentators, in "English Virgil: The *Aeneid* in the Eighteenth Century," *Philologica Pragensia*, 10 (1967), 1–11.

33. In Spence, I, 196. Spence's editor, James M. Osborn, notes the parallel in Chetwood's "Life of Virgil."

34. John H. Miller, "Pope and the Principle of Reconciliation," *Texas Studies in Literature and Language*, 9 (1967), 185–192.

35. Wasserman, *The Subtler Language*, p. 164.

36. Maynard Mack, ed., *An Essay on Man*, Twickenham edition, p. lxiii.

37. *The Guardian* no. 61 (1713), in *PW*, p. 109. Pope quotes approvingly Plutarch's view that man's humaneness should be extended "thro' the whole Order of Creatures, even to the meanest: Such Actions of Charity are the Over-flowings of a mild Good nature on all below us." The quotation shows that in 1713 Pope had already articulated the position regarding charity and hunting implicit in *An Essay on Man* twenty years later. The changing English attitudes toward hunting are part of Keith Thomas' subject in *Man and the Natural World: A History of the Modern Sensibility* (New York: Pantheon Books, 1983), pp. 160–165.

38. G. Wilson Knight, *The Poetry of Alexander Pope: Laureate of Peace* (1955; rpt. London: Routledge, 1965), p. 22.

39. In Schmitz, ed., *Pope's Windsor Forest, 1712*, p. 47. Schmitz cites the phrase from verses included in Pope's letter to John Caryll dated 29 November 1712 (*Correspondence*, I, 157).

## V. "The Visionary Maid"

Epigraph: Jean de La Bruyère, *The Characters, or The Manners of the Age*, trans. anonymously, 2d ed. (London, 1700), pp. 80–81. "Eloisa to Abelard" first appeared in 1717 in Pope's collected *Works*.

1. Johnson, *Lives of the Poets*, III, 101.

2. Ibid., p. 235.

3. *Correspondence*, I, 496 (1 September 1718). Pope is silently quoting from Dryden's *Palamon and Arcite:* "As noblest Metals are most soft to melt, / So Pity soonest runs in gentle minds" (ii.331–332). He also quotes this passage in a letter of 24 July 1711 (I, 130).

4. *Correspondence*, I, 447. Sherburn corrects the date to 23 October 1717.

5. Adler, *The Reach of Art*, p. 51. See also pp. 46–63.

6. Owen Ruffhead, *The Life of Alexander Pope* (London, 1769), pp. 171–172.

7. Howard D. Weinbrot, "Pope's 'Elegy to the Memory of an Unfortunate Lady,' " *Modern Language Quarterly*, 32 (1971), 255–267.

8. Dryden, *Of Dramatick Poesie* (1668), in *Essays*, I, 53. Pope's relation to Ovid has been explored by Hoyt Trowbridge, "Pope's *Eloisa* and the *Heroides* of Ovid," *Studies in Eighteenth-Century Culture*, vol. 3, ed. Harold E. Pagliaro (Cleveland: The Press of Case Western Reserve University, 1973), pp. 11–34. The best recent study of Pope's source is Howard Jacobson, *Ovid's "Heroides"* (Princeton: Princeton University Press, 1974).

9. In Spence, I, 15.

10. Thomas Babington Macaulay, "Addison" (1843), in *Critical and Historical Essays*, 2 vols. (1907; rpt. New York: Dutton, 1956), II, 503.

11. Austin Warren referred in passing to "Eloisa to Abelard" as a "soliloquy from tragedy, in the manner of Racine"; see *Rage for Order* (1948; rpt. Ann Arbor: University of Michigan Press, 1959), p. 41. This same idea is developed, too briefly, by Evelyn Hoover in "Racine and Pope's *Eloisa*," *Essays in Criticism*, 24 (1974), 368–374. On Pope's relation to drama, see Donald J. Greene, " 'Dramatic Texture' in Pope," in *From Sensibility to Romanticism: Essays Presented to Frederick A. Pottle*, ed. Frederick W. Hilles and Harold Bloom (New York: Oxford University Press, 1965), pp. 31–53; John Butt, *Pope's Taste in Shakespeare* (London: Oxford University Press, 1936); Goldstein, *Pope and the Augustan Stage.*

12. John Hughes, "The History of Abelard and Heloise," in *Letters of Abelard and Heloise*, 3d ed. (London, 1718), p. 39. For additional information concerning Eloisa, I have relied upon two very different but complementary studies: Étienne Gilson, *Heloise and Abelard*, trans. L. K. Shook (Ann Arbor: University of Michigan Press, 1960); D. W. Robertson, Jr., *Abelard and Heloise* (New York: Dial Press, 1972).

13. Quoted by Robertson, *Abelard and Heloise*, p. 58.

14. Hughes, "The History of Abelard and Heloise," p. 2.

15. Brendan O'Hehir rightly explains the much-criticized instances of "pathetic fallacy" in the poem—when altars blaze and statues tremble—as illustrating how Eloisa projects her own mental and emotional states on to her surroundings; see "Virtue and Passion: The Dialectic of *Eloisa to Abelard*" (1968), reprinted in *Essential Articles*, pp. 333–349.

16. For a description of Pope's alteration of Hughes's *Letters*, see Ed-

ward E. Foster's "Rhetorical Control in Pope's *Eloisa to Abelard*," *Tennessee Studies in Literature*, 13 (1968), 63–74. Robert P. Kalmey's helpful study—"Pope's *Eloisa to Abelard* and 'Those Celebrated Letters' " (1968), reprinted in *Recent Essays*, pp. 247–265—in my view underestimates the degree to which Pope's "intensified and tightly-knit drama of suffering and potential redemption" (p. 259) assimilates doctrinal content to a more pressing interest in psychological processes. Doctrinal content and contexts are also, at least in large part, the subjects of Patricia Carr Brückmann, " 'Religious Hope and Resignation': The Process of *Eloisa to Abelard*," *English Studies in Canada*, 3 (1977), 153–163; and Stephen J. Ackerman, "The Vocation of Pope's Eloisa," *Studies in English Literature*, 19 (1979), 445–457.

17. See Frances A. Yates, *The Arts of Memory* (London: Routledge, 1966), and Louis L. Martz, *The Poetry of Meditation: A Study in English Religious Literature*, rev. ed. (New Haven: Yale University Press, 1962). On the importance of memory and consciousness in "ordering" the individual, see Locke's chapter "Of Identity and Diversity" (added to the second edition): "For since consciousness always accompanies thinking, and 'tis that, that makes every one to be, what he calls *self;* and thereby distinguishes himself from all other thinking things, in this alone consists *personal identity, i.e.* the sameness of a rational Being: And as far as this consciousness can be extended backwards to any past Action or Thought, so far reaches the Identity of that *Person*"; *An Essay Concerning Human Understanding*, p. 335.

18. Maynard Mack, "Introduction," *The Augustans*, 2d ed. (Englewood Cliffs, N.J.: Prentice-Hall, 1961), p. 27. The relation between character and correspondence is part of James A. Winn's subject in "Pope Plays the Rake: His Letters to Ladies and the Making of the *Eloisa*," in *The Art of Alexander Pope*, ed. Erskine-Hill and Smith, pp. 89–118. As Pope wrote: "They say a letter should be a natural image of the mind of the writer" (*Correspondence*, I, 94).

19. *To a Lady* (1734/5), l. 268.

20. *Correspondence*, I, 200 (8 December 1713)—punctuation slightly altered.

21. *An Essay on Man*, iii.51–52. The concept of sympathy becomes a crucial issue in eighteenth-century philosophy because of its implications concerning theories of human nature. For an introduction to the philosophical literature, see John B. Radner, "The Art of Sympathy in Eighteenth-Century British Moral Thought," in *Studies in Eighteenth-Century Culture*, vol. 9, ed. Roseann Runte (Madison: University of Wisconsin Press, 1979), pp. 189–210.

22. Pope's placement of enduring stability outside the temporal order is expressed clearly in the conclusion to his "Messiah" (1712):

> The Seas shall waste; the Skies in Smoke decay;
> Rocks fall to Dust, and Mountains melt away;
> But fix'd *His* Word, *His* saving Pow'r remains:
> Thy *Realm* for ever lasts! thy own *Messiah* reigns!

23. "Epistle to Mr. Jervas" (1716), ll. 77–78.

24. *Correspondence*, I, 338 (March 1716).

25. *Correspondence*, I, 239 (28 July 1714). Pope describes his activities, ironically, as "sleep" (imagination) and "musing" (memory)—which further suggests how far Eloisa's defining mental attributes link her with Pope as poet.

26. Thomas R. Edwards, Jr., rightly describes the nature of Eloisa's conflict: "For all its brilliance as drama and its attractive sympathy for its heroine, *Eloisa to Abelard* lacks the Augustan mediation between opposites that is the great achievement of Pope's early career" (*This Dark Estate*, p. 25). Other major readings include: Henry Pettit, "Pope's *Eloisa to Abelard:* An Interpretation" (1953), reprinted in *Essential Articles*, pp. 320–332; Barrett John Mandel, "Pope's 'Eloisa to Abelard,' " *Texas Studies in Literature and Language*, 9 (1967–1968), 57–68; Murray Krieger, " 'Eloisa to Abelard': The Escape from Body or the Embrace of Body," *Eighteenth-Century Studies*, 3 (1969–1970), 28–47; Spacks, *An Argument of Images*, pp. 234–240.

## VI. Rereading Pope

Epigraph: Voltaire, *Philosophical Letters*, trans. Ernest N. Dilworth (Indianapolis, Ind.: Bobbs-Merrill, 1961), pp. 147–148. Voltaire added this passage (which he wrote in English) to the 1756 edition of his works. Later his attitude toward the poem was more critical—but in 1756 he was over sixty, so his warm praise cannot be dismissed as a youthful indiscretion. The most important treatment of Pope's poem is undoubtedly by Douglas H. White, *Pope and the Context of Controversy: The Manipulation of Ideas in "An Essay on Man"* (Chicago: University of Chicago Press, 1970).

1. Swift, *Correspondence*, IV, 263 (1 November 1734). Although Swift claims that he "never doubted" Pope's authorship, in an earlier letter to Pope he clearly joins himself with the general belief that the author was Edward Young (IV, 153).

2. Quoted in *Pope: The Critical Heritage*, ed. John Barnard (London: Routledge & Kegan Paul, 1973), p. 279. On the international response, see Robert Shackleton, "Pope's *Essay on Man* and the French Enlightenment," *Studies in the Eighteenth Century II: Papers Presented at the Second David Nichol Smith Memorial Seminar* (Canberra: Australian National University Press, 1973), pp. 1–15; and Richard Gilbert Knapp, "The Fortunes of Pope's *Essay on Man* in Eighteenth Century France," *Studies on Voltaire and the Eighteenth Century*, 82 (1971), 5–156.

3. Thomas Sprat, *The History of the Royal Society*, ed. Jackson I. Cope and Harold Whitmore Jones (St. Louis: Washington University Press, 1958), p. 113. On theories of language and projects for linguistic reform in the seventeenth and eighteenth centuries, see (among many) Russell A. Fraser, *The Language of Adam: On the Limits and Systems of Discourse*

(New York: Columbia University Press, 1977); and Murray Cohen, *Sensible Words: Linguistic Practice in England, 1640–1785* (Baltimore: Johns Hopkins University Press, 1977).

4. Lord Hervey, *"A Letter to Mr. C–b–r"* (1742), in *Pope: The Critical Heritage*, ed. Barnard, p. 316.

5. Swift, *Correspondence*, IV, 153 (1 May 1733); and Pope, *Correspondence*, III, 433 (15 September 1734). As Pope explains the general response: "I was thought a divine, a philosopher, and what not?" (III, 433).

6. *Correspondence*, IV, 171 (11 April 1739). Pope's modest skills at the parry and thrust of learned debate are suggested by his confession that at fourteen he had studied a collection of church controversies "and the consequence was, that I found my self a Papist and a Protestant by turns, according to the last book I read" (I, 453–454).

7. Dryden, "Preface to *Sylvae*" (1685), in *Essays*, I, 259–260. Pope's debt to Lucretius has been studied by Miriam Leranbaum, *Alexander Pope's "Opus Magnum," 1729–1744* (Oxford: Clarendon Press, 1977), pp. 38–63; and by Bernhard Fabian, "On the Literary Background of the *Essay on Man*: A Note on Pope and Lucretius" (1975), in *Recent Essays*, pp. 416–427. Pope's debt to Lucretius in *An Essay on Man*—as distinguished from the Horatian influence in *An Essay on Criticism*—was observed by Jacob H. Adler in "Balance in Pope's *Essays*," *English Studies*, 43 (1962), 457–467.

8. Arthur Murphy, "An Essay on the Life and Genius of Henry Fielding, Esq." (1762), in *Pope: The Critical Heritage*, ed. Barnard, p. 452.

9. Johnson, *Lives of the Poets*, III, 243.

10. These responses are conveniently collected in *Pope: The Critical Heritage*, ed. Barnard, pp. 279–281.

11. *Correspondence*, II, 333 (15 October 1725). Warburton had dated the earliest beginnings of *An Essay on Man* as September 1725. In his treatment of self-love, Pope deprives La Rochefoucauld of his most scandalous and damaging topic: the unredeemed selfishness of all human acts.

12. Pascal, *The Pensées*, trans. J. M. Cohen (Baltimore: Penguin Books, 1961), p. 41.

13. "On the Bravery of the English Common Soldiers," in *The Works of Samuel Johnson, LL.D.*, 9 vols. (Oxford, 1825), VI, 149.

14. Friedrich Nietzsche, *The Genealogy of Morals: An Attack* (1887), in *The Birth of Tragedy and the Genealogy of Morals*, trans. Francis Golffing (New York: Doubleday, 1956), p. 157, slightly altered. The richness and elusiveness of the maxim as a literary form is discussed by Philip E. Lewis in *La Rochefoucauld: The Art of Abstraction* (Ithaca: Cornell University Press, 1977). Clearly, not all maxims or aphorisms prove equally rich.

15. *Correspondence*, III, 155 (6 December 1730).

16. In Spence, I, 186.

17. *The Advancement of Learning* (1605), in *The Works of Francis*

*Bacon,* ed. James Spedding, Robert L. Ellis, and Douglas D. Heath, 14 vols. (Boston, 1864–1874), VI, 292. Two helpful studies which treat Bacon's use of aphorism are: Lisa Jardine, *Francis Bacon: Discovery and the Art of Discourse* (London: Cambridge University Press, 1974): and James Stephens, *Francis Bacon and the Style of Science* (Chicago: University of Chicago Press, 1975).

18. Bacon, *The Great Instauration* (1620), in *Works,* VIII, 32.

19. William Warburton, *A Critical and Philosophical Commentary on Mr. Pope's Essay on Man* (London, 1742), p. 6.

20. Thomas De Quincey, in *North British Review* (August 1848), in *Pope: A Critical Anthology,* ed. Bateson and Joukovsky, p. 224.

21. *Complete Prose Works of John Milton,* ed. Don M. Wolfe, II (New Haven: Yale University Press, 1953), 549.

22. Griffin, *Alexander Pope: The Poet in the Poem,* p. 162.

23. The modern studies of paradox are voluminous (especially after paradox achieved honorific status in the New Criticism) but mostly disappointing. An impressive exception is Rosalie L. Colie's *Paradoxia Epidemica: The Renaissance Tradition of Paradox* (Princeton: Princeton University Press, 1966), to which I am much indebted.

24. Hugh Kenner, *Paradox in Chesterton* (London: Sheed & Ward, 1948), p. 17.

25. W. V. Quine, *The Ways of Paradox and Other Essays,* rev. ed. (Cambridge, Mass.: Harvard University Press, 1976), p. 3.

26. Review of Soame Jenyns' *A Free Enquiry into the Nature and Origin of Evil* (1757), in *The Works of Samuel Johnson,* VI, 52.

27. The standard account is Leo Spitzer's *Classical and Christian Ideas of World Harmony: Prolegomena to an Interpretation of the Word "Stimmung,"* ed. Anna Granville Hatcher (Baltimore: The Johns Hopkins University Press, 1963). This volume reprints the study first published in *Traditio,* 2 (1944), 409–464; and 3 (1945), 307–364.

28. Dunton, *Athenian Sport,* p. 1.

29. "A Discourse upon the *Moral Reflections,* and *Maxims,*" in *Moral Reflections and Maxims, Written by the late Duke de la Rochefoucauld,* trans. anonymously (London, 1706), p. xii.

30. A. R. Humphreys, "Pope, God, and Man," in *Alexander Pope,* ed. Peter Dixon (London: G. Bell & Sons, 1972), p. 91.

31. In Hermann Frankel, *Early Greek Poetry and Philosophy* (1962), trans. Moses Hadas and James Willis (New York: Harcourt Brace Jovanovich, 1973), p. 115. Pope, as he demonstrated in *Windsor-Forest,* where Pan represents both pastoral harmony and feral violence, understood the ancient practice of attributing opposite natures to a single figure: "Thus as *Venus* suggests unlawful as well as lawful Desires, so *Minerva* may be described as the Goddess not only of Wisdom but of Craft, that is, both of true and false Wisdom" (note to *Iliad* VIII.439).

32. "To the Unknown AUTHOR of the *Essay on Man,*" *The Gentle-*

*man's Magazine* (1734), in *Pope: The Critical Heritage*, ed. Barnard, p. 280. Italics added.

33. *An Epistle to Mr. Pope, Occasion'd by his Essay on Man* (1734), in *Pope: The Critical Heritage*, ed. Barnard, p. 281.

34. Swift, *Correspondence*, IV, 263 (1 November 1734).

35. *Correspondence*, III, 354 (8 March 1732/3).

## VII. Property, Character, and Money in the *Moral Essays*

Epigraph: Sir William Blackstone, *Commentaries on the Laws of England*, ed. Edward Christian, 12th ed., 4 vols. (London, 1794), II, 2.

1. In Spence, I, 261.

2. The work Warburton titled (after Pope's death) the *Moral Essays* is composed of the following four verse epistles, which I list in sequence. The list makes use of shortened and standardized titles, with each title followed by the date of initial publication:

    i. *To Cobham: Of the Knowledge and Characters of Men* (16 January 1733/34)

    ii. *To a Lady: Of the Characters of Women* (8 February 1734/35)

    iii. *To Bathurst: Of the Use of Riches* (15 January 1732/33)

    iv. *To Burlington: Of the Use of Riches* (13 December 1731)

I cite specific poems and verses by roman numeral (as keyed to the titles above) followed by the line number. All quotations are from the volume of the Twickenham edition entitled *Epistles to Several Persons* (ed. F. W. Bateson). I use Warburton's title *Moral Essays*, first appearing in 1751, because it has the sanction of long usage.

3. *Correspondence*, III, 348 (16 February 1732/33). In addition to Thomas R. Edwards, Jr. (*This Dark Estate*, p. 77), Howard Erskine-Hill is among the relatively few critics who emphasize that the four separate epistles of the *Moral Essays* compose a unified work ("Heirs of Vitruvius: Pope and the Idea of Architecture," *The Art of Alexander Pope*, ed. Erskine-Hill and Smith, p. 151). Because I am not undertaking a traditional quest for hidden unities, I will not attempt to discuss each of the four epistles in the same ways or at equal length.

4. *The Second Epistle of the Second Book of Horace, Imitated*, l. 304. On the earlier history of avarice, see John A. Yunck, *The Lineage of Lady Meed: The Development of Mediaeval Venality Satire* (South Bend, Ind.: University of Notre Dame Press, 1963).

5. William Letwin, *The Origins of Scientific Economics* (Garden City, N.Y.: Doubleday, 1964), p. 235. See also Joyce Oldham Appleby, *Economic Thought and Ideology in Seventeenth-Century England* (Princeton: Princeton University Press, 1978): "A close examination of the writings on economic topics in seventeenth-century England reveals dis-

tinctly radical reworkings of the meaning of wealth, money, private initiative, economic growth, and the motive of gain" (pp. 18–19).

6. See P. G. M. Dickson, *The Financial Revolution in England: A Study in the Development of Public Credit, 1688–1756* (London: St. Martin's Press, 1967). The best study of Pope's relation to financial change is Howard Erskine-Hill, "Pope and the Financial Revolution," in *Alexander Pope*, ed. Dixon, pp. 200–29. See also Peter Dixon, *The World of Pope's Satires: An Introduction to the "Epistles" and "Imitations of Horace"* (London: Methuen, 1968), pp. 122–152.

7. *The First Epistle of the First Book of Horace, Imitated* (1738), l. 79.

8. *An Essay on the Increase and Decline of Trade . . .*, in Dorothy George, *London Life in the Eighteenth Century (1925*; rpt. Hammondsworth: Penguin Books, 1965), p. 313. Two sources to which I am indebted for information contained in this paragraph are Isaac Kramnick, *Bolingbroke and His Circle: The Politics of Nostalgia in the Age of Walpole* (Cambridge, Mass.: Harvard University Press, 1968); and W. A. Speck, *Stability and Strife: England, 1714–1760* (London: Edward Arnold, 1977).

9. In Kramnick, *Bolingbroke and His Circle*, p. 48. See also Charles Duguid, *The Story of the Stock Exchange: Its History and Position* (London: Richards, 1901).

10. "It needed the financial skill of Walpole and not merely the healing hand of time to restore confidence in the nation's financial system. Walpole exploited this opportunity and displayed his remarkable abilities, while some of the leading ministers in the Government were ruined"; see H. T. Dickinson, *Walpole and the Whig Supremacy* (London: The English Universities Press, 1973), p. 56. See also Vincent Carretta, "Pope's *Epistle to Bathurst* and the South Sea Bubble," *Journal of English and Germanic Philology*, 77 (1978), 212–231.

11. *Correspondence*, II, 42 (c. 1 May 1720). South Sea stock did not begin its precipitous decline until August 1720—so that Sherburn's tentative dating must be questioned. Pope invested much of his modest wealth in annuities.

12. *Epilogue to the Satires* (1738), ii.58, punctuation slightly altered. Peter Walter appears also, of course, as the rapacious Peter Pounce in *Joseph Andrews*.

13. *An Essay on Man*, ii.198.

14. C. B. Macpherson, "Capitalism and the Changing Concept of Property," in *Feudalism, Capitalism and Beyond*, ed. Eugene Kamenka and R. S. Neale (London: Edward Arnold, 1975), p. 110.

15. *Two Treatises of Government* (1690), ed. Peter Laslett, rev. ed. (Cambridge: Cambridge University Press, 1963), p. 395 (II.ix.124). On the influence of Locke's *Two Treatises*, see John Dunn, "The Politics of Locke in England and America in the Eighteenth Century," in *John Locke: Problems and Perspectives*, ed. John W. Yolton (Cambridge: Cam-

bridge University Press, 1969), pp. 45–80. Two useful books related to Lockean ideas of property are: *Life, Liberty, and Property: Essays on Locke's Political Ideas,* ed. Gordon J. Schochet (Belmont, Cal.: Wadsworth, 1971); and James Tully, *A Discourse on Property: John Locke and His Adversaries* (Cambridge: Cambridge University Press, 1980). As is well known, property for Locke need not refer to material objects alone.

16. Pat Rogers, *The Augustan Vision* (London: Weidenfeld and Nicolson, 1974), p. 99. David Hay reports: "The most recent account suggests that the number of capital statutes grew from about 50 to over 200 between the years 1688 and 1820. Almost all of them concerned offenses against property"; see "Property, Authority and the Criminal Law," in *Albion's Fatal Tree: Crime and Society in Eighteenth-Century England* (New York: Random House, 1975), p. 18. This volume has five co-authors: David Hay, Peter Linebaugh, John G. Rule, E. P. Thompson, and Cal Winslow.

17. E. P. Thompson, *Whigs and Hunters: The Origin of the Black Act* (New York: Random House, 1975), p. 197. See also Thompson's important appendix "Alexander Pope and the Blacks" (pp. 278–294). On developments in copyright law, see Lyman Ray Patterson, *Copyright in Historical Perspective* (Nashville: Vanderbilt University Press, 1968), pp. 143–150.

18. J. Moore, "A Comment on Pocock," in *Theories of Property: Aristotle to the Present,* ed. Anthony Parel and Thomas Flanagan (Waterloo, Ontario: Wilfrid Laurier University Press, 1979), p. 167. Moore here summarizes the description of civic humanism developed in a series of studies by J. G. A. Pocock. The strongest argument for the rhetorical expediency of Bolingbroke's position is by Quentin Skinner, "The Principles and Practice of Opposition: The Case of Bolingbroke versus Walpole," in *Historical Perspectives: Studies in English Thought and Society, in Honour of J. H. Plumb,* ed. Neil McKendrick (London: Europa, 1974), pp. 93–128.

19. "A Dissertation on Parties" (1734), in *The Works of the late Right Honorable Henry St. John, Lord Viscount Bolingbroke,* ed. David Mallet, 5 vols. (London, 1777), II, 247. We need to be clear about what the sometimes vague concepts of "land" and "money" actually meant: "By the 'landed interest' contemporaries did not mean landowners at large, but only those who lived exclusively on their incomes from rents, deriving no supplementary revenues from other sources such as office-holding, commerce or even the mineral resources of their estates. The 'monied interest' was an even more precise term. It referred not to traders and merchants in general, but to those elements in society who were involved in the new machinery of public credit which was created after the Revolution along with the setting up of the Bank of England in 1694"; see W. A. Speck, "Conflict in Society," in *Britain after the Glorious Revolution, 1689–1714,* ed. Geoffrey Holmes (London: Macmillan, 1969), p. 135. Opposition propaganda, of course, did not always observe such strict usage.

20. David Hume, "Of Public Credit" (1752), *Essays and Treatises on Several Subjects*, 2 vols. (London, 1764), I, 387. E. P. Thompson offers this reading of eighteenth-century culture: "What one notices about it first of all is the importance of money. The landed gentry are graded not by birth or other marks of status but by rentals: they are worth so many thousand pounds a year. Among the aristocracy and ambitious gentry, courtship is conducted by fathers and by their lawyers, who guide it carefully towards its consummation, the well drawn marriage settlement. Place and office could be bought and sold (provided that the sale did not seriously conflict with the lines of political interest); commissions in the Army; seats in parliament. Use-rights, privileges, liberties, services—all could be translated into an equivalent in money"; see "Eighteenth-Century English Society: Class Struggle without Class?" *Social History*, 3 (1978), 138.

21. See J. G. A. Pocock, "Machiavelli, Harrington and English Political Ideologies in the Eighteenth Century," in *Politics, Language, and Time: Essays on Political Thought and History* (New York: Atheneum, 1971), p. 131.

22. Johnson, *Lives of the Poets*, III, 219.

23. Ibid., p. 85.

24. On Pope's relation to earlier traditions of character, see Benjamin Boyce, *The Character-Sketches in Pope's Poems* (Durham, N.C.: Duke University Press, 1962); and *The Theophrastan Character in England to 1642* (Cambridge, Mass.: Harvard University Press, 1947).

25. "Preface" to the *Iliad*, in *PW*, pp. 229–230.

26. "Preface" to *The Works of Shakespeare*, in *Eighteenth-Century Critical Essays*, ed. Elledge, I, 279.

27. Montaigne, *Essays*, II, 5 and 9.

28. *The First Epistle of the First Book of Horace, Imitated*, ll. 136–137. Pope's couplet closely follows Horace's Latin. The contributions of Horace and of Montaigne to Pope's idea of character no doubt demonstrate the "mingled Features" which Pope praised in allusion.

29. Dryden, "Preface to *Troilus and Cressida*, containing The Grounds of Criticism in Tragedy" (1679), in *Essays*, I, 215.

30. *The First Epistle of the First Book of Horace, Imitated*, ll. 181–184.

31. *Correspondence*, IV, 364 (10 October 1741).

32. Montaigne, "Of Solitude," in *Essays*, I, 453.

33. *Correspondence*, IV, 136 (19 October 1738).

34. J. G. A. Pocock, "Early Modern Capitalism—the Augustan Perspective," in *Feudalism, Capitalism and Beyond*, ed. Kamenka and Neale, p. 79.

35. *Correspondence*, IV, 13 (30 April [1736]). This paragraph is indebted to Maynard Mack's *The Garden and the City: Retirement and Politics in the Later Poetry of Pope, 1731–1743* (Toronto: University of Toronto Press, 1969).

36. *Correspondence*, IV, 526 (19–29 May 1744).

37. Swift, *Correspondence*, IV, 169 (8 July 1733).

38. *Correspondence*, IV, 262 (3 September 1740).

39. *The Second Epistle of the Second Book of Horace, Imitated*, ll. 230–231.

40. "He knows to live, who keeps the middle state, / And neither leans on this side, nor on that"; *The Second Satire of the Second Book of Horace, Paraphrased* (1734), ll. 61–62. Pope's middle state is far more flexible than the version attributed here to Hugh Bethel.

41. *The First Epistle of the First Book of Horace, Imitated*, ll. 24–34.

42. Ibid., l. 169.

43. *Correspondence*, II, 112 (2 April 1722).

44. Ibid., p. 302 (29 June [1725]). Pope in a similar vein laments the wordly distractions that "keep me from Myself" (*The First Epistle of the First Book of Horace, Imitated*, l. 41).

45. *The Second Satire of the Second Book of Horace, Paraphrased*, ll. 131–132.

46. *The First Epistle of the First Book of Horace, Imitated*, l. 188.

47. In Spence, I, 160.


# VIII. The Muse of Pain

Epigraph: Joshua Poole, *The English Parnassus: or, A Helpe to English Poesie* (1657).

1. Warton, *An Essay on the Genius and Writings of Pope*, I, 211; II, 6. On the early history of satire, see Ulrich Knoche, *Roman Satire* (1949), trans. Edwin S. Ramage (Bloomington: Indiana University Press, 1975). The scholarly and critical studies of English satire are too numerous to mention here, but see John R. Clark et al., "Satire: A Selective Critical Bibliography," *Seventeenth-Century News*, 33 (1975), 1–10. Three useful starting points for studying eighteenth-century satire are Ian Jack, *Augustan Satire: Intention and Idiom in English Poetry, 1660–1750* (Oxford: Clarendon Press, 1952); Howard D. Weinbrot, *The Formal Strain: Studies in Augustan Imitation and Satire* (Chicago: University of Chicago Press, 1969); and *The Satirist's Art*, ed. H. James Jensen and Malvin R. Zirker, Jr. (Bloomington: Indiana University Press, 1972). On modern critical approaches to satire, see Leonard Feinberg, "Satire: The Inadequacy of Recent Definitions," *Genre*, 1 (1968), 31–37. The best all-purpose collection is *Satire: Modern Essays in Criticism*, ed. Ronald Paulson (Englewood Cliffs, N.J.: Prentice-Hall, 1971).

2. "Satire is a poem of a difficult nature in itself"; *Essays*, II, 74. As Mikhail Bakhtin observes of the later eighteenth century: "In no other time was Rabelais so little understood and appreciated"; see *Rabelais and His World* (1965), trans. Helene Iswolsky (Cambridge, Mass.: MIT Press, 1968), p. 116.

3. Maynard Mack, "The Muse of Satire," *Yale Review*, 41 (1951), 85. "What is desperately needed today," Mack wrote in 1951, "is inquiry that

deals neither with origins nor effects, but with artifice" (p. 82).

4. George Berkeley, in *Essay, Principles, Dialogues, with Selections from Other Writings,* ed. Mary Whiton Calkins (New York: Charles Scribner's Sons, 1929), pp. 118–119 (paragraphs 19–20).

5. In Halsband, *Lord Hervey,* p. 177.

6. Dryden, "Discourse concerning the Original and Progress of Satire," in *Essays,* II, 44.

7. Quoted in Robert C. Elliott, *The Power of Satire: Magic, Ritual, Art* (Princeton: Princeton University Press, 1960), p. 12. In discussing the primitive history of satire I rely considerably on Elliott's fascinating first chapters. Unfortunately, Elliott is too hasty in claiming that Swift and (I assume) other Augustan satirists wholly rejected "the irresponsibility of the primitive mode" to assume "the plenary responsibilities of art" (p. 221). Augustan satire, I am suggesting, still retained the connection with its primitive past that Elliott finds characteristic of Roman verse satire (p. 129).

8. Walter Harte, *An Essay on Satire, Particularly on the "Dunciad"* (London, 1730), p. 14.

9. See Thomas B. Gilmore, Jr., *The Eighteenth-Century Controversy over Ridicule as a Test of Truth: A Reconsideration,* School of Arts and Sciences Research Papers, no. 25 (Atlanta: Georgia State University, 1970).

10. *The First Epistle of the Second Book of Horace, Imitated* ll. 257–258. On the relation of satire to the laws of libel, see Frederick Seaton Siebert, *Freedom of the Press in England, 1476–1776: The Rise and Decline of Government Control* (Urbana: University of Illinois Press, 1952); J. A. Downie, *Robert Harley and the Press: Propaganda and Public Opinion in the Age of Swift and Defoe* (London: Cambridge University Press, 1979); and C. R. Kropf, "Libel and Satire in the Eighteenth Century," *Eighteenth-Century Studies,* 8 (1974–75), 153–168.

11. Dryden, *Essays,* II, 75.

12. In P. K. Elkin, *The Augustan Defence of Satire* (Oxford: Clarendon Press, 1973), p. 74.

13. Swift, *Correspondence,* III, 103 (29 September 1725).

14. André Dacier, *An Essay upon Satyr,* in *Miscellany Poems upon Several Occasions,* ed. Charles Gildon (London, 1692), n.p.

15. "An Epistle to a Lady" (1733), ll. 177–180, in *The Poems of Jonathan Swift,* ed. Harold Williams, 2d ed., 3 vols. (Oxford: Clarendon Press, 1958). "Hoyse" means "hoist."

16. Swift, *A Tale of a Tub,* ed. A. C. Guthkelch and D. Nichol Smith, 2d ed. (Oxford: Clarendon Press, 1958), p. 48. The flogging of schoolboys continued well into the nineteenth century; see Ronald Pearsall, *Night's Black Angels: The Forms and Faces of Victorian Cruelty* (New York: David McKay Co., 1975).

17. Swift, *Journal to Stella,* ed. Williams, I, 59. In *Swift and the Satirist's Art* (Chicago: University of Chicago Press, 1963), Edward W. Rosenheim distinguishes between "punitive" and "persuasive" satire. (This

distinction appears in the section reprinted as "The Satiric Spectrum" in *Satire*, ed. Paulson, pp. 305–329.) I am suggesting a view of Augustan satire which emphasizes the punitive power of all but the most abstract and toothless satiric works. Satire without the power to inflict pain is like a rubber sword: its pleasures depend on a denial of the normal power to injure.

18. Dryden, *Essays*, II, 79.

19. In Spence, I, 149.

20. *Epilogue to the Satires*, ii.181–182.

21. Johnson, *Lives of the Poets*, III, 242.

22. *The First Epistle of the Second Book of Horace, Imitated*, l. 38 and note. On Renaissance satirical theory and practice, see Alvin B. Kernan, *The Cankered Muse: Satire of the English Renaissance* (New Haven: Yale University Press, 1959). The medical tradition of satire is discussed by Mary Claire Randolph, "The Medical Concept in English Renaissance Satiric Theory: Its Possible Relationships and Implications," *Studies in Philology*, 38 (1941), 125–157. I do not agree with U. C. Knoepflmacher, who sees this medical tradition still active in *Arbuthnot*. See his "The Poet as Physician: Pope's *Epistle to Dr. Arbuthnot*," *Modern Language Quarterly*, 31 (1970), 440–449.

23. *The First Epistle of the Second Book of Horace, Imitated*, l. 262.

24. On the theory and practice of legal punishment, see Leon Radzinowicz, *A History of English Criminal Law and Its Administration from 1750*, 4 vols. (New York: Macmillan, 1948–1968), especially vol. 1; James Heath, *Eighteenth Century Penal Theory* (New York: Oxford University Press, 1963); *Crime in England, 1550–1800*, ed. J. S. Cockburn (Princeton: Princeton University Press, 1977); Hay et al., *Albion's Fatal Tree*; and Michael Ignatieff, *A Just Measure of Pain: The Penitentiary in the Industrial Revolution, 1750–1850* (New York: Pantheon Books, 1978). Also of great interest is Michel Foucault, *Discipline and Punish: The Birth of the Prison* (1975), trans. Alan Sheridan (New York: Pantheon Books, 1977).

25. Cesar de Saussure, *A Foreign View of England in the Reigns of George I. & George II.*, trans. Madame Van Muyden (London: John Murray, 1902), p. 341.

26. See L. A. Parry, *The History of Torture in England* (Montclair, N.J.: Patterson Smith, 1975), pp. 167–168. Although punished during the reign of James II, Oates received a state pension under William III.

27. *Epilogue to the Satires*, i.168.

28. "Upon a Printer," in *The Works of Mr. John Oldham, Together with his Remains* (London, 1686), p. 132.

29. Dryden, *Essays*, II, 93.

30. Ibid. Dryden is borrowing from his preface to *Absalom and Achitophel*: "*There's a sweetness in good Verse, which Tickles even while it hurts.*"

31. *The First Satire of the Second Book of Horace, Imitated*, l. 42.

32. See Horace Bleackley, *The Hangmen of England* (London: Chapman and Hall, 1929), p. 61.

33. *Correspondence*, III, 419 and 423 (26 July/2 August 1734).

34. Warton, *An Essay on the Genius and Writings of Pope*, II, 250.

35. Swift, *Correspondence*, III, 289 (1 June 1728).

36. Edward Bloom and Lillian Bloom, *Satire's Persuasive Voice* (Ithaca: Cornell University Press, 1979), p. 54.

37. Swift, *Correspondence*, IV, 383 (3 September 1735)—italics added. Dante's kick is discussed in an essay by Gerald L. Bruns, "Allegory and Satire: A Rhetorical Meditation," *New Literary History*, 11 (1979), 121–132.

38. *Correspondence*, II, 341 (23 November 1725).

39. Dryden, "Discourse concerning Satire," *Essays*, II, 84.

40. Montaigne, *Essays*, II, 9–10.

41. Dryden, "Discourse concerning Satire," *Essays*, II, 95. See William S. Anderson, *Anger in Juvenal and Seneca*, University of California Publications in Classical Philology, vol. 19 (Berkeley: University of California Press, 1964). Anderson views Juvenal's representations of anger as rhetorical, the manipulations of a satiric persona, a kind of literary game. I take a very different approach to the place of anger in satire.

42. Warton, *An Essay on the Genius and Writings of Pope*, II, 250, 211.

43. In Spence, I, 42.

44. Dryden, "Discourse concerning Satire," *Essays*, II, 84. Howard D. Weinbrot, *Alexander Pope and the Traditions of Formal Verse Satire* (Princeton: Princeton University Press, 1982), notes that Persius, as well as Horace and Juvenal, helped to shape Pope's self-conception as satirist.

45. *The First Satire of the Second Book of Horace, Imitated* (1733), l. 41.

46. In Spence, I, 116.

47. *Correspondence*, III, 419 (26 July 1734).

48. *Epilogue to the Satires*, i.65.

49. Ibid., ii.10.

50. *Correspondence*, III, 255 (16 December 1731).

51. *Epilogue to the Satires*, ii.212–215. Wyndham Lewis provides an effective response to the platitude that satire necessarily affirms a dominant moral ideology. See "The Greatest Satire is Nonmoral" (1934), in *Satire*, ed. Paulson, pp. 66–79. Two essays I especially admire for their emphasis upon matters which complement the prevailing studies of satiric artifice are William Kinsley, " 'The Malicious World' and the Meaning of Satire," *Genre*, 3 (1970), 137–155; and Alvin B. Kernan, "Aggression and Satire: Art Considered as a Form of Biological Adaptation," in *Literary Theory and Structure: Essays in Honor of William K. Wimsatt*, ed. Frank Brady, John Palmer, and Martin Price (New Haven: Yale University Press, 1973), pp. 115–129.

52. James R. Kincaid, " 'Be Ye Lukewarm!' The Nineteenth-Century

Novel and Social Action," *Bulletin of the Midwest Modern Language Association*, 6 (1973), 89.

53. Swift, *Correspondence*, IV, 152 (1 May 1733). Swift had earlier expressed his animosity toward mankind in a famous letter to Pope: "I hate and detest that animal called man, although I hartily love John, Peter, Thomas and so forth" (III, 103).

54. Ibid., IV, 207 (1 December 1739). On the general relation between language and injury—where satire, strangely, is not discussed—see the chapter entitled "Words and Wounds" in Geoffrey H. Hartman's *Saving the Text: Literature / Derrida / Philosophy* (Baltimore: Johns Hopkins University Press, 1981), pp. 118–157.


# IX. Politics, Time, and Deformity

1. Abraham Cowley, "The Danger of Procrastination," in *Complete Works*, II, 338.

2. The explanation was added by Pope as a note (first published in Warburton's edition of 1751) at the conclusion to the *Epilogue to the Satires*.

3. *Correspondence*, II, 226 (9 April 1724).

4. Ibid., p. 435 (10 May 1727). Pope's view that the "whole course" of his life would change after the death of his mother appears in a letter to John Caryll (III, 375).

5. Ibid., IV, 6 (25 March 1736). Punctuation slightly altered.

6. *The Second Epistle of the Second Book of Horace, Imitated*, ll. 72–79. Swift recognized that Pope's translation of Horace's lines was actually a form of interpretation, saying, "you have put them in a strong and admirable light" (Swift, *Correspondence*, V, 5).

7. *Correspondence*, III, 455 (12 May 1735).

8. Ibid., II, 321–322 (14 September 1725).

9. Swift, *Correspondence*, III, 293 (16 July 1728).

10. "The Freedom of Epistles is rarely disputed" (*The Guardian* no. 12). Three studies emphasizing the "Freedom" of Augustan poetic composition are D. J. Greene, " 'Logical Structure' in Eighteenth-Century Poetry," *Philological Quarterly*, 31 (1952), 315–336; Peter Thorpe, "The Non-structure of Augustan Verse," *Papers on Language and Literature*, 5 (1969), 235–251; and Reuben A. Brower, "Form and Defect of Form in Eighteenth-Century Poetry: A Memorandum," in *Eighteenth-Century Studies in Honor of Donald F. Hyde*, ed. W. H. Bond (New York: Grolier Club, 1970), pp. 365–382. Thomas R. Edwards, Jr., discusses the "extravagance" of Pope's language and poetic stance in an excellent study of the *Epilogue* entitled "Heroic Folly: Pope's Satiric Identity" (1962), reprinted in *Recent Essays*, pp. 565–584.

11. *The Second Satire of the Second Book of Horace, Paraphrased*, ll. 137–146. The tradition of retirement verse is part of Maynard Mack's sub-

ject in *The Garden and the City*. See also Maren-Sofie Røstvig, *The Happy Man: Studies in the Metamorphoses of a Classical Ideal*, 2 vols., 2d ed. (Norwegian Universities Press, 1962). Volume 2 covers the period 1700–1760.

12. In Spence, I, 13.

13. *Correspondence*, IV, 406 (23 July 1742).

14. Ibid., p. 169 (27 March 1739). It is clear that Pope recognized the analogies between his own situation and Cato's. "Indeed my Heart is sick of This bad World, (as Cato said)," he writes in 1742 (p. 429). It is also clear that he recognized his own changed stance toward the state. In 1739 he confesses: "The Public is indeed more my Concern than it used to be, as I see it in more danger" (p. 398).

15. In Paul Gabriner, "Pope's 'Virtue' and the Events of 1738" (1973), reprinted in *Recent Essays*, p. 605. H. T. Dickinson sketches the larger picture which Pope and Marchmont could not see: "From 1734 to 1736 the Opposition despaired and Walpole seemed at the height of his political career ... From 1737, however, Walpole began to encounter serious difficulties and considerable resistance" (*Walpole and the Whig Supremacy*, pp. 176–177). The death of Queen Caroline on November 20, 1737, helped considerably to weaken Walpole's dominance over the king and the Commons.

16. Bolingbroke, *The Idea of a Patriot King* (1749), in *Works*, III, 73. This work, although not published until 1749, was written some ten years earlier, about the time when (on his return to England in 1738) Bolingbroke rejoined the Opposition, now centered around Frederick, the Prince of Wales.

17. Joseph Warton, ed., *Works of Pope*, IV, 317, n.

18. James M. Osborn, "Pope, the Byzantine Empress, and Walpole's Whore" (1955), reprinted in *Essential Articles*, pp. 577–590. For other (less certain) sources at play in Pope's description, see Vincent Carretta, "Two More Analogues to Pope's Vice Triumphant," *Modern Philology*, 77 (1979), 56–57.

19. *Correspondence*, IV, 364 (10 October 1741).

20. Ibid., p. 112 (31 July 1738). Punctuation altered.

21. *Selected Prose of Robert Frost*, ed. Hyde Cox and Edward Connery Lathem (New York: Holt, Rinehart & Winston, 1959), p. 106.

22. Quoted by F. W. Bateson, ed., *Epistles to Several Persons*, Twickenham edition, p. 6.

23. In Sir James Prior, *Life of Edmond Malone* (London, 1860), p. 429. For the history of Pope's illnesses—he desribed himself as someone who "is never to have health a week together"—see Marjorie Hope Nicolson and G. S. Rousseau, *"This Long Disease, My Life": Alexander Pope and the Sciences* (Princeton: Princeton University Press, 1968).

24. Maynard Mack, "Pope: The Shape of the Man in His Work," *Yale Review*, 67 (1978), 493–516.

25. In *Portraits by Sir Joshua Reynolds*, ed. Frederick W. Hilles (New

York: McGraw-Hill, 1952), p. 24. Joseph Warton reports of Pope: "He was too sensible of the Deformity of his Person to allow the whole of it to be represented" (*Works of Pope*, I, ix).

26. Bolingbroke, *Letters on the Study and Use of History* (1752), in *Works*, II, 501–502. Bolingbroke composed these letters in France between 1735 and 1738. For evidence that Pope knew (and used) the *Letters*, see Thomas Akstens, "Pope and Bolingbroke on 'Examples': An Echo of the *Letters on History* in Pope's Correspondence," *Philological Quarterly*, 52 (1973), 232–238.

27. Dryden, "Discourse concerning Satire," in *Essays*, II, 87.

28. Paul Gabriner, "Pope's 'Virtue' and the Events of 1738," pp. 585–611. The pictorial tradition representing Virtue as an armed goddess is discussed by Cedric D. Reverand II, "*Ut pictura poesis*, and Pope's 'Satire II, i' " (1976), reprinted in *Recent Essays*, pp. 373–391.

29. *Correspondence*, I, 173 (February 1712/13).

30. Alasdair MacIntyre, *After Virtue: A Study in Moral Theory* (South Bend, Ind.: University of Notre Dame Press, 1981), pp. 34–48. Pope's treatment of virtue offers an alternative to the philosophical arguments MacIntyre discusses.

31. *Correspondence*, I, 191 (20 September 1713).

32. *Correspondence*, Ibid., IV, 351 (18 July 1741).

33. Bolingbroke, *The Idea of a Patriot King*, in *Works*, III, 37.

34. Ibid., pp. 72–73.

35. *Correspondence*, IV, 364 (10 October 1741).


# X. The Kinship of Madness in *The Dunciad*

Epigraph: Warburton notes that Pope had bound up a "complete collection" of all the libels published against him—and to each volume in the collection he prefixed this motto from Job 31:35.

1. Unless otherwise noted, all quotations from *The Dunciad* refer to the 1743 version, edited in the Twickenham edition by James Sutherland (3d ed., 1963). Two useful studies of madness in its eighteenth-century literary and social contexts are Michael V. DePorte, *Nightmares and Hobbyhorses: Swift, Sterne, and Augustan Ideas of Madness* (San Marino, Cal.: Huntington Library, 1974); and Max Byrd, *Visits to Bedlam: Madness and Literature in the Eighteenth Century* (Columbia: University of South Carolina Press, 1974), which includes a chapter entitled "The *Dunciad* and Augustan Madness." Patricia Meyer Spacks has treated thematic implications of madness throughout Pope's work in *An Argument of Images*.

2. Cited by Robert Rentoul Reed, Jr., *Bedlam on the Jacobean Stage* (Cambridge, Mass.: Harvard University Press, 1952), p. 25. Swift's account of his trip to Bedlam appears in the *Journal to Stella* (13 December 1710). For other contemporary descriptions of Bedlam, see Tom Brown's

*Amusements Serious and Comical* (1700), Edward Hatton's *A New View of London* (1708), and *The Tatler* no. 30 (1709). Standard accounts of Bedlam are Daniel Hack Tuke's *Chapters in the History of the Insane in the British Isles* (London, 1882) and Edward Geoffrey O'Donoghue's *The Story of Bethlehem Hospital . . .* (London: Unwin, 1914).

3. George Rosen, *Madness in Society: Chapters in the Historical Sociology of Mental Illness* (Chicago: University of Chicago Press, 1968), pp. 164–165.

4. The standard account of general form is Aubrey L. Williams' discussion of the "translation of empire" motif imitated from Virgil. "Placed in this light," he notes, "Pope's alliance of the events of his poem with the 'action' of the *Aeneid* can be seen to serve two functions. It supplies a type of 'narrative' progression and structure, and it permits a complex interplay of different realms of value"; see his *Pope's Dunciad: A Study of Its Meaning* (1955; rpt. Hamden, Conn.: Archon Books, 1968), pp. 24–25. Although Pope in his annotations helped his readers to recognize the parodies of conventional epic action and structure, he extends parody to the point at which action and structure tend to dissolve. In this respect, John E. Sitter seems correct in stressing the relationship between Pope's *Dunciad* and the "plotless" display poems of his age: "The *Dunciad* is primarily a descriptive poem dealing with the emblematic manifestations of an abstraction—Dulness. It is an allegorical vision, in other words, and to ask for a precise account of 'what is going on' would be as inappropriate as a criticism contending that the *Temple of Fame* 'lacks action.' Both poems have a slender thread of narrative which helps give them unity, but their essential 'design' is the relation of a vision rather than the narration of a story"; see *The Poetry of Pope's "Dunciad"* (Minneapolis: University of Minnesota Press, 1971), p. 80.

5. Swift, *Correspondence*, III, 293 (16 July 1728).

6. William Kinsley, "The *Dunciad* as Mock-Book" (1971), reprinted in *Recent Essays*, p. 707.

7. *Peri Bathous: or . . . the Art of Sinking in Poetry*, ed. Edna Leake Steeves (New York: King's Crown Press, 1952), p. 18. Throughout I assume that Pope maintains a close relationship between *Peri Bathous* and *The Dunciad*. (The appearance of Martinus Scriblerus in both works is an initial and obvious point of similarity.) Although it is often said that Pope issued the Scriblerian *Peri Bathous* in order to stir up the dunces and thus to justify publication of *The Dunciad* in response, it also seems likely that Pope intended the *Peri Bathous* as a companion piece to *The Dunciad*, containing a detailed *aesthetic* justification of his attacks.

8. For a vivid picture of the antiparade, see Ned Ward's *The London Spy* (1698–1709), ed. Arthur L. Hayward (London: Cassell, 1927), pp. 218–221.

9. Emrys Jones, "Pope and Dulness" (1968), reprinted in *Recent Essays*, p. 639. Less convincingly than Jones, Donald T. Siebert, Jr., emphasizes Pope's comic vision in *The Dunciad* while ridiculing (as the

"School of Deep Intent") readers who do not share his view of the poem as "more good fun than anything else"; see his "Cibber and Satan: *The Dunciad* and Civilization," *Eighteenth-Century Studies*, 10 (1976–77), 203–221.

10. *Peri Bathous*, p. 69.

11. Locke, *An Essay Concerning Human Understanding*, p. 161.

12. Quoted by Rosen in *Madness in Society*, p. 164. The term *irrational* applied to men, as I have used it in this essay, does not follow eighteenth-century usage, since the primary definition in Johnson's *Dictionary* is "Void of reason, void of understanding; without the discoursive faculty." In using *irrationality* as synonymous with *madness*, I am deliberately using the term in its modern sense of reason overwhelmed, reason splintered, or reason deceived.

13. Michel Foucault, *Madness and Civilization: A History of Insanity in the Age of Reason* (1961), trans. Richard Howard (New York: Pantheon Books, 1965), p. 95.

14. Locke, *An Essay Concerning Human Understanding*, p. 161.

15. Samuel Johnson, *The History of Rasselas, Prince of Abissinia* (1759), ed. J. P. Hardy (New York: Oxford University Press, 1968), pp. 104–105.

16. *Peri Bathous*, p. 81.

17. "Inspiration is a real feeling of the Divine Presence, and enthusiasm a false one"; see Shaftesbury, *A Letter Concerning Enthusiasm* . . . (1708), in *Characteristics*, I, 37.

18. Foucault, *Madness and Civilization*, p. 104.

19. Boswell, *Life of Johnson*, p. 281.

20. "The truth is, *Pride* may justly be said to be the chief *Procatarick*, or remote original cause of *Madness*"; see Thomas Tryon, *A Treatise of Dreams and Visions* (London, 1689), p. 256.

21. Arthur Koestler, *The Act of Creation* (New York: Macmillan, 1964), p. 358.

22. *Peri Bathous*, p. 13. For a discussion of Pope's attitude toward solipsism, see Rebecca Price Parkin's *The Poetic Workmanship of Alexander Pope*, pp. 223–230.

23. Tony Tanner, "Reason and the Grotesque: Pope's *Dunciad*" (1965), reprinted in *Essential Articles*, p. 835.

24. Foucault, *Madness and Civilization*, p. 103. Although is is clear that his historical arguments need some revision, Foucault is considerably undervalued and misunderstood by critics who judge him according to the goals and standards of orthodox historiography. See, for example, G. S. Rousseau, "Whose Enlightenment? Not Man's: The Case of Michel Foucault," *Eighteenth-Century Studies*, 6 (1972–73), 238–256; Allan Megill, "Foucault, Structuralism, and the Ends of History," *Journal of Modern History*, 51 (1979), 451–503; and H. C. Erik Midelfort, "Madness and Civilization in Early Modern Europe: A Reappraisal of Michel Foucault," in *After the Reformation: Essays in Honor of J. H. Hexter*, ed. Barbara C.

Malament (Philadelphia: University of Pennsylvania Press, 1980), pp. 247–265.

25. Ezra Pound, *ABC of Reading* (New York: New Directions, 1960), p. 170. In noting Pope's habit of removing from the poem dunces who had repented, Michael Rosenblum observes that *The Dunciad* is "the only masterpiece of literature whose contents are negotiable"; see "Pope's Illusive Temple of Infamy" (1972), reprinted in *Recent Essays*, p. 669.

26. *Peri Bathous*, p. 11. Cibber's incorrigible dullness, as Aristarchus explains in his preliminary dissertation on the hero, is the literary equivalent of death, and this equivalence allows the poet to deal with Cibber "as if he had been dead as long as an old Egyptian hero; that is to say, *embowel* and *embalm him for posterity*" (p. 265). Cibber's literary remains, then, consist of a mummified carcass—a role which he had assumed with great acclaim in *Three Hours after Marriage* (1717).

27. Foucault, *Madness and Civilization*, pp. 107 and 115. John E. Sitter's comment on the poem seems pertinent here: "The amoral and mindless Cibber moves and sleeps in a degenerate world of inaction . . . Action is the change from one state of existence to another, but the movement described in the *Dunciad* is from being to nothingness"; *The Poetry of Pope's "Dunciad,"* p. 62. For two excellent studies of *The Dunciad* which propose very different readings of Pope's attitude toward the disorder he depicts, see R. G. Peterson, "Renaissance Classicism in Pope's *Dunciad,"* *Studies in English Literature*, 15 (1975), 431–445; and Howard Erskine-Hill, *Pope: "The Dunciad"* (London: Edward Arnold, 1972).

28. In Spence, I, 177. Pope composed a mock-epitaph for one of the dunces, James Moore Smythe, which observed the following approach toward nothingness:

> Here lyes what had nor *Birth*, nor *Shape*, nor *Fame*;
> No Gentleman! no *man! no-thing!* no *name!*　　　　　　　(ll. 1–2)

The dis-integrative powers of Dulness are explored by Fredric V. Bogel, "Dulness Unbound: Rhetoric and Pope's *Dunciad,"* *PMLA*, 97 (1982), 844–855.

## Conclusion

Epigraph: Quoted in *Works of Pope*, ed. Warton, I, 229, n. Punctuation slightly altered.

1. This sentence from the manuscript preface to Pope's *Works* (1717) was deleted from the published version (see Maynard Mack, "Pope's 1717 Preface," in *Augustan Worlds*, p. 98). A full history of sense would trace its origins, in the last three decades of the seventeenth century, in the comedies of Molière and in the criticism of Boileau and Rymer.

2. For the controversy surrounding wit, see Richard C. Boys, *Sir Richard Blackmore and the Wits: A Study of "Commendatory Verses on the Author of the Two Arthurs and the Satyr against Wit"* (1700) (1949; rpt.

New York: Octagon Books, 1969). It is the Restoration mode which Pope has in mind when claiming in 1740 that "the Way of a Wit . . . never was the character of me or my writing" (*Correspondence*, IV, 258).

3. Daniel Defoe, *The Pacificator* (1700), p. 2.

4. In Boswell, *Life of Johnson*, p. 68.

5. Pope's half-sister reports: "I never saw him laugh very heartily in all my life" (in Spence, I, 6). Swift was reputed to have laughed only twice.

6. C. S. Lewis, *Studies in Words*, 2d ed. (Cambridge: Cambridge University Press, 1967), p. 141. On the word *sense*, see also William Empson, *The Structure of Complex Words* (1951; rpt. Ann Arbor: University of Michigan Press, 1967), pp. 250–310.

7. Sprat, *History of the Royal Society*, p. 112.

8. *To Burlington*, l. 44.

9. Jean de La Bruyère, "Characters" (1687), in *The Continental Model*, p. 330.

10. In Spence, I, 25. In a letter, Pope writes that Dryden was "very learn'd, but not polite"; *Correspondence*, I, 28 (12 or 13 July 1707).

11. "The whole religious business of mankind," Pope wrote, consists in "resignation to our Maker, and charity to our fellow creatures"; *Correspondence*, I, 335 (20 March 1715/16).

12. Voltaire, *Philosophical Letters*, p. 111.

13. Johnson, *Lives of the Poets*, III, 216.

14. In *PW*, pp. 292 and 289–290.

15. Johnson, *Lives of the Poets*, III, 236. "It is certainly the noblest version of poetry which the world has ever seen; and its publication must therefore be considered as one of the great events in the annals of learning" (III, 119).

16. William Kurtz Wimsatt, *The Portraits of Alexander Pope* (New Haven: Yale University Press, 1965), p. 23. See also John Riely and William Kurtz Wimsatt, "A Supplement to *The Portraits of Alexander Pope*," in *Evidence in Literary Scholarship: Essays in Memory of James Marshall Osborn*, ed. René Wellek and Alvaro Ribeiro (Oxford: Clarendon Press, 1979), pp. 123–164.

17. Horace Walpole, *Anecdotes of Painting in England* (1762–1771), ed. Ralph N. Wornum, 3 vols. (London, 1862), I, xvii.

18. In Wimsatt, *Portraits of Pope*, p. 23.

19. It is repeated not only by Jervas. It also appears in paintings by Kneller (one of which was later reproduced in mezzotint engraving by George White) and in the widely reproduced painting by Jean Baptiste Van Loo which was later engraved by J. Houbraken. I am deeply indebted to Wimsatt's fine *Portraits of Pope* for this—and other—information on representations of Pope.

20. Robert Burton, *The Anatomy of Melancholy* (1621), ed. A. R. Shilleto, 3 vols. (London: Bell, 1896), I, 461. On the history of melancholy in art, see Rudolf and Margot Wittkower, *Born under Saturn: The Character and Conduct of Artists, A Documented History from Antiquity to*

*the French Revolution* (1963; rpt. New York: Norton, 1969). There are actually *two* traditions of melancholy, one identified with Galen, one with Aristotle. In the Galenic tradition, melancholy in its association with the cold and dry bodily humors is hostile to life, depressive, heavy, inert. The Aristotelian tradition, especially as reinterpreted by Marsilio Ficino, found melancholy favorable to imaginative and intellectual activity.

21. "Sibylline Oracles," *Encyclopedia of Religion and Ethics* (1958).

22. In Wimsatt, *Portraits of Pope*, p. 94.

23. Irving Lavin, "Divine Inspiration in Caravaggio's Two *St. Matthews,*" *Art Bulletin*, 56 (1974), 62.

24. Charles de Saint-Evremond, "Of Poetry" (1671), in *The Continental Model*, p. 140. Charles de Marguetel de Saint-Denis, seigneur de Saint-Evremond (1610–1703) spent his last forty years living in England. Dryden wrote an introductory essay for Saint-Evremond's two-volume *Miscellaneous Essays* (1692–1694), and Saint-Evremond's work was well known in Pope's day through the translation in 1714 by Pierre Des Maizeaux.

25. The central texts include William Sharpe's *Dissertation on Genius* (1755), Edward Young's *Conjectures on Original Composition* (1759), William Duff's *Essay on Original Genius* (1767), James Beattie's *The Minstrel; or, The Progress of Genius* (1771–1774), and Alexander Gerard's *An Essay on Genius* (1774). The most recent study of such writings—still without an adequate recognition of Pope—is by James Engell, *The Creative Imagination: Enlightenment to Romanticism* (Cambridge, Mass.: Harvard University Press, 1981).

26. Preface to the *Works* (1717), in *PW*, p. 290. On the early history of the term *genius*, see Margaret Lee Wiley, "Genius: A Problem in Definition," *Texas Studies in English*, 16 (1936), 77–83.

27. Dryden, "A Parallel of Poetry and Painting," in *Essays*, II, 138. René Rapin—one of the great spokesmen for French neoclassicism—puts it this way: "No man can be a Poet without a Genius: the want of which, no art or industry is capable to repair. This Genius is that celestial fire ... which enlarges and heightens the Soul"; *Reflections on Aristotle's Treatise of Poesie ...*, trans. Thomas Rymer (London, 1674), p. 7.

28. *Correspondence*, IV, 28 (17 August 1736).

29. Ibid., II, 138 (18 October 1722).

30. Ibid., p. 229 (9 April 1724).

31. Johnson, *Lives of the Poets*, III, 217. On the failures of sense, see Hugh Kenner, *The Counterfeiters: An Historical Comedy* (Bloomington: Indiana University Press, 1968), pp. 65–67. What is missing from Kenner's excellent account is an understanding of the *strengths* of sense, especially when sense is united with other virtues.

32. *Correspondence*, I, 238–239 (25 July 1714).

33. Prologue to *Three Hours after Marriage* (1717), l. 5.

34. In *The Artist as Critic: Critical Writings of Oscar Wilde*, ed. Richard Ellmann (London: W. H. Allen, 1970), p. 95. Pope's description

of poetry as a "dangerous weapon" appears in a letter dated 28 October 1710 (*Correspondence*, I, 100). Wilde, it should be added in fairness, belongs to the modern adversaries of Pope, of whom the latest is James Reeves, *The Reputation and Writings of Alexander Pope* (New York: Barnes & Noble, 1976).

# ❧ Index

Abelard, Peter, 137, 139–142, 144, 145, 147, 151. *See also* "Eloisa to Abelard"

Ackerman, Stephen J., 340n16

Addison, Joseph: as Atticus, 242; *Cato*, 143, 146, 252; on character, 18; commerce, 325n12; coquettes, 94, 334n23; *Essay on Criticism*, 48; genius, 316; party-writing, 68; philosophy, 177; *Rape of the Lock*, 102; revision, 10, 332n10; satire, 217, 218; sense, 310; Virgilian indirection, 115–116; wit, 298

Aden, John M., 330n12

Adler, Jacob H., 328n33, 342n7; quoted, 134

Akstens, Thomas, 354n26

Allen, Ralph, 208, 267, 268

Amis, Kingsley, 327n19

Anderson, William S., 351n41

Anne, 104, 110, 130, 296

Appleby, Joyce Oldham, quoted, 344–345n5

Arbuthnot, Dr. John, 230, 236, 237, 242, 268; quoted, 186. See also *Epistle to Dr. Arbuthnot*

Archilochus, 215, 219; quoted, 217

Ariès, Phillipe, 329n39

Aristotle, 65; on character, 199; friendship, 67; melancholy, 359n20; pain and pleasure, 238; Pope compared to, 48; Renaissance criticism, 49; "Rules" and "Unities," 58, 60, 62; virtue as middle term, 201

Arnold, Matthew, 16; quoted, 82

Atkins, J. W. H., quoted, 47

Atterbury, Francis, 242, 268

Audra, E., quoted, 107

Augustus, 10, 117, 125, 265

Ault, Norman, 323, 335n7

Austen, Jane, 297

"Autumn," 244, 245

Bacon, Francis, 318; quoted, 165, 166

Bakhtin, Mikhail, quoted, 348n2

Bateson, F. W., 353n22

Bathurst, Allen, Earl Bathurst, 183, 194. See also *To Bathurst*

Battestin, Martin C., 332n10

Beattie, James, 359n25

Bedford, Emmett G., 330n13

Bell, Robert H., 338n32

Berkeley, George, 156; quoted, 215

Bethel, Hugh, 211, 212, 268, 348n40

Blackstone, Sir William, quoted, 179

Blake, William, 76, 180

Bleackley, Horace, 351n32

Bloom, Edward and Lillian, quoted, 232

Bloom, Harold, 4; quoted, 324n4

Bloomfield, Morton W., 328n31

Blount, Edward, 242

Blount, Martha (Patty), 17, 44, 100, 144, 150, 185, 203, 212. See also *To a Lady*

Blount, Teresa, 17, 185

Blunt, Sir John, 185, 186

Bogel, Fredric V., 357n28

Boileau, Nicholas, 73, 105, 218, 220, 336n11, 338n29, 357n1

Bolingbroke. *See* St. John, Henry

Boswell, James, 227; quoted, 284, 299

Boyce, Benjamin, 347n24

Boyle, A. J., quoted, 337n18

Boyle, John, 5th Earl of Orrery, 251

Boyle, Richard, 3rd Earl of Burlington, 133, 194, 195. See also *To Burlington*

Boys, Richard C., 357n2

# Index

Bristol. *See* Hervey, John
Brody, Baruch, 326n3
Brooke, Henry, quoted, 37
Broome, William, 23
Brower, Reuben A., 324n2, 352n10; quoted, 2
Brown, Tom, 354–355n2
Brückmann, Patricia Carr, 340n16
Bruns, Gerald L., 351n37
Bruss, Elizabeth W., 326n2
Brydges, James, 1st Duke of Chandos, 236
Buckingham. *See* Villiers, George
Buckingham and Normanby. *See* Sheffield, John
Bunn, James H., 325n11
Burlington. *See* Boyle, Richard
Burton, Robert, quoted, 310
Busby, Dr. Richard, 219, 220
Butler, Samuel, 197
Butt, John, 323, 327n23, 332n7, 339n11
Byrd, Max, 354n1
Byron, George Gordon, 17, 29, 76, 77, 85; quoted, 75

Cameron, J. M., quoted, 48
Caravaggio, 313
Carew, Thomas, 183
Caroline, 353n15
Caretta, Vincent, 345n10, 353n18
Caryl. *See* Caryll, John
Caryll, John, 17, 44, 104, 178, 243, 388n39
Casaubon, Isaac, 218
Chalker, John, 336n9
Chandos. *See* Brydges, James
Charles II, 50, 297
Chartres, Francis, 184, 185, 186, 239
Chaucer, Geoffrey, 82
Chesterfield. *See* Stanhope, Philip Dormer
Chetwood, Knightly, 123
Churchill, John, 1st Duke of Marlborough, 121, 122
Cibber, Caius-Gabriel, 270
Cibber, Colley, 17, 33, 223, 270–295 *passim*, 357n26; quoted, 283, 284, 293
Cicero, 68
Clark, John R., 348n1
Claudian, 325n10

Cobham. *See* Temple, Richard
Cockburn, J. S., 350n24
Cohen, Murray, 342n3
Cohen, Ralph, quoted, 329n40
Coleridge, Samuel Taylor, quoted, 77
Colie, Rosalie L., 343n23
Congreve, William, 10–11, 242, 268, 319
Conversation, Pope's: anger at Dennis, 235; Bacon as genius, 165; Cibber "stuck all over," 223; on Dryden, 3, 4, 6, 301–302; final edition of his works, 46; flattery, 213; imitation, 108, 324–325n10; mediocre poets, 293; moral writing, 123, 136, 179; Persian fable, 64; poetic technique, 25, 83, 247; on Rabelais, 90; revision, 79, 332n10; variety, 63; Virgil's judgment, 106; writing rules, 60; writing for stage, 137
Cooper, Anthony Ashley, 1st Earl of Shaftesbury, 20
Cooper, Anthony Ashley, 3rd Earl of Shaftesbury, 282; quoted, 20, 356n17
Corbet, Elizabeth, 39–44 *passim*, 328n35. *See also* "Epitaph. On Mrs. Corbet"
Corneille, Pierre, 49
Correspondence, Pope's: anger as goal, 233, 237; being "at home," 22; *Cato*, 266, 353n14; character in writing, 38–39; commerce and poetry, 9; concealment, 21; on Dryden, 132, 339n3, 358n10; "Eloisa to Abelard," 150; *Essay on Criticism*, 49; *Essay on Man*, 156; ethics, 241, 243–244; father's death, 133; fragmentary composing, 165; friendship, 208; game like life, 98–99; genius, 316; illness, 242; inconsistency, 17, 44, 342n6; La Rochefoucauld, 161; letter-writing, 46, 329n41, 340n18; life in imagination, 18; money-hearted Vanneck, 205; mother's death, 352n4; offending the violent, 104; Phaethon-like traveler, 336n12; poetry as weapon, 320–321; political pessimism, 251–252, 267–268; present versus past, 257; *Rape of the Lock*, 81, 101, 102; refusal to publish, 269; "relation" of works, 180; rereading, 178; resignation and charity, 358n11; revi-

# Index

# Index

# Index

# Index

Whiston, William, 45, 49, 329n42
White, Douglas H., 341
White, George, 358n19
Wilde, Oscar, 29, 360n34; quoted, 321
Wiles, Richard C., 325n14
Wiley, Margaret Lee, 359n26
Wilkinson, L. P., 336n9
William III, 50, 104, 113, 118, 182, 196
Williams, Aubrey, quoted, 107, 355n4
Williams, William Carlos, 1, 75
Wimsatt, William Kurtz, Jr., 328n33, 333n13, 334n28, 358nn16 and 19; quoted, 307
*Windsor-Forest*, 7, 79, 151, 163, 173, 243, 254, 343n31; quoted, 103–130 *passim*
Winn, James, A., 323, 324n3, 340n18
"Winter," 244, 245, 253; quoted, 245
Wittkower, Rudolf and Margot, 358–359n20
Wordsworth, William, 1, 76, 150; quoted, 41
Wycherley, William, 3, 92

Yates, Frances A., 143
Yeats, William Butler, 23
Young, Edward, 341n1
Yunck, John A., 344n4

370